Educating Exceptional Children

02/03

Fourteenth Edition

EDITOR

Karen L. Freiberg

University of Maryland, Baltimore County

Dr. Karen Freiberg has an interdisciplinary educational and employment background in nursing, education, and developmental psychology. She received her B.S. from the State University of New York at Plattsburgh, her M.S. from Cornell University, and her Ph.D. from Syracuse University. She has worked as a school nurse, a pediatric nurse, a public health nurse for the Navajo Indians, an associate project director for a child development clinic, a researcher in several areas of child development, and a university professor. Dr. Freiberg is the author of an award-winning textbook, *Human Development: A Life-Span Approach*, which is now in its fourth edition. She is currently on the faculty at the University of Maryland, Baltimore County.

McGraw-Hill/Dushkin

530 Old Whitfield Street, Guilford, Connecticut 06437

Visit us on the Internet
http://www.dushkin.com

Credits

1. **Inclusive Education**
   Unit photo—© 2002 by Cleo Freelance Photography.
2. **Early Childhood**
   Unit photo—© 2002 by Cleo Freelance Photography.
3. **Learning Disabilities**
   Unit photo—Courtesy of McGraw-Hill/Dushkin.
4. **Speech and Language Impairments**
   Unit photo—United Nations photo by L. Solmssen.
5. **Developmental Disabilities**
   Unit photo—United Nations photo by S. DiMartini.
6. **Emotional and Behavioral Disorders**
   Unit photo—Courtesy of Cheryl Greenleaf.
7. **Vision and Hearing Impairments**
   Unit photo—United Nations photo by Marta Pinter.
8. **Multiple Disabilities**
   Unit photo—United Nations photo by Jan Corash.
9. **Orthopedic and Health Impairments**
   Unit photo—United Nations photo by J. Isaac.
10. **Giftedness**
    Unit photo—Courtesy of Pamela Carley.
11. **Transition**
    Unit photo—United Nations photo by John Isaac.

Copyright

Cataloging in Publication Data
Main entry under title: Annual Editions: Educating Exceptional Children. 2002/2003.
1. Exceptional children—Education—United States—Periodicals. 2. Educational innovations—United States—Periodicals
I. Freiberg, Karen, *comp.* II. Title: Educating exceptional children.
ISBN 0–07–250678–4   371.9'05   ISSN 0198–7518

Fourteenth Edition

Cover image © 2002 by PhotoDisc, Inc.
Printed in the United States of America   1234567890BAHBAH5432   Printed on Recycled Paper

Editors/Advisory Board

Members of the Advisory Board are instrumental in the final selection of articles for each edition of ANNUAL EDITIONS. Their review of articles for content, level, currentness, and appropriateness provides critical direction to the editor and staff. We think that you will find their careful consideration well reflected in this volume.

Staff

To the Reader

In publishing ANNUAL EDITIONS we recognize the enormous role played by the magazines, newspapers, and journals of the public press in providing current, first-rate educational information in a broad spectrum of interest areas. Many of these articles are appropriate for students, researchers, and professionals seeking accurate, current material to help bridge the gap between principles and theories and the real world. These articles, however, become more useful for study when those of lasting value are carefully collected, organized, indexed, and reproduced in a low-cost format, which provides easy and permanent access when the material is needed. That is the role played by ANNUAL EDITIONS.

The Individuals with Disabilities Education Act (IDEA) is now over 25 years old. President Gerald Ford signed it into law in 1975 requiring that all students with disabilities be provided a free and appropriate education in the least restrictive environment possible. For about 95 percent of America's children with disabilities this now means education in regular classrooms in public schools. The number of children with disabilities requiring special services has jumped about 50 percent since the advent of IDEA. This is due to several factors: better diagnostic and assessment techniques, more children being kept alive after premature birth, "at-risk" births, earlier education, later education and transition services until age 21, and more awareness of conditions of disability. Current costs for special education in the United States are about $51 billion dollars a year, about 20 percent of total school spending.

The current United States president, George W. Bush, has promised that education will be a priority in his administration. He envisions new schools, new teachers, higher salaries for teachers, reductions in class size, improved curricula, and more school supplies, including computers. Will Congress appropriate the funds to fulfill his wish list? Currently the costs for educating children in the United States are paid predominantly by state and local governments. Federal assistance for education is currently about 10 percent of the actual expenditures. Will Congress agree to pay more? What impact will increased spending for special education have on lawmakers' decisions?

IDEA requires schools to work with parents as partners in the education of individuals with disabilities. Educational services must be provided to persons with special needs from time of diagnosis (birth, if applicable) through age 21. Educators, in collaboration with parents and other service providers, are required to provide individualized family service plans (IFSPs) for infants and young children who are at risk of developing disabilities or who acquire disabilities before they enter public school. Individualized transition plans (ITPs) must be provided for older students. For this reason, one-quarter of all the articles in *Annual Editions: Educating Exceptional Children 02/03* deal with family involvement.

Every child with a disability who is enrolled in public school has an annually updated individualized education plan (IEP). This describes how the child will receive special services, and where, when, why, and what services will be provided. It is team-written by teachers, the student, parents, and all applicable service providers. IDEA directs IEPs to be outcomes-oriented.

Is the education of children with exceptionalities best carried out in regular education classes? Proponents of inclusion cite benefits such as socialization of both the children with special needs and their peers without disabilities. Tolerance and acceptance begin with exposure and are taught by egalitarian teachers who focus on positive interaction and differential abilities. Opponents of inclusive education cite lack of preparation of regular education teachers, crowded and ill-equipped classrooms, monies being diverted from the education of the many to education of the few, and the negative effects of competition.

Annual Editions: Educating Exceptional Children 02/03 includes articles that discuss the pros and cons of inclusion. It explains how IDEA provisions are being implemented in all areas of special education. Selections have been made with an eye to conveying information, giving personal experiences, and offering many practical suggestions for implementation. Teachers will find articles that deal with all levels of education from preschool through transition to postsecondary education.

To help us improve future editions of this anthology, please complete and return the postage-paid article rating form on the last page. Your suggestions are valued and appreciated.

Good luck in using this anthology to make your own and others' lives easier and more rewarding.

Karen Freiberg

Karen L. Freiberg
Editor

Contents

UNIT 1
Inclusive Education

Four articles present strategies for establishing positive interaction between students with and without special needs.

Unit Overview   xvi

UNIT 2
Early Childhood

Three unit articles discuss the implementation of special services to preschoolers with disabilities.

Unit Overview   26

The concepts in bold italics are developed in the article. For further expansion, please refer to the Topic Guide and the Index.

UNIT 3
Learning Disabilities

The assessment and special needs of students with learning disabilities are addressed in this unit's three selections.

UNIT 4
Speech and Language Impairments

In this unit, three selections examine communication disorders and suggest ways in which students can develop their speech and language.

The concepts in bold italics are developed in the article. For further expansion, please refer to the Topic Guide and the Index.

UNIT 5
Developmental Disabilities

Three articles in this section discuss concerns and strategies for providing optimal educational programs for students with developmental disabilities, Down syndrome, and traumatic brain injuries.

The concepts in bold italics are developed in the article. For further expansion, please refer to the Topic Guide and the Index.

UNIT 6
Emotional and Behavioral Disorders

Ways to teach emotionally and behaviorally disordered students are discussed in the unit's three articles.

UNIT 7
Vision and Hearing Impairments

Three selections discuss the special needs of visually an hearing impaired children from infancy through secondary school.

The concepts in bold italics are developed in the article. For further expansion, please refer to the Topic Guide and the Index.

The concepts in bold italics are developed in the article. For further expansion, please refer to the Topic Guide and the Index.

UNIT 10
Giftedness

UNIT 11
Transition

The concepts in bold italics are developed in the article. For further expansion, please refer to the Topic Guide and the Index.

Topic Guide

This topic guide suggests how the selections in this book relate to the subjects covered in your course. You may want to use the topics listed on these pages to search the Web more easily.

On the following pages a number of Web sites have been gathered specifically for this book. They are arranged to reflect the units of this *Annual Edition*. You can link to these sites by going to the DUSHKIN ONLINE support site at *http://www.dushkin.com/online/*.

ALL THE ARTICLES THAT RELATE TO EACH TOPIC ARE LISTED BELOW THE BOLD-FACED TERM.

Adult development

5. From Philosophy to Practice in Inclusive Early Childhood Programs

Aggression

7. Emergent Literacy in an Early Childhood Classroom: Center Learning to Support the Child With Special Needs

Assessment

8. Learning Disabilities
10. Chaos in the Classroom: Looking at ADHD
11. For the Love of Language
12. Approaching Families: Facilitating Culturally/Linguistically Diverse Family Involvement
15. Don't Water Down! Enhance: Content Learning Through the Unit Organizer Routine
16. Identifying Depression in Students With Mental Retardation
17. Anger, Dismay, Guilt, Anxiety—The Realities and Roles in Reporting Child Abuse
18. Wraparound Services for Young Schoolchildren With Emotional and Behavioral Disorders
24. The Unexpected Benefits of High School Peer Tutoring
25. Using Technology to Construct Alternate Portfolios of Students With Moderate and Severe Disabilities
29. Uncommon Talents: Gifted Children, Prodigies and Savants
30. Using the Internet to Improve Student Performance
31. Gifted Students Need an Education, Too
33. Choosing a Self-Determination Curriculum

Brain disorders

7. Emergent Literacy in an Early Childhood Classroom: Center Learning to Support the Child With Special Needs
14. Collaborative Planning for Inclusion of a Student With Developmental Disabilities
15. Don't Water Down! Enhance: Content Learning Through the Unit Organizer Routine
16. Identifying Depression in Students With Mental Retardation
28. Accessible Web Site Design
32. Listening to Student Voices About Postsecondary Education

Child development

5. From Philosophy to Practice in Inclusive Early Childhood Programs

Collaboration

2. Here Comes the SUN Team! Collaborative Inclusion at Work
3. Four Inclusion Models That Work
5. From Philosophy to Practice in Inclusive Early Childhood Programs
13. Family and Cultural Alert! Considerations in Assistive Technology Assessment
14. Collaborative Planning for Inclusion of a Student With Developmental Disabilities
18. Wraparound Services for Young Schoolchildren With Emotional and Behavioral Disorders
21. Seeking the Light: Welcoming a Visually Impaired Student
23. Training Basic Teaching Skills to Paraeducators of Students With Severe Disabilities
25. Using Technology to Construct Alternate Portfolios of Students With Moderate and Severe Disabilities

30. Using the Internet to Improve Student Performance

Computers

9. Graphic Organizers to the Rescue! Helping Students Link—and Remember—Information
13. Family and Cultural Alert! Considerations in Assistive Technology Assessment
21. Seeking the Light: Welcoming a Visually Impaired Student
22. Visual Teaching Strategies for Students Who Are Deaf or Hard of Hearing
25. Using Technology to Construct Alternate Portfolios of Students With Moderate and Severe Disabilities
26. I Learned How to Take Turns and Other Important Early Childhood Lessons Helped Along by Computers
28. Accessible Web Site Design
30. Using the Internet to Improve Student Performance

Conflict resolution

13. Family and Cultural Alert! Considerations in Assistive Technology Assessment
17. Anger, Dismay, Guilt, Anxiety—The Realities and Roles in Reporting Child Abuse
18. Wraparound Services for Young Schoolchildren With Emotional and Behavioral Disorders
19. Student Mentors and Proteges Learning Together

Developmental disability

14. Collaborative Planning for Inclusion of a Student With Developmental Disabilities
15. Don't Water Down! Enhance: Content Learning Through the Unit Organizer Routine
16. Identifying Depression in Students With Mental Retardation
25. Using Technology to Construct Alternate Portfolios of Students With Moderate and Severe Disabilities
28. Accessible Web Site Design
29. Uncommon Talents: Gifted Children, Prodigies and Savants
32. Listening to Student Voices About Postsecondary Education

Disabilities

7. Emergent Literacy in an Early Childhood Classroom: Center Learning to Support the Child With Special Needs
14. Collaborative Planning for Inclusion of a Student With Developmental Disabilities
15. Don't Water Down! Enhance: Content Learning Through the Unit Organizer Routine
16. Identifying Depression in Students With Mental Retardation
28. Accessible Web Site Design
32. Listening to Student Voices About Postsecondary Education

Diversity

4. Creating Culturally Responsive, Inclusive Classrooms
5. From Philosophy to Practice in Inclusive Early Childhood Programs
12. Approaching Families: Facilitating Culturally/Linguistically Diverse Family Involvement
13. Family and Cultural Alert! Considerations in Assistive Technology Assessment
17. Anger, Dismay, Guilt, Anxiety—The Realities and Roles in Reporting Child Abuse

World Wide Web Sites

The following World Wide Web sites have been carefully researched and selected to support the articles found in this reader. The easiest way to access these selected sites is to go to our DUSHKIN ONLINE support site at *http://www.dushkin.com/online/*.

AE: Educating Exceptional Children 02/03

The following sites were available at the time of publication. Visit our Web site—we update DUSHKIN ONLINE regularly to reflect any changes.

General Sources

The Big Pages of Special Education Links
http://www.mts.net/~jgreenco/special.html

This site leads to links that deal with disabilities related to special education.

ERIC Clearinghouse on Disabilities and Gifted Education
http://www.ericec.org

This ERIC clearinghouse has information on everything important to special education professionals. It links also to The Council for Exceptional Children and the National Clearinghouse for Professions in Special Education.

Family Village
http://www.familyvillage.wisc.edu/index.htmlx

Here is a global community of disability-related resources that is set up under such headings as library, shopping mall, school, community center, and others.

National Information Center for Children and Youth With Disabilities (NICHCY)
http://www.nichcy.org/index.html

NICHCY provides information and makes referrals in areas related to specific disabilities, early intervention, special education and related services, individualized education programs, and much more. The site also connects to a listing of Parent's Guides to resources for children and youth with disabilities.

National Rehabilitation Information Center (NARIC)
http://www.naric.com

A series of databases that can be keyword-searched on subjects that include physical, mental, and psychiatric disabilities, vocational rehabilitation, special education, assistive technology, and more can be found on this site.

Special Education Exchange
http://www.spedex.com/main_graphics.htm

SpEdEx, as this site is more commonly known, offers a wealth of information, links, and resources to everyone interested in special education.

UNIT 1: Inclusive Education

Consortium on Inclusive Schooling Practices
http://www.asri.edu/cfsp/brochure/abtcons.htm

The Consortium represents a collaborative effort to build the capacity of state and local education agencies to provide inclusive educational services in school and community settings, focusing on systemic reform rather than on changes in special education only.

Kids Together, Inc.
http://www.kidstogether.org

Based on the IDEA law about teaching children with disabilties in regular classrooms, this site contains all the information on inclusion you might need.

New Horizons for Learning
http://www.newhorizons.org

Based on the theory of inclusion, this site is filled with information on special needs inclusion, technology and learning, a brain lab, and much more, presented as floors in a building.

UNIT 2: Early Childhood

Division for Early Childhood
http://www.dec-sped.org

A division of the Council for Exceptional Children, the DEC advocates for the improvement of conditions of young children with special needs. Child development theory, programming data, parenting data, research, and links to other sites can be found on this site.

Institute on Community Integration Projects
http://ici.umn.edu/projectscenters/

Research projects related to early childhood and early intervention services for special education are described here.

National Early Childhood Technical Assistance System
http://www.nectas.unc.edu

An exceptionally complete site on children with special needs, NECTAS explores many areas, including the IDEA and inclusion, and includes a projects database.

Special Education Resources on the Internet (SERI)
http://seriweb.com

SERI offers helpful sites in all phases of special education in early childhood, including disabilities, mental retardation, behavior disorders, and autism.

UNIT 3: Learning Disabilities

Children and Adults With Attention Deficit/Hyperactivity Disorder (CHADD)
http://www.chadd.org

CHADD works to improve the lives of people with AD/HD through education, advocacy, and support, offering information that can be trusted. The site includes fact sheets, legislative information, research studies, and links.

The Instant Access Treasure Chest
http://www.fln.vcu.edu/ld/ld.html

Billed as the Foreign Language Teacher's Guide to Learning Disabilities, this site contains a very thorough list of resources for anyone interested in LD education issues.

Learning Disabilities and Disorders
http://fly.hiwaay.net/~garson/learnd.htm

This is a good source for information about all kinds of learning disabilities with links to other related material.

www.dushkin.com/online/

Learning Disabilities Association of America (LDA)
http://www.ldanatl.org

The purpose of the LDA is to advance the education and general welfare of children of normal and potentially normal intelligence who show handicaps of a perceptual, conceptual, or coordinative nature.

Teaching Children With Attention Deficit Disorder
http://www.kidsource.com/kidsource/content2/add.html

This in-depth site defines both types of ADDs and discusses establishing the proper learning environment.

UNIT 4: Speech and Language Impairments

Speech Disorders WWW Sites
http://www.socialnet.lu/handitel/wwwlinks/dumb.html

A thorough collection of Web sites, plus an article on the relationship between form and function in the speech of specifically language-impaired children, may be accessed here.

UNIT 5: Developmental Disabilities

Arc of the United States
http://www.thearc.org

Here is the Web site of the national organization of and for people with mental retardation and related disabilities and their families. It includes governmental affairs, services, position statements, FAQs, publications, and related links.

Autism Society Early Interventions Package
http://www.autism-society.org/packages/early_intervention.pdf

Answers to FAQs about early intervention in cases of autism as well as online help with obtaining early intervention services, reading lists, and organizations to contact for further information are located on this Web site.

Disability-Related Sources on the Web
http://www.arcofarizona.org/dislnkin.html

This resource's many links include grant resources, federally funded projects and federal agencies, assistive technology, national and international organizations, and educational resources and directories.

Gentle Teaching
http://www.gentleteaching.nl

Maintained by the foundation for Gentle Teaching in the Netherlands, this page explains a nonviolent approach for helping children and adults with special needs.

UNIT 6: Emotional and Behavioral Disorders

Resources in Emotional or Behavioral Disorders (EBD)
http://www.gwu.edu/~ebdweb/index.html

At this page, link to a collection of Web resources for teachers of students with serious emotional disturbances.

UNIT 7: Vision and Hearing Impairments

Info to Go: Laurent Clerc National Deaf Education Center
http://clerccenter.gallaudet.edu/InfoToGo/index.html

Important for parents and educators, this Web site from Gallaudet University offers information on audiology, communication, education, legal, and health issues of deaf people.

The New York Institute for Special Education
http://www.nyise.org/index.html

This school is an educational facility that serves children who are blind or visually impaired. The site includes program descriptions and resources for the blind.

UNIT 8: Multiple Disabilities

Activity Ideas for Students With Severe, Profound, or Multiple Disabilities
http://www.palaestra.com/featurestory.html

The Fall 1997 issue of the *Palaestra* contains this interesting article on teaching students who have multiple disabilities. The complete text is offered here on line.

UNIT 9: Orthopedic and Health Impairments

Association to Benefit Children (ABC)
http://www.a-b-c.org

ABC presents a network of programs that includes child advocacy, education for disabled children, care for HIV-positive children, employment, housing, foster care, and day care.

Introduction: Community Travel
http://isd.saginaw.k12.mi.us/~mobility/ctpintro.htm

The purpose of community-based education is to help students in special education to become more independent. Here is an excellent description of how it is being done in at least one community.

Resources for VE Teachers
http://cpt.fsu.edu/tree/ve/tofc.html

Effective practices for teachers of varying exceptionalities (VE) classes are listed here.

UNIT 10: Giftedness

Kenny Anthony's Gifted and Talented and General Educational Resources
http://www2.tsixroads.com/~kva/

In addition to definitions and characteristics of giftedness and needs of the gifted, an excellent list of education resources for the gifted can be found at this site.

National Association for Gifted Children (NAGC)
http://www.nagc.org/home00.htm

NAGC, a national nonprofit organization for gifted children, is dedicated to developing their high potential.

UNIT 11: Transition

National Transition Alliance (NTA) Home Page
http://www.dssc.org/nta/index.html

This NTA site provides state transition resources, searchable databases on transition, school-to-work model programs, and links to other online databases. It includes a database of model transition programs.

We highly recommend that you review our Web site for expanded information and our other product lines. We are continually updating and adding links to our Web site in order to offer you the most usable and useful information that will support and expand the value of your Annual Editions. You can reach us at: *http://www.dushkin.com/annualeditions/*.

UNIT 1

Inclusive Education

Unit Selections

1. **What's Good? Suggested Resources for Beginning Special Education Teachers**, Sharon A. Maroney
2. **Here Comes the SUN Team! Collaborative Inclusion at Work**, Donna M. Sobel and Nancy S. Vaughn
3. **Four Inclusion Models That Work**, Dori Elliott and Merry McKenney
4. **Creating Culturally Responsive, Inclusive Classrooms**, Winifred Montgomery

Key Points to Consider

- What does the 1997 reauthorization of IDEA require of states who fail to include children with disabilities in regular education classes? What impact will this have on twenty-first century education?

- How does the parent panel approach to parental/educator collaboration work?

- What is a SUN team? How does this support unit make inclusion easier?

- What other methods can facilitate inclusive education? Does specialized instruction really help? What are the three biggest challenges facing inclusive education?

 **Links: www.dushkin.com/online/**
These sites are annotated in the World Wide Web pages.

Consortium on Inclusive Schooling Practices
http://www.asri.edu/cfsp/brochure/abtcons.htm

Kids Together, Inc.
http://www.kidstogether.org

New Horizons for Learning
http://www.newhorizons.org

The numbers of students with exceptionalities who are being educated in regular education classes is increasing annually. During its 25 years in existence, the Individuals with Disabilities Education Act (IDEA) has reduced the numbers of special needs students being educated in residential centers, hospitals, homes, or special schools to less than 5 percent. Children who once would have been turned away from public schools are now being admitted in enormous numbers. In the United States today there are over 6 million students with conditions of exceptionality being educated in public school, and their numbers continue to grow.

This trend necessitates more knowledge and expertise on the part of regular education teachers. Educating children with exceptionalities can no longer be viewed as the responsibility of special education teachers. This trend also mandates more knowledge and expertise on collaboration and advisory activities on the part of all special educators. Teamwork is essential as special education and regular education are becoming more and more intertwined.

Public schools have an obligation to provide free educational services in the least restrictive environment possible to all children who have diagnosed conditions of exceptionality. Although laws in Canada and the United States differ slightly, all public schools have an obligation to serve children with exceptional conditions in as normal an educational environment as possible. Inclusive education is difficult. It works very well for some students with exceptionalities in some situations, and marginally or not at all for other students with exceptionalities in other situations.

For inclusion to succeed within a school, everyone must be committed to be part of the solution: superintendent, principal, teachers, coaches, aides, ancillary staff, students, parents, and family members. Special education teachers often find that their jobs involve much more than instructing students with special needs. They serve as consultants to regular education teachers to ensure that inclusion is meaningful for their students. They collaborate with parents, administrators, support personnel, and community agencies as well as with regular education teachers. They plan curriculum and oversee the writing of individualized family service plans (IFSPs), individualized education plans (IEPs) and individualized transition plans (ITPs). They schedule and make sure that services are provided by all team-involved persons. They keep up with enormous amounts of paperwork. They update parents even when parents are too involved, or not involved enough. They keep abreast of new resources, new legal processes, and new instructional techniques. They make projections for the futures of their students and set out ways to make such good things happen. They also struggle to be accountable, both educationally and financially, for all they do.

The term "least restrictive environment" is often mistakenly understood as the need for all children to be educated in a regular education classroom. If students can learn and achieve better in inclusive programs, then they belong there. If students can succeed only marginally in inclusive education classrooms, some alternate solutions are necessary. A continuum of placement options exists to maximize the goal of educating every child. For some children, a separate class, or even a separate school, is still optimal.

Every child with an exceptional condition is different from every other child in symptoms, needs, and teachability. Each child is, therefore, provided with a unique individualized education plan (IEP). This plan consists of both long- and short-term goals for education, specially designed instructional procedures with related services, and methods to evaluate the child's progress. The IEP is updated and revised annually. Special education teachers, parents, and all applicable service providers must collaborate at least this often to make recommendations for goals and teaching strategies. The IEPs should always be outcomes-oriented with functional curricula.

The first article included in this unit suggests resources for beginning special education teachers. Experienced educators have given their expertise to Sharon Maroney to pass on to novice teachers. Advice is included on developing professionalism, instructing effectively, managing behavior, and using special techniques such as a cognitive-behavioral curriculum. The author also counsels readers to try new things and have fun in their chosen professions. Educating exceptional children is challenging. It should also be exciting and fun.

The second selection was chosen to help change attitudes about the trend toward inclusion. It documents the growth and development of neighborhood inclusive education in the Boulder Valley school district, serving 25,000 students in eastern Colorado. As in schools everywhere, there was opposition to the closing of special education classes and schools. Could students with special needs be educated well in general classes? An affirmative answer was sounded, thanks to the use of the SUN team. The authors describe how this support unit achieved its successes.

The third selection offers four other ways to help achieve successful inclusion of students with exceptionalities in general education classes: consultation, team teaching, aide services, and limited pullout services. Dori Elliott, a regular education teacher, and Merry McKenney, a special education teacher, give many realistic and practical suggestions for success with each of these models. They expect positive outcomes and help the reader understand how they can be achieved.

The last article included in this unit speaks plainly about the problems encountered by teachers with students from minority cultures in inclusive education classrooms. Many culturally diverse students with special needs are not served well by regularized education. The dropout rate from school is twice as high in students with exceptionalities as it is in nondisabled students. Many dropouts are students who encounter problems due to their cultural differences as well as their conditions of disability. This problem is multiplied when one considers the certainty that some children from minority cultures are not correctly assessed as students with one or more types of disability until late in elementary school or even into middle school. By this time they are too far behind their peers to ever catch up. On occasion, students from minority cultures are diagnosed as learning disabled because they have not been taught to read or write or calculate adequately. Winifred Montgomery gives advice to teachers on how to create culturally responsive inclusive classrooms. If students from diverse groups can connect with the teachers and the classroom materials and methods, they will learn more efficiently.

What's Good?

Suggested Resources for Beginning Special Education Teachers

"What's good?" "What do I need?" "What will I actually use?"
"What should I buy with my limited budget?"

Sharon A. Maroney

These are the questions most often asked by beginning teachers when seeking advice on acquiring materials and locating resources for classroom use. Faced with too many responsibilities and too little time, wanting to be fully prepared but not knowing exactly how, seeing catalogs filled with teaching materials but having no experience with any, and having limited financial resources, beginning teachers need assistance in selecting teaching resources. Teachers need strategies that are effective, efficient, easy to use, practical, and adaptable. Information must reflect current best practices in education.

SPECIAL EDUCATION
TEACHERS CAN DEVELOP
PROFESSIONALISM THROUGH
MEMBERSHIP IN
PROFESSIONAL
ORGANIZATIONS AND
KNOWLEDGE OF THE
LEGAL REQUIREMENTS
OF THE FIELD.

This article includes a set of classroom resources identified by experienced teachers as recommended resources for beginning teachers. The resources are grouped into six areas of priority for beginning special education teachers: (a) developing professionalism, (b) basics for effective instruction, (c) academic instruction, (d) cognitive-behavioral instruction, (e) behavioral management, and (f) classroom extras.

Developing Professionalism

We need to view teaching as a profession, not just a job. Teachers continually work to become true professionals by obtaining access to information, keeping current with the developments in the field, and being knowledgeable of what it means to be a professional special educator. Special education teachers can develop professionalism through membership in professional organizations and knowledge of the legal requirements of the field.

As newly established special education professionals, beginning teachers should become members of a professional organization that advocates for special educators, special education, and the students and families who receive special educa-

tion services. With membership in The Council for Exceptional Children (CEC), teachers have access to high-quality, timely information and the CEC Web site (http://www.cec.sped.org); reap the benefits of CEC's advocacy activities; and receive the following publications: *TEACHING Exceptional Children* (6 issues/year), *Exceptional Children* (4 issues/year), *CEC Today* (10 issues/year), and *Research Connections in Special Education* (2 issues/year). Membership in the CEC offers opportunities to become involved in the profession at the local, state, national, and international levels through professional development, leadership, advocacy, publications, and networking activities. Membership is also available in the 17 divisions of CEC, representing areas of interest within special education.

Special education teachers should be proficient in using the resources of the federally-funded Educational Resources Information Center—the ERIC system. This includes knowing how to search the ERIC database and use the resources of the ERIC Clearinghouses. The ERIC Clearinghouse on Disabilities and Gifted Education is located at The Council for Exceptional Children in Reston, VA.

All special education teachers should have copies of current district, state, and federal rules, regulations, and policies for special education. This is especially important for beginning teachers, who are expected to be knowledgeable of and adhere to rules and regulations immediately. As soon as beginning teachers accept positions, they should contact the director of special education within the school district, the intermediate special education agency, and the state department of special education to request and obtain this information. All teachers need to have their own copy of the rules and regulations so [as] not to rely on others for the interpretation of or access to these documents.

THE WEB SITE OF THE U.S. OFFICE OF SPECIAL EDUCATION PROGRAMS PROVIDES ACCESS TO INFORMATION ON FEDERAL INITIATIVES, LEGAL ISSUES, AND NATIONAL RESOURCES IN SPECIAL EDUCATION.

The book, *IDEA 1997: Let's Make It Work* (1998) uses a question-and-answer format to present the content of the Individuals with Disabilities Education Act (IDEA) of 1997. Recently a first-year special education teacher shared that although she had prepared for and completed several individualized education program (IEP) meetings, she still felt that the other professionals on the IEP team understood the IEP process much better than she did. This teacher found *IDEA 1997: Let's Make It Work* (1998) to be especially useful, understandable, and full of the information she needed.

The compact disk, *Discover IDEA CD '99* (1999), allows teachers to access the actual text of the IDEA 1997, in addition to providing a frequently asked questions (FAQs) section and keyword search capability. This resource is especially useful for locating exact wording and references to specific topics throughout the law. Teachers can visit the IDEA Practices Web site (http://www.ideapractices.org) to preview this CD and learn about the IDEA Partnerships Projects of the U.S. Department of Education.

Several Web sites devoted to special education currently exist on the Internet. The National Center for Children and Youth with Disabilities (NICHY) Web site (http://www.nichy.org) and Special Education Resources on the Internet (SERI; http//www.hood.edu/seri) are two teacher- and parent-friendly Internet resources for information on special education and people with disabilities. The NICHY site distributes numerous publications and information sheets on different disabilities and topics in special education. SERI posts information and links to several other Web sites on special education and related topics. The Web site of the U.S. Office of Special Education Programs (http://www.ed.gov/offices/OSERS/OSEP/index.html) provides access to information on federal initiatives, legal issues, and national resources in special education.

The *Survival Guide for the First Year Special Education Teacher* (Cohen, Gale, & Meyer, 1994) is a teacher-friendly book that many beginning teachers have found extremely helpful. Teachers especially liked the use of lists and the good basic advice and information. Survival topics include shunning the need to be superman or superwoman, preparing emergency lesson plans for when all else fails, the dos for working with general educators, and hints for positive report card comments. This resource can provide an informal approach to address the responsibilities required of special education teachers.

Effective Instruction

Research has identified several strategies that constitute effective teaching that can be applied to academic and behavioral instruction; special education and general education classrooms; and individual, small-group, and large-group instruction. Because students currently identified as needing special education services typically experience severe deficits in several academic and behavioral skills, teachers need to be knowledgeable of and able to implement effective teaching strategies.

The First Days of School: How to Be an Effective Teacher (Wong & Wong, 1998) is an excellent resource for first-year teachers and one that experienced teachers will use throughout their careers. The authors identify three characteristics of effective teachers: holding positive expectations for student success; being good classroom managers; and designing lessons to help students teach mastery. The book presents comprehensive, almost step-by-step information to enable teachers to attain all three characteristics. Sections titled "Your very first priority when class starts is to get the students to work" and "Are you an invitational or disinvitational teacher?" are examples of the common sense approach of this book.

An extensive collection of research-based techniques is presented in *Strategies and Tactics for Effective Instruction* (Algozzine, Ysseldyke, & Elliott, 1997) and *Time Savers for Educators* (Elliott, Algozzine, & Ysseldyke, 1997). The strategies are presented to address four components of effective instruction: planning instruction, managing instruction, delivering instruction, and evaluating instruction. Teachers will especially appreciate the reproducibles provided so strategies can be used immediately and with little preparation. An additional resource on research-based teaching strategies is the Educational Resources Information Center Clearinghouse on Teaching and Teacher Education (ERIC—on the Web: http://www.ericsp.org). The ERIC Clearinghouse, a program of the National Library of Education, U.S. Department of Education, is the largest database on teaching and teacher education.

THE MOST IMPORTANT ACADEMIC RESOURCES SPECIAL EDUCATION TEACHERS MUST HAVE ARE THE CURRENT GENERAL EDUCATION CURRICULAR MATERIALS, INCLUDING ALL STUDENT MATERIALS, TEACHER'S MANUALS, AND ANCILLARY MATERIALS.

Effective instruction also requires the effective use of time. As many special education teachers know, the time students spend waiting (wait time) can easily turn into disruption time. Beginning teachers can review resources such as *Five-Minute Warm-ups for the Middle Grades: Quick and Easy Activities to Reinforce Basic Skills* (Green, Schlichting, & Thomas, 1994) and create an index card file of activities that can quickly engage students during those 5–10 minutes of wait time. Although the title indicates application to the middle grades, the activities in this book can be adapted easily for other ability levels, grade levels, or content. This is a helpful resource for any teacher looking to decrease waiting time, increase student engagement, and prevent disruptive behavior.

Academic Instruction

Unfortunately for some beginning teachers, teacher training programs in special education often include limited course work in teaching methods and materials in academic curricula areas, especially science, social students, language arts, and the general education curricula. As a result, special education teachers frequently feel unprepared to teach all the academic content areas they are required to teach. Therefore, many beginning teachers must prepare themselves for this teaching responsibility.

The most important academic resource special education teachers must have are the current general education curricular materials, including all student materials, teacher's manuals, and ancillary materials. These materials are invaluable for beginning teachers in that they include a scope and sequence of skills to be taught, comprehensive lesson plans, and a variety of assessment tools. Many current curricula also include instructional strategies and accommodations for students with special needs. As mandated by IDEA 1997, all students receiving special education must have access to the general education curriculum. Special education teachers need to approach their school administrators and request their own copies of these materials. Limited access to these resources will decrease the effectiveness and efficiency of instruction.

TeachNet.com (http://www.teachnet.com) and Education World (http://www.education-world.com) are two Web sites suggested for teachers interested in accessing teaching resources on the Internet. These interactive sites are designed for classroom teachers and provide a variety of resources for teachers with varying interests and needs. TeachNet.com offers lesson plans, how-to information sheets, and a teacher-to-teacher message center. Education World offers resources and information in general education and special education, across curriculum areas, and links to related sites. Both of these sites are easy to navigate, and the information is clearly presented.

Motivating students is a challenge for all teachers, especially when students have had a history of academic difficulty. *If You're Going to Teach Kids to Write, You've Gotta Have This Book* (Frank, 1995) is an extremely entertaining approach to teaching and motivating students to write. This book is filled with creative, fun, motivating writing activities and illustrations while at the same time presenting a sound process for developing writing skills. A second resource to help motivate students to write is the *Scholastic Rhyming Dictionary* (Young, 1994). Some teachers have commented that after some of their students were introduced to this book, the students couldn't wait to use this dictionary to write rap lyrics in their free time.

TEACHERS NEED STRATEGIES THAT ARE EFFECTIVE, EFFICIENT, EASY TO USE, PRACTICAL, AND ADAPTABLE.

Cognitive-Behavioral Instruction

Cognitive-behavioral instruction involves teaching students to think before they act and to become aware of the role their thoughts play in determining their behavior. Many special education teachers successfully change student behavior by rewarding desired behavior, and many students demonstrate certain types of behavior in efforts to earn rewards. But what happens when there isn't someone available to reward behavior? Cognitive-behavioral instruction, on the other hand, enables students to control their own behavior independently and throughout their lives. The following are four cognitive-behavioral instruction curricula. Beginning teachers are advised to select one of these curricula and to use it earnestly. Cutting and pasting activities from different curricula is not recommended.

1. Clear Thinking (Nichols, 1998) is an instructional curriculum designed to teach adolescents and young adults cognitive restructuring for clearer and more logical thinking, as based on the rational emotive therapy model. Teachers of students with behavioral disorders have been pleased with this program and with how well students have received it. This program includes an instructor's guide, *Clear Thinking: Talking Back to Whispering Shadows* (Nichols, 1998) and a student text, *Whisper-*

ing Shadows; Think clearly & Claim Your Personal Power (Nicholas & Shaw, 1998).

2. For the elementary grades, *Thinking, Feeling, Behaving* (Vernon, 1989a, and 1989b) is a curriculum also based on rational emotive therapy. It is designed to teach students the connections between their thoughts, feelings, and behavior, and that rational thoughts lead to rational feelings and rational behaviors. This curriculum is available at two grade levels: *Thinking, Feeling, Behaving: An Emotional Education Curriculum for Children* (Vernon, 1989b) and *Thinking, Feeling, Behaving: An Emotional Education Curriculum for Adolescents* (Vernon, 1989a).

3. *I Can Problem Solve: An Interpersonal Cognitive Problem-Solving Program* (Shure, 1992), is an instructional curriculum containing 77 lessons designed to teach students how to think and to use thinking to solve their own problems. This program is available at three grade levels: pre-school, kindergarten and primary, and intermediate elementary grades.

4. The skillstreaming curriculum by Goldstein and McGinnis (1997) is a complete prosocial skills curriculum following a direct instruction approach involving teacher modeling and student role playing. Each curriculum provides teachers with assessment tools, strategies for conducting group lessons, and activities for generalization. This curriculum is available at three grade levels: *Skillstreaming the Elementary School Child* (McGinnis & Goldstein, 1997), *Skillstreaming the Adolescent* (Goldstein & McGinnis, 1997); and *Skillstreaming in Early Childhood* (McGinnis & Goldstein, 1997).

Behavior Management

When asked to identify the most important factor related to the success or failure of beginning teachers, school administrators frequently cite behavior management. Beginning special education teachers must be prepared with classwide and individual behavior management techniques that they can effectively and efficiently use. Teachers have found these resources helpful:

- *The Tough Kid Book* (Rhode, Jenson, & Reavis, 1993) materials provide beginning teachers with the basics in behavior management in a teacher-friendly, ready-to-use format. Both beginning and practicing teachers have found these materials extremely useful. *The Tough Kid Book* (Rhode, Jenson, & Reavis) presents several practical strategies to increase or decrease student behavior, as well as strategies for academic instruction. *The Tough Kid Tool Box* (Jenson, Rhode, & Reavis, 1994) provides the reproducibles for the implementation of the strategies presented in *The Tough Kid Book*.

- *The Teacher's Encyclopedia of Behavior Management: 100 Problems and 500 Plans* (Sprick & Howard, 1995) presents in-depth descriptions of three or more interventions for each of 100 kinds of common problem behavior. The step-by-step descriptions, with sample recording and evaluation materials, provide beginning teachers with the information they need to implement each intervention. The book serves as a model of the comprehensive application of several behavioral change strategies.

TEACHER TRAINING PROGRAMS IN SPECIAL EDUCATION OFTEN INCLUDE LIMITED COURSE WORK IN TEACHING METHODS AND MATERIALS IN ACADEMIC CURRICULA AREAS, ESPECIALLY SCIENCE, SOCIAL STUDENTS, LANGUAGE ARTS, AND THE GENERAL EDUCATION CURRICULA.

- *The Pre-referral Intervention Manual: The Most Common Learning and Behavior Problems Encountered in the Educational Environment* (McCarney & Cummins, 1988) is a book of ideas for classroom interventions. It can be extremely helpful when brainstorming ideas for prereferral interventions, classroom accommodations, and behavioral interventions for students. Included in this book are 193 academic and social behavior problems with approximately 20 or more intervention suggestions for each.

Internet Addresses for Suggested Web Sites

The Council for Exceptional Children (CEC): www.cec.sped.org
ERIC Clearinghouse on Disabilities and Gifted Education: www.ericec.sped.org
ERIC Clearinghouse on Teaching and Teacher Education: http://www.ericsp.org
Education World: http://www.education-world.com
IDEA Practices: http://www.ideapractices.org
National Information Center for Children and Youth with Disabilities (NICHY): http://www.nichy.org
Special Education Resources on the Internet (SERI): http://www.hood.edu/seri
TeachNet.com: http://www.teachnet.com

Classroom Extras

School should be academically focused, challenging, supportive, exciting, and fun. With the never-ending demands faced by beginning teachers and the uncertainty that goes along with beginning a career, some teachers forget to have fun in the classroom or feel they don't have the time to try something new. On the other hand, some very enthusiastic teachers quickly burn out by trying to do something new and different each day. Here's a more re-

---

Recommended Resources for Beginning Teachers

Clear Thinking: Talking Back to Whispering Shadows: Instructor's Guide (Nichols, 1998). ISBN 0-9649142-2-0, $30.

The Council for Exceptional Children (CEC). Membership information, 1-800-232-7733, annual fee $75–$85.

Discover IDEA CD '99 (1999). Available from IDEA Partnerships Projects, http://www.ideapractices.org, $10.

The First Days of School: How to Be an Effective Teacher (Wong & Wong, 1998). ISBN 0-9629360-0-0-6, $30.

Five-Minute Warmups for the Middle Grades: Quick and Easy Activities to Reinforce Basic Skills (Green, Schlichting, & Thomas, 1994). ISBN 0-86530-263-4, $10

I Can Problem Solve: An Interpersonal Cognitive Problem-Solving Program for the Intermediate Elementary Level (Shure, 1992). ISBN 0-87822-340-1, $40.

I Can Problem Solve: An Interpersonal Cognitive Problem-Solving Program for the Kindergarten and Primary Level (Shure, 1992). ISBN 0-87822-339-8, $40.

I Can Problem Solve: An Interpersonal Cognitive Problem-Solving Program for the Preschool Level (Shure, 1992). ISBN 0-87822-338-X, $40.

IDEA 1997: Let's Make It Work (1998). ISBN 0-86586-303-2. Available from CEC, 1-800-232-7733, $15.

If You're Going to Teach Kids to Write, You've Gotta Have This Book (Frank, 1995). ISBN 0-86530-317-7, $15.

Instructor, published by Scholastic Inc., 1-800-544-2917, $15 per year.

The Laughing Classroom: Everyone's Guide to Teaching with Humor and Play (Loomans & Kolberg, 1993), ISBN # 0-915811-44-8, $15.

The Pre-referral Intervention Manual: The Most Common Learning and Behavior Problems Encountered in the Educational Environment (McCarney & Cummins, 1988). ISBN 1-87837-211-4, $30.

Scholastic Rhyming Dictionary (Young, 1994). ISBN 0-590-49461-9, $13.

Skillstreaming the Adolescent (Goldstein & McGinnis, 1997). ISBN 0-87822-369-X, $18.

Skillstreaming in Early Childhood (McGinnis & Goldstein, 1997). ISBN 0-87822-321-5, $14.

Skillstreaming the Elementary School Child (McGinnis & Goldstein, 1997). ISBN 0-87822-372-X, $18.

Strategies and Tactics for Effective Instruction (Algozzine, Ysseldyke, & Elliott, 1997). ISBN 1-57035-119-8, $30.

Survival Guide for the First Year Special Education Teacher (Cohen, Gale, & Meyer, 1994). ISBN 0-86586-256-7. Available from CEC, 1-800-232-7733, $12.

The Teacher's Encyclopedia of Behavior Management: 100 Problems and 500 Plans (Sprick & Howard, 1995). ISBN 1-57035-031-0, $40.

Teaching Tolerance, available from Teaching Tolerance, 400 Washington Avenue, Montgomery, AL 36104, at no cost.

Thinking, Feeling, Behaving: An Emotional Education Curriculum for Adolescents (Vernon, 1989). ISBN 0-87822-306-1, $26.

Thinking, Feeling, Behaving: An Emotional Education Curriculum for Children (Vernon, 1989). ISBN 0-87822-305-3, $26.

Time Savers for Educators (Elliott, Algozzine, & Ysseldyke, 1997). ISBN 1-57035-118-X, $20.

The Tough Kid Book (Rhode, Jenson, & Reavis, 1993). ISBN 0-944584-55-1, $20.

The Tough Kid Tool Box (Jenson, Rhode, & Reavis, 1994). ISBN 1-57035-000-0, $20.

Whispering Shadows: Think Clearly & Claim Your Personal Power: Student Text (Nichols & Shaw, 1998). ISBN 0-9649142-1-2, $15

Note: All costs are approximate.

---

alistic plan for using the resources described in this section: First, plan one night each month to read one magazine, book chapter, or other resource; second, select one new idea or activity to try that month. Selecting, planning for, and implementing one new idea each month is a reasonable and achievable goal for a beginning teacher.

SCHOOL SHOULD BE ACADEMICALLY FOCUSED, CHALLENGING, SUPPORTIVE, EXCITING, AND FUN.

Of all the teacher-oriented magazines, *Instructor* consistently has much to offer beginning teachers: high-quality content, noteworthy educators as authors, and attractive and teacher-friendly presentation. *Instructor* magazine, available at the primary or intermediate level, includes monthly feature articles, posters for classroom use, student activity sheets, and information related to teachers and teaching. *Teaching Tolerance* magazine includes many articles on teacher and school developed programs to promote tolerance toward all types of diversity. Of special interest are the articles describing actual teachers and their projects, programs, and student activities. Beginning teachers find the activities and resources especially helpful for gathering ideas for culturally diverse classrooms.

The Laughing Classroom: Everyone's Guide to Teaching with Humor and Play (Loomans & Kolberg, 1993) is a collection of the authors' teaching experiences and reflections with several ideas for classroom activities. After an experienced special education teacher described how her attitude toward laughter and fun in classroom had changed as a result of this book, several other teachers purchased *The Laughing Classroom* and had similar positive experiences. This resource encourages teachers to reflect on their teaching and offers suggestions for change.

Final Thoughts

This article has described many useful resources for beginning teachers;

but these teachers will find themselves inundated with additional resources they will be *required* to use in the classroom. These materials will include curricula, benchmarks or standards, discipline plans, and other resources established by the school, district, or state. Beginning teachers should first consult building administrators, directors or coordinators of special education, and teaching colleagues to obtain these required resources and implementation information.

As beginning teachers obtain and use various resources, they should remember that *more is not always better.* It is preferable to have a few excellent resources and to study and use them completely and correctly, rather than to have several resources and become overwhelmed or confused by all the ideas presented.

References

Algozzine, B., Ysseldyke, J. E., & Elliott, J. (1997). *Strategies and tactics for effective instruction.* Longmont, CO: Sopris West.

Cohen, M. K., Gale, M., & Meyer, J. M. (1994). *Survival guide for the first year special education teacher* (Rev. ed.) Reston, VA: The Council for Exceptional Children.

The Council for Exceptional Children. (1998). *IDEA 1997: Let's make it work.* Reston, VA: Author.

Elliott, J., Algozzine, B., & Ysseldyke, J. E. (1997). *Time savers for educators.* Longmont, CO: Sopris West.

Frank, M. (1995). *If you're going to teach kids to write, you've gotta have his book* (2nd ed.). Nashville, TN: Incentive Publications.

Goldstein, A. P., & McGinnis, E. (1997). *Skillstreaming the adolescent* (2nd ed.). Champaign, IL: Research Press.

Green, B., Schlichting, S., & Thomas, M. E. (1994). *Five-minute warmups for the middle grades: Quick and easy activities to reinforce basic skills.* Nashville, TN: Incentive Publications.

Jenson, W., Rhode, G., & Reavis, H. K. (1994). *The tough kid tool box.* Longmont, CO: Sopris West.

Loomans, D., & Kolberg, K. (1993). *The laughing classroom: Everyone's guide to teaching with humor and play.* Tiburon, CA: H. J. Kramer Inc.

McCarney, S. B., & Cummins, K. K. (1988). *The pre-referral intervention manual: The most common learning and behavior problems encountered in the educational environment.* Columbia, MO: Hawthorne Press.

McGinnis, E., & Goldstein, A. P. (1997). *Skillstreaming the elementary school child* (2nd ed.). Champaign, IL: Research Press.

McGinnis, E., & Goldstein, A. P. (1997). *Skillstreaming in early childhood* (2nd ed.). Champaign, IL: Research Press.

Nichols, P. (1998). *Clear Thinking: Talking back to whispering shadows.* Iowa City, IA: River Lights Publishing.

Nichols, P., & Shaw, M. (1998). *Whispering shadows: Think clearly & claim your personal power.* Iowa City, IA: River Lights Publishing.

Rhode, G., Jenson, W., & Reavis, H. K. (1993). *The tough kid book.* Longmont, CO: Sopris West.

Shure, M. B. (1992). *I can problem solve: An interpersonal cognitive problem-solving program.* Champaign, IL: Research Press.

Sprick, R. S., & Howard, L. M. (1995). *The teacher's encyclopedia of behavior management: 100 problems and 500 plans.* Longmont, CO: Sopris West.

Vernon, A. (1989a). *Thinking, feeling, behaving: An emotional education curriculum for adolescents.* Champaign, IL: Research Press.

Vernon, A. (1989b). *Thinking, feeling, behaving: An emotional education curriculum for children.* Champaign, IL: Research Press.

Wong, H. K., & Wong, R. T. (1998). *The first days of school: How to be an effective teacher* (Rev. ed.). Sunnydale, CA: Wong Publications.

Young, S. (1994). *The Scholastic rhyming dictionary.* New York: Scholastic Inc.

Sharon A. Maroney *(CEC Chapter #682), Professor in Special Education, Western Illinois University, Macomb, Illinois.*

Address correspondence to the author at Western Illinois University, Special Education Department, 25 Horrabin Hall, Macomb, IL 61455 (e-mail: SA-Maroney1@wiu.edu).

From *Teaching Exceptional Children,* September/October 2000, pp. 22-27. © 2000 by The Council for Exceptional Children. Reprinted with permission.

Here Comes the SUN Team!
Collaborative Inclusion at Work

The SUN team provided intensive support to individual schools so that all students would experience more success in their neighborhood schools.

Donna M. Sobel
Nancy S. Vaughn

A young boy in kindergarten will benefit from the collaborative, inclusive approach to special education in this elementary school. The school is part of an innovative district that has developed a collaborative program in response to the need for technical assistance and support for students with severe disabilities being served at various neighborhood schools.

This project provided intensive support to individual schools so that all students would experience more success in their neighborhood schools. Multidisciplinary team members provided consultation, collaboration, and modeling to better prepare staff members to meet the unique educational challenges that they were encountering.

This article highlights the inclusion model, which resulted in enhanced classroom and school practices and programming for students with significant educational needs. Here, we describe

- The collaborative program development and design.
- Student, family, and educator outcomes during and after the intervention.
- Benefits to the district-level special education department.

Inclusion in Boulder Valley

The Boulder Valley School District in Colorado covers a geographical area of 575 square miles and educates approximately 25,000 students within 56 different schools. During the spring of 1993, the Boulder Valley School District's Special Education Department held many meetings with teachers, parents, and administrators to discuss current inclusionary practices. At that time, the general trend of the school district was clearly toward more neighborhood schooling of students with severe or multiple needs. Of the almost 3,000 students that were identified with special needs and receiving services, approximately 80% were attending their neighborhood school, while the remaining students were transported to a magnet or self-contained program. This trend during the early 1990s toward neighborhood schooling obviously caused the numbers in local "center based" programs to drop while the need for teacher expertise in all schools broadened.

Organizational Framework

Beginning initially as a brainstorming session among the district level special education management team, one coordinator and a special education teacher were identified to explore delivery options. These professionals conducted individual focus meetings with various parent, community, and school district groups. Participants were asked to suggest options for how services could best be delivered. The groups spent a long time in conversations negotiating the common themes among the groups. Figure 1 shows a framework of themes that emerged from those discussions.

Through these extensive discussions with stakeholders, we determined that the district needed an innovative system. It appeared critical that this new system be driven by the key elements of *flexibility, creativity*, and *professionalism*. The name SUN team stands for *Supporting Unique Needs*.

Staffing

Administratively, we obtained staff for our team solely by restructuring current personnel. This included itinerant staff, as well as reallocating the time of staff members who formerly worked with intensive/self-contained or focus programs that were now being shifted to neighborhood schools. Specific staff allocations to the SUN team have varied each year to align with the needs of the district's special education services.

Yearly allocations have ranged from 3.5 to 6.5 certified staff positions, in addition to 1 full-time coordinator position. The composition of these positions is based on expertise in specialty areas, such as speech/language, literacy, and behavioral or cognitive challenges. Because of the characteristics of the specialty areas and the needs of the students, student caseloads are ever changing; therefore, a consultant does not have a set number of students on his or her caseload.

Figure 1. Organizational Framework

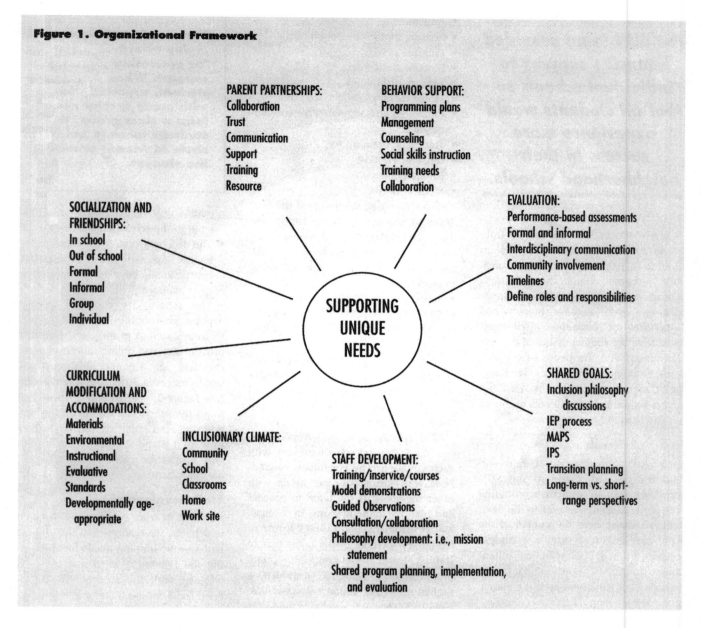

Student Referrals

Each year, approximately 50 new student referrals are made to the SUN team, with 30–40 students continuing with services from one year to the next. Referrals occur over the course of the year. The length of service a student receives from a SUN team consultant ranges from one "in-person" contact to extended consultations over the course of the school year.

Funding

Funding for this inclusion model is provided by the yearly budget and is driven by this data and the identified needs within the special education department.

Roles and Responsibilities

Through a restructuring of staff allocations, the SUN team included parents, teachers, and service providers who could provide technical expertise and resources to share in many areas, such as these:

- Literacy.
- Severe perceptual communicative disabilities.
- Autism.
- Sensory motor integration needs.
- Multiple needs.
- Emotional disorders.
- Sensory disabilities.
- Motor therapy.

- Facilitated and augmentative communication.
- Traumatic brain injury.
- Circle of Friends.
- Family support.
- Medical needs.

From its onset, we designed the SUN Team to provide intensive support so that all students could experience success in their neighborhood schools. Initial efforts outlined the following roles of SUN team members:

- Supporting inclusive practices.
- Developing positive peer interactions.
- Bridging home, school, and community resources.

Table 1. Roles and Responsibilities for SUN Team and Home School Members

SUN Team Members	Home School Team Members
	Initiate referral to SUN Team through current procedures and arrange a preliminary meeting time.
Conduct a preliminary meeting to establish anticipated SUN Team involvement: * Compile student history. * Compile student needs & strengths. * Identify possible SUN Team roles and responsibilities. * Clarify reason(s) for referral.	Identify school case manager to communicate with SUN Team.
Review current records. Conduct teacher and parent interviews to gather background information.	Assume responsibility for meeting the needs of student as established through IEP process. * Continue to gather data. * Continue collaboration with family. * Continue modification/adaptations as delineated. * Maintain contact with general education team.
Conduct observation of the student in the learning environment: * Analyze environmental, instructional, behavioral, and classroom management systems that the student is placed in. * Identify elements of the existing inclusive environment. * Identify student needs.	Above process continues.
Submit a summary of observations and information gathered to the student's case manager and the SUN Team office: * Discussion of observation, interviews and record reviewed. * Interpretation of findings. * Recommendations of services to be provided by the SUN Team.	Above process continues.
Meet with the school team to develop an action plan: * Conduct a review staffing or addendum to clarify IEP revisions. * Establish/define outcomes with an accompanying timeline.	Participate in the development and implementation of an action plan that supports the successful inclusion of this individual: * Facilitate ongoing communications regarding meeting times and programmatic issues with parents or other advocates for the students.
Follow-up and Evaluations: * Participate in meetings, annual review, review, or triennial staffings, as necessary.	Follow-up and Evaluations: Participate in meetings, annual review, review or triennial staffings as necessary.

• Developing, implementing, and evaluating realistic instructional strategies and techniques for adaptations and modifications to individualized education programs (IEPs).

The specific roles and responsibilities of a SUN team consultant vary with each situation. The consultant collaborates with the coordinator along with other members of the team to process and plan recommendations. In a sense, a SUN team consultant then becomes a temporary member of the home school staffing team, facilitating appropriate programming. Table 1 provides a sequence of this support process. We have used this sequence as a guide for SUN and home-school staffing team members.

Referral Process

As the SUN team began to evolve as a service delivery model, we began to see the need for a systematic referral process. In our work with each school in the district, we recognized that each referral was a unique experience, one that took shape based on several complex factors, such as these:

Figure 2. Supporting Unique Needs (SUN) Team Referral Form

Person initiating referral:_____ Building Contact Person: _____

Student Information

Name:_____ School: _____ Phone: _____

Age: _____ Grade: _____ Classroom Teacher: _____

Special Education Case Manager: _____ Phone: _____

Disability: _____

Family Information

Parent Names (mother): _____ (father): _____

Street Address (mother): _____ (father): _____

Home/Work Phone (mother): _____ (father): _____

Known Outside Service Providers Involved

Community Agencies/Contact Person: _____ Phone: _____

Therapists: _____ Phone: _____

Physicians: _____ Phone: _____

Other: _____ Phone: _____

DESCRIBE CONCERN:	**DESIRED OUTCOME:**

Referral assigned to: _____ Date: _____
SUN Team Consultant

- The student and his or her specific needs, history, and developmental level.
- The parents and their experiences, their own personal history with school, beliefs, skills and knowledge, parenting style, and history with their child in the school system.
- The teachers and their experiences, beliefs, and skills in environmental, instructional, behavioral, and classroom management.
- The school, its climate, physical plant, philosophies, and leadership.

In an attempt to initiate the referral process and also obtain thorough documentation for accountability purposes, we developed a SUN team referral form (see Figure 2) and distributed it to all the schools in the district. When referring staff complete the form, they forward it to the SUN team coordinator, who assigns the referral to the appropriate consultant.

Staff Development

As the SUN team began to be involved in schools, we realized that the schools had specific training needs for supporting the referred student and the staff working with the student. We developed some formal training and presented it in the form of inservice and district-level courses. In addition, the district worked collaboratively with universities to develop and provide university courses for teachers, administrators, paraeducators, parents, and support staff. Here are some topics of the courses:

- General information about the history and intent of special education law.
- Special education identification and process.
- Roles of general educators in accommodation and modification efforts.
- Specific information about individual disabilities relevant to an existing situation.
- Teaching strategies.
- Alternative assessments.

In addition to these formal staff development efforts, members of the SUN team often focused on informal training through conversation and modeling to address the needs of specific students. The SUN team consultant quickly learned to be alert and sensitive to seizing consultative opportunities, sometimes referred to as "teachable moments."

While many topics/issues for training became evident as the work to support inclusive programming progressed, several became recurrent areas of focus. *The most requested topics related to the need for staff training included specific conditions such as autism, emotional disturbance, and attention deficit disorder.* Issues that were less requested and possibly perceived as less obvious included changing roles of special educators; sensitivity to general education concerns; collaboration and consultation skills; co-teaching and team involvement; differentiated instruction; facilitation skills for problem-solving; providing for parent education and support; alternative assessment strategies for general educators; behavioral planning, analysis, interventions and management; and data collection and useful application for programming.

In considering the wide range of possible training formats, the SUN team selected and successfully implemented an array of methods. Table 2 lists the formats for addressing these "need-to-know" topics, along with a sample application description. These formats have worked effectively for sharing information and empowering school staffs to provide for all students of diversity.

Table 2. Description of Staff Training Formats

FORMAT	DESCRIPTION
University Course	A three-credit, 45-contact-hour course on Collaboration and Consultation, taught by university faculty.
Workshop	A 2-day training for recertification credit on bilingual assessment taught by a local consulting firm.
Faculty Meeting Presentations	Collaboratively, a SUN team consultant and building level special education personnel provide a joint presentation on Fragile X Syndrome.
Small Group Trainings	A SUN team consultant facilitates a training session for paraeducators on positioning and handling.
Parent Support Groups	Collaboratively, school personnel and the SUN team consultant facilitate evening parent groups to discuss issues such as "Homework Power Struggles."
Mini-Presentations	A SUN team consultant shares pertinent information in staffings or planning meetings around issues such as "Matrix Planning."
Mailings	A SUN team consultant drops articles in the school mail or hand delivers articles or research information related to specific topics such as "Circle of Friends."
Modeling or Co-teaching	A SUN team consultant demonstrates or models strategies for situations such as conflict resolution or problem-solving.

Program Evaluation

Over a 6-year period, the SUN team has evolved as a service delivery model. In an attempt to maintain a thorough understanding of the benefits and drawbacks of this program, we have used two different evaluation measures. The first method of monitoring outcomes of service delivery has been through a monthly caseload update list. This information is processed in monthly team meetings and allow consultants to use each other's expertise on difficult cases.

These meetings serve as an organizational tool, provide a form of supervision and accountability, and add another layer of collaboration on behalf of the students. An analysis of the monthly update data yields valuable evaluation information. In addition to accountability issues, such as numbers of students serviced, numerous programmatic issues have surfaced. The district's special education department has prioritized staff development efforts as a direct result of those highlighted programmatic issues.

Second, in continued efforts to increase and sustain an effective model, the SUN team consultants seek direct feedback through informal surveys. During the spring of each school year, the team asks major stakeholders—parents, administrators, students, general educators, special educators, and related service providers—to anonymously respond to an evaluation survey.

The team collates direct transcriptions from all respondents by question and by specific stakeholder group. SUN team members read all evaluations and identify common themes. We then allocate sufficient time periods to discuss and prioritize specific team goals for the upcoming year.

Program Benefits

An analysis of the responses from the different stakeholders involved in this project revealed positive, recurring themes. The general and special educators responded consistently that the SUN team consultants shared knowledge, skills, and strategies for working with students with challenging needs. They often did this through direct work with the student, plus modeling effec-

tive practices for teachers and paraeducators. Here are some quotations from evaluations:

- Schools noted that the consultant came in with "a fresh perspective" and "new ideas in often difficult situations."
- A principal described the SUN team consultant as displaying "helpful and positive interactions with our whole staff" and a "larger frame of reference aside from specific knowledge."
- Another administrator stated, "One consultant single-handedly salvaged the educational future of a sixth grader. Prior to her involvement, the staff was considering recommending placement other than public school for this student. She met with teachers and parents and developed strategies and plans for the student. Things changed very dramatically and positively for this student."
- Teachers have repeatedly emphasized that they have been given "wonderful suggestions" and "insight" for developing plans of action and "support for difficult situations."

A Day in the Life of a SUN Team Consultant

In addition to coordinating staff development efforts, SUN consultants were called on for model or demonstration teaching, assistance with the securement of materials or resources, facilitation of staffings and meetings, and collaborative planning. Team members have stressed that just as creativity, flexibility, and a willingness to risk and try new ideas are attributes that are critical for success in the schools, they must also be traits they must model as they endeavor to assist in the improvement of inclusive school programming. In their own words: The notations that follow reflect the typical day of a SUN team consultant.

Elementary School #1. Second-grade boy with Tourette Syndrome showing increased aggressive behaviors, oppositional behavior, increased anxiety, and attention deficit symptoms. Team meeting scheduled with special education teacher, paraeducator, principal, and parents. Parents cancel. Team meets to examine programming issues, and process recent incidents of aggression. Reschedule with parents and determine current course of action to reduce inappropriate behaviors and support both the student and staff.

Observe student and paraeducator in second-grade classroom and recess. Speak with general education teacher and parae-ducator. Record anecdotal notes and develop a draft checklist to collect data and monitor behavior.

Wrap-up with special education teacher, sharing notes and suggestions. Check messages and leave for next school.

Middle School #1. Sixth-grade girl with severe attentional difficulties, impulsivity, mood swings, and sexually provocative behaviors. Follow-up meeting with special education teacher from annual review to analyze behavior management program, restructuring where needed and to discuss consultant's observations of student in general education classroom. Check messages, return necessary phone calls, lunch, and next school.

Elementary School #2. Fifth-grade boy with social problems resulting in isolation, labeling, and shunning by peers, erratic mood swings and behavior, unique problems resulting from mother's own mood disorder. Follow-up meeting with special education teacher, paraeducator, mental health counselor, and general education teacher following initial observation by consultant 1 week earlier. Discussion about existing programming, current needs of student and staff, and possible interventions to implement immediately. Schedule annual review. Check messages and leave for next school.

Elementary School #3. Kindergarten boy who is in remission from seizure disorders has had marked behavior changes. Conversation with special educator and observation of the student. Notations regarding classroom climate and environment, interaction with peers, physical therapist, and paraeducator. Notes include a sketch of a suggested rearrangement of the room and a listing of handouts to pull regarding matrix planning. Schedule a follow-up meeting during teacher's planning period for the end of the week. Note: Matrix Planning is a process where a student's needs are delineated vertically on a sheet of paper and the naturally occurring events/ schedule of the day are noted horizontally. Collaboratively the team plots out how the student's needs can best be met.

High School #1. Ninth-grade boy with Asperger's syndrome demonstrating regressive behaviors as a result of the transition to high school. Former student of consultant. Conference with student to process the suspension from school for hitting a classmate and his negative interactions with peers because of teasing. It is requested by student, staff, and parents to have these weekly meetings until the student feels comfortable with his transition.

- Numerous teachers have responded to the "positive benefits we have seen from the friendship groups that the consultant has helped us get going."
- Other teachers have noted, "just the opportunity to talk to someone else and sometimes be reassured that what I'm doing is right on track."
- The director of the special education department maintains, "I believe that the district as a whole has benefited from this service delivery."
- Parents also saw this model as very positive and a valued resource for information and support. One parent felt that her child's "education and social-emotional well-being would be compromised," and "it would be stressful and a struggle working as a team without this much needed support."
- Another parent responded, "I couldn't imagine trying to do this without her."

- Another parent described the benefit as helping her adjust her "parenting to my son's condition."
- One parent stated that, "Others benefited by knowing what to expect from my son. The consultant gave him (and the staff) the coping strategies and suddenly my son went from being a problem student to a productive one who added a great deal to the class, both from the teacher's point of view and other students'. From a parental view, my son had an advocate. That consultant was the critical connection that enabled him not just to survive as a regular student, but to succeed and to succeed well."

Challenges and Needs

When asked what more the SUN team could provide, teachers, administrators and parents alike reported that more time with the consultants either in providing direct instruction to the student or support to the staff was needed. They shared a recognition that the SUN team member's time was stretched too thin, that they were worried about getting the consistent help they needed and that adding more consultants would have been helpful.

Other programmatic recommendations included providing ongoing, organized training sessions to teach special education teachers how to "put out fires, run Individual Planning Sessions and Circle of Friends." In addition, assistance in the planning and implementation of program recommendations was sought.

Feedback is critical in the ongoing refinement of this innovative model for meeting the unique needs of the students. One consultant maintained that the *fluidity* of this consulting process makes it successful and well received: "Each situation is responded to with respect to its uniqueness and not simply plugged into a canned solution or response." Creativity and individualization are the norm for a successful consultation.

Perspectives on Inclusion

In the two decades since the U.S. Congress passed the Individuals with Disabilities Education Act (IDEA; originally the Education for All Handicapped Children Act, Public Law 94-142, 1975), philosophy, theory, and technology in general and special education have changed. As states and districts have reformed and restructured their educational systems, individual schools have had greater opportunities to implement inclusionary practices. Increasing numbers of schools have discovered the benefits of inclusion for all students, while simultaneously asking how to best meet the needs of those students (Doelling, Bryde, Brunner, & Martin, 1998; Elliott & McKenney, 1998; Webb, 1994).

According to Ryndak and Alper (1996), the challenge of special education services is to disseminate that body of knowledge, to move beyond philosophy and generality, and to detail strategies for day-to-day instruction. In disseminating information, schools and districts need to include the following issues:

- Philosophical stance (Daniels & Bizar, 1998; Davis, Monda-Amaya, & Hammitte, 1996; Pugach & Warger, 1996; Skrtic, Sailor, & Gee, 1996; Turner & Louis, 1996).

- Staff training (Anderson, Herr, & Nihlen, 1994; Rankin et al., 1994; Sparks & Hirsh, 1997).
- Resources (Greenwald, Hedges, & Laine, 1996; Hoover & Patton, 1997; Osborne & Dimattia, 1994; Webb, 1994).
- Caseload/class size (Karge, McClure, & Patton, 1995).
- Collaboration skills (Blanton, Griffin, Winn, & Pugach, 1997; Friend & Cook, 1996; Kampwirth, 1999).
- Shared planning (Friend, Reising, & Cook, 1993; Reinhille, 1996; Wood, 1998).
- Coordinating services (Giangreco, 1996; Lugg & Boyd, 1993).
- Service delivery systems (Deering, 1998; Jones & Carlier, 1995; Villa & Thousand, 1992).

Osborne (1994) maintained that as districts redesign their service delivery systems, planners must consider the needs of students with severe disabilities. These authors stated that if school districts do not take the initiative to restructure their educational programs so that inclusive practices can be fully implemented, they will be forced to do so under court orders.

Implications for Practice

Schalock, Fredricks, Dalke, and Alberto (1994) stated that systems change in the education of students with severe disabilities poses many challenges. These researchers pointed out that systems need to advocate for better and different services for students with disabilities. Our experiences indicate that the inclusionary system described here can be a highly effective means of improving services for all learners. As indicated previously, at the onset of this project, approximately 80% of the nearly 3,000 students identified with special needs were attending their neighborhood school.

Overall district efforts in this continued direction have proven successful; 4 years later, nearly 95% of the students with identified needs are now attending their neighborhood school. Our analysis of current efforts has provided us with a firm foundation from which to grow and improve services. The picture emerging from the analysis of this project indicates many positive gains, as well as the following areas of continued emphasis and improvement:

- *Staff Selection.* Professional staff on the SUN team must demonstrate expertise in the following areas: cognitive needs; organization and moving through a variety of settings and situations in a day; and consultation and collaboration in a way that empowers

school staffs to meet challenges in inclusionary practices. Beginning staff allocations were based more on personnel placement needs rather than staffing for areas of expertise. Over the years, it became clear that the expert model was critical for all stakeholders.

- *Staff Development and Training.* Training for staff growth and development must be ongoing. Development of training opportunities should meet the unique needs of each school, keeping in mind the broad scope as well as the specific student needs. Initial perceptions regarding the "luxury" of staff development were quickly replaced with the realization of its necessity. Ongoing changes in the field necessitate that a proactive plan for staff training must be included in this service delivery design. Additionally, ongoing opportunities for parent training and support would enhance this delivery model.

- *Administrative Support.* The district needs to provide support in several critical ways. In the area of leadership there must be clarity of focus toward the immediate and future direction and goals regarding inclusionary practice. The district should model and facilitate good communication with parents, teachers, auxiliary staff, and community supports toward these goals. Fi-

nally, the district must commit initial and ongoing financial and resource support to achieve those goals. At the school level, it is critical openness to outside supports, productive communication systems internally, and the team approach when working to improve inclusionary practices.

References

Anderson, G. L., Herr, K., & Nihlen, A. S. (1994). *Studying your own school: An educator's guide to qualitative practitioner research.* Thousand Oaks, CA: Corwin Press.

Blanton, L. P., Griffin, C. C., Winn, J. A., & Pugach, M. C. (1997). *Teacher education in transition: Collaborative programs to prepare general and special educators.* Denver, CO: Love.

Daniels, H., & Bizar, M. (1998). *Methods that matter: Six structures for best practice classrooms.* York, ME: Stenhouse.

Davis, P. S., Monda-Amaya, L. E., & Hammitte, D. (1996). Where have we been and where are we going? Views from the presidents. *Teacher Education and Special Education, 19,* 235–247.

Derring, P. D. (1998, January). Making comprehensive inclusion of special needs students work in a middle school. *Middle School Journal, 29* (3), 12–19.

Doelling, J. E., Bryde, S., Brunner, J., & Martin, B. (1998). Collaborative planning for inclusion of a student with developmental disabilities. *Middle School Journal, 29* (3), 34–39.

Elliott, D., & McKenney, M. (1998, March/April). Four inclusion models that work. *TEACHING Exceptional Children, 30* (4), 54–58.

Friend, M., & Cook, L. (1996). *Interactions: Collaboration skills for school professionals* (2nd ed.). New York: Longman.

Friend, M., Reising, M., & Cook, L. (1993). Co-teaching: An overview of the past, a glimpse at the present, and considerations for the future. *Preventing School Failure, 37* (4), 6–10.

Giangreco, M. F. (1996, February). What do I do now? A teacher's guide to including students with disabilities. *Educational Leadership, 53* (5), 56–59.

Greenwald, R., Hedges, L., & Laine, R. (1996). The school resources on student achievement. *Review of Educational Research, 66,* 361–396.

Hoover, J. J., & Patton, J. R. (1997). *Curriculum adaptations for students with learning and behavior problems. Principles and practices* (2nd ed.). Austin, TX: Pro-Ed.

Jones, M. M., & Carlier, L. L. (1995). Creating inclusionary opportunities for learners with multiple disabilities: A team-teaching approach. *TEACHING Exceptional Children, 27* (3), 23–27.

Kampwirth, T. J. (1999). *Collaborative consultation in the schools: Effective practices for students with learning and behavior problems.* Upper Saddle River, NJ: Prentice Hall.

Karge, B. D., McClure, M., & Patton, P. L. (1995). The success of collaboration resource programs for students with disabilities in grades 6 through 8. *Remedial and Special Education, 16* (2), 79–89.

Lugg, C. A., & Boyd, W. L. (1993). Leadership for collaboration: Reducing risk and fostering resilience. *Phi Delta Kappan, 75,* 253–258.

Osborne, A. G. (1994). The IDEA's least restrictive environment mandate: Legal implications. *Exceptional Children, 61* (1), 6–14.

Pugach, M. C., & Warger, C. L. (1996). *Curriculum trends, special education, and reform.* New York: Teachers College Press.

Rankin, D., Hallick, A., Ban, S., Hartley, P., Bost, C., & Uggla, N. (1994). Who's dreaming? A general education perspective on inclusion. *Journal of the Association for Persons with Severe Handicaps, 19,* 235–237.

Reinhille, N. (1996). Co-teaching: New variations on a not-so-new practice. *Teacher Education and Special Education, 12* (1), 34–48.

Ryndak, D. L., & Alper, S. (1996). *Curriculum content for students with moderate and severe disabilities in inclusive settings.* Boston: Allyn & Bacon.

Schalock, M., Fredricks, B., Dalke, B., & Alberto, P. (1994). The house that traces built: A conceptual model of service delivery systems and implications for change. *The Journal of Special Education, 28,* 203–223.

Skrtic, T., Sailor, W., & Gee, K. (1996). Voice, collaboration, and inclusion. *Remedial and Special Education, 17,* 142–157.

Sparks, D., & Hirsh, S. (1997). *A new vision for staff development.* Oxford, OH: National Staff Development Council. [ERIC Document Reproduction Service No. ED 410 201]

Turner, C. S. V., & Louis, K. S. (1996). Society's response to differences: A sociological perspective. *Remedial and Special Education, 17,* 134–141.

Villa, R. A., & Thousand, J. S. (1992). How one district integrated special and general education. *Educational Leadership, 50* (2), 39–41.

Webb, N. (1994, July/August). With new court decisions backing them, advocates see inclusion as a question of values. *The Harvard Education Letter, 4,* 3.

Wood, J. W. (1998). *Adapting instruction to accommodate students in inclusive settings* (3rd ed.). Upper Saddle River, NJ: Prentice Hall.

From *Teaching Exceptional Children,* November/December 1999, pp. 4–12. © 1999 by *The Council for Exceptional Children.* Reprinted by permission.

Consultation •Team Teaching •Aide Services •Limited Pullout Services

Four Inclusion Models That Work

Dori Elliott •••• Merry McKenney

Being a special education teacher and a general education teacher who believe in inclusion doesn't always make us the most popular teachers on staff. After 4 years of implementing inclusion in our school, we still face complaints and opposition from our colleagues. Many teachers are concerned with teacher workload and who has the most course preparations. Some colleagues believe that if students with special needs are included with the general class, then the special education teacher has nothing to do but read the newspaper or visit in the teachers' lounge. If the success of inclusion were dependent on positive feedback from teachers, whether that be in planning meetings or in casual conversation among staff, the program would not survive. On the other hand, complaints from parents and students have been almost nonexistent.

Our philosophy of education is what drives our belief in inclusion. We believe that all students learn better within a single-system approach, instead of separation of general and special education services (Stainback & Stainback, 1989). All students have the right to an education in the least restrictive environment possible (P.L. 94–142). Interactions with students, parents, and teachers have led us to believe that inclusion is more successful than a dual system. We believe that for students to be included, they must be a regular part of the classroom routine, feel a sense of belonging within that group, and have the opportunity to be a contributing member. In our district, we are working toward a single educational system that serves all children, with special and general education sharing resources rather than co-existing side by side. (Stainback & Stainback, 1989).

Special Education Law and Outcomes

Looking back on history, we've basically come around in a full circle, at least concerning students with learning disabilities. Before legislation in 1975, students were always integrated within the general classroom, unless their disabilities were so severe that they were institutionalized. In fact, it wasn't until P.L. 94–142 came along that we started changing education for students with disabilities. Students with disabilities were to be assessed and labeled with a disability so that their individual needs could be addressed. In theory all students were to be given equal educational opportunities.

Added to this law was the concept of least restrictive environment (LRE), which gave students with disabilities a chance to be with their peers as much as possible. LRE favored integration, but allowed for segregation. A free, public education is not available in different degrees. LRE, however, depends on the degree of disability, the degree of services available, and therefore a subjective decision for the child study team to make at the individualized education program (IEP) meeting. Regarding LRE, it is difficult to distinguish the difference between students' rights versus students' needs. Thus, people often debate the theory and practice of least restrictive environment, which may result in due process.

After P.L. 94–142, educators designed new assessments, teaching strategies, and materials to better the education for students with learning disabilities. Special education teachers were supposed to possess specialized skills that would benefit these children. They learned *direct instruction* through task analysis and reduction. Through all these painstaking methods, what have we learned? Do these students learn more quickly than if they were in the classroom, retain greater amounts of information or generalize the learned concepts to other areas? The practices within our professional experience do not indicate this to be so. The outcomes of special education programs seem to indicate that they are not working. Children served in special education programs have not made the expected progress in academic, social, or vocational areas (Rogers, 1993).

Which Delivery Model Works for You?

Here are two questions that we believe both general and special educators should ask:

1. How do kids learn best?
2. Does specialized instruction really work to the extent we had hoped it would?

Our goal is not to set up a program that is accommodating for us as teachers, but which is best for students' long-term needs. What we do know is that a pull-out program is easier for all teachers involved to schedule and implement; but we do not feel it is in the best interest of the students.

Before researching and choosing approaches to inclusion, determine what attitudes individual staff members have about students with special needs. Ultimately, a school's approach to inclusion depends on staff beliefs. Because negative attitudes tend to inhibit the potential of inclusion, it is important to address these attitudes in the form of different delivery models. Ideally, we would like to see a school adhere to one belief and thus one model of inclu-

Team teaching approaches can involve both general and special education teachers instructing the entire class or working with small groups to make classroom experiences successful.

sion. Realistically, we find that teachers, just like students, work in an environment that accommodates their needs.

According to current research (Berres & Knoblock, 1987; Rogers, 1993), several approaches are effective in including students with special needs in the general classroom setting. These include consultation, team teaching, aide services, and limited pullout services.

Consultation

Consultation involves no direct services to students in the classroom setting, except for assessment, observation, and planning meetings. General and special educators use special time allotments to meet and discuss student needs and services, and they make adaptations and modifications, as needed. The special education teacher may also provide additional instructional materials based on individual needs.

In this model, we suggest modifying the student's environment to meet attention, vision, hearing, and behavior needs. We also suggest reductions and modifications of classroom assignments. Teachers may provide materials to help students with spatial or organizational difficulties and may supply different writing tools, paper, assignment format, or a word processor.

Consultation requires a strong trust and communication system between the two teachers, as well as parents. It is imperative that the inclusion belief is intact before attempting this model. Since this is the *least* restrictive model, we consider it ideal in theory, but general education teachers may find it the most difficult to buy into. They may have concerns that other children in the classroom may be neglected because of the needs of the students with disabilities. Teachers may feel ineffective and taken

advantage of by the special education teacher. Other, less inclusive models, such as team teaching, may work for some teachers.

Team Teaching

Team teaching can be done in a variety of ways, but involves both general and special education teachers working together in the classroom and instructing the entire class. The least restrictive approach is co-teaching, where both teachers teach together at the same time, or switch subjects or days teaching. Other team-teaching approaches involve small-group work, as well as individual tutorial or assistance to make classroom experiences successful. This approach lends itself to flexibility in delivery, depending on the lesson and students' daily needs. The advantage of team teaching over consultation is the ability to modify and adapt, as needed, on the spot.

When in a co-teaching model, we may work alongside the classroom teacher or deliver instruction independently to the entire class. The amount of time spent in this role depends highly on the number of students and the degree of need in that particular classroom. If a special education teacher possesses a strength or interest in a particular area, he or she will typically be more comfortable teaching this subject. Or if the student is in great need in one area, the general education teacher may plan for the special education teacher to teach that lesson.

Once again, while this is less restrictive in delivery and practice, one or both teachers may not be comfortable with it. We have found ourselves in situations where the co-teachers do not hold the same belief systems. In this case, it is not a comfortable work environment for the teachers or stu-

dents. However, compatible teams have found this approach to be successful and positive.

Benefits and Challenges of Inclusion

Benefits • • • •

• Cooperative learning allows diverse groups of students to succeed.
• Performance-based assessments involve both general and special education teachers in setting goals and evaluating students' progress.
• In a middle school, inclusionary practices are essential to students' self-esteem.

Challenges • • • •

• Training and funding of professional personnel are essential for success.
• Programming for students with multiple disabilities and emotional disturbance must be carefully considered.
• Teachers must provide instruction for all without slowing the pace of the curriculum.

Aide Services

One way to avoid tracking students by ability is to use instructional aides in the classroom, as we have done in our district. Realistically, special education teachers cannot meet the needs of students placed in

Learners with disabilities work alongside those without to benefit both learners in life skills and academics.

several different classrooms at different grade levels without the use of instructional assistance or ownership by the general education teacher. The success of this approach depends on the professional abilities of the aides and on a district's willingness to budget sufficiently. We recommend that the special education teacher have at least monthly contact with the students in their classrooms, to observe and assess progress.

Our aides typically go into a classroom where one to four students with disabilities are placed. Their job is to check the students' progress, provide individual or small-group tutorial assistance, assist the classroom teacher, and report back to the special education teacher. Occasionally, to avoid distractions, the aide may take a small group of students out of the classroom to work on a test or project.

In our experience, most classroom teachers are willing to work with this delivery system as long as the aides are well trained and helpful to them. The problem with this model is the inconsistency with funding and personnel from year to year.

Limited Pullout Service

When most people think of the job of a special education teacher, they think of a pullout program. It is more traditional, and it relieves the general education teacher from a lot of responsibility involving students with disabilities. The special education teacher does not need to plan or collaborate as frequently with the general

education teacher; therefore, both teachers can independently direct their curriculum and classroom.

A pullout program often allows for more individualized instruction. However, it breaks apart the student's day, as well as the student's learning. Students must leave their general classroom at specific times and travel to and from the resource room. Thus, time is wasted gathering supplies and traveling the halls. Most of the lessons learned are not transferred to the general education class because what is learned in the resource room is sometimes out of context. It is almost impossible to coordinate and align curriculum on a daily basis and expect students to transfer this learning. Students often don't feel part of their general class because they are not "smart enough" to remain in there the whole day. Thus, there is a stigma attached to pullout programs, with negative implications.

An example of the need for pullout services is in the case of students with more severe disabilities. For instance, we have pulled students out to work on skills that are extremely low for their grade placement and cannot realistically be adapted or taught within the general classroom. Another case is when the disability creates a distraction that prevents other students from learning or the teacher from teaching.

A pullout option is available only in a limited capacity within an inclusion model. Students should be pulled out only during noninstructional times, as needed. It is our goal to pull students out only when there is no way for them to succeed in the classroom without the more individualized

instruction and tutoring. It is clearly the most restrictive model within our program.

Advantages of Inclusion in an Intermediate School

Allows for Best Teaching Practices

Cooperative learning appears to be effective and practical within the classroom. Learners with disabilities work alongside those without to benefit both learners in life skills and academics. Cooperative learning is essential in an inclusive environment since students of varying abilities are placed together and need to function as a whole unit. Diversity among students is accepted and appreciated. We have found that students of lower abilities benefit greatly from working cooperatively with students of higher abilities. Cooperative learning, developing independent life skills, and improving academics is a common goal among general education and special education. Thus, this practice is accepted and beneficial.

Allows for Active Assessment Practices

Inclusion allows for more realistic assessment of what students can and cannot do, based on performance rather than individually administered tests. IEP goals and objectives in an inclusive model became more practical for the teacher and the student. The classroom teacher also becomes more involved in writing and reviewing the IEP, allowing them to take more ownership for the student. Our purpose of assessment is learning, along with assessment for accountability.

Allows for Personal Growth

Self-esteem and a strong, trusting relationship with a classroom teacher are critical to a student's success through the intermediate grades. To be segregated from age-level peers, work with different curriculum and materials, and be excluded from activities and discussion can in no conceivable way strengthen a student's self-confidence and bonding with a teacher. Students need a self-contained, heterogeneous setting to nurture development at this stage in their lives (Merenbloom, 1988).

Challenges with Inclusion

Successful inclusion programs involve trained personnel. To prevent tracking, more teachers are required than with a pullout program. Funding for inclusion is costly, and many question if this is cost prohibitive. Without adequate funding, inclusion is likely to fall short as a means of servicing learners with disabilities.

There are concerns regarding the inclusion of learners with multiple disabilities, or emotional disturbances, in the classroom all day. Adaptive equipment, the extra personnel required to meet needs of students with more severe needs, and extreme behavioral occurrences are concerns of teachers, parents, and administrators. Our program primarily focuses on students with learning disabilities. However, our school includes students with multiple disabilities and behavioral challenges as much as possible.

Some teachers and administrators worry that to accommodate students with disabilities, the curriculum pace is slowed or altered in a way that is detrimental to students in the classroom. Is this fair to the other students? Is this true, or is it a misconception? We believe these concerns are valid, but they can be dealt with proactively without adverse affects on classroom learning.

Inclusion and Civil Rights

In our intermediate school setting, we have used all the approaches to inclusion we described here. The size of our district warrants several classrooms per grade; therefore, the issue of placing students each year may cause a lack of continuity in our inclusion program. Our administrators would like to see all classroom teachers, Grades 4–6, involved in inclusion. However, this has not happened. We study and evaluate local issues, such as classroom size, beliefs of current teachers on staff, and funding for special education as we continue to develop and improve our inclusive model.

Inclusion, or the integration of students with special needs into the general classroom, is not going to fade away. The focus on civil rights in the United States is more predominant than ever, and inclusion is quite simply an extension of the fight for human equality.

Although the pendulum tends to swing in education, many educators have broken new ground regarding the rights of students with disabilities, and it cannot be covered up. This process of breaking new ground brings unspoken beliefs and feelings to the surface. Many people have concerns that are difficult to deal with. In developing a new educational approach, we meet obstacles that must be dealt with proactively and with an open mind, instead of impeding program development. The positive affects of inclusion have been proven; and it is clearly in the best interest of our nation that we continue to consider and develop inclusive programs in our schools. Success and failures within inclusion programs are evident and compelling; thus, we are becoming more realistic and practical in our expectations and practices.

References

Berres, M., & Knoblock, P. (1987). *Program models for mainstreaming*. Rockville, MD: Aspen.

Merenbloom, E. (1988). *Developing effective middle schools through faculty participation*. Columbus, OH: National Middle School Association.

Rogers, J. (1993). The inclusion revolution. *Research Bulletin, 1*(11), 1–6.

Stainback, W., Stainback, S., & Bunch, G. (1989). Introduction and historical background. In Stainback, Stainback, and Forest (Eds.), *Educating all students in the mainstream of regular education*, (pp. 3–14 and 15–26). Baltimore, MD: Paul H. Brooks.

Resources

Angle, B. (1996). 5 steps in collaborative teaching and enrichment remediation. *TEACHING Exceptional Children, 29*(1), 8–10.

Biklen, D. (1985). *The complete school: Integrating special and regular education*. New York: Columbia University, Teacher's College Press.

Chalmers, L., & Fairede, T. (1996). Successful inclusion of students with mild/moderate disabilities in rural school settings. *TEACHING Exceptional Children, 29*(1), 22–25.

Dieker, L., & Barnett, C. (1996). Effective co-teaching. *TEACHING Exceptional Children, 29*(1), 5–7.

Eichhorn, D. (1983). Focus on the learner leads to a clearer middle school picture. *NASSP Bulletin, 67*(463), 45–48.

Fuchs, D., Fernstrom, P., Scott, S., Fuchs, L., & Vandermeer, L. (1994). Classroom ecological inventory: A process for mainstreaming. *TEACHING Exceptional Children, 26*(3), 11–15.

Kluwin, T., Gonsher, W., & Samuels, J. (1996). The E. T. class: Education together. *TEACHING Exceptional Children, 29*(1), 11–15.

Stainback, W., & Stainback, S. (1987). Educating all students in regular education. *Association for Severely Handicapped Newsletter, 13*(4), 1–7.

Wang, M., & Zollers, N. (1990). Adaptive instruction: An alternative service delivery approach. *Remedial and Special Education, 11*(1), 7–21.

Dori Elliott, *fifth-grade teacher, and* **Merry McKenney,** *fourth- and fifth-grade special education teacher, Belgrade Intermediate School, Belgrade, Montana.*

Address correspondence to Dori Elliott, 702 Hoffman, Belgrade, MT 59714 (e-mail: jelliott@imt.com).

Creating Culturally Responsive, Inclusive Classrooms

Winifred Montgomery

Culturally responsive classrooms specifically acknowledge the presence of culturally diverse students and the need for these students to find relevant connections among themselves and with the subject matter and the tasks teachers ask them to perform.

Let's repeat that: *Culturally responsive classrooms specifically acknowledge the presence of culturally diverse students and the need for these students to find relevant connections among themselves and with the subject matter and the tasks teachers ask them to perform.* In such programs teachers recognize the differing learning styles of their students and develop instructional approaches that will accommodate these styles. In light of the value of culturally responsive instructional practices, schools and districts need to support teachers in their quest to learn about the use of these strategies (see box, "Our Increasingly Diverse Classrooms"). This article provides guidelines for creating culturally responsive, inclusive classrooms. Teachers can use these guidelines with students from culturally and linguistically diverse backgrounds in all kinds of classrooms, but particularly in inclusive settings where general and special educators work together to promote the academic, social, and behavioral skills of all students. First, teachers need to take an honest look at their own attitudes and current practice.

Many teachers are faced with limited understanding of cultures other than their own and the possibility that this limitation will negatively affect their students' ability to become successful learners.

Conduct a Self-Assessment

Many teachers are faced with limited understanding of cultures other than their own and the possibility that this limitation will negatively affect their students' ability to become successful learners. Hence, teachers must critically assess their relationships with their students and their understanding of students' cultures (Bromley, 1998; Patton, 1998). The self-assessment in Figure 1, based on the work of Bromley, 1998), is one tool teachers can use to examine their assumptions and biases in a thoughtful and potentially productive way.

Teachers need to use instructional methods that are tailored to suit the setting, the students, and the subject.

Following self-assessment, teachers need to take time to reflect on their responses (what they have learned about themselves) and make some critical decisions regarding ways to constructively embrace diversity and, thus, create learning environments that respond to the needs of their students.

Use a Range of Culturally Sensitive Instructional Methods and Materials

In addition to self-assessment, an important component of effective culturally responsive classrooms is the use of a range of instructional methods and materials (Bromley, 1998). Teachers need to use instructional methods that are tailored to suit the setting, the students, and the subject. By varying and adapting these methods and materials, teachers can increase the chances that their students will succeed. The following are effective culturally sensitive instructional methods.

Explicit, strategic instruction shows students what to do, why, how, and when.

Figure 1. Diversity Self-Assessment

- What is my definition of diversity?
- Do the children in my classroom and school come from diverse cultural backgrounds?
- What are my perceptions of students from different racial or ethnic groups? With language or dialects different from mine? With special needs?
- What are the sources of these perceptions (e.g., friends, relatives, television, movies)?
- How do I respond to my students, based on these perceptions?
- Have I experienced others making assumptions about me based on my membership in a specific group? How did I feel?
- What steps do I need to take to learn about the students from diverse backgrounds in my school and classroom?
- How often do social relationships develop among students from different racial or ethnic backgrounds in my classroom and in the school? What is the nature of these relationships?
- In what ways do I make my instructional program responsive to the needs of the diverse groups in my classroom?
- What kinds of information, skills, and resources do I need to acquire to effectively teach from a multicultural perspective?
- In what ways do I collaborate with other educators, family members, and community groups to address the needs of all my students?

Source: Adapted from Bromley (1998).

Explicit, Strategic Instruction

Explicit, strategic instruction shows students what to do, why, how, and when. An effective strategy is the think-aloud method, a procedure that takes advantage of the benefits of modeling. In a "think-aloud," the teacher reads a passage and talks through the thought processes for students. The objective is to show students how to ask themselves questions as they comprehend text.

Another important strategy is reciprocal questioning where teachers and students engage in shared reading,

discussion, and questioning (Leu & Kinzer, 1999). The primary goal of this strategy is to help students learn to ask questions of themselves about the meaning they are constructing as they read.

Many classrooms are organized around an interdisciplinary, or cross-curricular theme.

Interdisciplinary Units

Interdisciplinary units include and connect content area learning with language arts and culturally diverse literature (Cooper, 2000; Leu & Kinzer, 1999). Many effective classrooms are organized around an interdisciplinary, or cross-curricular, theme with students participating in meaningful reading, writing, listening, and speaking tasks as they explore the theme through a variety of activities and books. The topic can be drawn from children's lives and interests and sometimes from the curriculum. Teachers can help their students successfully engage in cross-curricular activities by demonstrating how to make connections across the curriculum through literature, by making explicit connections among books, and by helping them recall how previous activities and experiences relate to current studies.

Teachers can design instruction that provides just enough scaffolding, or support, for students to be able to participate in tasks that currently are beyond their reach.

Instructional Scaffolding

Instructional scaffolding involves the use of teacher demonstration and the modeling of strategies that students need to be successful with content area texts (Galda, Cullinan, & Strickland, 1997; Leu & Kinzer, 1999). In scaffolded instruction, teachers determine the difference between what students can accomplish independently and what they can accomplish with instructional support. Teachers then design instruction that provides just enough scaffolding for students to be able to participate in tasks that currently are beyond their reach. Over time, as the tasks become more under the control of the learner, the teacher can introduce more difficult tasks.

Journal Writing

Journal writing provides opportunities for students to share their personal understanding regarding a range of literature in various cultural contexts that inform, clarify, explain, or educate them about our culturally diverse society (Montgomery, in press). For example, character study journals permit students to make their own personal connections with a specific character as they read the story. Students develop their own insight into the characters and the events in the story, and they are given the independence to write what they want about the character. The teacher provides time for students to share their journal writings in small cooperative learning groups, with their teachers, with their tutor(s), or with a reading buddy.

Open-Ended Projects

Open-ended projects allow students to contribute at their varying levels of ability. Such projects work well with diverse learners because they need not start or finish at the same time. Students can explore a topic of interest drawn from their readings of culturally rich literature or a content area topic they are currently studying. They may choose to write reports or prepare oral presentations and create artwork to illustrate some of the major concepts embedded in their topic. Goforth (1998) suggests a project in which interested students make artifacts such as dolls or "story cloths" representing an ethnic or cultural group. They may also want to write stories or poems about their artifacts.

Establish a Classroom Atmosphere That Respects Individuals and Their Cultures

Teachers can enhance students' self-esteem when they construct learning environments that reflect the cultural membership in the class. This strategy goes beyond wall decoration to atmosphere: Teachers must attend to all students and try to involve them equally in all class activities. This recognition gives students a positive feeling about their worth as individuals and as productive members in their classroom. Some strategies to accomplish a positive classroom atmosphere include:

- *Current and relevant bulletin boards* that display positive and purposeful activities and events involving culturally diverse people. Include, for example, newspaper articles (local and national) reporting newsworthy events or accomplishments that involve people of color, photographs of community leaders from culturally diverse backgrounds, student-made posters depicting culturally relevant historical events, and original (student-written) stories and poems with culturally diverse themes.
- *A book corner* with a variety and range of culturally diverse literature, fiction and nonfiction (see box, "Culturally Complex Atmosphere"). The books that are chosen must also deal fairly with disabilities and special needs. The characters should be integrated naturally into the story and not depicted as anomalies or peculiarities in society (Russell, 1994).

Our Increasingly Diverse Classrooms

For many reasons, U.S. schools are serving a growing number of students from culturally and linguistically diverse backgrounds (Obiakor & Utley, 1997; Salend, 2001). In fact, the student population in the United States is growing fastest in those segments with which American education has traditionally been least successful—African Americans and Hispanics.

- *Special Education Overrepresentation.* A disproportionate number of students from culturally and linguistically diverse backgrounds are inappropriately referred to and placed in special education (Yates, 1998). Data from the Office of Civil Rights reveal that African-American and Hispanic-American students, particularly males, are overrepresented in terms of their identification in the disability categories of serious emotional disturbance and mental retardation (Oswald, Coutinho, Best, & Singh, 1999). These data also indicate that students from culturally and linguistically diverse backgrounds identified as needing special education services are more likely to be provided these services in more restrictive settings than their caucasian counterparts.
- *The Negative Effects of Tracking.* The overrepresentation of students from culturally and linguistically diverse backgrounds in special education can have a negative effect on students and their school performance because it places them in a separate and unequal track that denies them access to the general education curriculum. In addition, once placed in special education classes, these students often encounter lowered teacher expectations, a watered down curriculum, and less effective instruction that can have deleterious effects on their school performance, self-esteem, behavior, education and career goals, and motivation to achieve (Nieto, 1996). As a result, these students often do not return to general education placements and frequently leave school before graduating.
- *Need for Culturally Responsive Instruction.* Though several factors contribute to the disproportional representation of students from culturally and linguistically diverse backgrounds in special education (Artiles & Zamora-Duran, 1997), one important factor is the failure of general education teachers to use culturally responsive instructional practices that address their educational, social, and cultural needs (Smith, Finn, & Dowdy, 1993).

- *Cross-cultural literature discussion groups* in which students discuss quality fiction and nonfiction literature that authentically depicts members of diverse cultural groups. Discussion groups help all students feel pride in themselves and in their culture when they see their backgrounds valued in classroom reading and study activities. In small groups, students can read a single work of literature on their own, follow the experiences of a particular character and his or her problems, form opinions about a specific issue put forward in the text, or respond to a significant event that occurred during the character's life (Montgomery, 2000). For example, the content and characterizations in culturally diverse books such as *Amazing Grace* (Hoffman, 1991), *Local News* (Soto, 1993), *Smoky Night* (Bunting, 1994), *The Story of Ruby Bridges* (Coles, 1995) and *Black Cowboys, Wild Horses* (Lester & Pinkney, 1998) can stimulate greater interest in reading *and* in reading to learn.

- *Language arts and social studies programs* provide opportunities for students to share written and oral reports pertaining to their heritage and cultural traditions. Teachers can introduce thematic units that offer excellent opportunities for children to explore a range (in terms of readability) of different forms of literature that look intensively into a single cultural or ethnic experience (Leu & Kinzer, 1999). If learners are to be successful in understanding cultural traditions, trade books must be available in the classroom and in the school library to support these strategies.

Culturally Complex Atmosphere

Creating a *book corner* that appeals to all children can be a challenge for the teacher. The Internet has become an excellent resource for the kind of quality literature that will introduce children to other cultural contexts. Teachers will find valuable links to appropriate children's literature that will help their students appreciate and begin to understand the range of human experiences and cultural backgrounds.

- The Web site *Multicultural Resources* provides articles, reviews, and literature selections organized around specific cultural groups (http://falcon.jmu.edu/~ramseyil/multipub.html).
- An excellent Web resource for children's literature that addresses cultural differences is *The Children's Literature Web Guide* (http://www.acs.ucalgary.ca/~dkbrown/lists.html)
- *The Reading Zone of the Internet Public Library* (http://www.ipl.org/youth/lapage.html) is a central site that is useful for teachers and students.

Foster an Interactive Classroom Learning Environment

Students must have opportunities to interact with each other—to engage in shared inquiry and discovery—in their efforts to solve problems and complete tasks. The following are suggested activities for interactive engagement in the learning process:

- *Cooperative learning groups.* Cooperative groups bring students together within a variety of supportive and collaborative learning activities. The use of this kind of learning group allows all children to see the benefits of bringing together people with diverse backgrounds for problem-solving tasks. They use listening, speaking, reading, and writing together to achieve common goals and in the process become accountable since their performance affects group outcomes. They become active language users and learn to respect each other's opinions (Bromley, 1998). For example, the I-Search Strategy (Leu & Kinzer, 1999) is an interdisciplinary, student-centered inquiry process that emphasizes participation and sharing of research findings in small cooperative learning groups, as well as in whole-group settings. To implement this strategy, children choose a motivating theme; with the teacher's assistance, they formulate their own research plans; next, they follow and revise their plans as they gather information, and then they prepare papers, posters, or presentations using computer software, or they prepare oral reports.

Through the Internet, second-language learners may communicate in their native language with children from similar cultural and linguistic backgrounds.

- *Guided and informal group discussions.* Informal discussions provide opportunities for able students and less able students to collaborate in constructing meaning from text and enable them to learn from each other by sharing their reflections, opinions, interpretations, and questions. The teacher models discussion techniques and guides the students through early discussion sessions. As students develop their discussion skills and begin to feel comfortable talking about story content and their opinions, they will begin to try out ideas without worrying about being wrong or sounding as if they do not understand the story.
- *The Internet.* On the Web, children can experience exciting cultural exchanges. Keypals (see box) is the online equivalent of pen pals. It is an e-mail activity that may be particularly beneficial to second-language learners because the students are able to communicate in their native language with children from similar cultural and linguistic backgrounds. Moreover, important friendships can develop among *all* students as they find out about life in another part of the world, share useful Web sites, and

even help one another with homework (Leu & Kinzer, 1999).

Employ Ongoing and Culturally Aware Assessments

In culturally responsive classrooms, teachers employ ongoing and systematic assessment of student abilities, interests, attitudes, and social skills. This information provides a basis for instructional decision making and offers insights into what to teach and how to teach. In addition, there is an emphasis on student involvement in the assessment process. When students are permitted to participate in their assessment, they are able to reflect on their own progress and offer insights that adults may not have. Examples of culturally sensitive assessment include the following:

- *Daily observation of students' social and learning behaviors in all classroom situations.* Observations can be recorded on checklists, in notebooks, on file cards, or in any way that permits the teacher to summarize observations in a consistent and meaningful way. For example, the class roster can be used as a convenient recording form for observations. The teacher lists the names of the students in the class and then heads subsequent columns across the top of the roster to identify the project, activity, or behavior that is observed.
- *Portfolio assessment.* Student and teacher select samples of work that reveal the diverse needs and abilities of the student. Teachers, students, and family members reflect on what students have done over time, how well they are doing, and what areas need to be improved.
- *Teacher-made tests that are closely tied to the instructional program.* Special attention is given to the cognitive styles of all the students and their evolving academic skills. For example, teachers can design a test to assess students' knowledge or performance within a particular content area lesson.

Keypals

The Internet expands the appeal of pen pal activities in the classroom. A great site for Keypal contacts is: **http://www.stolaf.edu/network/iecc**

At this site, intercultural *E-Mail Classroom Connections,* teachers will find a good source for developing keypals from different countries. There are several mailing lists for teachers looking for partner classrooms. Teachers can subscribe directly from this Web page.

- *Student self-assessment.* Students can respond to questions about their learning during periodic teacher/student conferences. Portfolios can be used during these conferences. For example, students can be shown their work, discuss it with their teachers, and then assess their own progress.
- *Teacher self-evaluation.* Self-evaluation is an integral part of teaching effectiveness. The kinds of questions teachers ask themselves about their choices of teaching behaviors and strategies, the effectiveness and cultural relevance of their lessons, and their reactions and responses to the cultural diversity in their classrooms can greatly contribute to continuing growth in teaching and learning.

Collaborate with Other Professionals and Families

Collaboration and communication with culturally diverse families and with other professionals are essential elements of culturally responsive classrooms. Families are a critical component of a strong instructional program and should be regularly informed about students' progress and encouraged to participate in class and school activities whenever possible. It is also important to establish strong collaborative relationships with colleagues to develop instructional programs that broaden the learning opportunities of all students. The following are specific collaborative activities that teachers and families might use:

Send newsletters to all families providing an overview of culturally responsive curriculum goals, classroom activities, and selected student-written stories and poems.

- *Consult and share ideas regularly with other teachers with whom students work.* Meet with teachers to discuss students' academic and social progress, as well as specific learning needs.
- *Communicate regularly with families.* For example, send newsletters to all families providing an overview of culturally responsive curriculum goals, classroom activities, and selected student-written stories and poems.
- *Invite families to participate in classroom cultural celebrations and to assist in planning such events.* Encourage culturally diverse families to visit the classroom to learn what occurs in the learning environment and to see how well their children are doing—academically and socially.
- *Initiate a parent volunteer tutorial program.*

- *Use culturally diverse community resources.* Invite to your classroom culturally diverse civic leaders, business leaders, artists and writers, members of the police and fire department, college professors, and academically successful high school students.

- *Attend culturally diverse community or neighborhood events.*

Final Thoughts

Of primary importance in any culturally responsive classroom is the teacher's belief that children from culturally diverse backgrounds want to learn. Second, instructional strategies and specific teaching behaviors can encourage all students to engage in learning activities that will lead to improved academic achievement. Third, the development of instructional programs that prevent failure and increase opportunities for success should be the goal of every teacher. The strategies delineated in this article can become important ways of helping all children find purpose, pride, and success in their daily efforts to learn.

Learn More About It

The following resources can help teachers evaluate the results of self-assessment:

Books

Au, K. (1993). *Literacy instruction in multicultural settings.* New York: Harcourt Brace.

Garcia, E. (1994). *Understanding and meeting the challenge of student cultural diversity.* Boston: Houghton Mifflin.

Journal Articles

Montgomery, W. (2000). Literature discussion in the elementary school classroom. *Multicultural Education, 8*(1), 33–36.

Nieto, S. (1994). Lessons from students on creating a chance to dream. *Harvard Educational Review, 64,* 392–426.

Web Sites

Cultural Diversity in the Classroom (http://education.indiana.edu/cas/tt/v212/cultural.html)

ERIC Digests on Cultural Diversity (http://www.uncg.edu/edu/ericcass/diverse/digests/tableoc.htm)

References

Artiles, A. J., & Zamora-Duran, G. (1997). *Reducing disproportionate representation of culturally and linguistically diverse students in special and gifted education.* Reston, VA: The Council for Exceptional Children.

Bromley, K. D. (1998). *Language art: Exploring connections.* Needham Heights, MA: Allyn & Bacon.

Bunting, E. (1994). *Smoky night.* New York: Harcourt Brace.

Coles, R. (1995). *The story of Ruby Bridges.* New York: Scholastic.

Cooper, J. D. (2000). *Literacy: Helping children construct meaning.* Boston: Houghton Mifflin.

Galda, L., Cullinan, B., & Strickland, D. S. (1997). *Language, literacy, and the child* (2nd ed.). Fort Worth, TX: Harcourt Brace.

Goforth, F. S. (1998). *Literature and the learner.* Belmont, CA: Wadsworth.

Hoffman, M. (1991). *Amazing grace.* New York: Scholastic.

Lester, J., & Pinkey, J. (1998). *Black cowboys, wild horses.* New York: Dial Books.

Leu, D. J., & Kinzer, C. K. (1999). *Effective literacy instruction, K–8* (4th ed.). Upper Saddle River, New Jersey: Merrill.

Montgomery, W. (2000). Literature discussion in the elementary school classroom: Developing cultural understanding. *Multicultural Education, 8*(1), 33–36.

Montgomery, W. (in press). Journal writing: Connecting reading and writing in mainstream educational settings. *Reading and Writing Quarterly.*

Nieto, S. (1996). *Affirming diversity* (2nd ed.). New York: Longman.

Obiakor, F. E., & Utley, C. A. (1997). Rethinking preservice preparation for teachers in the learning disabilities field: Workable multicultural strategies. *Learning Disabilities Research and Practice, 12*(2), 100–106.

Oswald, D. P., Coutinho, M. J., Best, A. M., & Singh, N. N. (1999). Ethnic representation in special education: The influence of school-related economic and demographic variables. *The Journal of Special Education, 32,* 194–206.

Patton, J. M. (1998). The disproportionate representation of African Americans in special education. *The Journal of Special Education, 32*(1), 25–31.

Russell, D. (1994). *Literature for children* (2nd ed.). New York: Longman.

Salend, S. (2001). *Creating inclusive classrooms: Effective and reflective practices* (4th ed.). Columbus, OH: Merrill/Prentice Hall.

Smith, T. E. C., Finn, D. M., & Dowdy, C. A. (1993). *Teaching students with mild disabilities.* Fort Worth: Harcourt Brace Jovanovich.

Soto, G. (1993). *Local news.* Orlando, FL: Harcourt Brace.

Yates, J. R. (1998, April). *The state of practice in the education of CLD students.* Presentation at the annual meeting of the Council for Exceptional Children, Minneapolis, MN.

Winifred Montgomery, *Associate Professor, Department of Elementary Education, State University of New York at New Paltz.*

Address correspondence to the author at Department at Elementary Education, State University of New York, 75 S. Manheim Blvd., New Paltz, NY 12561-2443 (e-mail: montgomw@matrix.newpaltz.edu).

UNIT 2
Early Childhood

Unit Selections

5. **From Philosophy to Practice in Inclusive Early Childhood Programs**, Tom Udell, Joyce Peters, and Torry Piazza Templeman
6. **Together Is Better: Specific Tips on How to Include Children With Various Types of Disabilities**, Jane Russell-Fox
7. **Emergent Literacy in an Early Childhood Classroom: Center Learning to Support the Child With Special Needs**, Margaret Genisio and Mary Drecktrah

Key Points to Consider

- How can early childhood educators merge developmentally appropriate practices with special education strategies in inclusive preschool programs?

- How can a preschool teacher set up a classroom and offer choices to children with a variety of types of disabilities so that all students can learn together?

- What is emergent literacy? Why does an early childhood center support emergent literacy better than at-home services?

- Why should books that include representations of children with disabilities be read to all preschoolers? Give examples of some possible books.

 **Links: www.dushkin.com/online/**
These sites are annotated in the World Wide Web pages.

Division for Early Childhood
http://www.dec-sped.org

Institute on Community Integration Projects
http://ici.umn.edu/projectscenters/

National Early Childhood Technical Assistance System
http://www.nectas.unc.edu

Special Education Resources on the Internet (SERI)
http://seriweb.com

Fifteen years ago the U.S. Congress established a grant incentive aimed at providing services for young children at risk of disability, beginning at age 3. By 1991, this amendment to the Individuals with Disabilities Education Act (IDEA) was fully enacted. Child Find organizational groups found many babies, toddlers, and preschoolers with conditions of obvious disability (for example, blindness, deafness, orthopedic handicap). These young children could receive special educational services according to IDEA's mandate: "a free and appropriate education in the least restrictive environment." Many infants and young children were also found who were at "high risk" of developing educational disabilities (for example, low vision, hard of hearing, developmental delay) unless education began before age 6. The 1997 reauthorization of IDEA supported and augmented the mandate for early childhood special education and especially for very early family/child intervention at home. Special services were initiated for children from birth to age 3 when they were assessed as in need of such very early help.

The United States is faced with multiple questions about the education of its future citizens—its young children. Many U.S. babies are born preterm, small for their gestational age, and/or with extremely low birth weight. This is a direct result of the United States' high rate of teenage pregnancy (nearly double that of most European countries and Canada) and its low rate of obtaining adequate prenatal care, especially among young and/or poor mothers. These infants are at high risk for developing disabilities and conditions of educational exceptionality. Early intervention can help these babies.

All services to be provided for any infant, toddler, or preschooler with a disability, and for his or her family, are to be articulated in an individualized family service plan (IFSP). The IFSP is to be written and implemented as soon as the infant or young child is determined to be at risk. IFSPs specify what services will be provided for the parents, for the diagnosed child, for siblings, and for all significant caregivers. Children with pervasive disabilities (for example, autism, traumatic brain injuries, blindness, deafness, orthopedic impairments, health impairments, or multiple disabilities) may require extensive and very expensive early childhood interventions.

IFSPs are written in collaboration with parents, experts in the area of the child's exceptional condition, teachers, home service providers, and other significant providers. They are updated every 6 months until the child enters public school and receives an individualized education plan (IEP). A case manager is assigned to oversee each individual child with an IFSP to ensure high quality and continuous intervention services.

In the United States, an association called Child Find locates and identifies infants, toddlers, and young children who qualify for early childhood special education and family services. An actual diagnosis, or label of condition of exceptionality, is not required. Assessment is usually accomplished in a multidisciplinary fashion. It can be very difficult. As much as possible, it is conducted in the child's home in a nonthreatening fashion. Diagnosis of exceptionalities in children who cannot yet answer questions is complicated. Personal observations are used as well as parent reports. Most of the experts involved in the multidisciplinary assessment want to see the child more than once to help compensate for the fact that all children have good days and bad days.

Despite the care taken, many children who qualify for, and would benefit from, early intervention services are missed. Underfunding of Child Find groups and constant short supplies of time, materials, and multidisciplinary professionals to do assessments are prodigious problems. Occasionally the availability of funds for early childhood interventions encourage the overdiagnosis of risk factors in infants from low-income, minority, or rural areas.

A challenge to all professionals providing early childhood special services is how to work with diverse parents. Some parents welcome any and all intervention, even if it is not merited. Other parents resist any labeling of their child as "disabled" and refuse services. Professionals must make allowances for cultural, economic, and educational diversity, multiple caregivers, and single parents. Regardless of the situation, parental participation is the sine qua non of early childhood intervention.

At-home services may include instruction in the educational goals of the IFSP and in skills such as discipline, behavior management, nutrition, and health maintenance. At-home services also include counseling for parents, siblings, and significant others to help them deal with their fears, and to help them accept, love, and challenge their special child to become all he or she is capable of being. A case manager helps ensure that there is cooperation and coordination of services by all team and family members.

Most children receiving early childhood services have some center-based or combined center- and home-based special education. Center care introduces children to peers and introduces the family to other families with similar concerns. It is easier to ensure quality education and evaluate progress when a child spends at least a part of his or her time in a well-equipped educational center.

The first selection for this unit on early childhood takes the reader on a journey from the philosophical roots of programs for young children to the practice of special education in early childhood education inclusion programs for children with disabilities. The authors believe that research-supported special education practices should not be excluded from inclusive preschool curricula. Rather there should be a merging of developmentally appropriate practices for serving young children with intervention practices focused on special education goals and services.

The second article in this unit provides specific tips on how to include children with various types of disabilities in a preschool program. Jane Russell-Fox, a preschool teacher, has had success working in inclusive classrooms and writes about her tried-and-true techniques enthusiastically.

The third article defines emergent literacy as an awareness of print in the environment. It is especially fostered in young children by listening, talking, reading, and writing in center-based programs. The authors address the needs of young children with learning disabilities, mental retardation, emotional-behavioral disorders, speech and language disabilities, special gifts and talents, and visual impairments. They give specific suggestions for center-based learning to support each of these categories.

From Philosophy to Practice in Inclusive Early Childhood Programs

Tom Udell
Joyce Peters
Torry Piazza Templeman

Two 4-year-olds are playing at the water table. Their teacher observes that Michelle splashes her hand on the surface repeatedly, chortling with delight. Carlos is busy pouring water from a large container into several smaller ones and then arranging them in a pattern to his liking.

These children of the same age are at different developmental points in their lives. How can a teacher or a child care provider allow Michelle to do all the splashing she needs to do, teach her social skills in water play, and also encourage Carlos to continue his absorption in measuring and artistic design—as well as learn the social skills of playing with Michelle? A simple water table activity is more complicated than it seems. Why is this play activity important? How can an inclusive program meet the needs of both children?

The Individuals with Disabilities Education Act has challenged all providers of service to young children with disabilities to provide services in natural community settings where young children without disabilities participate. Educators are looking for ways to merge developmentally appropriate practices with practices found effective in the field of early childhood special education. Although these two sets of practices converge at certain points, professionals agree that differences remain (Bredekamp & Rosegrant, 1992).

The Teaching Research Early Childhood Program has developed a conceptual framework to meet the challenge of blending developmentally appropriate practices with early childhood special education recommended practices. This blended approach has resulted in the delivery of quality services within an inclusive preschool/child care setting.

Elements of an Inclusive Program

In the context of early childhood education, what are the differences among practices known as *mainstreaming, reverse mainstreaming, integration*, and *inclusion?* All these terms denote the introduction of children with disabilities into a "typical" environment for some portion of the day, or in the case of reverse mainstreaming, the introduction of some typically developing peers into what is essentially a special education program.

Inclusion goes further in that no one is introduced into anyone else's program. All children attend the same program, all of the time. Each child is given the support he or she needs to be successful in the setting. For children age 3 to school age, these settings are most often public and private community preschool and child care programs.

The most comprehensive and widely disseminated guidelines defining quality services in these settings are *developmentally appropriate practices*, as defined by the National Association for the Education of Young Children (NAEYC).

PRINCIPLES OF EARLY CHILDHOOD SPECIAL EDUCATION

- Intervention focused on functional goals
- Family-centered services
- Regular monitoring and adjustment of intervention
- Transition planning
- Multidisciplinary services

Research in early childhood special education indicates that those using these developmental guidelines as the *sole* principles for providing services to young children with disabilities would fall short of providing the full range of services these children need. Carta, Schwartz, Atwater, and McConnell (1991) warned against the adoption of these guidelines to the potential exclusion of principles and practices that we know are effective for children with disabilities, but also suggest that educators not overlook developmentally appropriate practices in providing inclusive services for these children. Indeed, Bredekamp and Rosegrant stated in a 1992 NAEYC publication:

> Experiences with mainstreaming over the past two decades suggest a conclusion that probably will be made concerning the guidelines... and children with special needs 20 years from now: The guidelines are the context in which appropriate early education of children with special needs should occur; however, a program based on the guidelines alone is not likely to be sufficient for many children with special needs. (p. 106)

Let's look at both recommended practices—developmentally appropriate practices and early childhood special education practices—and find points where educators, children, families, and communities can work together to make inclusive programs successful.

Developmentally Appropriate Practice

NAEYC published a widely used position statement about developmentally appropriate practices for serving young children from birth to age 8 in early childhood programs (Bredekamp, 1987). The association compiled and published this statement in reaction to the concern of early childhood educators with the increasing academic demands made of young children in early childhood programs and general misconceptions about how teachers should provide instruction to young children.

This position statement became the most widely recognized guideline in the field of early childhood education. In 1997 NAEYC published the revised *Developmentally Appropriate Practice in Early Childhood Programs* (Bredekamp & Copple, 1997), clarifying the misunderstandings and misinterpretations that arose from a decade of extensive dissemination of the original position statement.

Based on the developmental theories of Piaget and Vygotsky, the NAEYC guidelines convey the primary message that *learning occurs through exploratory play activities* and that formal instruction beyond the child's current developmental level will result in nonfunctional, rote learning at best. Developmentally appropriate practice suggests that teachers should not attempt to direct or tightly structure learning experiences and that formal academic instruction at the preschool level should not occur.

These guidelines have three dimensions, as follows:

1. *Age appropriateness.* According to child development knowledge and research, all children grow and change in a universal, predictable sequence during the first 9 years of life. This knowledge about typical child development allows teachers to plan appropriate environments and experiences.
2. *Individual appropriateness.* Each child has his or her own unique pattern of growth, strengths, interests, experiences, and backgrounds. Both the curriculum and adults' interactions with children should be responsive to these individual differences.
3. *Cultural appropriateness.* To truly understand each child, teachers and child care providers must recognize and respect the social and cultural context in which the child lives. When teachers understand the cultural context in which children live, they can better plan meaningful experiences that are relevant for each child (Bredekamp & Copple, 1997).

Teachers should use knowledge of child development to identify the range of appropriate behaviors, activities, and materials for a specific age group. As well, they should use this knowledge in conjunction with an understanding of each child in the classroom and his or her unique personalities, backgrounds, and abilities to design the most appropriate learning environment.

Effective early childhood instructional practices emphasize child-initiated, child-directed play activities, based on the assumption that young children are intrinsically motivated to learn by their desire to understand their environment.

NAEYC recommends that instructional practices emphasize child-initiated, child-directed play activities, based on the assumption that young children are intrinsically motivated to learn by their desire to understand their environment. Teaching

strategies include hands-on exploratory activities with emphases on the use of concrete, real, and relevant activities.

Rationale of Early Childhood Special Education

Early childhood special education is based on the premise that early and comprehensive intervention maximizes the developmental potential of infants and children with disabilities. Such intervention produces child outcomes that would likely not occur in the absence of such intervention (McDonnell & Hardman, 1988).

Since the initiation of publicly supported services for preschool children with disabilities in the mid-1970s, professionals in early childhood special education have developed a body of practices. This body of practice has evolved from research, model demonstration, and evaluation efforts and is currently referred to as *early childhood special education recommended practices*. Researchers have documented syntheses of desired characteristics, or recommended practices, of exemplary, early childhood special education models (DEC, 1993; McDonnell & Hardman, 1988; Wolery, Strain & Bailey, 1992; Wolery & Wilbers, 1994). We have selected components of these models and practices that researchers have shown to be essential, effective, and compatible with the NAEYC guidelines (see Carta et al., 1991, for evaluation criteria). These components include setting functional goals and monitoring children's progress toward these goals, planning for transitions, and working closely with families.

Intervention Focused on Functional Goals

Intervention for children with disabilities should focus on producing specific and measurable child goals. To make meaningful changes in children's behavior, these goals need to be functional for each child and for the environments in which the child participates. A *functional* skill is one that is essential to participation within a variety of integrated environments. In early childhood settings, functional skills are those that assist children to interact more independently and positively with their physical and social environments.

For example, it is probably more functional for a child to be able to carry out his or her own toileting functions independently than to be able to name 10 farm animals. Shouldn't we give preference to skills that will enable the child to participate more fully in an integrated setting, as opposed to those skills that would be indicated in the developmental hierarchy or sequence? If our answer is yes, these goals then become the focus for providing individualized intervention. Teachers or care providers design services and instruction to produce a specific outcome—like independent toileting—and this outcome becomes the standard against which the success of an intervention is measured.

Family-Centered Services

The family is the heart of all early childhood programs. Families participate in planning and decision making in all aspects of their children's program.

A good school-family partnership includes a system for a child's family to have regular communication with the classroom staff and have frequent opportunities to participate in their child's program. Quality programs also include procedures for helping families link into existing community resources.

Regular Monitoring and Adjustment of Intervention

Educators and care providers should systematically monitor the effects of specific interventions. Researchers have shown the effectiveness of using *formative* assessment data to monitor children's progress toward their individual goals and objectives. (McDonnell & Hardman, 1988).

Key Aspects of Developmentally Appropriate Practices
- **Developmental evaluation of children for program planning and implementation**
- **High staff qualifications**
- **High ratio of adults to children**
- **Strong relationship between home and program**

We know that such data must be gathered frequently enough to monitor the subtleties of progress or failure. Data-collection systems must measure child progress toward the acquisition of predetermined goals, including the application of skills in a variety of settings.

Transition Planning

Educators and care providers of all children—and particularly children with disabilities—must plan for transition from one school or child care setting to the next one. Early childhood special educators are particularly concerned with transition from preschool to kindergarten because this move signals a major change for the child and the family from familiar and secure surroundings to a new, unknown setting.

This is a time of considerable stress, and teachers and child care providers must engage in careful, timely planning to smooth the process. Many people are involved in the transition planning process: the child's family, the sending teacher, the early intervention specialist, support personnel, and the future receiving teacher. An effective transition plan often begins 1–2 years before the actual move. This preliminary planning enables the sending teachers to identify skills needed in the future environment. These skills are included in the child's curriculum during the last preschool years.

Multidisciplinary Services

Professionals from many disciplines need to participate in the planning of comprehensive services for children with disabilities and their families. Because many of these children and their families have complex needs, no single professional and no one discipline can provide a full range of services.

The specific needs of each child and family determine what disciplines should be involved in assessing, planning, implementing, and monitoring services. The following disciplines are commonly involved in early childhood special education:

- Speech and language therapy.
- Occupational and physical therapy.
- Health and medical services.
- Audiology.
- Disability-specific specialists, such as a vision specialist or autism specialist.

Professionals in these disciplines provide services in an integrated manner: They share knowledge and methods across disciplines, and the entire team develops and implements one comprehensive plan. Following this plan, team members provide consultation services within the early childhood environment.

Merging Programs Through Developmentally Appropriate Practices

The first step to merging these approaches is to recognize the advantages a program adhering to developmentally appropriate practices offers for the successful inclusion of children with disabilities. Such a program will have high-quality components, many of which facilitate the inclusion process.

Facilitating Inclusion

The nature of developmentally appropriate practices allows for the inclusion of children with great variation in development within the same setting. Even in a group of young children without disabilities, of the same age, children can be as much as 2 years apart developmentally.

Thus, planning developmentally appropriate activities and providing equipment and materials for the preschool setting already accommodates children in a wide development range. This allowance in planning and material selection makes it possible to include children with mild and moderate disabilities without additional adaptation.

This developmental approach to planning creates an ideal environment for embedding instruction on individually targeted skills. The developmental emphasis on learning as a process rather than a product also facilitates targeting a variety of individualized objectives. To illustrate the process-versus-product approach, let's look at ways teachers might provide art experiences—and individualized instruction—for children.

The *process* approach to art allows children to explore available materials, experiment, and create individual designs with little regard for the end product. This approach also allows for intervention on a variety of instructional objectives for children with disabilities while all children are involved in the same activity. For example, all children are involved in a fingerpainting activity; one child may be working on requesting objects, another on identifying colors, and yet another on staying with the group.

Providing Quality Indicators

Developmentally appropriate practices are not a curriculum, nor do they dictate a rigid set of standards. Developmental programs will not all look the same, but they will have a similar framework that pays careful attention to child development knowledge and will assist educators in providing quality services for children. The use of developmentally appropriate practices ensures quality in programs in many ways, such as developmental evaluation of children for program planning and implementation, high staff qualifications, a high ratio of adults to children, and strong relationship between home and program.

- *Developmental evaluation.* Decisions about enrollment and placement have a major effect on children. Educators and care providers base these decisions on multiple assessment data emphasizing observations by teachers and parents. Teachers use developmental assessment of child progress and achievement to adapt curriculum, communicate with families, and evaluate program effectiveness. Developmental evaluations of children use valid instruments developed for use with young children; these assessment tools are gender, culture, and socio-economically appropriate (Bredekamp, 1987).

Children of the same age can be as much as 2 years apart developmentally.

- *Staff qualifications.* The NAEYC guidelines for developmentally appropriate practice emphasize the need for staff with preparation and supervised experiences specific to working with young children. Early childhood teachers should have college-level preparation in early childhood education and child development.

- *High adult/student ratios.* A key to implementing developmentally appropriate practices is to have a small number of children per classroom and a high ratio of adults to children. Ratios suggested in the NAEYC position statement are higher than those required for licensing in most states. NAEYC recommended standards describe a ratio of 2 adults to 20 children ages 4–5, with younger children requiring smaller groups with higher adult-to-child ratios.

- *Home-to-program relationship.* NAEYC guidelines recommend parent involvement in all decision making, regular communication between parents and teacher, and encouragement of parent involvement in the day-to-day happenings of the program. These practices help in building a strong relationship between home and the child's community program.

Developing a Conceptual Base

We have developed a conceptual base, recognizing the two sets of practice, that will allow both developmentally appropriate practices and special education principles to exist within the same setting. The Teaching Research Early Childhood Program has developed a philosophy that views developmentally appropriate practices as the foundation on which individualized programs are built, adding special education instruction when needed for individual children. We believe that the two approaches to early childhood are not mutually exclusive.

Figure 1 illustrates this dilemma. The builder has two sets of clearly different materials and cannot decide which to use. The key to moving beyond this dilemma is to recognize that these practices serve distinctively different purposes—and we can view them as different types of resources.

- *Developmentally appropriate practices* are used to design an age-appropriate, stimulating environment supportive of all children's needs. These practices, however, were not developed to reflect or address specific individual needs of children with disabilities and offer little information about specific intervention strategies needed to serve these children.

- *Early childhood special education* practices are used to complement the basic program for children with exceptional developmental needs and to emphasize individualized strategies to maximize children's learning opportunities. These practices, however, do not provide guidelines for designing a quality early childhood learning environment.

When educators recognize these practices as being different, but compatible, they can then plan a single comprehensive program, as shown in Figure 2. The completed school uses developmentally appropriate practices as the material from which the foundation is built and special education practices as the material that completes the structure.

Implementing Both Practices Within the Same Setting

Let's look more closely at how this merger might work. A well-designed early childhood education program, following developmentally appropriate practices, uses a planned, well-organized environment where children interact with materials, other children, and adults. Here the NAEYC guidelines are apparent: Young children are intrinsically motivated to learn by their desire to understand their environment; the program is set up to allow children to self-select activities from a variety of interest centers.

When children show they need further support, educators use special education strategies that are made available in the program. These strategies include the following:

- *Directly prompting practice* on individually targeted skills, based on functional behavioral outcomes.
- *Reinforcing* children's responses.
- *Collecting data* to monitor children's progress and make intervention changes.

Some educators view these strategies as conflicting with developmentally appropriate practices. Some people liken this direct prompting to the formal instruction that NAEYC deplored for use with young children. We believe that this view is a misinterpretation of NAEYC's position statement and the guidelines for developmentally appropriate practices.

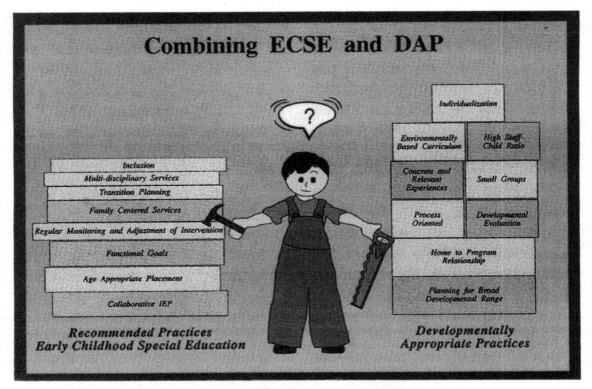

Figure 1

As we mentioned earlier, however, NAEYC guidelines do not exclude intervention strategies for children with identified special needs (Bredekamp & Rosegrant 1993). We hope that by clarifying this misinterpretation, we might encourage teachers to view these intervention strategies as individually appropriate for some children.

As educators begin to merge these two approaches to early childhood education, we will find all children participating in the same well-organized, systematically planned environment—with direct instruction being provided to children who need this type of intervention. This direct instruction is blended into naturally occurring opportunities throughout the ongoing daily routine, such as play at the water table or learning independent toileting. An early childhood program adhering to developmentally appropriate practices provides a strong foundation for the provision of consultation services from professionals across different disciplines.

Consider transition services—an area of special education services that some educators believe conflicts with a child-centered developmental program. The transition planning process has an apparent conflict with developmentally appropriate practice because it presumes that the needs of some future environment should drive the child's curriculum at present. Guidelines for developmentally appropriate practices reject the idea of current curriculums being driven by the needs of a future environment.

To resolve this conflict we can look to the *foundation* concept. In developmentally appropriate practice, we find children participating in an environment planned to fit their current developmental demands and individual backgrounds and interests. Within this environment, children with special needs receive instruction on specific skills that will assist them to be successful in their next setting. Teachers have selected these specific skills or objectives with direct regard to the child's current needs and level of functioning, with some, but not predominant, focus on transition skills needs as dictated by future environments. Skills selected because of the demands of a future environment are ones that can be facilitated without disruption in the current environment. These skills are also within the boundaries of being developmentally appropriate in the future environment.

Mutually Beneficial, Not Mutually Exclusive

In inclusive early childhood education programs, we must caution against adopting developmentally appropriate practices to the exclusion of research-supported special education practices. Similarly, we must not fail to recognize the benefits offered by placing children with disabilities in developmentally appropriate programs. We need to develop an understanding of both sets of practices and to develop a program, from philosophy to practice, that merges practices.

References

Bredekamp, S. (Ed.). (1987). *Developmentally Appropriate Practices in Early Childhood Programs Serving Children from Birth Through Age 8* (Exp. ed.). Washington, DC: National Association for the Education of Young Children.

Bredekamp, S., & Copple, C. (Eds.). (1997). *Developmentally Appropriate Practices in Early Childhood Programs* (Rev. ed.) Washington, DC: National Association for the Education of Young Children.

Bredekamp, S., & Rosegrant, T. (Eds.). (1992). *Reaching potentials: Appropriate curriculum and assessment for young children* (Vol. 1, pp. 92–112). Washington, DC: National Association for the Education of Young Children.

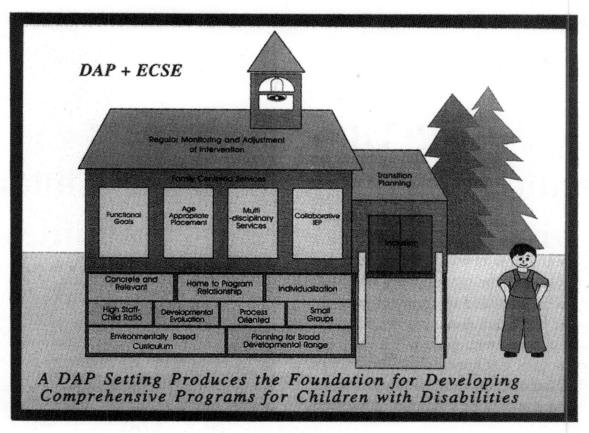

DAP + ECSE

Regular Monitoring and Adjustment of Intervention

Family Centered Services

Transition Planning

| Functional Goals | Age Appropriate Placement | Multi-disciplinary Services | Collaborative IEP |

Inclusion

| Concrete and Relevant | Home to Program Relationship | Individualization |

| High Staff-Child Ratio | Developmental Evaluation | Process Oriented | Small Groups |

| Environmentally Based Curriculum | Planning for Broad Developmental Range |

A DAP Setting Produces the Foundation for Developing Comprehensive Programs for Children with Disabilities

Figure 2

Carta, J. J., Schwartz, I. S., Atwater, J. B., & McConnell, S. R. (1991). Developmentally appropriate practice: Appraising its usefulness for young children with disabilities. *Topics In Early Childhood Special Education 11*(1), 1–20.

DEC Task Force on Recommended Practices. (1993). *DEC recommended practices: Indicators of quality in programs for infants and young children with special needs and their families.* Reston, VA: The Council for Exceptional Children, Division of Early Childhood Education. (ERIC Document Reproduction Service No. ED 370 253)

McDonnell, A., & Hardman, M. (1988). A synthesis of "best practice" guidelines for early childhood services. *Journal of the Division of Early Childhood, 12,* 328–337.

Wolery, M., Strain, P. S., & Bailey, D. B. (1992). Reaching potentials of children with special needs. In S. Bredekamp & T. Rosegrant (Eds.), *Reaching potentials: Appropriate curriculum and assessment for young children* (Vol. 1, pp. 92–112). Washington, DC: National Association for the Education of Young Children.

Wolery, M., & Wilbers, J. S. (Eds.). (1994). *Including children with special needs in early childhood programs.* Washington, DC: National Association for the Education of Young Children.

Tom Udell, *Assistant Research Professor;* **Joyce Peters**, *(CEC Oregon Federation), Associate Research Professor;* **Torry Piazza Templeman**, *(CEC Oregon Federation), Associate Director, Teaching Research Division, Western Oregon University, Monmouth.*

Address correspondence to Tom Udell, Teaching Research Division, Western Oregon University, 345 N. Monmouth Ave., Monmouth, OR 97361 (e-mail: udellt@wou.edu).

We would like to thank Kathy Haydon for her illustrations.

Together Is Better:
Specific Tips on How to Include Children with Various Types of Disabilities

Jane Russell-Fox

My experiences with both inclusive and noninclusive environments has led me to conclude that "together is better." I believe that early childhood professionals who are including children with special needs in their classrooms can set up the environment so that it accommodates these children as well as typically developing children. In doing this the professional takes the first steps toward successful inclusion.

While working in several different self-contained settings, I spent most of my time negotiating with my peers and administrators to plan for inclusion of the special needs children in my group. Usually my plan was for inclusion that would operate 15 to 20 minutes of the school day to give my children a chance at least to hear others model language, involve themselves in cooperative play, and establish friendships.

Staff members who knew I was a strong supporter of inclusive classrooms tended continually to say to me, "That sounds like a good idea; we should try that next week." Next week always came, and we were no closer to the beginning of an inclusive environment than we were the week before.

After my experiences in inclusive environments, I know now that everyone has to be sold on inclusion before it can work successfully. After one is sold on inclusion, it's the job of the team to set

up the environment and offer choices to all children at a variety of levels so that all can learn together in the same room.

It is also the job of the team to continue updating skills and working to improve the effectiveness of the program. Children with special needs do need specialized services based on individual needs, including predictable routines, accurate record keeping of goals, effective teaching strategies, all performed in a developmentally appropriate environment.

There is no blueprint to follow—each person is an individual.

PHOTOGRAPHS (2) © THE GROWTH PROGRAM.

Develop a professional relationship with the child's parents. Keep communication lines open among all involved—parents, physicians, special education teachers, and other relevant people.

The following ideas are only a way to get you started. A range of services needs to be provided to most children with special needs. You can't do it all by yourself. Expect your team members to be there for you. Team members can include everyone from a child care provider to an occupational therapist.

The following processes are adaptations that are easy and use many commonsense ideas and readily available materials. For example, Jennifer has a vision impairment and is not able to see some of the books you read during circle time. What can you do? Try storytelling, enlarging the books, using flannel-board characters, or giving Jennifer a designated spot toward the front during circle time.

Working with a child who has exceptional health needs

- Develop a professional relationship with the child's parents and physician, and in some cases with other care providers who may come in contact with the child.
- Keep communication lines open among all.
- Get informed about the child's health needs, including medicine and diet.
- Invite the school nurse to become a part of the team.
- Develop a program plan for the child who may be out of the classroom for long periods of time. Home visits, telephone calls, classmate phone lists, and care packages from classmates or activity packets from the teacher can assist the child and his or her family in continuing to be a part of the classroom.*

Working with a child who has exceptional hearing needs

- Develop a professional relationship with the child's parents, audiologist, hearing specialist, sign language interpreter, and speech and language therapist.
- Keep communication lines open with them.
- Learn to change a hearing aid battery and cord.
- Use visual and tactile aids as much as you can.
- Use the child's name when seeking the child's attention.
- Make sure you have the child's attention before beginning the activity, giving directions, or introducing additional material.
- Speak at normal speed and volume without exaggerating lip movements.
- Make certain the child sits up close for good visibility of the teacher, activity, and other children.

- Encourage language in group activities by allowing time for the child to start and finish speaking.*

PHOTOGRAPH © THE GROWTH PROGRAM.

Facilitating social skills is an essential part of facilitating true inclusion. Teachers will want to keep groups relatively small so children can interact as children typically do.

Working with a child who has exceptional learning needs

- Concentrate on the child's strengths, not weaknesses.
- Present content in short segments using a multisensory approach (audio, visual, manipulative). Provide for as much overlearning or repeated practice as necessary.
- Praise the child's progress.
- Use task analysis.
- Be patient when it is necessary to show a child how to do something many times.
- Give directions one at a time until a child can handle more than one.
- Help parents to recognize their children's small successes.
- Plan for modeling and imitation.
- Provide clear transitions; try to avoid abrupt changes in activities.
- Present developmental-level challenges.
- Allow time and opportunity to practice new skills needed for activities.

Specific intervention strategies for working with a child with visual impairments

- Consult with the child's parents and vision specialists to determine what the child can see and what play materials would be most appropriate.
- Orient the child to the classroom layout and locations of materials. Give a new orientation whenever changes are made.
- Provide the child with a rich variety of tactile, manipulative, and auditory experiences.
- Encourage independence both by your actions and in the way the room is arranged.
- Be alert to the need for physical prompts.
- Before beginning a new activity explain what is going to happen.*

Working with a child who has exceptional communication needs

- Be a good listener.
- Use parallel talk. Broadcasting play-by-play action of the child's activity helps to stimulate the acquisition of language (e.g., "You're putting the ball in the basket").
- Use alternative communications as needed (e.g., sign language, augmentative communication).
- Have everyone in the classroom model good language by talking about and labeling what they are doing.
- Promote specific reasons for expressing language (i.e., giving information, requesting and getting attention, protesting, and commenting).

Working with a child who has exceptional physical needs

- Get input from the physical therapist on the proper handling and positioning of the child. Get specific directions on the length of time the child should be in a given position. Seek suggestions from the occupational therapist on adapting fine-motor materials so that the child participates in all of the classroom projects. (Of course parents must be included in all planning for the child.)

- Make sure materials and toys are accessible to the child.
- Remember that physical delays don't always have an accompanying mental disability.
- Become familiar with adaptive equipment and know how to use and care for it.
- Arrange the environment to accommodate adaptive equipment.
- Allow extra time for making transitions.
- Support and encourage that which the child can do physically.
- Foster independence by focusing on the child's nonphysical abilities.

FACILITATING SOCIAL SKILLS IS AN ESsential part of facilitating true inclusion. Teachers will want to keep groups relatively small so children can interact as children typically do. Rewarding remarks reinforce specific desired behaviors. Materials appropriate to the skills of interaction desired need to be provided. For example, if your desired outcome is cooperation, set up situations in the classroom to encourage teamwork—"After we pick up the blocks, then we can get ready for [a] snack." Making suf-

ficient materials available helps promote cooperation and imitation.

With each new child with special needs, a few accommodations can be made to a classroom environment and the instruction to allow these children to be included. Placing children with special needs in a learning environment with their typical peers offers many challenges for families and staff, but the rewards reaped and the teamwork accomplished are well worth the effort.

Coming into a work environment that is already sold on inclusion and is *practicing* it has been one of the greatest rewards of my professional career. I strongly urge you to develop inclusive classrooms in *your* setting!

Note

4. *Source: Adapted by permission from R. E. Cook, A. Tessier, and M. D. Klein, *Adapting Early Childhood Curricula for Children with Special Needs*, 3d ed. New York: Merrill/Macmillan, 1992, 206–07, 209.

For further reading

Allen, K.E. 1980. *Mainstreaming in early childhood education.* Albany, NY: Delmar.

Barnes, E., C. Berrigan, & D. Biklen. 1978. *What's the difference: Teaching positive*

attitudes toward people with disabilities. Syracuse, NY: Human Policy Press.

Buscaglia, L. 1983. *The disabled and their parents: A counseling challenge.* New York: Holt, Rinehart, & Winston.

Chandler, P.A. 1994. *A place for me: Including children with special needs in early care and education settings.* Washington, DC: NAEYC.

Cook, R.E., A. Tessier, & M.D. Klein. 1987. *Adapting early childhood curricula for children with special needs.* 3d ed. New York: Harcourt Brace Jovanovich.

Deiner, P.L. 1983. *Resources for teaching young children with special needs.* New York: Harcourt Brace Jovanovich.

Debelak, M., J. Herr, & M. Jacobson. 1981. *Creative innovative classroom materials for teaching young children.* New York: Harcourt Brace Jovanovich.

Froschl, M., L. Colon, E. Rubin, & B. Sprung. 1984. *Including all of us—An early childhood curriculum about disabilities.* New York: Project Educational Equity Concepts.

Fullwood, D. 1990. *Chances and choices: Making integration work.* Baltimore: Paul H. Brookes.

Trainer, M. 1991. *Differences in common. Straight talk on mental retardation, Down syndrome and life.* Bethesda, MD: Woodbine House.

Jane Russell-Fox, M.Ed., is a preschool teacher for the inclusive "Wee Wildcat" program for the Eastmont School District in East Wenatchee, Washington.

From *Young Children*, May 1997, pp. 81–83. © 1997 by the National Association for the Education of Young Children (NAEYC). Reprinted by permission.

Emergent Literacy in an Early Childhood Classroom: Center Learning to Support the Child with Special Needs

Margaret Genisio[1,2] and Mary Drecktrah[1]

A child with special needs will flourish and benefit from an early childhood environment that empowers learning. Center learning empowers a child to be actively engaged in self-directed learning based on strength, ability, and interest. Center learning can enhance interactive language, story response, art, reading and writing-like behavior, collaboration, buddy activity, and independence. All of these empowering areas of development are strongly related to the child's emergent literacy development. The variety of center learning experiences is limited only by the imagination; this article provides a selection of start-up ideas for the early childhood educator.

KEY WORDS: emergent literacy; early childhood; special needs.

INTRODUCTION

Choice, engagement, experimentation, risk taking, opportunity to see and use print, and hear and use language, are all closely linked early childhood education components related to emergent literacy development in the young child (Allen & Mason, 1989; Teale, 1986). The child with special needs requires scaffolding crafted to empower the child to progress towards personal literacy fulfillment (Salinger, 1996).

Center learning is one way to offer a personally nurturing and stimulating environment that scaffolds learning, sometimes taking it beyond the classroom walls and into the home.

The *child with special needs* is one who learns in different ways and at different rates. Children ages 3 to 5 years with disabilities must be educated in the least restrictive environment according to Public Law 99-457, which means that today's classrooms will enhance learning opportunity for all children (Wood, 1993).

Although many educators use the broad term of developmental delays to categorize young children with disabilities, we use particular categories with specific characteristics to help define the type of child for which our suggestions would be suited. The following are areas of special need (Tompkins, 1995, pp. 59–61), with a range of suggestions for early childhood educators (Ysseldyke & Algozzine, 1995). Center learning is one positive, empowering option that can effectively address the suggestions that follow:

Students with Specific Learning Disabilities (Tompkins, 1995). These children are capable of learning, but demonstrating significant problems in one or more of the following areas: listening, speaking, reading (reading-like activity), writing (writing-like activity).

Suggestions for Teachers of Students with Learning Disabilities

- Help youngsters focus on important activities
- Use concrete examples when demonstrating new ideas
- Provide more experiences for practice than necessary for classmates
- Allow youngsters to progress at their own speed
- Modify activities to compensate for learning problems

Students with Mental Retardation (Tompkins, 1995). These children have below average intellectual functioning, coupled with limitations in two or more of the following areas: communicating, self-care, home living, social skills, self-direction, health, safety, and play.

Suggestions for Teachers Working with Mental Retardation

- Use varied and concrete examples when demonstrating new ideas
- Break activities into smaller parts
- Provide more experiences for practice than necessary for classmates
- Give corrective and supportive feedback more often than for others
- Repeat teaching and experiences more often than necessary than for peers

Student with behavior disorders (Tompkins, 1995): these children exhibit frequent frustration and find it difficult to communicate frustrations to another either verbally, in art or in drama. The limited ability to communicate may make this child feel uncomfortable at school.

A center in the classroom that focuses on the alphabet not only reinforces activity that is engaged in at home between parent and child, but also extends this learning into the classroom and perhaps back home once again.

Suggestions for Teachers of Students with Emotional Disturbance

- Establish rules and consequences for behavior with the youngster
- Teach appropriate behaviors, modeling and practicing often
- Praise and reward youngsters for appropriate behaviors
- Be consistent with all youngsters
- Help youngsters monitor their own behavior

Students with language disorders (Tompkins, 1995): This area includes children with needs in listening and speaking; the child finds difficulty in using language to express ideas, interest, feelings or to engage in conversation, descriptions, retelling or made up stories.

Suggestions for Teachers of Students with Speech/Language Disabilities

- Encourage youngsters to talk to each other and adults
- Provide good speech models

- Integrate language activities into all centers
- Value speech and language diversity
- Be aware of developmental language levels, use areas of strength

Students who are gifted (Tompkins, 1995): These children demonstrate the need for more challenge, are able to engage in more advanced reading and writing activities, can communicate ideas and stories and can activate conversation at an advanced level.

Suggestions for Teachers of Students Who Are Gifted and Talented

- Model higher-level thinking skills and creative problem-solving
- Offer challenging activities in centers that generate different types of thinking and solutions
- Encourage independent learning activities
- Provide advanced content through enrichment activities
- Provide challenging instructional activities using youngster's interest and preferences

Students who are visually impaired

Suggestions for Teachers of Students with Visual Impairments

- Organize classroom so student knows where things are
- Verbalize information along with pictures, videos
- Give students freedom to move close to areas of interest and discussion
- Reduce distance between youngster and speaker
- Check that the youngster's glasses or other visual aids are working correctly

SCAFFOLDING THE EXPERIENCE: CRAFTING AN EMPOWERING LEARNING ENVIRONMENT

Darlene Nugent, an early childhood educator, described one parent's reaction to center learning:

Charlene frequently used baby talk and rarely conveyed ideas or messages from school to home. She has been enthusiastic about bringing home the class traveling alphabet book in the special "ABC" tote bag. This is the first time she has been able to tell us about her school activity. In fact, she wants me to help her find print to slip into each letter bag page in the binder. Last night she completed two pages in the book. She placed a box top from vanilla wafers in the "v" section, and an empty package from hot chocolate in the "h" section. Later, when I asked her to tell a story about the pages, she said she has hot chocolate and vanilla cookies when she comes home from school.

A center in the classroom that focuses on the alphabet not only reinforces activity that is engaged in at home between parent and child, but also extends this learning into the classroom and perhaps back home once again. An ABC Center, such as the one described below, enhances this learning:

ABC Center

Goal: To provide children with an opportunity to interact with a variety of materials that depict letters of the alphabet.

Number of Children: Four at one time.

Activity: In the alphabet center are magnetic alphabet letters, both upper and lower case. These can be used with individual magnetic trays, cookie sheets, or burner covers purchased at variety store in sets of four. Children experiment with letter combinations, copying words from books. The center also contains letter picture cards, alphabet stamps, jigsaw letter puzzles, and a traveling alphabet book. A traveling alphabet book is a loose-leaf binder, containing 26 clear plastic pockets, one for each letter of the alphabet. Use an inexpensive supermarket variety of an alphabet book that has been cut up, placing each letter of the alphabet at the top of each page as a guide. The book is sent home with a different child each night. The child then inserts environmental print that contains the featured letter of the alphabet within each pocket. **"Environmental print"** is print that features very familiar logos, such as "McDonalds." When the book is brought back to class each child reads the logo selection to the class, page by page.

Adaptation: A grabber that has a pincher on the end of a stick that a child can operate offers a motorically impaired child the opportunity to manipulate the letters in this center. Another way to participate is to use a flashlight to indicate which letters she/he wants a peer to move to form a sequence. This provides an opportunity for collaborative activity for all children. Wikki Stix are colorful 6-inch lengths of bendable, wax-like strips similar to pipe cleaners, that can be manipulated into letters by all children, providing a different tactile experience. Multisensory opportunities can encourage all students to experiment with letter writing. Sugar or corn meal, instead of sand for writing with their fingers, are environmentally friendly to children with allergies or breathing problems. Sandpaper letters and foam form letters are other three-dimensional materials that may intrigue children.

Nugent explained that Charlene's parent had been provided with supporting directions to use as needed. A main point of emphasis was to encourage Charlene's efforts to tell what she planned to do with the alphabet book she brought home. When Charlene was prompted with key phrases and given time to remember what had happened at school, she was able to tell her mother what she planned to do. Phrases such as the following were used to prompt Charlene: "This looks very interesting! What will we do with this book? What could these pockets be used for?" This language scaffolding was especially prepared by the teacher for Charlene because she had delayed language development.

"I give the children enrolled in my program time to decide what they would like to do, and time to try it. Center activity provides the backdrop for so much individual learning," said Nugent. Nugent has 16 children and 2 assistants in her Oshkosh, Wisconsin, classroom.

> When the children decide to spend time at a center they are making a choice based on their interest at the time. I encourage this. I want the children to enjoy themselves as they activate personal learning. To help children's experimentation and risk taking I suggest that they rotate among my changing centers and explore each one during free visit time. There is lots of opportunity for experimentation and small group activity. Some of my children have special needs or are developmentally delayed. I closely observe to make sure they benefit from the center time and can actively enjoy participating with their peers. Enhancing the emerging literacy of each child is the major goal of the center activity. I keep each child's strengths and needs in mind as I use center learning to promote literacy development.

What Nugent is stressing is based on sound educational principles. She creates a nurturing and safe environment by leading children through enjoyable activities in language-based centers, and then encourages movement, choice-making, and experimentation. This activity, coupled with language interaction and negotiation, cooperative learning, socialization, book handling, and reading- and writing-like activity, form core basics in the development of sound emergent literacy (Butler & Clay, 1979; Salinger, 1996; Teale, 1982).

EMERGENT LITERACY

Early childhood classroom environments that provide the child with authentic opportunity to become engaged in learning by listening, talking, reading, writing, and playing, nurture emerging literacy. The term *emergent literacy* (Clay, 1966) acknowledges children's natural growth and awareness of print in the environment. Literacy development is an ongoing, cumulative activity. This means that the child becomes acquainted with literacy in personally satisfying ways, building on what is learned as time passes. We know that the early childhood child in a literacy-rich home environment acquires a lot of personally satisfying and useful information about literacy through natural learning (Butler & Clay, 1979).

Pretending to write a letter to a friend, telling a story that is similar to one heard while holding the book and turning pages, talking to stuffed animals, and engaging in dramatic play are all literacy-related activities that begin first as home-based endeavors for most children. Observing parents and caregivers as they perform everyday literacy-related activities, such as reading the newspapers, or writing out a grocery list, contributes to the child's natural learning about literacy.

Some children with special needs or disabilities may not have had a literature-rich home environment.

Some children with special needs or disabilities may not have had a literature-rich home environment. The early childhood classroom may be their first encounter with rhyming chants, dramatic play, telling stories, or being read to in a nurturing environment. This background presents a particular challenge to the early childhood professional. Scaffolding and modeling techniques used with center learning strengthen the opportunity for learning success.

SCAFFOLDING AND MODELING FOR THE YOUNG CHILD

Verbal interaction between teacher and child that helps the child to solve a problem, carry out a task or achieve a goal beyond efforts that are unassisted is referred to as *scaffolding* (Applebee & Langer, 1983). Talking about the way the Reading Center is used, and then providing the child with an opportunity to use the Center, is strong verbal scaffolding.

Modeling an activity at the same time scaffolding is provided further enhances the learning opportunity. Modeling involves physical demonstration, showing the child what needs to occur, while demonstrating the activity for the child. For example, if the activity involves using a pointer to "Read the Room," the teacher demonstrates holding the pointer, drawing it under words and pictures in the room (modeling), while telling the child

I am going to start reading the room at the door. Even though I may not be able to read like mom,

dad or the teacher, I can do kid reading, and I can say what I think words are. The first thing I see is Susan's picture with her name, "Susan" on it. When I use the pointer I hold it at this end, and I can put the other end under the word "Susan," and read it. When I come to words I cannot read, I can say what I remember about them, until I have read the room from here where I am standing at the door.

A verbal framework and a physical demonstration have been modeled and scaffolded, providing the child with positive motivation to continue exploring literacy-related activity. For some children, the teacher may have to lead them through the activity. The teacher may have to help guide the pointer so words are not skipped, verbally prompting the child with words.

CENTER LEARNING: ADAPTATIONS TO ENHANCE EMERGENT LITERACY

Learning environments, such as the Center, enhance opportunities to grow in emerging literacy and to interactively use the communicative arts of speaking, listening, reading, and writing. Centers are exciting learning environments for the child. At once small groups of friends gather to meet to share in an activity that has become familiar through modeling and scaffolding. Yet, there are some unresolved mysteries, choices, and a little risk available for the child to consider. Here, the child can anticipate success. Perhaps there are artifacts at the center that are so intriguing that she/he wants to carry learning beyond the classroom, sharing it with a parent or sibling, as was the case with Charlene and the ABC tote bag containing the traveling alphabet book.

Providing the child with information about how to enter a center, and about center scheduling, is part of the learning associated with participating in this learning experience.

In order to be an ordered environment out of which learning can occur, the center should have a designated location accessible to all, focused on a particular topic, using a prescribed routine to enter and exit, as well as to use the artifacts contained within it. Center goals and outcomes are predetermined by the teacher, with the strengths and needs of each child in mind. Several centers can be in operation at the same time in a classroom, depending on the arrangement of the room. A center may be a spot in the room, or it may be a collection of items the child carries to a particular spot to use. A Dress-up/Costuming Center, for example, may be a carton containing costuming items which can be carried from the closet to a location in the classroom for use. A Reading Center is usually a permanent classroom location outfitted with cushions, rugs, a rocking chair, and baskets of books, along with stuffed animals that can be read to.

Providing the child with information about how to enter a center, and about center scheduling, is part of the learning associated with participating in this learning experience. At the early childhood level, a 10- to 15-minute time frame is a maximum length of time to be within a center. The child can rotate from one center to another center during specific periods using charts with names and time frames to enhance movement, which is also supervised by the teacher.

Centers are most effective when there is high anticipation by the children about choices and participation. Activity in each center can be for small groups or for one child alone.

"Jason and Lor spent ten minutes at the Sequencing Center reordering loose, duplicated pictures from *Mrs. Wishy-washy* (Cowley, 1980), a story read with a small group of children in the morning. They paged through *Mrs. Wishy-washy* deciding what happened first, next, and so on. The children organized the pages and put them into plastic page savers, placing the pages in a three-ring binder to make their own book. Lor's first language is Hmong and he requires extensive language immersion activity. This activity provided Lor with an opportunity to orally plan with his partner about the organization and order of the story they were working with. The project was visual, linguistic, cooperative and was based on the auditory comprehension of a story. After the children created their picture book they sat together, turned the pages and talked about the story. They had the option of taking their book to the Shared Reading (or Library) Center, a station in close proximity to the Sequencing Center, to 'read' it to a stuffed rabbit, or to the Overhead Projector Corner, to make an overhead drawing to share," continued Nugent. This scenario took 20 minutes, and included two center activities chosen by the 4½ year-old boys.

Centers that reinforce this learning and scaffold new adventures, such as the Sequencing Center, Shared Reading Center, Library Center, Read the Room Center, and Overhead Projector Corner, extend learning through choice, movement, language interaction, art, reading and dexterity.

Sequencing Center

Goal: To provide an opportunity to understand the order of a story by looking at the pictures and placing them in sequence, and to provide children with an opportunity to work together in a small group.

Number of Children: Four children at one time.

Activity: Purchase several identical copies of inexpensive and very familiar supermarket variety books. Videos with accompanying books work well with this project when viewing is followed by reading the story. Share the story in small groups. Disassemble one copy of the book, placing each page in a plastic page saver pocket. Provide a small three-ring binder and the pages of the story at a table. The children work together to reassemble the story, telling about their decisions, placing their pages inside the binder. They can retell the story by reading it, or by retelling using the pictures as a guide. Another version of the story can be made by reordering the pages in a different way. Pages that are cut to fit inside the remaining cardboard cover can be clipped together so that another version of the story can be drawn.

Adaptation: Children who have difficulty putting items in order can be paired with children who can sequence. They can complement and enhance one another as they work together. For example, children who respond to the story though listening and viewing the video can work with children who enjoy oral interaction and planning. Together they can sequentially organize the story.

Shared Reading Center

Goal: To provide the child with an opportunity to reread, or re-experience, a familiar, class shared big book in personal ways.

Number of Children: Two children at one time.

Activity: In this center an easel displays the recently read big book. Children can decide to "reread" the book, taking turns reading it, or retelling while turning the pages, to one another. Or, they can buddy read, with one child reading a page to a partner. They can chorally read, which focuses on reading the story together.

Library Center

Goal: To engage the children in reading activity within a comfortable area of the classroom dedicated to encouraging self-selection of a wide variety of children's books, enhancing reading and reading-like activity, comfort and relaxation.

Number of Children: Four at one time.

Activity: The books should represent a variety of early childhood education literature, such as picture books, big books, predictable books, fairy tales, poetry, nursery rhymes, and short stories. Books within the library center should be rotated about every 2 weeks, and the quantity should be approximately four books per child within the center. Books can be categorized by the children in plastic, color-coded cartons for ease of selection (e.g., green cartons contain books about animals; blue cartons contain books about friends and family; red cartons contain Big Books; orange cartons contain books that you can read along with, that are predictable). Books made by the children should also be included in the library center. Children should be aware of how to check out books, and they should know how long they may be inside the center. Books read to the class by the teacher should be available at the library center.

Adaptation: For the child with visual problems, or special needs in screening out external stimuli, earphones with recorded books on tape can enhance the enjoyment here. Pairing children with special needs who have beginning print awareness with children who are more aware of the conventions of print in the sharing of a book can benefit both. The child who knows how books are read (front to back, top to bottom, left to right) can demonstrate her/his knowledge in relaxed activity as they both hold the book.

Goal: To engage the child in reading and reading-like activity involving familiar, prominently posted classroom material.

Number of Children: Four at one time.

Activity: This center comprises a container housing three pointers and three sets of lenses-out sunglasses. Children pick up the container, obtain a pointer and pair of sunglasses without lenses (optional). They walk around their classroom, pointing the pointer at posted material, "reading" it. If they are unable to read they name what they see. This causes the child to read in a continuous manner, and is a satisfying experience. Reading occurs in a soft whisper to one's self, or to an accompanying child. For example, holding a pointer, John read the calendar and said: "This is the November month, and today is Thursday." He pointed to the words as he read. He also said, "This is Calley's picture," when he pointed to his classmate's art. Prior to reading the room the teacher should provide modeling and scaffolding so that what is displayed around the room is familiar. Naming what is pointed to is as important as is actual reading. Children can walk around the room alone, or in pairs of two.

Adaptation: For children with motor impairments, a flashlight can substitute for the pointer so they can more easily participate in this activity. It should be pointed out here that the classroom must be barrier free, and the flashlight serves only to enhance bridging distance at the option of the child.

Overhead Projector Corner

Goal: To facilitate manual dexterity in the handling of materials that are used with the overhead projector, and to aid in story comprehension. This center fosters planning together and conveying ideas to others in the class.

Number of Children: Four children at one time.

Activity: Following careful modeling and scaffolding four children move to the location of the overhead projector. The projector is located in a confined space, such between two file cabinets, or in a corner. Four tickets are near the projector. When four tickets are taken no others will enter the space for the projector. Children know how to turn the machine on and off and they know that the machine casts shadows on the wall. In fact, they probably have already had a chance to experiment in this capacity!

The children also know how to draw on acetate sheets. A maximum of 4–6 acetate sheets are provided to the group accompanied by washable markers in a variety of colors. The children select a familiar book to work with, and before retelling the story on the acetate sheets, they sit together to talk about the story and about who will draw what. They then plan to retell the story by illustrating major ideas on the acetate sheets. After they complete the art, they retell it using the art. During retelling the acetate sheets are displayed on the overhead. Acetates can be washed and reused by other youngsters in the class.

Adaptation: Some children require additional guidance through spatial learning activity. To enhance learning Styrofoam trays can serve as a frame for the acetate sheets and help contain the pictures.

CONCLUSION: BENEFITING THE CHILD WITH SPECIAL NEEDS

Engaging children in activities that enhance the natural progression of emergent literacy includes opportunity for active learning and participation in decision making. We know that language interaction, handling of literacy-related materials, and social communication is part of emergent literacy that can be enhanced during the scaffolding and modeling of experiences at center play. The centers presented in this article provide strong opportunity to strengthen emergent literacy through literacy-related play.

Emergent literacy early childhood classrooms with center activity support the child with special needs by providing a variety of literacy-related opportunities that build on strength (Morrow, 1993). Participation and choice are crucial elements of center activity.

Nugent's contact with 4-year-old Charlene and her family continues. Her parents, familiar with Child Find, a process that identifies children with disabilities and provides parents with information about typical childhood development, want more information about her development in the crucial area of language. Following a series of oral exchanges between Charlene and her mother observed by a trained practitioner, her family learned that she was experiencing some developmental delay in language. The observation led to the crafting of a plan (Individual Family Service Plan) intended to address her strengths and needs [to] benefit Charlene, her teachers, as well as her family.

Nugent talks about responding to Charlene's personal plan within her emergent literacy program: Charlene continues baby talk at school, even though she is 4½ years old. She sometimes does not respond to her name, and finds it hard to listen to a story in small groups during shared book reading time. After we were given information about Charlene's language differences, we focused on providing Charlene with more opportunity to listen to familiar stories followed by time for one-on-one interaction, such as we make available for her at the Sequencing Center. A variety of scaffolded and modeled experiences, designed to be brief, such as drawing on acetate with markers in response to reading and sharing this with a small group at Overhead Corner, scaffold Charlene's active language opportunities. Charlene wears a name tag, as do other children. We notice that she is calling others by their name, and responding as well to hers. As Charlene progresses at her personal rate, she will have a buddy to work with on special projects to encourage additional language interaction.

Center learning has provided Charlene, and others with special needs, with a sense of empowerment, choice, and excitement in daily learning adventures. Ideas for center learning grow throughout the school year and become part of the learning environment as needs of the children are understood and met.

NOTES

1. College of Education and Human Services, The University of Wisconsin-Oshkosh, Oshkosh, Wisconsin 54901.

2. Correspondence should be directed to Margaret Genisio, Department of Reading, University of Wisconsin-Oshkosh, 800 Algoma Boulevard, Oshkosh, Wisconsin 54901.

REFERENCES

Allen, J., & Mason, J. (Eds.). (1989). *Risk makers, risk takers, risk breakers*. Portsmouth, NH: Heinemann.

Applebee, A. N., & Langer, J. (1983). *Instructional scaffolding: Reading and writing as natural language activities. Language Arts*, 60, 168–175.

Butler, D., & Clay, M. (1979). *Reading begins at home*. Portsmouth, NH: Heinemann.

Breen, M. J., & Fiedler, C. R. (1996). *Behavioral approach to assessment of youth with emotional/behavioral disorders*. Austin, TX: Pro-Ed.

Cowley, J. (1980). *Mrs. Wishy-washy*. Bothell, WA: Wright Group.

Clay, M. M. (1966). *Emergent reading behavior*. Doctoral dissertation, University of Auckland, New Zealand.

Morrow, L. (1993). *Literacy development in the early years: Helping children read and write*. Boston: Allyn & Bacon.

Salinger, T. (1996). *Literacy for young children*. Columbus, OH: Merrill.

Teale, W. (1982). Toward a theory of how children learn to read and write naturally. *Language Arts*, 58, 555–570.

Teale, W. (1986). The beginnings of reading and writing: Written language development during the preschool and kindergarten and preschool years. In M. Sampson (Ed.), *The pursuit of literacy: Early reading and writing*. Dubuque, IA: Kendall Hunt.

Tompkins, G. E. (1995). *Language arts: Content and teaching strategies*. Englewood Cliffs, NJ: Merrill/Prentice-Hall.

Wood, J. W. (1993). *Mainstreaming: A practical approach for teachers*. (2nd ed.). New York: Merrill/MacMillian.

Ysseldyke, J. E., & Algozzine, B. (1995). *Special education: A practical approach for teachers*. Boston: Houghton Mifflin.

From *Early Childhood Education Journal*, Vol. 26, No. 4, 1999, pp. 225-231. © 1999 by Human Sciences Press, Inc. Reprinted by permission.

UNIT 3
Learning Disabilities

Unit Selections

Key Points to Consider

- How prevalent are LDs? How early can they be assessed? When can intervention begin? What intervention programs are most effective?

- How do graphic organizers benefit students with LDs? Can teachers introduce graphic organizers into inclusive regular education classrooms?

- Helping students with ADHD requires the collaboration of parents, teachers, and students. Name three strategies an educator can use to aid the student's concentration level.

 **Links: www.dushkin.com/online/**
These sites are annotated in the World Wide Web pages.

Children and Adults With Attention Deficit/Hyperactivity Disorder (CHADD)
http://www.chadd.org
The Instant Access Treasure Chest
http://www.fln.vcu.edu/ld/ld.html
Learning Disabilities and Disorders
http://fly.hiwaay.net/~garson/learnd.htm
Learning Disabilities Association of America (LDA)
http://www.ldanatl.org
Teaching Children With Attention Deficit Disorder
http://www.kidsource.com/kidsource/content2/add.html

Today's general education teachers and special educators must seriously attend to the growing numbers of students who have a wide range of different learning disabilities (LDs). LD enrollments in inclusive, regular education classes have skyrocketed. They are the fastest growing and largest category of exceptionalities in elementary, middle, and high schools. Children with LD now make up over 50 percent of those receiving special educational services.

The ways in which students with LDs are identified and served has been radically transformed with the reauthorization of PL94-142 in 1997 as PL105-17, or IDEA (Individuals with Disabilities Education Act). New assessment methods have made the identification of students with LDs easier and far more common. However, many lawmakers and educators feel that students who have other problems (for example behavior disorders, poor learning histories, or dysfunctional families) are erroneously being diagnosed with LDs. IDEA requires states to place students with disabilities in regular classrooms as much as possible or lose their federal funding. A landmark U.S. Supreme Court case in November of 1993 (*Carter v. Florence Co., SC*) ruled that public schools must give appropriate educational services to students with LDs or pay the tuition for private schools to do so. This ruling opened a floodgate of new litigation by parents. IDEA has turned out to be much more expensive than Congress envisioned when it enacted this education bill 25 years ago.

Is the rapid increase of students assessed with learning disabilities really an artifact of misdiagnoses, exaggeration, and a duping of the system that makes available funding for special needs? Neonatal medical technology and achievements in preventive medicine and health maintenance have greatly reduced the numbers of children who are born deaf, blind, or severely physically disabled with multiple exceptional conditions. The very same medical technology has greatly increased the numbers of children who are kept alive who were born prematurely, small for their gestational age, of low birth weight, and "at-risk" for less severe disabilities such as LDs.

A learning disability is usually defined by the lay public as difficulty with reading and/or calculating. IDEA defines it as a disorder in the processes involved in understanding or in using language, spoken or written, that may manifest itself in an imperfect ability to listen, speak, read, write, spell, or to do mathematical calculations. Learning disabilities are identified differently outside of education. *The Diagnostic and Statistical Manual of Mental Disorders* (4th edition) divides LDs into academic skills disorders (reading, mathematics, written expression) and attention deficit hyperactive disorder (ADHD). The National Joint Committee for Learning Disabilities (NJCLD) separates LDs into specific problems related to the acquisition and use of listening, speaking, reading, writing, reasoning, or mathematical abilities. Attention deficit hyperactive disorder, if not accompanied by any specific learning problem or any specific behavioral/emotional disorder, can be assessed as a health disability by both IDEA and NJCLD, especially if it can be ameliorated with medication. Due to parental pressures, the IDEA definition of LDs has been amended administratively to include ADHD if the deficit in attention leads to difficulty in learning.

The rest of the definition of an LD is an exclusionary definition. It helps clarify the nature of LDs: They are not developmental disabilities, deficiencies in any of the sensory systems (vision, hearing, taste, touch, smell, kinesthetics, vestibular sensation), problems associated with health or physical mobility, emotional or behavioral disorders, or disabilities of speech or language. They can be assessed as true LDs only if there is a discrepancy between the child's ability to learn and his or her actual learning.

IDEA's strong emphasis on a free and appropriate educational placement for every child with a disability has forced schools to be more cautious about all assessments and labeling. Increasing numbers of children are now being assessed as LD who once might have been labeled developmentally disabled or disabled by speech, language, emotions, behavior, or one of the senses. A child with an LD may concurrently have a disability in any of these other areas, but if this occurs, both the LD and the other disability/ies must be addressed in an individualized education plan (IEP) designed especially for that unique child.

The causes of LDs are unknown. Usually some central nervous system dysfunctions are believed to underlie the disabilities, even if their existence cannot be demonstrated. Other suspected causes include genetic inheritance, poor nutrition, or exposure to toxic agents. The NJCLD definition of LD presumes biological causation and lifetime chronicity.

About two out of every five students assessed as having a learning disability leaves school before graduation. Frequently the school failure begins early with delayed reading. Special education directed at reading frequently chooses either a phonic or a whole language strategy. Phonics seems to work better for children who do not automatically grasp what reading is about, while whole language seems to work better for students who grasp reading and writing but have difficulty accomplishing them. The need for individualized strategies for individual LD students is paramount.

This unit on learning disabilities addresses both the successes and the frustrations of educating children with LDs. The first article in the section is an overview of LDs. It especially speaks about the remediation of reading disorders, both because reading is critically important to academic success and because more is known about dyslexia (difficulty with words). G. Reid Lyon states that about 80 percent of children with LDs have their primary difficulties in learning to read. Teachers are not as well prepared as they should be to intervene when students have reading disabilities.

The second article contains practical suggestions for effecting curriculum changes that will assist with the education of students with LDs in inclusive regular education classes in neighborhood schools. Graphic organizers really help students learn.

The third article addresses the need to help students with attention deficit hyperactive disorder (ADHD) in the regular classroom. Debates still exist about their assessment as learning disabled and their entitlement to special educational services. Despite the use of medication (usually Ritalin), students with ADHD may make classrooms chaotic. Steven and Vivien Schlozman suggest a number of teaching techniques to reduce confusion and help students with ADHD learn more effectively.

Learning Disabilities

G. Reid Lyon

Abstract

Approximately 5% of all public school students are identified as having a learning disability (LD). LD is not a single disorder, but includes disabilities in any of seven areas related to reading, language, and mathematics. These separate types of learning disabilities frequently co-occur with one another and with social skill deficits and emotional or behavioral disorders. Most of the available information concerning learning disabilities relates to reading disabilities, and the majority of children with learning disabilities have their primary deficits in basic reading skills.

An important part of the definition of LD is its exclusions: learning disabilities cannot be attributed primarily to mental retardation, emotional disturbance, cultural difference, or disadvantage. Thus, the concept of LD focuses on the notion of a *discrepancy* between a child's academic achievement and his or her apparent capacity to learn.

Recent research indicates, however, that disability in basic reading skills is primarily caused by deficits in phonological awareness, which is independent of any achievement-capacity discrepancy. Deficits in phonological awareness can be identified in late kindergarten and first grade using inexpensive, straightforward testing protocol. Interventions have varying effectiveness, depending largely on the severity of the individual child's disability. The prevalence of learning disability identification has increased dramatically in the past 20 years. The "real" prevalence of LD is subject to much dispute because of the lack of an agreed-upon definition of LD with objective identification criteria. Some researchers have argued that the currently recognized 5% prevalence rate is inflated; others argue that LD is still underidentified. In fact, it appears that there are both sound and unsound reasons for the increase in identification rates.

Sound reasons for the increase include better research, a broader definition of disability in reading, focusing on phonological awareness, and greater identification of girls with learning disabilities. Unsound reasons for the increase include broad and vague definitions of learning disability, financial incentives to identify students for special education, and inadequate preparation of teachers
by colleges of education, leading to overreferral of students with any type of special need.

There is no clear demarcation between students with normal reading abilities and those with mild reading disability. The majority of children with reading disabilities have relatively mild reading disabilities, with a smaller number having extreme reading disabilities. The longer children with disability in basic reading skills, at any level of severity, go without identification and intervention, the more difficult the task of remediation and the lower the rate of success.

Children with extreme deficits in basic reading skills are much more difficult to remediate than children with mild or moderate deficits. It is unclear whether children in the most severe range can achieve age- and grade-approximate reading skills, even with normal intelligence and with intense, informed intervention provided over a protracted period of time. Children with severe learning disabilities are likely to manifest an increased number of and increased severity of social and behavioral deficits. When children with disabilities in reading also manifest attention deficit disorder, their reading deficits are typically exacerbated, more severe, and more resistant to intervention.

While severe reading disorders are clearly a major concern, even mild deficits in reading skills are likely to portend significant difficulties in academic learning. These deficits, too, are worthy of early identification and intervention. Even children with relatively subtle linguistic and reading deficits require the expertise of a teacher who is well trained and informed about the relationships between language development and reading development. Unfortunately, such teachers are in short supply, primarily because of a lack of professional certification programs providing this training.

This article focuses primarily on deficits in basic reading skills, both because of their critical importance to academic success and because relatively more is known about these deficiencies. However, other academic, social, and behavioral manifestations of learning disability are also important and cannot be assumed to be adequately addressed by programs to improve basic reading skills. While early intervention is necessary, it should not be assumed to be sufficient to address the multiple manifestations of learning disability.

Approximately one-half of all children receiving special education services nationally, or about 5% of the total public school population, are identified as having a learning disability (LD) when the federal definition of LD is used by schools to formulate identification criteria.[1] At the same time, LD remains one of the least understood and most debated disabling conditions that affect children. Indeed, the field continues to be beset by pervasive, and occasionally contentious, disagreements about the definition of the disorder, diagnostic criteria, assessment practices, treatment procedures, and educational policies.[2–6]

Learning disability is not a single disorder, but is a general category of special education composed of disabilities in any of seven specific areas: (1) receptive language (listening), (2) expressive language (speaking), (3) basic reading skills, (4) reading comprehension, (5) written expression, (6) mathematics calculation, and (7) mathematical reasoning. These separate types of learning disabilities frequently co-occur with one another and also with certain social skill deficits and emotional or behavioral disorders such as attention deficit disorder. LD is not synonymous with reading disability or dyslexia although it is frequently misinterpreted as such.[7,8] However, most of the available information concerning learning disabilities relates to reading disabilities, and the majority of children with LD have their primary deficits in reading.[2]

Box 1

Definition of Learning Disability Under the Individuals with Disabilities Education Act

"Specific learning disability" means a disorder in one or more basic psychological processes involved in understanding or in using language, spoken or written, that may manifest itself in an imperfect ability to listen, speak, read, write, spell, or to do mathematical calculations. The term includes such conditions as perceptual disabilities, brain injury, minimal brain dysfunction, dyslexia, and developmental aphasia. The term does not apply to children who have learning problems that are primarily the result of visual, hearing, or motor disabilities, of mental retardation, of emotional disturbance, or of environmental, cultural, or economic disadvantage.

Source: Code of Federal Regulations, Title 34, Subtitle B, Chapter III, Section 300.7(b)(10).

Box 1 shows the statutory definition of learning disabilities contained in the Individuals with Disabilities Ed-

ucation Act (IDEA). An important part of the definition of learning disabilities under the IDEA is the exclusionary language: learning disabilities cannot be attributed primarily to mental retardation, emotional disturbance, cultural difference, or environmental or economic disadvantage. Thus, the concept of learning disabilities embedded in federal law focuses on the notion of a discrepancy between a child's academic achievement and his or her apparent capacity and opportunity to learn. More succinctly, Zigmond notes that "learning disabilities reflect unexpected learning problems in a seemingly capable child."[9]

Although poverty and disability are often found together and each tends to exacerbate the other (*see the article* by Wagner and Blackorby in *The Future of Children*, Spring 1996), Congress has established separate programs to serve children with disabilities (the IDEA) and children in poverty (Title 1). Title 1 of the Elementary and Secondary Education Act provides funding for supplemental programs in schools serving large numbers of economically disadvantaged children. Because individual children with disabilities have strong entitlements to services under the IDEA, Congress's intent was that the IDEA serve only children with "true disabilities" and that the IDEA specifically exclude those students whose underperformance is primarily attributable to poverty. However, in the category of learning disability, and perhaps also in the category of mental retardation, this distinction is difficult or impossible to draw, and no empirical data exist to support this exclusionary practice.

While there is some agreement about these general concepts, there is continued disagreement in the field about diagnostic criteria, assessment practices, treatment procedures, and educational policies for learning disabilities. A number of influences have contributed to these disagreements which, in turn, have made it difficult to build a generalizable body of scientific and clinical knowledge about learning disabilities and to establish reliable and valid diagnostic criteria.[4,5] While some progress has been made during the past decade in establishing more precise definitions and a theoretically based classification system for LD,[8–10] it is useful to understand these historical influences because of their continuing impact on diagnostic and treatment practices for children with learning disabilities.

The next section of this article reviews briefly the historical events that have molded the field of learning disabilities into its present form. Subsequent sections address issues related to the prevalence of learning disabilities, the validity of current prevalence estimates, impediments to the identification and teaching of the child with LD, advances in identification, classification, intervention practices in the area of reading disability, comorbidity of types of learning disabilities (reading, written expression, mathematics disabilities) with disorders of attention and social skills deficits, outcomes for individuals with learning disabilities, and the implications for teacher preparation and school policies.

Figure 1

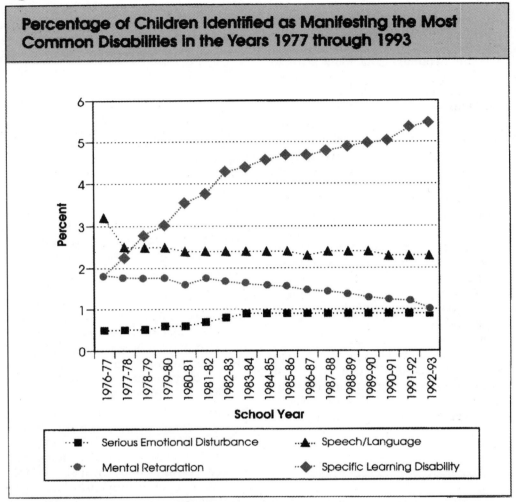

Percentage of Children Identified as Manifesting the Most Common Disabilities in the Years 1977 through 1993

Source: Office of Special Education Programs. *Implementation of the Individuals with Disabilities Education Act: Fifteenth Annual Report to Congress.* Washington, DC: U.S. Department of Education, 1993.

Historical Influences

The study of learning disabilities was initiated in response to the need (1) to understand individual differences among children and adults who displayed *specific* deficits in spoken or written language while maintaining integrity in *general* intellectual functioning and (2) to provide services to these students who were not being adequately served by the general educational system.[6,9,10] Overall, the field of learning disabilities emerged primarily from a social and educational need and currently remains a diagnostic practice that is more rooted in clinical practice, law, and policy than in science. Advocates for children with learning disabilities have successfully negotiated a special education category as a means to educational protection at the same time that the schools have seen an increase in the identification of LD.[6]

The unexpected pattern of *general* strengths and *specific* weaknesses in learning was first noted and studied by physicians during the early twentieth century, thus giving the field its historical biomedical orientation.[10] Doctors noted that children with learning disabilities were similar to adults and children with focal brain damage in that specific impairments in some areas of learning could occur without diminishing strengths in general cognitive ability.

Although the clinical work conducted during the first half of the twentieth century recognized the existence of learning disabilities, such information had little influence on public school policies until the mid-1960s. At this time, behavioral scientists, educators,[11] and parents expressed concern that some children had learning handicaps that were not being served effectively by general educational practices.[9] At the same time, these children were ineligible for special education services because their characteristics did not correspond to any recognized categories of disability. This disenfranchisement stimulated an advocacy movement to provide special educational services to students with learning disabilities,[4,6,9] leading many states to establish a special education category for LD during the late 1960s and 1970s.

Prevalence

The influence of advocacy has, in turn, contributed to a substantial proliferation in the number of children who have been identified with learning disabilities relative to other handicapping conditions (see Figure 1). Clearly, the prevalence of LD identification has increased dramatically.

The "real" prevalence of learning disabilities is subject to much dispute because of the lack of an agreed-upon definition of LD and objective diagnostic criteria.[4,8,12] Some have argued that the currently recognized 5% prevalence rate is excessive and is based on vague definitions, leading to inaccurate identification. On the other hand, research efforts to identify objective early indicators of LD in basic reading skills have concluded that virtually all children scoring below the 25th percentile on standardized reading tests can meet the criteria for having a reading disorder.[12] While less is known about LD in written expression, researchers estimate its true prevalence at between 8% and 15% of the school population.[13] Research also indicates that approximately 6% of the school population has difficulties in mathematics which cannot be attributed to low intelligence, sensory deficits, or economic deprivation.[14]

Increase in Identification

The substantial increase in the identification of children with learning disabilities shown in Figure 1 has led many to question the validity and reliability of LD as a diagnostic category or its "realness" as a handicapping condition.[15] In fact, it appears likely that there are both sound and unsound reasons for the increase, as is discussed later.

It should be made clear that difficulties in the identification of children with learning disabilities do not make the disabilities any less "real" to the student who cannot learn to read, write, or understand mathematics despite good intelligence, an adequate opportunity to learn, and ostensibly good teaching. However, such an anecdotal understanding of learning disability and its prevalence seems inadequate now, given the increase in diagnoses of LD, the consequences of learning failure in children, and the tremendous financial resources that are applied to the identification and teaching of children with learning disabilities. Given what is at stake, it is critical that the construct of learning disability and procedures for identifying children and adults with LD be valid and accepted by the scientific and clinical communities.

The question remains, however, of how to go about increasing the ability to identify individuals with LD accurately. Valid prevalence estimates depend upon a set of

criteria for identification that are clear, observable, measurable, and agreed upon.

The Discrepancy Standard

There is currently no universally accepted test, test battery, or standard for identifying children with LD. While a discrepancy between intelligence quotient (IQ) and achievement has been a widely accepted criterion for the identification of LD and still serves as the driving clinical force in the diagnosis of LD, there is considerable variation in how the discrepancy is derived and quantified.[9,16] Federal regulations and extant clinical criteria[17] do not specify particular formulas or numerical values to assess discrepancy objectively. The effect of this lack of specification on both clinical and research practices is substantial. From a clinical standpoint, a child can be identified as having a learning disability in one school district but not in a neighboring district because of differences in the measure of discrepancy used. From a research perspective, different approaches to the discrepancy measurement lead to substantially different sample characteristics and different prevalence estimates, which undermine the ability to replicate and generalize findings.[5,6,8,9] For the individual child, use of the discrepancy standard clearly promotes a wait-to-fail policy because a significant discrepancy between IQ and achievement generally cannot be detected until about age eight or nine. In fact, most school districts do not identify children with learning disabilities until a child is reading well below grade level, generally in third or fourth grade.[18] By this time the child has already experienced at least a few years of school failure and probably has experienced the common attendant problems of low self-esteem, diminished motivation, and inadequate acquisition of the academic material covered by his classmates during the previous few years.

It is clear that the longer children with learning disabilities, at any level of severity, go without identification and intervention, the more difficult the task of remediation becomes and the harder it is for the children to respond. Specifically, the data strongly suggest that children at risk for reading failure should be identified before the age of nine if successful intervention results are to be anticipated.[13] For example, a longitudinal investigation of 407 students[19] found that 74% of the children whose disability in reading was first identified at nine years of age or older continued to read in the lowest quintile throughout their middle and high school years. In addition, the longer children, at all severity levels, are faced with failure in reading in the classroom setting, the greater the probability that comorbid learning and behavioral difficulties will arise, further complicating the remediation task.

Developing a Diagnostic Standard

If current definitions of learning disability are not useful and if the discrepancy standard is a poor one, why have schools not adopted other means of defining and identifying LD? There are a number of conceptual and methodological barriers to the accurate identification of learning disabilities, and these impediments lead to confusion about definitions, diagnostic issues, and rising prevalence rates.

Multidisciplinary Nature of the Field

Opinions about what constitutes a learning disability vary[6,10] in part because LD is the concern of many disciplines and professions, including education, psychology, neurology, neuropsychology, optometry, psychiatry, and speech and language pathology, to name a few. Each of these disciplines has traditionally focused on different aspects of the child or adult with learning disability, so divergent ideas and contentious disagreements exist about the importance of etiology, diagnostic methods, intervention methods, and professional roles and responsibilities.[10] It is not surprising that so many children are identified because each professional may view the child through his or her own idiosyncratic clinical lens. For example, optometrists may identify a child as having a learning disability if the youngster displays difficulties in visual tracking. Speech and language pathologists, on the other hand, become concerned if the child's vocabulary and syntactic development are not commensurate with expectations. Educators become concerned primarily when development in reading, writing, and mathematics is deficient.

Lack of Specific Identification Criteria

Probably the most significant and persistent problem in the field is the lack of a precise definition and a theoretically based classification system that would allow (1) the identification of different types of learning disabilities and (2) a means of recognizing distinctions and interrelationships between types of learning disabilities and other learning disorders such as mental retardation, attention deficit disorder, speech and language difficulties, and general academic underachievement.[20] At present, the field continues to construct and use vague and ambiguous definitions that rely heavily on the exclusion of alternative diagnoses, such as the IDEA definition shown in Box 1.

Overly Broad Label

Some observers argue that the term "learning disability" is too broad to be of any diagnostic value. Stanovich,[16] a leading proponent of this view, proposes that the general term learning disabilities be abandoned and that definitional and research efforts focus on the specific types of disabilities that are now identified in ambiguous terms.

As noted earlier, the generic term learning disabilities encompasses disabilities in seven categories: (1) listening, (2) speaking, (3) basic reading skills, (4) reading comprehension, (5) written expression, (6) mathematical calculation, and (7) mathematical reasoning. Given the complexity and heterogeneity of each of these disabilities,

it seems unrealistic to expect that any definitional clarity can be achieved by grouping them together under one label. To do so only obscures the critical features of each disability and makes research findings difficult to interpret.

Definitions of specific learning disabilities can be more easily and successfully operationalized than generic definitions, as the research on disabilities in basic reading skills shows.[8] To establish valid prevalence estimates for the number of individuals with learning disabilities, the first step should be to establish explicit diagnostic criteria for *each* of the seven specific disability domains. At present, the greatest progress toward this goal has been in the area of disability in basic reading skills.[8]

LD as a Sociological Phenomenon

The simplest explanation for the increasing numbers of children identified with learning disabilities and for the difficulty in understanding and defining LD is that "LD" is not a distinct disability, but an invented category created for social purposes. Some argue that the majority of students identified as having learning disabilities are not intrinsically disabled but have learning problems because of poor teaching, lack of educational opportunity, or limited educational resources.[15] In addition, because the label of LD is not a stigmatizing one, parents and teachers may be more comfortable with a diagnosis of LD than with labels such as slow learner, minimal brain dysfunction, or perceptual handicap. A diagnosis of LD does not imply low intelligence, emotional or behavioral difficulties, sensory handicaps, or cultural disadvantage. Thus, more positive outcomes are expected for children with learning disabilities than for those with mental retardation or emotional disturbance.

Reasons for Increase in Identification of LD

As pointed out, the substantial increase in the identification of LD, as shown in Figure 1, has caused many researchers to question the validity of the data. No doubt, the failure to develop an agreed-upon, objective, operational definition of learning disability gives credence to the concern about the validity of the identification process. Thus, it seems reasonable to assume that at least some of the increase in prevalence can be linked to conceptual, methodological, social, and political factors that spuriously inflate the identification of children with learning disabilities.[5] However, despite the conceptual and methodological shortcomings that have plagued the field with respect to definition and identification practices, there exist a number of possible sound reasons that could account for an increase in the number of children identified with LD.

Some Sound Reasons

As knowledge about learning disabilities grows, some academic difficulties not previously recognized as LD can be identified as such. Greater knowledge also affects the behavior and practices of teachers and parents. Sound reasons for the increase in identification rates are described and discussed in the sections that follow.

• *Better Research.* Research in the past decade measures underachievement in reading as it occurs naturally in large population-based samples[12,13] rather than as identified by schools, which use widely varying criteria. In addition, much of this new research is longitudinal and has been replicated, providing the necessary foundation for epidemiological studies.[2,12,13,19,21–24] Finally, many of these studies have been specific to LD in reading, rather than LD in general, allowing greater precision.

• *Broader Definitions.* Prevalence is directly linked to definition. LD in reading has been defined in recent research as *significant difficulties in reading single words accurately and fluently, in combination with deficits in phonological awareness.*[8] Using this definition and stronger longitudinal research methods outlined above, the prevalence for reading disability alone has increased from estimates of less than 5% in 1976 to approximately 17% in 1994.[12]

Phonological awareness is a critical attribute in learning to read, and children who lack this awareness can be identified in late kindergarten and early first grade. Typical diagnostic questions for kindergartners or first graders involve rhyming skills (for example, "Tell me three words that rhyme with 'cat'") and phoneme deletion skills (for example, "Say 'cat' without the /t/ sound"). The majority of children pick up phonological awareness skills easily by six to seven years of age, but a large minority of children (about 17%) have significant difficulty with these skills and will have great difficulty learning to read, regardless of their intelligence, unless these skills are acquired.

• *Identification of LD in Girls.* A substantial portion of this increase can be attributed to the fact that females have been found to manifest reading disabilities at rates equal to males, in contrast to previous reports that males with reading disabilities outnumbered females with reading disabilities at a ratio of four to one.[25] This finding necessarily increases the prevalence rate.

• *Increased Awareness.* Information disseminated in the past decade, particularly concerning the characteristics of reading disability, has increased the number of children referred for assessment of a learning disability.[6]

• *Understanding of the Impact.* There has been an increase in the recognition that even "mild" deficits in reading skills are likely to portend significant difficulties in academic learning and are, therefore, worthy of early identification, diagnosis, and intervention.[26,27]

Some Unsound Reasons

There is no shortage of horror stories about the misidentification of LD and reports that the category serves as a "catch all" for any youngster who is not meeting the expectations of parents and teachers. Are there legitimate reasons for these criticisms? The answer appears to be yes. Examples are described and discussed in the sections that follow.

• *Ambiguous Definitions.* The ambiguity inherent in the general definitions of LD (see Box 1) leaves the identification process open for wide interpretation and misinterpretation. Flexible identification decision making allows some children to be identified as having learning disabilities when they do not, while others with learning disabilities may be overlooked.[5] This latitude can be manipulated to increase prevalence rates in response to financial incentives (for example, to qualify for increased state funding), to decrease prevalence rates in response to political movements (for example, inclusion), or to abandon programs that appear too costly.[28]

Both market and legal forces can stimulate the development of new professional specialties whose members have financial incentives to diagnose students with learning disabilities.

• *Social and Political Factors.* Social and political factors also contribute to the inflation of prevalence rates for learning disabilities. In 1976–77, the first year of full implementation of Public Law 94-142, 2.16% of all schoolchildren were served in programs for children with mental retardation (MR) and 1.80% in programs for children with learning disabilities (Figure 1). By the 1992–93 school year, placements for children with MR had decreased to 1.1% while placements for children with LD had increased to 5.4% of the total school population (Figure 1). While these reversed trends mask substantial variations among states, the dramatic changes in identification rates of the two types of disability suggest that attempts to apply less stigmatizing labels may be influencing the identification process.

• *Number of Professional Specialties Involved.* The large number of professional specialties involved in the identification process provides fertile ground for the overidentification of LD because each specialty brings its own set of diagnostic assumptions, theories, and measures to the assessment task. Inconsistent identification practices allow prevalence rates to escalate. This is a significant problem when there are financial incentives to encourage identification (see the article by Parrish and Chambers in *The Future of Children,* Spring 1996). Both market and legal forces can stimulate the development of new professional specialties (such as language/learning disorder specialist) whose members have financial incentives to diagnose students with learning disabilities, which the specialists will often be employed to treat. Although it may be uncomfortable to mention these factors, they exist and play some role in the increase of prevalence of LD. At the same time, the majority of professionals serving children with learning disabilities appear well intentioned and well informed.

• *Inadequate Preparation of Teachers.* Unfortunately, a major factor contributing to invalid prevalence estimates may be the inadequate preparation of teachers by colleges of education. Recent studies have found that a majority of regular classroom teachers feel that they are not prepared to address individual differences in learning abilities within classroom settings.[29] Even more alarming, research suggests that special educators themselves do not possess sufficient content knowledge to address the language and reading needs of children with learning disabilities.[30] Without adequate preparation, teachers have a tendency to over-refer children for specialized assistance because they feel ill-equipped to provide the necessary services.[31]

Interpreting Prevalence Rates

The prevalence of learning disabilities is completely dependent upon the definition used. In most areas, the identification of LD is based largely upon the discrepancy standard and, thus, provides a count of the number of older elementary students (third grade and above) who are achieving significantly below expectations based on IQ. This is, at best, an incomplete definition of LD and one that, for the majority of students with learning disabilities, is based upon an invalid criterion, namely, the discrepancy standard.

Clearly, current definitions allow both overidentification and underidentification of L.D. Depending upon the magnitude of financial incentives and upon unrelated factors (for example, class size, goals for increasing test scores) that often shape the decisions of classroom teachers to refer students with special needs, an individual school district may drastically overidentify or underidentify students with learning disabilities. Therefore, local or national statistics on identification rates for students with LD must be interpreted with caution.

Efforts to Improve Identification

To improve the diagnosis and remediation of learning disabilities, a classification system is needed to identify different types of learning disabilities as well as the distinctions and interrelationships among types of LD and other childhood disorders.[2,20,32] Prospective longitudinal studies are one of the most powerful means to study the different types of LD and their relationships to other disorders and to obtain data for a focused and succinct definition.

Prospective, longitudinal studies of LD can serve as a platform to (1) identify critical learning and behavioral characteristics that may be manifested in different ways at different developmental periods, (2) develop early predictors of underachievement for different academic domains (for example, reading, written language, math), (3) map the developmental course of different types of learning disabilities, (4) identify commonly co-occurring disorders and secondary behavioral consequences and develop in response to failure in school, and (5) assess the efficacy of different treatment and teaching methods for different types of learning disabilities.

Approximately 80% of children identified as having learning disabilities have their primary difficulties in learning to read.

To address this compelling need to establish a valid classification system and definition for LD, Congress enacted the Health Research Extension Act of 1985 (Public Law 99-158). This act called for the development of an Interagency Committee on Learning Disabilities (ICLD), under the lead of the National Institute of Child Health and Human Development (NICHD), to identify critical research needs in LD and to implement comprehensive studies to address issues relevant to identification, prevention, etiology, and treatment.

New Knowledge of Reading Disabilities

Since the inauguration of the NICHD Learning Disability Research Network in 1987, researchers have learned the most about learning disabilities that affect linguistic, reading, and spelling abilities and the least about learning disabilities in mathematics.[2] A number of new findings have also been obtained in the area of attention deficit disorder (ADD) and its relationship to different types of LD, particularly disorders in reading.[12] For brevity, the major discoveries made during the past several years are presented in Table 1. Selected findings are reviewed here. The reader should note that many findings have been replicated by multiple research groups, as cited in Table 1, and that the findings are primarily based on large longitudinal samples. Finally, readers should note that studies being conducted in Canada by Stanovich and Siegel at the Ontario Institute for Studies in Education are included in Table 1 because of their impact on the field and because Stanovich and Siegel serve as consultants to the Yale Learning Disability Research Center (LDRC).

As Table 1 shows, a majority of discoveries made during the past decade have been in the area of reading disabilities. This is appropriate. As Lerner pointed out from her analysis of public school referral data in 1989,[33] approximately 80% of children identified as having learning disabilities have their primary difficulties in learning to read. This high rate of occurrence of reading difficulties among youngsters with LD has also been reported by Kavale in his meta-analytic studies.[34] More recent longitudinal and cross-sectional studies have supported the high rate of reading difficulty among children with learning disabilities, but have also found that reading deficits frequently co-occur with other academic and attentional difficulties. For example, Fletcher and his associates at the

Yale Center for the Study of Learning and Attention have, as part of a larger classification effort, studied 216 children, 7.5 to 9.5 years of age, who were identified as normal readers, reading disabled, math disabled, both reading and math disabled, normal reading with ADD, and reading disabled with ADD.[21,35] From this sample of children with a variety of learning disabilities, only 25 youngsters were reading at age-appropriate levels.

Research indicates that reading disorders reflected in deficient decoding and word-recognition skills are primarily caused by deficiencies in the ability to segment syllables and words into constituent sound units called phonemes.[16,22,36–38] For example, in a large study of 199 seven- to nine-year-old children who had significant difficulties in decoding and word recognition, more than 85% of the youngsters manifested deficits on measures of phonological awareness. In this investigation, children with and without IQ-reading-achievement discrepancies appeared equally impaired on both the phonological and reading measures.[21] This extremely high frequency of phonological awareness deficits in children with reading disabilities has led Share and Stanovich to conclude: "We know unequivocally that less-skilled readers have difficulty turning spellings into sounds…. This relationship is so strong that it deserves to be identified as one, if not the defining, feature of reading disability."[39]

Biological Bases

Several NICHD investigations have indicated that these phonologically based reading disabilities are linked to neurobiological and genetic factors.[2,8,13,40] Functional and structural neuroimaging studies indicate that the poor phonological skills which limit the development of basic reading abilities, are highly related to aberrant neurophysiological processing.[22,40] Moreover, there is increasing evidence from behavioral and molecular genetic studies that the phonological deficits observed in reading disability are heritable.[41,42] Taken together, longitudinal studies of the linguistic, neurobiological, and genetic factors in reading disabilities provide strong and converging evidence that reading disability is primarily caused by deficits in phonological processing and, more specifically, phonological awareness.[8,13,30,37,38,40]

Likewise, the data derived from genetic and neurobiological studies suggest that some reading disabilities are associated with subtle chromosomal[42] and neurological differences,[22,40] indicating that such disabilities are biologically "real" rather than sociopolitically created.

Interventions applied after a child has failed in reading for two or three years may not be effective for several reasons, including the student's declining motivation and impared self-concept.

Discrepancy Standard

In addition to the previously discussed problems of the discrepancy standard, Table 1 indicates that the use of a discrepancy formula, which calculates differences between IQ reading scores, is not a valid indicator of reading disability; that is, children with reading disabilities both with and without such discrepancies have similar deficits in phonological awareness and similar genetic and neurophysiological characteristics.[36] At this time, it is not clear whether children with higher IQs respond more favorably to intervention.[7]

Persistent Deficit

Unfortunately, as Table 1 indicates, reading disabilities appear to reflect a persistent deficit rather than a developmental lag. That is, children with delays in understanding phonological concepts in first grade are unlikely to catch up later without explicit and informed teaching. Longitudinal studies show that, of the youngsters who are identified in the third grade, approximately 74% remain reading disabled through the ninth grade.[19,43] This appears to be true even when special education has been provided. It should be made clear, however, that interventions applied *after* a child has failed in reading for two or three years may not be effective for several reasons, including the student's declining motivation and impaired self-concept. Instructional difficulties in later intervention abound. For example, the teacher carrying out the interventions may not be properly trained, the interventions may not include explicit and informed instruction in the development of phonological awareness and sound-symbol relationships, the interventions may not be consistently applied and/or may be limited in intensity and duration, and there may be insufficient follow-up or explicit instruction to enable the student to generalize the specific concepts learned to material presented in regular classroom settings.

Distribution of Severity

A significant finding from the Yale LDRC is that reading disability represents the extreme of a normal distribution of reading ability so that there is an unbroken continuum from reading ability to reading disability.[43] The finding that reading disability is part of continuum now places the disorder in the context of other biologically based disorders such as hypertension and obesity.[43] The discovery that reading disability is best conceptualized as occurring along a normal distribution of reading skills underscores the fact that children will vary in their level of severity of the disorder running along a mild-to-severe spectrum, with the majority of children with reading disabilities falling at the mild end. This finding has significant implications. For example, what are the criteria for identifying a child as having a *severe* reading disability, and does this degree of disability warrant entitlement to a greater intensity and duration of specialized interventions?

Table 1

Major Findings from Research Programs Supported by the National Institute of Child Health and Human Development		
Research Domain	Findings	Research Group*
Definition of learning disabilities	Definitions that measure the discrepancy between IQ and achievement do not adequately identify learning disabilities, particularly in the area of basic reading skills.	Yale Ontario
Reading processes	Disabled readers with and without an IQ-achievement discrepancy show similar information processing, genetic, and neurophysiological profiles. This indicates that the existence of a discrepancy is not a valid indicator of disability in basic reading skills.	Colorado Bowman Gray Yale Ontario
Reading processes	Epidemiological studies indicate that as many females as males manifest dyslexia; however, schools identify three to four times more boys than girls.	Bowman Gray Colorado Yale
Reading processes	Reading disabilities reflect a persistent deficit rather than a developmental lag. Longitudinal studies show that, of those children who are reading disabled in the third grade, approximately 74% continue to read significantly below grade level in the ninth grade.	Yale Ontario
Reading processes	Children with reading disability differ from one another *and* from other readers along a continuous distribution. They *do not* aggregate together to form a distinct "hump" separate from the normal distribution.	Yale Bowman Gray Colorado Ontario
Reading processes	The ability to read and comprehend depends upon rapid and automatic recognition and decoding of single words. Slow and inaccurate decoding are the best predictors of deficits in reading comprehension.	Yale Bowman Gray Colorado Johns Hopkins Florida Houston
Reading processes	The ability to decode single words accurately and fluently is dependent upon the ability to segment words and syllables into phonemes. Deficits in phonological awareness reflect the core deficit in dyslexia.	Yale Colorado Bowman Gray Miami Johns Hopkins Florida Houston
Reading processes	The best predictor of reading ability from kindergarten and first-grade performance is phoneme segmentation ability.	Bowman Gray Yale Florida Houston
Attention	A precise classification of disorders of attention is not yet available; however, operational definitions are emerging.	Yale
Attention	Approximately 15% of students with reading disability also have a disorder of attention. Approximately 35% of students with disorders of attention also have reading disability. However, the two disorders are distinct and separable.	Bowman Gray Yale

*See the related endnote at the end of this article for a detailed description of research groups.

(continued)

Table 1 (continued)

Major Findings from Research Programs Supported by the National Institute of Child Health and Human Development		
Research Domain	**Findings**	**Research Group***
Attention	Disorders of attention exacerbate the severity of reading disability.	Bowman Gray Miami
Genetics	There is strong evidence for a genetic basis for reading disabilities, with deficits in phonological awareness reflecting the greatest degree of heritability.	Colorado Bowman Gray
Neurology	Regional blood studies indicate that deficient word recognition skills are associated with less than normal activation in the left temporal region.	Bowman Gray
Neurology	PET studies indicate that dyslexic adults have greater than normal activation in the occipital and prefrontal regions of the cortex.	Miami
Intervention	Disabled readers do not readily acquire the alphabetic code because of deficits in phonological processing. Thus, disabled readers must be provided highly structured programs that explicitly teach application of phonological rules to print.	Bowman Gray Florida Houston
Intervention	Longitudinal data indicate that systematic phonics instruction results in more favorable outcomes for disabled readers than does a context-emphasis (whole language) approach.	Bowman Gray Florida Houston

*See the related endnote at the end of this article for a detailed description of research groups.

Even children with relatively subtle linguistic and reading deficits require the expertise of a teacher who is well trained.

To answer such questions, the NICHD is embarking on a series of studies to identify the most valid points along the distribution of reading scores that distinguish levels of severity. In part, the validity of different cutoff points for mild, moderate, and severe reading disability is being determined by how children in each severity group respond to different types and intensities of intervention. At this writing, some initial results derived from the Florida State Intervention Project show that children with scores at the extreme lower end of the distributions for both phonological awareness skills and basic reading skills are much more difficult to remediate than children who fall along the distribution in the mild and moderate ranges.[44-46] It is as yet unclear whether children in the more severe range can achieve age- and grade-approximate reading skills,

even with intense, informed intervention provided over a protracted period of time.

While children with severe reading disabilities will most likely require a greater amount of time in high-impact intervention programs than children with less severe deficits, as discussed earlier, it is clear that the longer children *at any level of severity* go without proper identification and intervention, the more difficult the task of remediation and the harder it becomes for the children to respond. It is also clear that even children with relatively subtle linguistic and reading deficits require the expertise of a teacher who is well trained and informed about the relationships between language development and reading development.[30] Unfortunately, such teachers are in short supply, primarily because of a lack of programs providing this training.[31]

Co-occurring Disorders

As noted, most children with learning disabilities have more than one of the seven subtypes of learning disabilities. It is also not unusual to find LD co-occurring with certain behavioral or emotional disorders. The most common co-occurring combinations are discussed briefly below.

Figure 2

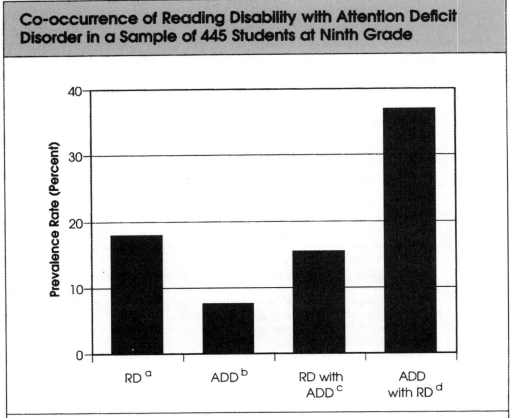

Co-occurrence of Reading Disability with Attention Deficit Disorder in a Sample of 445 Students at Ninth Grade

Study population: 445 children recruited through a random sample of those attending Connecticut public kindergarten during the 1983–84 school year. This cohort was followed for several years. This chart reflects measures taken during the subjects' ninth-grade year.

a **RD** is defined as either an ability-achievement discrepancy (based on a regression formula) or a reading standard score below the 25th percentile.

b **ADD** is defined as a score of greater than or equal to 1.5 above the mean on the inattention scale of the Multigrade Inventory for Teachers.

c **RD with ADD** is the percentage of all students meeting the criteria for RD in this study who also met the criteria for ADD.

d **ADD with RD** is the percentage of all students meeting the criteria for ADD in this study who also met the criteria for RD.

Source: Adapted with permission from Shaywitz, S.E., Fletcher, J.M., and Shaywitz, B.A. Issues in the definition and classification of the attention deficit disorder. *Topic in Language Disorders* (1994) 14:1-25

Reading and Attention Disorders

Attention deficit disorder (ADD) is an increasingly common diagnosis recognized in medicine[47] and psychology[17] although it is not a category of disability recognized under the IDEA. Like LD, ADD is the subject of considerable controversy, and diagnostic criteria for ADD continue to evolve. There is no litmus test for ADD, which is diagnosed on the basis of persistent and maladaptive behavior patterns (inattention, impulsivity, and hyperactivity) that are inappropriate for the child's age. The number of diagnoses of ADD has increased dramatically in the past decade,[48] and one

study[12] found 7% of a survey sample of 445 kindergarten students qualifying as "inattentive" on the Multigrade Inventory for Teachers.

Figure 2[12] indicates that a child identified with reading disabilities is twice as likely as a member of the general population to also meet the diagnostic criteria for inattention (15% versus 7%). Similarly, an individual diagnosed with ADD is at higher risk than a member of the general population of having a reading disability/phonological awareness deficit (36% versus 17%). Despite this co-occurrence, recent studies have indicated that reading disabilities and ADD are distinct and separable disorders.[12,22,49]

Unfortunately, when children with disabilities in reading also manifest ADD, their reading deficits are typically exacerbated, more severe, and more resistant to intervention.[22] In contrast to reading disabilities, ADD is more prevalent in males. Given the frequent co-occurrence of ADD with reading disabilities and given the tendency of boys with ADD to attract considerable attention from teachers, this combination may make boys with disabilities in reading much more likely than girls with disabilities in reading to come to the attention of teachers and to be referred for testing.

Social Adjustment Problems

In a broad sense, data indicate that learning disability, no matter what the specific type, has a tendency to co-occur with social adjustment problems.[50] Bruck,[51] in her review of the literature related to social and emotional adjustment, concluded that children with learning disabilities are more likely to exhibit increased levels of anxiety, withdrawal, depression, and low self-esteem compared with their nondisabled peers. This comorbidity is persistent. For example, Johnson and Blalock[52] found that, of the 93 adults studied in an LD clinic sample, 36% continued to receive counseling or psychotherapy for low self-esteem, social isolation, anxiety, depression, and frustration. In many instances, it appears that such emotional problems reflect adjustment difficulties resulting from academic failure.[13] Deficits in social skills have also been found to exist at significantly high rates among children with learning disabilities.[53] In general, social skill deficits include difficulties interacting with people in an appropriate fashion (for example, lack of knowledge of how to greet people, how to make friends, and how to engage in playground games or a failure to use knowledge of such skills in these situations). While not all children with learning disabilities exhibit deficits in social skills, there are certain common characteristics among those who do. For example, Bruck[51] reported that children with more severe manifestations of LD are likely to manifest both an increased number of and increased severity of social skills deficits. Moreover, the gender of the child appears to be a factor, with evidence suggesting that girls with LD are more likely to have social adjustment problems.[51]

Reading Disorders with Other Learning Disabilities

There is abundant evidence that it is rare for a child with learning disabilities to manifest only one specific type of learning disability.[3,53] The co-occurrence of learning disorders should be expected given the developmental relationships between listening, speaking, reading, spelling, writing, and mathematics. For example, it is clear that deficits in phonological awareness lead to difficulties in decoding and word recognition which, in turn, lead to deficits in reading comprehension.[16,37,38] Likewise, children with disabilities in reading frequently experience persistent difficulties in solving word problems in math for the obvious reason that the printed word is difficult for them to comprehend.[14]

An important conclusion to draw from the literature on co-occurring disorders is that any intervention or remediation effort must take into account the range of deficits a child may have. More specifically, while an intensive reading intervention may consist of explicit instruction in phonological awareness, sound-symbol relationships, and contextual reading skills, the child may also require elements essential to bolstering self-esteem, and to fostering reading in other content areas such as mathematics, social studies, and science. One cannot expect the intervention for the reading deficit to generalize serendipitously to other domains of difficulty.

LD in Written Expression

Typically, children who display LD in written expression have difficulties in spelling, formulation and expression of ideas, handwriting, and knowledge of grammar and syntax. Unfortunately, well-designed research investigating disorders of written expression is relatively meager. Definitions for disorders of written expression remain vague.[54] Therefore it is not surprising that estimates of the prevalence of such disorders range from 8% to 15%.[13] What is known is that boys and girls display written language deficits at relatively equal rates.[54] Despite the lack of objective and detailed identification criteria, a number of excellent studies have been conducted to identify effective assessment and intervention programs for problems in written expression.[55–57]

The most successful programs tend to ensure that clear linkages are drawn between oral language, reading, and written language. Successful programs also ensure that basic skills development in spelling and writing (graphomotor production) are explicitly taught and/or accommodated and that the student is also taught how to employ strategies to guide the formulation of ideas for writing and the organization of these ideas in writing. These elements are common to many writing programs; however, successful instruction for students with disabilities in written expression depends upon their intensity and explicitness.

LD in Mathematics

Children identified as manifesting LD in mathematics can demonstrate deficits in arithmetic calculation, mathematics reasoning, or both. In general, authorities agree that approximately 6% of the school population have difficulties in mathematics that cannot be attributed to low intelligence, sensory deficits, or economic deprivation.[14,58] While the data are sparse at this time, it appears that deficits in arithmetic calculation skills are more frequently identified than deficits in arithmetic reasoning.[14] However, common sense would suggest that attempts to reason mathematically would be constrained by limitations in calculations skills. Unfortunately, a major difficulty in identifying math learning disabilities accurately is that, like learning to read, learning mathematics concepts is dependent upon the teacher's knowledge of the concepts and ability to present them.[13]

Interventions for Learning Disabilities

Space does not permit an extended review of research on intervention methods for different types of learning disabilities. However, high-quality prospective longitudinal research methods are now being applied to the study of treatment methods for reading disabilities, and that research is summarized here.

Research attempting to identify effective treatment methods for different types and severity levels of reading deficits has been enormously difficult. This is because typical treatment studies have not been able to reliably determine whether the outcomes seen were attributable

---

Instruction in phonological awareness at the kindergarten level has significant positive effects on reading development during the first grade.

For example, Blachman and her colleagues[59–61] have shown that instruction in phonological awareness at the kindergarten level has significant positive effects on reading development during the first grade. Within this context, research has demonstrated that proper instruction carried out by informed teachers can prevent reading failure both for children with inherent LD in basic reading skills and for children whose lack of exposure to "language rich" environments and language development activities during the first five years of life places them at risk for reading deficits. For instance, in a series of studies, Blachman[60,61] provided 84 low-income, inner-city children with 11 weeks of intensive instruction, 20 minutes per day, with one teacher instructing a small group of four to five students in several aspects of phonological awareness. Prior to instruction, classroom teachers also received 14 hours of intensive training. At the end of the 11 weeks, children receiving the interventions significantly (p < 0.0001) outperformed control children at reading phonetically regular words and at related tasks. A follow-up study conducted in February and May of the first-grade year showed that the gains were maintained if the first-grade curriculum continued the same emphasis on phonological skill development. Similar studies of kindergarten and first-grade children conducted by other researchers[62–64] have yielded similar results.

to the treatment method, the child's general development, the child's previous instruction, the concurrent instruction being provided in the regular classroom, or combinations of these factors. In addition, a majority of treatment studies have been hampered by not having control over teacher expertise and training. Thus, if a treatment method does or does not work effectively, one does not know if it is because of the characteristics of the method, the characteristics of the teacher, or the characteristics of the child.

Since the late 1980s, a number of well-designed longitudinal treatment studies have been conducted. Because these studies have the capability to intervene with children early on and follow them over time, many of the methodological problems described above have been addressed. These intervention studies have provided information about how to prevent reading disabilities as well as how to address reading disabilities once they are detected at later ages.

Unfortunately, not all children with reading disabilities have the benefit of appropriate early interventions. As discussed earlier, most children whose reading disability is not recognized until third grade or later and who receive standard interventions fail to show noticeable improvement. However, intensive instruction of appropriate duration provided by trained teachers can remediate the deficient reading skills of many children. For example, in one study, Alexander and her colleagues[65] provided 65 severely dyslexic children with 65 hours of individual instruction in addition to group instruction in phonemic awareness and synthetic and analytic skills. This intensive treatment approach improved the reading skills of the children from an initial reading score of 77 to an average of 98.4 (mean = 100) on a measure of alphabetic reading skills. Longitudinal studies continue to demonstrate the efficacy of intensive and informed multidimensional treatment programs.[64,66]

Several additional findings have emerged from these longitudinal treatment studies. It is clear that children with severe phonological deficits, leading to poor decoding and word recognition skills, respond to treatment at slower rates than youngsters with mild to moderate deficits.[44,67] In addition, instruction and interventions for reading failure, which focus primarily on context and reading comprehension without commensurate attention paid to phonological awareness, decoding, and word recognition, show limited results.[67–6] Finally, the success of even the best-designed reading intervention program is highly dependent upon the training and skills of the teacher.[22,29–31,38]

Disability in basic reading skills has been a prime candidate for treatment studies because it is the most common form of LD, it is the most objectively identifiable, and more knowledge is available concerning its causes and developmental course. Interventions for other types of learning disabilities have been developed but not studied as extensively and not studied in prospective, longitudinal research. There is as yet no solid indication whether early, effective interventions for disability in basic reading skills will affect the developmental course of other forms of learning disability.

Outcomes

Learning disabilities, sometimes inappropriately conceptualized as a "mild" disorder, may be anything but—they may be persistent and may not respond to general instruction or to inappropriate (for example, whole language) instruction. Unless identified early on and taught by expert teachers using detailed and intensive approaches emphasizing teaching both in phonological awareness and phonics instruction, children who learn poorly in the third grade can be expected to learn poorly throughout middle- and high-school grades. Unfortunately, the majority of children with learning disabilities are still not identified until the third or fourth grade and do not receive appropriate and timely reading instruction. In turn, those students with learning disabilities who graduate from high school are destined for few postschool opportunities. The minority of children with LD who received appropriate early intervention have not been identified for long-term follow-up so their long-term outcomes are speculative, but there is reason for optimism in their significantly improved short-term outcomes.

At present, the long-term outcomes for the majority of individuals with learning disabilities who did not receive appropriate early reading instruction are frequently bleak. It is known from the epidemiological data cited earlier that 75% of the children with disabilities in reading who are not identified until the third grade continue to have reading disabilities in the ninth grade.[24] In a recent review, Martin[70] reported that a considerable percentage (26.7%) of high school students identified as having learning disabilities drop out of school prior to graduation. Another 16% of students with learning disabilities exit school for "unknown" reasons without a diploma. Equally disturbing, Fairweather and Shaver[71] found that only 17.1% of the individuals with learning disabilities whom they followed for three to five years after high school were enrolled in any postsecondary course, including vocational courses. Only 6.7% of the students with learning disabilities participated in two-year higher education programs, and only 1.8% participated in four-year programs.

While these data suggest that individuals with learning disabilities do not markedly improve their academic skills (particularly reading skills) and face limited educational and vocational opportunities, it should not be concluded that individuals with LD cannot be taught. They can, but, as stated throughout this paper, interventions are most likely to be successful if applied early and carried out by expert teachers.

Conclusions

The past decade has witnessed a significant improvement in the quality of research on learning disabilities. Much of this recent research has been longitudinal in nature, thus opening the door to the identification of better predictors of different types of LD, their prevalence, their developmental course, and their response to intervention. Specifically,

• The definitional issues addressed in this article continue to be the single greatest impediment to understanding learning disabilities and how to help children and adults with LD.

• Maintaining the term "learning disabilities" makes little sense for scientific purposes, clinical purposes, or school policy purposes. Instead, the field must grapple with the clear need to address each type of learning disability individually to arrive at clear definitional statements and a coherent understanding of etiology, developmental course, identification, prevention, and treatment.

• Reading disability in the form of deficits in phonological awareness is the most prevalent type of learning disability and affects approximately 17% of school-age children to some degree.

• While other factors will, no doubt, be identified as contributing to reading disability, deficits in phonological awareness will most likely be found to be the core deficit. Research during the past decade has shown that deficits in phonological awareness can be identified in late kindergarten and first grade using inexpensive, straightforward testing protocols, and the presence of these deficits is a strong indicator that reading disability will follow.

• Although it is now possible to identify children who are at-risk for reading failure, and some of the instructional conditions that must be in place from the beginning of formal schooling are understood, it is still true that the majority of LD children are not identified until the third grade. Therefore, policy initiatives should focus on the dissemination of existing early identification and early intervention programs.

• Interventions for reading disability must consist of explicit instructional procedures in phonological awareness, sound-symbol relationships, and meaning and reading comprehension, and should be provided by expert teachers in the kindergarten and first-grade years.

• In general, teachers remain seriously unprepared to address individual differences in many academic skills but particularly in reading. However, teachers cannot be expected to know what they have not been taught, and clearly colleges of education have let students down. Regrettably, being unprepared takes a toll on teachers. Many teachers worry about their failures with hard-to-teach students, become frustrated, lose confidence, and leave the profession, or discontinue attempting to teach children with special needs. This cycle of events calls for honest and aggressive reform in higher education.

• While early intervention is *necessary*, it should not be assumed to be *sufficient* to address the multiple manifestations of learning disability. Even those students who receive appropriate phonological instruction at a young age may require continuous and intensive support to deal with other co-occurring disorders.

• When policymakers consider "inclusionary" models of instruction, they must consider carefully whether those models can provide the critical elements of intensity and the appropriate duration of instruction, along with teacher expertise in multiple teaching methods and in accommodating individual learning differences.

Notes

1. Office of Special Education Programs. *Implementation of the Education of the Handicapped Act: Eleventh annual report to Congress*. Washington, DC: U.S.Department of Education, 1989.
2. Lyon, G. R. Research initiatives and discoveries in learning disabilities. *Journal of Child Neurology* (1995) 10: 120–26.
3. Lyon, G. R., ed. *Frames of reference for the assessment of learning disabilities: New views on measurement issues*. Baltimore: Paul H. Brookes, 1994.
4. Lyon, G. R., and Moats, L. C. An examination of research in learning disabilities: Past practices and future directions. In *Better understanding learning disabilities: New views from research and their implications for education and public policies*. G. R. Lyon, D. B. Gray, J. F. Kavanaugh, and N. A. Krasnegor, eds. Baltimore: Paul H. Brookes, 1993, pp. 1–14.
5. Lyon, G. R. Learning disabilities research: False starts and broken promises. In *Research in learning disabilities: Issues and future directions*. S. Vaughn and C. Bos, eds. San Diego, CA: College-Hill Press, 1987, pp. 69–85.
6. Moats, L. C., and Lyon, G. R. Learning disabilities in the United States: Advocacy, science, and the future of the field. *Journal of Learning Disabilities* (1993) 26:282–94.
7. Lyon, G. R. IQ is irrelevant to the definition of learning disabilities: A position in search of logic and data. *Journal of Learning Disabilities* (1989) 22:504–19.
8. Lyon, G. R. Toward a definition of dyslexia. *Annals of dyslexia* (1995) 45:3–27.
9. Zigmond, N. Learning disabilities from an educational perspective. In *Better understanding learning disabilities: New views from research and their implications for education and public policies*. G. R. Lyon, D. B. Gray, J. F. Kavanagh, and N. A. Krasnegor, eds. Baltimore: Paul H. Brookes, 1993, pp. 251–72.
10. Torgesen, J. K. Learning disabilities: Historical and conceptual issues. In *Learning about learning disabilities*. B. Y. L. Wong, ed. New York: Academic Press, 1991, pp. 3–29.
11. Kirk, S.A. Behavioral diagnosis and remediation of learning disabilities. In *Conference on the Exploration of the Perceptually Handicapped Child*. Evanston, IL: Fund for Perceptually Handicapped Children, 1963, pp. 1–7.
12. Shaywitz, S. E., Fletcher, J. M., and Shaywitz, S. E. Issues in the definition and classification of attention deficit disorder. *Topics on Language Disorders* (1994) 14:1–25.
13. Lyon, G. R. Learning disabilities. In *Child psychopathology*. E. Marsh and R. Barkley, eds. New York: Guilford Press, 1996, pp. 390–434.
14. Fleishner, J. E. Diagnosis and assessment of mathematics learning disabilities. In *Frames of reference for the assessment of*

learning disabilities: New views on measurement issues*. G. R. Lyon, ed. Baltimore: Paul H. Brookes, 1994, pp. 441–58.
15. Coles, G. *The learning mystique: A critical look at learning disabilities*. New York: Pantheon Press, 1987.
16. Stanovich, K. E. The construct validity of discrepancy definitions of reading disability. In *Better understanding learning disabilities: New views on research and their implications for education and public policies*. G. R. Lyon, D. B. Gray, J. F. Kavanaugh, and N. A. Krasnegor, eds. Baltimore: Paul H. Brookes, 1993, pp. 273–307.
17. American Psychiatric Association. *Diagnostic and statistical manual of mental disorders*. 4th ed. rev. Washington, DC: APA, 1994.
18. Foorman, B. R., Francis, D. J., Shaywitz, S. E., et al. The case for early reading intervention. In *Cognitive and linguistic foundations of reading acquisition: Implications for intervention*. B. Blachman, ed. Mahwah, NJ: Erlbaum. In press.
19. Francis, D. J., Shaywitz, S. E., Steubing, K. K., et al. Measurement of change: Assessing behavior over time and within a developmental context. In *Frames of reference for the assessment of learning disabilities: New views on measurement issues*. G. R. Lyon, ed. Baltimore: Paul H. Brookes, 1994, pp. 29–58.
20. Fletcher, J. M., Francis, D. J., Rourke, B. P., et al. Classification of learning disabilities: Relationships with other childhood disorders. In *Better understanding learning disabilities: New views on research and their implications for education and public policies*. G. R. Lyon, D. B. Gray, J. F. Kavanagh, and N. A. Krasnegor, eds. Baltimore: Paul H. Brookes, 1993, pp. 27–56.
21. Fletcher, J. M., Shaywitz, S. E., Shankweiler, D. P., et al. Cognitive profiles of reading disability: Comparisons of discrepancy and low achievement definitions. *Journal of Educational Psychology* (1994) 95:1–18.
22. Wood, F., Felton, R., Flowers, L., and Naylor, C. Neurobehavioral definition of dyslexia. In *The reading brain: The biological basis of dyslexia*. D. D. Duane and D. B. Gray, eds. Parkton, MD: York Press, 1991, pp. 1–26.
23. Lyon, G. R., Gray, D. B., Kavanagh, J. F., and Krasnegor, N. A., eds. *Better understanding learning disabilities: New views from research and their implications for education and public policies*. Baltimore: Paul H. Brookes, 1993.
24. Shaywitz, B. A., and Shaywitz, S. E. Measuring and analyzing change. In *Frames of reference for the assessment of learning disabilities: New views on measurement issues*. G. R. Lyon, ed. Baltimore: Paul H. Brookes, 1994, pp. 29–58.
25. Shaywitz, B. A., and Shaywitz, S. E., Fletcher, J. M., and Escobar, M. D. Prevalence of reading disability in boys and girls: Results of the Connecticut longitudinal study. *Journal of the American Medical Association* (1990) 264:998–1002.
26. Fletcher, J. M., and Foorman, B. R. Issues in definition and measurement of learning disabilities: The need for early identification. In *Frames of reference for the assessment of learning disabilities: New views on measurement issues*. G. R. Lyon, ed. Baltimore; Paul H. Brookes, 1994, pp. 185–200.
27. Blachman, B. A. Getting ready to read: Learning how print maps to speech. In *The language continuum: From infancy to literacy*. J. F. Kavanagh, ed. Parkton, MD: York Press, 1991, pp. 41–62.
28. Senf, G. Learning disabilities as a sociological sponge: Wiping up life's spills. In *Research in learning disabilities: Issue and future directions*. S. Vaughn and C. Bos, eds. Boston: College-Hill Press, 1987, pp. 87–101.
29. Lyon, G. R., Vaasen, M., and Toomey, F. Teachers' perceptions of their undergraduate and graduate preparation. *Teacher Education and Special Education* (1989) 12:164–69.
30. Moats, L. C. The missing foundation in teacher education: Knowledge of the structure of spoken and written language. *Annals of Dyslexia* (1994) 44:81–102.

31. Moats, L. C., and Lyon, G. R. Wanted: Teachers with knowledge of language. *Topics in Language Disorders* (1996) 16, 2:73–86.

32. Interagency Committee on Learning Disabilities. *A report to Congress*. Bethesda, MD: The National Institutes of Health, 1987.

33. Lerner, J. W. Educational interventions in learning disabilities. *Journal of the American Academy of Child and Adolescent Psychiatry* (1989) 28:326–31.

34. Kavale, K. A. Potential advantages of the meta-analysis technique for special education. *Journal of Special Education* (1984) 18:61–72.

35. Fletcher, J., Morris, R., Lyon, G.R., et al. Sub-types of dyslexia: An old problem revisited. In *Cognitive and linguistic foundations of reading acquisition: Implications for intervention research*. B. Blachman, ed. Mahwah, NJ: Erlbaum. In press.

36. Stanovich, E. E., and Siegel, L. S. Phenotypic performance profile of children with reading disabilities: A regression-based test of the phonological-core variable-difference model. *Journal of Educational Psychology* (1994) 86:24–53.

37. Adams, M. J. *Beginning to read: Thinking and learning about print*. Cambridge, MA: Cambridge University Press, 1990.

38. Adams, M. J., Bruck, M. Resolving the great debate. *American Educator* (1995) 19:7–10.

39. Share, D. L., and Stanovich, K. E. Cognitive processes in early reading development: Accommodating individual differences into a mode of acquisition. *Education: Contributions for Educational Psychology* (1995) 1:34–36.

40. Lyon, G. R., and Rumsey, J., eds. *Neuroimaging: A window to the neurological foundations of learning and behavior in children*. Baltimore: Paul H. Brookes. In press.

41. DeFries, J. C., and Gillis, J. J. Etiology of reading deficits in learning disabilities: Quantitative genetic analyses. In *Neuropsychological foundations of learning disabilities: A handbook of issues, methods, and practice*. J. E. Obrzut and G. W. Hynd, eds. San Diego: Academic Press, 1991, pp. 29–48.

42. Pennington, B. F. Genetics of learning disabilities. *Journal of Child Neurology* (1995) 10:69–77.

43. Shaywitz, S. E., Escobar, M. D., Shaywitz, B. A., et al. Evidence that dyslexia may represent the lower tail of a normal distribution of reading ability. *New England Journal of Medicine* (1992) 326:145–50.

44. Torgesen, J. K. A model of memory from an information processing perspective: The special case of phonological memory. In *Attention, memory, and executive function*. G. R. Lyon and N. A. Krasnegor, eds. Baltimore: Paul H. Brookes, 1996, pp. 157–84.

45. Torgesen, J. K., and Davis, C. Individual difference variables that predict response to training in phonological awareness. Unpublished manuscript. Florida State University, 1994.

46. Wagner, R. From simple structure to complex function: Major trends in the development of theories, models, and measurements of memory. In *Attention, memory, and executive function*. G. R. Lyon and N. A. Krasnegor, eds. Baltimore: Paul H. Brookes, 1996, pp. 139–56.

47. Dalton, R., and Forman, M. Attention deficit hyperactivity disorder (ADHD). In *Nelson textbook of pediatrics*. 15th ed. R. Behrman, R. Kliegman, and A. Arvin, eds. Philadelphia: W. B. Saunders, 1996, pp. 91–93.

48. Barkley, R. *Attention deficit hyperactivity disorder: A handbook for diagnosis and treatment*. New York: Guilford, 1990.

49. Gilger, J. W., Pennington, B. P., and DeFries, J. D. A twin study of the etiology of comorbidity: Attention-deficit hyperactivity disorder and dyslexia. *Journal of the Academy of Child and Adolescent Psychiatry* (1992) 31:343–48.

50. Bryan, T. Social problems in learning disabilities. In *Learning about learning disabilities*, B. Y. L. Wong, ed. New York: Academic Press, 1991, p. 195–226.

51. Bruck, M. Social and emotional adjustments of learning disabled children: A review of the issues. In *Handbook of cognitive, social, and neuropsychological aspects of learning disabilities*. S. J. Cedi, ed., Hillsdale, NJ: Erlbaum, 1986, pp. 230–50.

52. Johnson, D. J., and Blalock, J., eds. *Adults with learning disabilities: Clinical studies*. New York: Grune & Stratton, 1987.

53. Gresham, F. M. Conceptual issues in the assessment of social competence in children. In *Children's social behavior: Development, assessment, and modification*. P. Strain, M. Guralink, and H. Walker, eds. New York: Academic Press, 1986, pp. 143–86.

54. Hooper, S. R., Montgomery, J., Swartz, C., et al. Measurement of written language expression. In *Frames of reference for the assessment of learning disabilities: New views on measurement issues*. G. R. Lyon, ed. Baltimore: Paul H. Brookes, 1994, pp. 375–418.

55. Beringer, V. W. *Reading and writing acquisition: A developmental neuropsychological perspective*. Madison, WI: Brown and Benchmark, 1994.

56. Graham, S., Harris, K., MacArthur, C., and Schwartz, S. Writing and writing instruction with students with learning disabilities: A review of a program of research. *Learning Disability Quarterly* (1991) 14:89–114.

57. Gregg, N. Disorders of written expression. In *Written language disorders: Theory into practice*. A. Bain, L. Bailet, and L. Moats, eds. Austin, TX: PRO-ED, 1991, pp. 65–97.

58. Norman, C. A., and Zigmond, N. Characteristics of children labeled and served as learning disabled in school systems affiliated with Child Service Demonstration Centers. *Journal of Learning Disabilities* (1980) 13:542–47.

59. Blachman, B. A., ed. *Cognitive and linguistic foundations of reading acquisition: Implications for intervention research*. Mahwah, NJ: Erlbaum. In press.

60. Blachman, B. A., Ball, E., Black, R., and Tangel, D. Kindergarten teachers develop phoneme awareness in low-income inner-city classrooms: Does it make a difference? *Reading and Writing: An Interdisciplinary Journal* (1994) 6:1–17.

61. Tangel, D. M., and Blachman, B. A. Effect of phoneme awareness instruction on the invented spelling of first grade children: A one year follow-up. *Journal of Reading Behavior* (June 1995) 27,2:153–85.

62. Torgesen, J. K., Wagner, R. K., and Rashotte, C. A. Approaches to the prevention and remediation of phonologically based reading disabilities. In *Cognitive and linguistic foundations of reading acquisition: Implications for intervention research*. B. A. Blachman, ed. Mahwah, NJ: Erlbaum. In press.

63. Torgeson, J. K., Morgan, S., and Davis, C. The effects of two types of phonological awareness training on word learning in kindergarten children. *Journal of Educational Psychology* (1992) 84:364–70.

64. Foorman, B. R. *Early interventions for children with reading problems*. Progress Report. NICHD Grant HD 30995. Bethesda, MD: The National Institute of Child Health and Human Development, December 1995.

65. Alexander, A., Anderson, H., Heilman, P. C., et al. Phonological awareness training and remediation of analytic decoding deficits in a group of severe dyslexics. *Annals of Dyslexia* (1991) 41:193–206.

66. Torgesen, J. D. *Prevention and remediation of reading disabilities*. Progress Report. NICHD Grant HD 30988. Bethesda, MD: The National Institute of Child Health and Human Development, December 1995.

67. Torgesen, J. K., Wagner, R. K., and Rashotte, C. A. Longitudinal studies of phonological processing and reading. *Journal of Learning Disabilities* (1994) 27:276–86.

68. Iversen, S., and Tunmer, W. E. Phonological processing skills and the Reading Recovery Program. *Journal of Educational Psychology* (1993) 85:112–26.

69. Foorman, B. R. Research on the great debate: Code-oriented versus whole-language approaches to reading instruction. *School Psychology Review* (1995) 24:376–92.

70. Martin, E. W. Learning disabilities and public policy: Myths and outcomes. In *Better understanding learning disabilities: New views from research and their implications for education and public policy*. G. R. Lyon, D. B. Gray., J. F. Kavanagh, and N. A. Krasnegor, eds. Baltimore: Paul H. Brookes, 1993, pp. 325–42.

71. Fairweather, J. S., and Shaver, D. M. Making a transition to postsecondary education and training. *Exceptional Children* (1990) 57:264–70.

Sources for Table 1:

The Yale Research Group

The principal investigator for the Yale Learning Disability Research Center is Dr. Bennett Shaywitz, professor of pediatrics and professor and chief of pediatric neurology, the Yale University School of Medicine, 333 Cedar Street, New Haven, CT 06510. The Yale Group also consists of Drs. Sally Shaywitz, John Gore, Pawel Skudlarski, Robert Fulbright, Todd Constable, Richard Bronen, and Cheryl Lacadie from Yale University; Drs. Alvin Liberman, Kenneth Pugh, Donald Shankweiler, Carol Fowler, Ann Fowler, and Leonard Katz from the Haskins Laboratories; Drs. Jack Fletcher and Karla Steubing from the University of Texas Medical School; Drs. David Francis and Barbara Foorman form the University of Houston; Dr. Dorothy Aram from Emerson College; Dr. Benita Blachman from Syracuse University; Dr. Keith Stanovich and Linda Siegel from the Ontario Institute for Studies in Education; Dr. Rafael Kloorman from the University of Rochester; and Dr. Irwen Kirsch from the Educational Testing Service.

The Ontario Research Group

Drs. Keith Stanovich and Linda Siegel are professors of psychology and special education at the Ontario Institute for Studies in Education (OISE), Department of Special Education, Toronto, Ontario, Canada M5S 1V6 Canada. They are affiliated with the Yale University Learning Disability Research Center funded by the NICHD, as well as senior level scientists at OISE where funding is obtained primarily through the Canadian Research Council.

The University of Colorado Research Group

The principal investigator for the University of Colorado Learning Disability Research Center is Dr. John DeFries, professor and director of the Institute for Behavioral Genetics, the University of Colorado, Campus Box 447, Boulder, CO 80309-0447. The Colorado research team consists of Drs. Richard Olson, Barbara Wise, David Fulker, and Helen Forsberg from the University of Colorado, Boulder; Dr. Bruce Pennington from the University of Denver; Drs. Shelly Smith and William Kimberling from the Boys Town National Research Hospital in Omaha; Dr. Pauline Filipek from the University of California, Irvine; and Drs. David Kennedy and Albert Galaburda from Harvard University.

The Bowman Gray School of Medicine Research Group

The principal investigator for the Center for Neurobehavioral Studies of Learning Disorders is Dr. Frank Wood, professor of neurology and neuropsychology, Bowman Gray School of Medicine, 300 S. Hawthorne Road, Winston-Salem, NC 27103. Also from the Center are Drs. Rebecca Felton, Cecille Naylor, Mary McFarlane, John Keyes, Mark Espeland, Dale Dagenbach, and John Absher from the Bowman Gray School of Medicine; Dr. Raquel Gur from the University of Pennsylvania; Dr. Connie Juel from the University of Virginia; and Dr. Jan Loney from the State University of New York at Stony Brook.

The Johns Hopkins Research Group

The principal investigator for the Johns Hopkins Learning Disability Research Center is Dr. Martha Denckla, professor of neurology, pediatrics, and psychiatry, Johns Hopkins University School of Medicine, 707 North Broadway, Suite 501, Baltimore MD 21205. The Hopkins research team consists of Drs. Allan Reiss, Harvey Singer, Linda Schuerholz, Lisa Freund, Michelle Mazzocco, and Mark Reader from the Kennedy-Kriger Research Institute at Johns Hopkins; Drs. Frank Vallutino and Donna Scanlon at the State University of New York at Albany; Dr. Mark Appelbaum from Vanderbilt University; and Dr. Gary Chase from Georgetown University.

The Florida State University Research Group

The principal investigator of the Florida State University Learning Disabilities Intervention Project is Dr. Joseph Torgesen, professor of psychology, Florida State University, Tallahassee, FL 33124-2040. Members of the Florida State Research Group are Drs. Richard Wagner and Carol Rashotte from Florida State University; Drs. Ann Alexander and Kytja Voeller from the University of Florida, and Ms. Patricia Lindamood from Lindamood-Bell Learning Processes.

The University of Houston Research Group

The principal investigator for the University of Houston Learning Disabilities Intervention Project is Dr. Barbara Foorman, professor of educational psychology, University of Houston, 4800 Calhoun, Houston, TX 77204. The Houston group also consists of Drs. David Francis and Dorothy Haskell from the University of Houston; Drs. Jack Fletcher and Karla Steubing from the University of Texas Medical School; and Drs. Bennett and Sally Shaywitz from Yale University.

The University of Miami Research Group

The principal investigator for the University of Miami Learning Disabilities Program Project is Dr. Herbert Lubs, professor of pediatrics and genetics, University of Miami School of Medicine, MCCD, P.O. Box 18620, Miami, FL 33101. The Miami group also consists of Dr. Ranjan Dura, Bonnie Levin, Bonnie Jallad, Marie-Louis Lubs, Mark Rabin, Alex Kushch, and Karen Gross-Glenn, all from the University of Miami.

G. Reid Lyon, Ph.D., is a psychologist and director of extramural research in learning disabilities, language disorders, and disorders of attention at the National Institute of Child Health and Human Development at the National Institutes of Health, Bethesda, MD.

Graphic Organizers to the Rescue!

Helping Students Link— and Remember— Information

Gloria A. Dye

How do we remember things?

How do we take advantage of our short-term memory?

How does information get stored for the long term?

Do people remember things in different ways?

What can help students improve their memory of content?

What can teachers do to support students with disabilities in storing long-term memory?

Psychologists and neuroscientists are working on these questions as we read this article, and many answers are ready and waiting for savvy teachers to grab and use with their students.

Students with mild to moderate disabilities need strategies to help them achieve success in their content-area classes. As special education teachers, one of our goals is to ensure, to the best of our ability, that students are achieving success in all classes. If students are to become successful in content-area classes, we must present information in a manner that is clear and organized. A clear, organized style will assist students in the note-taking process and will help them link the new information to their existing schema of knowledge. Graphic organizers may help as we present new information to students and as we review previous lessons.

What Are Graphic Organizers?

Graphic organizers are "visual displays teachers use to organize information in a manner that makes the information easier to understand and learn" (Meyen, Vergason, & Whelan 1996, p. 132). Here are some examples of graphic organizers:

- Venn diagrams.
- Semantic webs.
- Genealogical trees.
- Frames.

Some of these examples can be found in works by Lazear (1991) and Staton (1991). The frame is a more detailed type of graphic organizer; Ellis (1998) described its use in the Content Enhancement Series entitled *The Framing Routine*. The frame is a "two-dimensional graphic organizer that allows the teacher to display in an organized manner important information related to the targeted key topic" (p. 5).

The graphic organizer has its roots in schema theory. In effect, schema theory states that *new information must be linked to preexisting knowledge*. The teacher's task is to ensure that the child has prior knowledge related to the concept and to provide a means to assist the child in making the necessary connections between what is being taught and the child's prior knowledge. When people learn something new, they must retain it for later use. Our knowledge is stored in a scaffold-like hierarchy, which includes our way of organizing the information. According to Slavin (1991), we encode, store, and retrieve information based on this system. Schema

theory can be better understood when we examine the cognitive approach to learning.

Cognitive Approach to Learning

"The cognitive approach to learning seeks to understand how incoming information is processed and structured into memory" (Weinstein & Mayer, 1986, p. 316). Figure 1, a graphic organizer, illustrates how information is processed through the short-term memory and the long-term memory.

According to cognitive theory, a student is bombarded with a great deal of information. This is what happens (imagine arrows showing choices and processes):

- All this information enters the sensory register and is held there for only a few seconds.

- The information is either processed immediately or is forgotten.

- If the student chooses to process the information, it then moves from the sensory register to short-term memory.

- At this point, the student must rehearse this newly received information or it will be lost. The rehearsal is important because the longer a piece of information remains in short-term memory and is actively used, the greater the chance that this information will move from short-term memory to long-term memory.

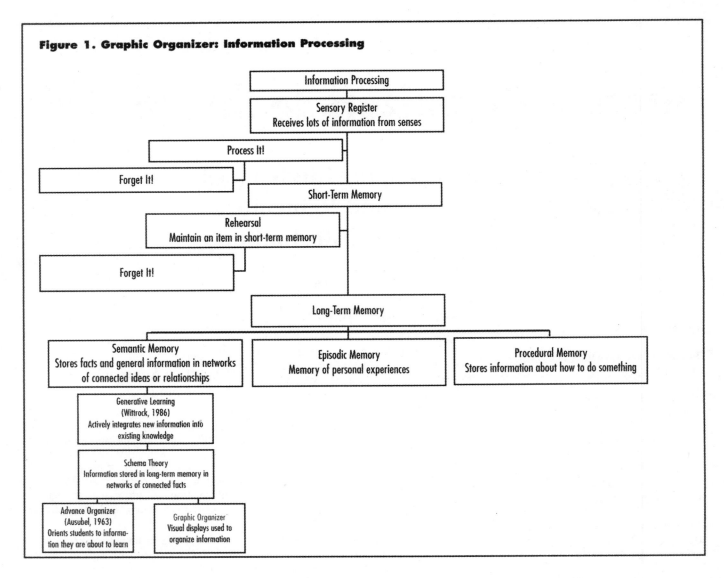

Figure 1. Graphic Organizer: Information Processing

Clearly, this is one of the key points in teaching—helping the student move pertinent information into long-term memory.

According to Slavin (1991) and Mercer (1997), long-term memory can be divided into three parts: procedural memory, episodic memory, and semantic memory.

- Procedural memory stores information about how to do something.
- Episodic memory stores information about personal experiences.
- Semantic memory is organized in a different fashion. Semantic memory stores facts and general information in networks of connected ideas or relationships. This concept of semantic memory is grounded in *generative-learning* (Wittrock, 1986), which states that if learners are to discover or truly

understand the new information, they must actively integrate this new information into their existing knowledge.

Schema Theory

Schema theory explains this integration even further. Schema theory states that a person takes this new information and stores it in preexisting hierarchies or channels. Clearly, schema theory sets the groundwork for advance organizers (Ausubel, 1963), which, when presented at the beginning of a lesson, orient the students to information that the teacher is about to present. The graphic organizers are visual displays used to organize information (Meyen et al., 1996). These processes help students integrate the new knowledge into their scaffolds.

Theory Comparison

Let's compare this approach to the behaviorist approach:

- The *behaviorist* approach "focuses on observable behaviors, and views learning as the establishing of functional relationships between a student's behavior and the stimuli in the environment" (Bos & Vaughn, 1998, pp. 55–56).
- The *cognitive* approach "focuses on what happens in the mind, and views learning as changes in the learner's cognitive structure" (Bos & Vaughn, 1998, p. 56).

Simply stated, the behaviorist approach focuses on the behaviors of the teacher and the student; and the cognitive approach focuses on the internal thinking processes of the student.

Application of Schema Theory to Children

The most critical component of schema theory to remember is as follows: "Information that fits into a (student's) existing schema is more easily understood, learned, and retained than information that does not fit into an existing schema" (Slavin, 1991, p. 164). If, for example, a student with a disability has difficulty learning information in a content-area class, one might ascertain, based on this schema theory, that the student may have a problem fitting the information he or she has learned into his or her existing scaffold of knowledge. Although there are many reasons for this, one explanation could be that the student may not have the proper background knowledge. As Ausubel (1963) explained it: "Potentially meaningful material is always learned in relation to an existing background of relevant concepts, principles, and information which provide a framework for its reception" (p. 76).

Early Childhood Uses

Here are some ways you may use graphic organizers with children at the early childhood level:

1. Teaching children about animals and helping them classify the animals.
2. Explaining the connection between characters in a story.
3. Developing language skills by including pictures along with the words within the graphic organizer to explain a certain concept.

We know that most students with learning disabilities have difficulties processing information; thus, "the most fundamental characteristic of students with learning disabilities is their lack of academic achievement in one or more areas" (Turnbull, Turnbull, Shank, & Leal, 1999, pp. 126–127). Given the lack of background knowledge and the inability to organize the information, it may be difficult for a student with learning disabilities to retain this newly learned information.

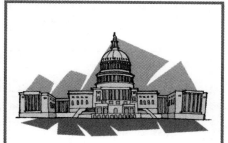

Elementary Uses

Here are some ways you might use graphic organizers with children at the elementary level:

1. Helping children remember or understand the specific parts of a story.
2. Using phonological awareness activities, teaching the children how and when to spell the various /s/ sounds, for example.
3. Helping the children remember the states and capitals and where they are located in the United States. For example, the eastern states, the western states, the midwestern states.

Helping the student link new information to an existing knowledge base is one way teachers can assist students in learning new information in content-area classes. The use of a graphic organizer is an underlying premise of schema theory. Understanding this theory can assist teachers in their presentation of the material and may help students make the necessary linkages for learning to occur (U.S. Department of Education, 1987).

If, for example, you were conducting a lesson about flight, you might use the graphic organizer shown in Figure 2. You could help students link concepts of flight to their existing knowledge base by orga-

nizing the relationships among topics in the graphic organizer.

Using this graphic organizer to present information about flight, you can help students compare some of the early attempts at flight made by people in the United States with the early attempts at flight made by Europeans. You can also add additional spaces for students to fill out, as seen by the blank spaces in Figure 2 under North Carolina, Germany, Montgolfier, and Bleriot. Students might add information about the Wright Brothers, for example, in the North Carolina box, to continue to develop the lesson about flight.

By using a graphic organizer like the "flight" organizer, students can have a copy of the information and can add to it as the instruction progresses. Similarly, you might add additional blanks under various levels to extend the amount of information you wish to present to the students on that topic. This also would assist the student in linking prior knowledge with the new information you present.

Middle School Uses

Here are some ways to use graphic organizers with middle school students:

1. Illustrating science concepts, such as how and when various types of clouds form.
2. Understanding history concepts, such as the key issues leading to the Civil War.
3. Associating the instruments in an orchestra with the particular section that instrument might be in. One section of the graphic organizer might be entitled "woodwind instruments," with the specific instruments noted.

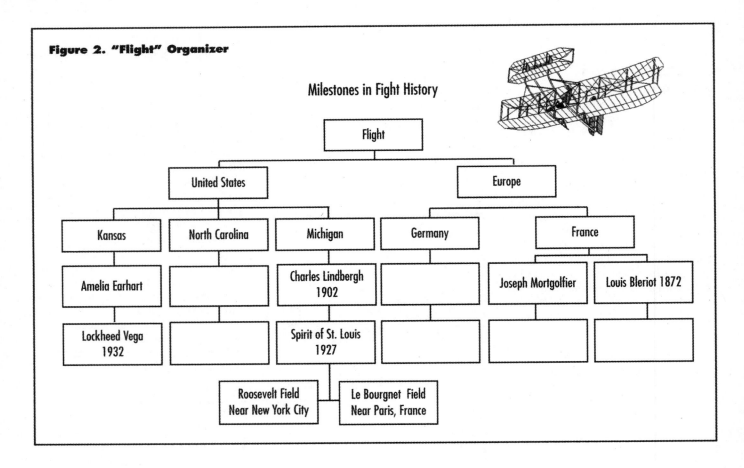

Figure 2. "Flight" Organizer

Milestones in Fight History

Flight
- United States
  - Kansas
    - Amelia Earhart
      - Lockheed Vega 1932
  - North Carolina
  - Michigan
    - Charles Lindbergh 1902
      - Spirit of St. Louis 1927
        - Roosevelt Field Near New York City
        - Le Bourgnet Field Near Paris, France
- Europe
  - Germany
  - France
    - Joseph Mortgolfier
    - Louis Bleriot 1872

Creating Your Own Graphic Organizer

Graphic organizers are relatively easy to create; they can enhance a student's understanding of many lessons. Here are four basic steps to follow:

1. Select the information you intend to present to the students. This may be a chapter, or a story, or a certain concept.
2. Decide what key components are necessary for the students to learn.
3. Create a graphic representation of that information, such as those illustrated in Figures 1 and 2. Your graphic chart should identify the key concepts of components and help illustrate the linkages among the key elements of the concept.
4. Help the students see the connections by examining the information in the graphic organizer.

Graphic organizers lend themselves to many different kinds of content and to uses with all age levels of students (see boxes on Early Childhood, Elementary, Middle, and High School uses).

Final Thoughts

Graphic organizers can benefit teachers, students, and parents. By using graphic organizers, teachers can have a clear understanding of what they want to address in their classes. Graphic organizers provide students with a road map to follow as they expand their schemas by linking them to existing knowledge. When looking at a graphic organizer, like the "Flight" organizer, parents can have a clearer view of what their children will learn or what they have learned in a content-area class. By serving as a means of helping students link the new information with their existing knowledge base, graphic organizers can contribute to our ultimate goal—student learning.

References

Ausubel, D. P. (1963). *The psychology of meaningful verbal learning*. New York: Grune & Stratton.

Bos, C. S., & Vaughn, S. (1998). *Strategies for teaching students with learning and behavior problems* (4th ed.). Needham Heights, MA: Allyn & Bacon.

Ellis, E. S. (1998). *The framing routine*. Lawrence, KS: Edge Enterprises.

Lazear, D. (1991). *Seven ways of teaching*. Palatine, IL: Skylight.

Mercer, D. C. (1997). *Students with learning disabilities*. Upper Saddle River, NJ: Prentice Hall.

Meyen, E. L., Vergason, G. A. & Whelan, R. J. (1996). *Strategies for teaching exceptional children in inclusive settings*. Denver, CO: Love.

High School Uses

Here are some ways to use graphic organizers with high school students:

1. Comparing two stories in literature.
2. Explaining the key components from a chapter in the history text.
3. Describing the key concepts from a chapter in the science text.

Slavin, R. E. (1991). *Educational psychology* (3rd ed.). Needham Heights, MA: Allyn & Bacon.

Staton, H. N. (1991). *The content connection: How to integrate thinking and writing in the content areas.* Glenview, IL: Goodyear Books.

Turnbull, A., Turnbull, R., Shank, M., & Leal, D. (1999). *Exceptional lives: Special education in today's schools* (2nd ed.). Upper Saddle River, NJ: Merrill, Prentice Hall.

U.S. Department of Education. (1987). *What works* (2nd ed.). Washington, DC: U.S. Government Printing Office.

Weinstein, C. E., & Mayer, R. E. (1986). The teaching of learning strategies. In M. C. Wittrock (Ed.), *Handbook of research on teaching* (pp. 315–327). New York: Macmillan.

Wittrock, M. C. (1986). Students' thought processes. In M. C. Wittrock (Ed.), *Handbook of research on teaching* (3rd ed.). New York: Macmillan.

Gloria A. Dye *(CEC Chapter #816), Assistant Professor, Secondary Special Education, Washburn University, Topeka, Kansas.*

Address correspondence to the author at Washburn University, 1700 S.W. College Avenue, Topeka, KS 66621 (e-mail: zzdye@washburn.edu).

From *Teaching Exceptional Children*, January/February 2000, pp. 72–76. © 2000 by The Council for Exceptional Children. Reprinted by permission.

Chaos in the Classroom: Looking at ADHD

Diagnosing and helping students with ADHD requires the collaboration of parents, clinicians, teachers, and students.

Steven C. Schlozman and Vivien R. Schlozman

Students increasingly walk through the classroom door wearing invisible labels and prescriptions. A list of psychiatric and learning disorders that was intended to clarify the difficulties different students experience has instead bewildered teachers and administrators. Educators must make sense of their students' new diagnostic criteria and glean from this information the most effective ways to assist their pupils. Given the enormous increase in the diagnosis and treatment of attention deficit hyperactivity disorder (ADHD) among school-age children, neuropsychiatric problems characterized by inattention and hyperactivity are pressing classroom issues.

Students diagnosed with ADHD often arrive in the classroom with medication and teaching recommendations that are based on completed psychological testing. In spite of these recommendations, teachers frequently have little or no contact with their students' clinicians. Tight budgets, large classrooms, and often multiple students with the same diagnosis who require different teaching strategies substantially challenge the educator's primary objective: to teach and inspire every student dynamically and efficiently. Reaching that goal starts with an understanding of ADHD and how teachers can help students who have been diagnosed with the disorder.

Describing and Diagnosing ADHD

ADHD is a neuropsychiatric disorder that begins before 7 years of age (American Psychiatric Association, 1994). Problems in the three core domains of *inattention, hyperactivity*, and *impulsivity* characterize the disorder.

Clinicians define *inattention* as age-inappropriate poor attention span and *hyperactivity* as age-inappropriate

increased activity in multiple settings. For example, an inattentive child may pay poor attention to details or appear as though his or her mind is elsewhere. Often, the child has difficulty sustaining a single activity. One mother describes her son's bedtime difficulties: He starts to brush his teeth, follows the cat into the playroom while his mouth is full of toothpaste, notices the blocks and sits down to play, and in two minutes turns on the computer at the other end of the room.

Most children will occasionally display many of the aspects ascribed to ADHD, and this recognition may account for much of the controversy surrounding the disorder.

Hyperactive children may fidget excessively and have difficulties playing quietly. Children with ADHD display, sometimes paradoxically, a level of inflexibility that leads them to experience intense frustration when asked to break from one activity and move on to something new. The child will appear to have well-honed attentional skills, but his or her rigidity will increasingly lead to tantrums and agitation.

Impulsivity refers to the tendency to act rashly and without judgment or consideration. A child might frequently interrupt others, take other children's toys, or appear consistently impatient and frustrated.

As these descriptions suggest, the symptoms of ADHD exist along a spectrum. Most children will occasionally display many of the aspects ascribed to ADHD, and this recognition may account for much of the controversy surrounding the disorder. To standardize the diagnosis, the Diagnostic and Statistical Manual-IV (DSM-IV) lists formal criteria (American Psychiatric Association, 1994). ADHD can be characterized as three types: predominantly inattentive, predominantly hyperactive-impulsive, or a combination of the two types. To some extent, these differentiations account for the increasingly recognized population of children—often girls—who display what appear to be difficulties primarily with attention but who respond to conventional treatments.

The brief adolescent tantrum or the distraction of an 8-year-old before vacation does not constitute sufficient data for a diagnosis of ADHD.

Finally, one of the most difficult and important aspects of understanding ADHD is to consider the child's developmental expectations. Obviously, we don't expect the same judgment or attention span from a 6-year-old and a teenager. In addition, symptoms must persist over time and exist in more than one setting. The brief adolescent tantrum or the distraction of an 8-year-old before vacation does not constitute sufficient data for a diagnosis of ADHD.

In fact, the heterogeneity and developmental aspects of ADHD make the diagnosis of the disorder potentially quite complicated (Cantwell, 1996). Ideally, the clinician should take a very careful history from as many sources as possible and note such important factors as the persistence of the symptoms and the extent to which these symptoms cause problems. Because emotionally troubled children often appear inattentive or agitated, the clinician should ask about difficulties in the child's life that might account for a change in the child's behavior. We must also remember, however, that many children experience difficult life changes but do not display symptoms of agitation or inattention.

Although research addresses the efficacy of specific laboratory tests, the descriptive criteria of ADHD remain the most effective means of making an accurate diagnosis. Clinicians must take the time to speak with parents and teachers, noting that children with ADHD will often appear normal in a brief office visit or in a one-on-one situation. As evidence mounts of a strong genetic component to the disorder, clinicians should ascertain whether siblings, parents, or close relatives suffer similar symptoms. Because many parents were not diagnosed as children, simply asking whether they were diagnosed with something similar to ADHD is usually not sufficient (Biederman et al., 1992). The clinician must probe parents for their memories of their childhood behavior.

Do inattention and hyperactivity always equal ADHD? In addition to the heterogeneity of ADHD, we must note that other psychiatric processes may account for many of the disorder's symptoms. Children with intense anxiety or depression are particularly likely to have problems that appear similar to ADHD, and evidence also exists that suggests that symptoms of depression—as the child's self esteem suffers in the face of continuing social and developmental failures—can complicate ADHD (Zametkin & Monique, 1999). Clinicians should also screen for problems with substance abuse, Tourette's syndrome, and psychosocial stressors. Clinicians, parents, or teachers may mistakenly attribute symptoms of these conditions to ADHD, and the symptoms may complicate the course of a child who happens also to suffer from ADHD.

In general, younger children with ADHD are happy. The preteen diagnosed with ADHD who is not generally in good spirits should be carefully scrutinized for other or additional psychological problems. Conversely, as children with untreated ADHD age, they may develop significant self-image problems. These difficulties come about as the young people continually endure academic and social failures; simply treating their ADHD will often not meet all of their social, developmental, and learning needs.

Although we don't clearly understand the causes of ADHD, current research suggests evidence of potentially causative brain abnormalities. Many of these studies implicate problems with frontal lobe function (Rubia et al., 1999). In general, the frontal lobe region of the cerebral cortex allows for the planning and execution of complex and complicated tasks. We often refer to the activity of this portion of the brain as executive function, and we think that children with ADHD have deficits in executive functioning.

Evidence for these deficits has been generated both by neuropsychological testing and by neuroimaging studies, as well as by the observation that individuals with frontal lobe injuries display behavior similar to that of people with ADHD. As stated earlier, strong evidence for a genetic component of the disorder also exists (Biederman et al., 1992). Further, mounting evidence suggests that psychological and environmental stress can lead to the development of the syndrome (Weiss, 1996). Although we know of no clear cause for the disorder, most theorists would argue that both environmental and biological factors play substantial roles in the development of ADHD.

Treating ADHD

Treatments for ADHD include behavioral and medical therapies. Stimulants such as methylphenidate (Ritalin) and dextroamphetamine (Dexedrine) continue to be first-line medical treatments, with more than 40 years of experience confirming the relative safety and effectiveness of these medications. Although the number of stimulants on the market proliferates, response to a specific stimulant remains idiosyncratic; some children will do better on one stimulant than the other, and it is difficult to predict which medication will work best. In addition to the stimulants, tricyclic antidepressants such as desipramine can be very effective, though their use is somewhat limited in younger children. Medications such as clonidine (Catapress) and guanfacine (Tenex), both high blood pressure medications, appear to treat the impulsive symptoms of the syndrome, but are not effective for inattention.

In general, if medical therapies work and the child receives the appropriate dose and stimulant, the child's behavior should improve relatively quickly. If a child does not improve or improves only minimally, both the proposed treatment regimen (dose and/or medication) and often the diagnosis itself should be re-evaluated. Nevertheless, we need to understand the limitations of medical therapies. Although such symptoms as overactivity, attention span, impulsivity, aggression, social interaction, and academic performance will often improve, such specific skills as reading and such antisocial behavior as cheating or stealing may not show marked progress without additional interventions (Zametkin & Monique, 1999). Children still must master the fundamental developmental task of learning to focus on activities or subjects that are not of immediate interest. No medication can take the place of the mastery of skills and attainment of maturity necessary for academic and social success.

Behavioral treatments of ADHD include daily report cards, positive reinforcement, social skills groups, and individual therapy (Barkley, 1990). As the child matures, these treatments may also address the child's self-image. Although psychodynamic therapies (play or talk therapies) may not be directly effective, we have found that the relationship between a child and an effective therapist often ameliorates many of the problem behaviors associated with ADHD.

Finally, when deciding on treatment, the parents and the child must take part in the decision-making process. Some families prefer behavioral remedies; others may request medications. Attention to such details as the meaning of each treatment modality, as well as the hopes and concerns of both the parents and the child, will have enormous benefits. Adolescents may not wish to take medications, for instance, but may be willing to implement equally effective study and behavioral strategies. Conversely, both time and financial constraints may limit the efficacy of psychotherapy. Clinicians must educate families about ADHD and its treatment and help the families make informed decisions. Clinicians should leave time at the end of an appointment for questions—if families cannot ask questions, their understanding of and compliance with treatment is severely threatened.

The issue of alcohol and drug abuse and ADHD deserves special mention. Because stimulants are addictive substances, we often worry that prescribing these medications will predispose children to addictive problems. Although caution is always necessary when using stimulants, recent research suggests that, in fact, the number of children developing substance abuse problems is substantially higher in those with ADHD who do not receive adequate treatment (Biederman, Wilens, Mick, Spencer, &

Faraone, 1999). Nevertheless, in adolescents with pre-existing problems with substances, clinicians often prefer treatment with medications other than stimulants.

ADHD in the Classroom

Just as diagnosing and treating children with ADHD is complex, working with the inattentive and hyperactive child challenges all teachers. The problems that children with ADHD experience may lead to chaotic classrooms, missed and incomplete assignments, and miserable teachers and students alike. Educators have found, however, a number of useful classroom techniques.

To assist the student with ADHD, educators need to exercise caution, creativity, and vigilance.

First, teachers must view the child as a whole person. The child is not a person with ADHD, or an "ADHDer," but a complete and unique individual. Although seemingly obvious, teachers must resist the tendency to label a child with unfair expectations. Most important, teachers can remind students that they are capable of learning and of enjoying the learning process. Many students diagnosed with ADHD will arrive in the classroom severely demoralized, having gleaned from their parents and peers that they are unable to excel academically. On the other hand, telling students that they can learn as easily as students without attentional deficits might reintroduce a pattern of failure and disappointment.

Educators, therefore, should be proactive when they suspect a psychiatric reason for a student's difficulties. Studies have demonstrated that teachers are valuable sources of clinical information. At the same time, teachers should be aware of their own biases. Many of the studies, for instance, suggest that teachers frequently suspect ADHD in boys more often than in girls (Dulcan, 1997).

To assist the student with ADHD, educators need to exercise caution, creativity, and vigilance. Teachers must employ all of their professional skills to structure classrooms and make assignments clear. Educators should let students with ADHD know that they will work creatively with the students to explore learning and organization strategies. An honest relationship between teacher and student is essential.

To be most effective, teachers should discuss the strategies with the student outside of class so that the student understands the teacher's expectations and the kinds of support the teacher will offer. Specific strategies might include nonverbal reprimands for out-of-control behavior. A simple and silent hand on the student's shoulder inconspicuously tells the student that his or her behavior is inappropriate. Similarly, relying on such cues as lost eye contact between a student and teacher might help a teacher recognize wavering attention. If a child is persistently unable to focus, move his or her seat to a less distracting part of the room. Some other strategies include the following:

Require meticulously organized assignment books. For every class, the student with ADHD must have each day's homework recorded. When the teacher doesn't assign homework, the student writes "no homework" in the appropriate place. If the student fails to keep the log current, he or she must get the teacher's signature in the assignment book at the end of class. The teacher should also both write the assignment on the board and repeat the assignment aloud. This time-honored teaching technique of appealing to multiple senses works well for children with ADHD.

Teach students with ADHD to break down assignments into smaller, less overwhelming components. When reading textbooks, for example, we have found a variation of Robinson's SQ3R method to be effective (Robinson, 1961). The student surveys each section of the text by first reading the boldfaced print, looking at the visuals, and reading the captions under the visual displays. The student then generates a general statement about what he or she will be reading, allowing him or her to focus on the content of the reading material. After each section, the student stops to recap the main idea of the completed segment. This strategy helps the student become actively engaged with and focused on the text.

Use flash cards. After students give themselves a pretest to determine what they have already mastered, they make flash cards of all of the material that they don't know. They then can separate the cards into three piles: mastered material that they know without hesitation, material that they've guessed correctly but without confidence, and material that they don't know. In this way, the students gain a sense of control over the learning situation and learn to transfer these strategies to other academic and non-academic learning settings. The corresponding sense of accomplishment for both teacher and students can be enormously rewarding.

Experienced teachers will note that many of these strategies have been around for years—long before we reached our present understanding of ADHD. We know now that ADHD leaves the student with deficits in executive functioning and that the time-honored classroom techniques create for the student a kind of external frontal lobe. Good teachers have simply hit upon these techniques in their quests to engage and teach their students.

Teachers need not be overwhelmed by the growing complexity of psychiatric and psychological diagnoses that follow their beleaguered students. As always, good educators remain central to a child's development.

Teachers should never hesitate to contact a child's clinician. If a student appears different or suffers a behavioral change, a physician or psychologist will use this valuable information to determine a diagnosis and treatment. Although clinicians and teachers have just begun to work together, educational and clinical collaborations need to evolve and prosper. The teacher, the clinician, and most important, the student, will benefit enormously.

References

American Psychiatric Association. (1994). *Diagnostic and statistical manual for mental disorders* (4th ed.). Washington, DC: Author.

Barkley, R. A. (Ed.). (1990). *Attention deficit hyperactivity disorder: A handbook for diagnosis and treatment.* New York: Guilford.

Biederman, J., Faraone, S. V., Keenan, K., Benjamin, K., Krifcher, B., Moore, C., Sprich-Buckminster, S., Ugaglia, K., Jellinck, M. S., & Steingard, R. (1992). Further evidence for family-genetic risk factors in attention deficit hyperactivity disorder: Patterns of comorbidity in probands and relatives in psychiatrically and pediatrically referred samples. *Archives of General Psychiatry,* 49, 728–38.

Biederman, J., Wilens, T., Mick, E., Spencer, T., & Faraone, S. V. (1999). Pharmacotherapy of attention deficit hyperactivity disorder reduces risk for substance use disorder. *Pediatrics,* 104, e20.

Cantwell, D. P. (1996). Attention deficit disorder: A review of the past 10 years. *Journal of the American Academy of Child and Adolescent Psychiatry,* 35, 978–87.

Dulcan, M. (1997). Practice parameters for the assessment and treatment of children, adolescents and adults with attention deficit/hyperactivity disorder. *Journal of the American Academy of Child and Adolescent Psychiatry,* 36 (Suppl. 10), 85S–121S.

Robinson, F. P. (1961). *Effective study.* New York: Harper and Row.

Rubia, K., Overmeyer, S., Taylor, E., Brammer, M., Williams, S. C., Simmons, A., & Bullmore, E. T. (1999). Hypofrontality in attention deficit hyperactivity disorder during higher order motor control: A study with functional MRI. *American Journal of Psychiatry,* 156, 891–6.

Weiss, G. (1996). Attention deficit hyperactivity disorder. In M. Lewis (Ed.), *Child and adolescent psychiatry: A comprehensive textbook* (pp. 544–63). Baltimore, MD: Williams and Wilkins.

Zametkin, A. J., & Monique, E. (1999). Current concepts: Problems in the management of attention deficit hyperactivity disorder. *New England Journal of Medicine,* 340, 40–46.

Steven C. Schlozman, M.D., is Clinical Instructor in Psychiatry, Massachusetts General Hospital/Harvard Medical School, 15 Parkman St., WACC-725, Boston, MA 02114; and Lecturer in Education, Harvard Graduate School of Education; 617-724-6300, ext. 133-1114; sscholzman@partners.org. **Vivien R. Schlozman** is a private practice educator at the Pembroke Hill School. She may be reached at 6600 Overhill Rd., Shawnee Mission, KS 66208.

From *Educational Leadership,* November 2000, pp. 28–33. © 2000 by the Association for Supervision and Curriculum Development. All rights reserved. Reprinted by permission.

UNIT 4

Speech and Language Impairments

Unit Selections

11. **For the Love of Language**, Geoffrey Cowley
12. **Approaching Families: Facilitating Culturally/Linguistically Diverse Family Involvement**, Howard P. Parette and Beverly Petch-Hogan
13. **Family and Cultural Alert! Considerations in Assistive Technology Assessment**, Jack J. Hourcade, Howard P. Parette Jr., and Mary Blake Huer

Key Points to Consider

- What is specific language impairment (SLI)? How can a teacher assist in language acquisition?

- How can parents of culturally/linguistically diverse students be involved with their child's language development?

- Are assistive devices always desirable prescriptions for students with speech and language impairments?

 **Links: www.dushkin.com/online/**
These sites are annotated in the World Wide Web pages.

Speech Disorders WWW Sites
http://www.socialnet.lu/handitel/wwwlinks/dumb.html

Speech and language impairments, although grouped together as a category of disability by the IDEA (Individuals with Disabilities Education Act) are not synonomous. Speech is the vocal utterance of language. It is considered disordered in three underlying ways: voice, articulation, and fluency. Voice involves coordinated efforts by the lungs, larynx, vocal cords, and nasal passages to produce recognizable sounds. Voice can be considered disordered if it is incorrectly phonated (breathy, strained, husky, hoarse) or if it is incorrectly resonated through the nose (hyper-nasality, hypo-nasality). Articulation involves the use of the tongue, lips, teeth, and mouth to produce recognizable sounds. Articulation can be considered disordered if sounds are added, omitted, substituted, or distorted. Fluency involves appropriate pauses and hesitations to keep speech sounds recognizable. Fluency can be considered disordered if sounds are very rapid with extra sounds (cluttered) or if sounds are blocked and/or repeated, especially at the beginning of words (stuttered).

Language is a rule-based use of voice sounds to communicate. Language problems refer to the use of voice sounds in combinations and patterns that fail to follow the arbitrary rules for that language or to a delay in the use of voice sounds relative to normal development in other areas (physical, cognitive, social). Language delays can also be diagnosed in conjunction with other developmental delays (health, sensory, motor, mental, emotional, behavioral).

The prevalence rates of speech and language disorders are higher than the rates for any other condition of disability in primary school. However, the exact extent of the problem has been questioned because assessment of communication takes a variety of forms. Shy children may be diagnosed with delayed language. Bilingual or multilingual children are often mislabeled as having a language disorder when they simply have different language because they come from linguistically and culturally diverse backgrounds. Many bilingual children do not need the special services provided by speech-language clinicians but do benefit from instruction in English as a second language.

All children with language and/or speech disorders are entitled to assessment and remediation as early in life as the problem is realized. In addition, they are entitled to a free and appropriate education in the least restrictive environment possible and to transitional help into the world of work, if needed, after their education is completed.

Disordered language is usually more difficult to remedy than delayed language. Disordered language may be due to a receptive problem (difficulty understanding voice sounds), an expressive problem (difficulty producing the voice sounds that follow the arbitrary rules for that language), or both. Language disorders include aphasia (no language) and dysphasia (difficulty producing language). Many language disorders are the result of a difficulty in understanding the syntactical rules and structural principles of the language (form), or are the result of a difficulty in perceiving the semantic meanings of the words of the language (content). Many language disorders are also due to a difficulty in using the language pragmatically, in a practical context (function).

Most speech and language impairments have been remediated by high school. An exception to this is speech problems that persist due to physical impairments such as damage to or dysfunction of lungs, larynx, vocal cords, or nasal passages. Other exceptions are language problems that persist due to concurrent disabilities such as deafness, autism, compromised mentation, traumatic brain injuries, and/or some emotional and behavioral disorders.

Speech-language clinicians usually provide special services to children with speech and language impairments in pull-out sessions in resource rooms. Computer technology is also frequently used to assist these children in both their regular education classes and in pull-out therapy sessions.

The first article provides a conceptual framework for the development of language in early childhood. Geoffrey Cowley reviews how infants and toddlers acquire language. He also enumerates many of the things that can undermine the process of learning to talk (autism, hearing defects, brain lesions, or social isolation). The problem of specific language impairments (SLIs) is presented as a fairly common problem that occurs in children with normal hearing and normal intelligence. The two possible explanations for it, auditory-processing or grammatical deficit, are discussed. A list of abnormalities in language at 3, 6, and 12 months and 2, 3, and 4 years developed by the American Speed-Language-Hearing Association (ASLHA) is included to warn parents, teachers, and significant others of red flags for possible speed problems. Recommendations for how to foster good language are also given.

The second article discusses the importance of recognizing communication and speech-language patterns of culturally/linguistically diverse children. Several practice tips are given to facilitate family involvement. From early use of interpreters to choosing language acquisition curricula that are family-friendly, these tips can help integrate diverse children with language differences to schools before they develop language delays or disorders.

The third article included in this unit addresses the question of if and when to provide assistive devices to improve speech and language. The mere fact that the technology exists to improve a speech or language impairment does not make it the most desirable prescription. Decisions about the use of technology must involve families and be sensitive to their routines and needs. Decisions must also be culturally sensitive and be appropriate to each unique student's skill levels.

For the Love of Language

Learning to speak seems nothing short of a miracle.
Scientists are discovering how social and biological
forces let children master their native tongue.

By Geoffrey Cowley

AGE IS AN ADVANTAGE IF YOU'RE trying to learn geometry or swing dancing. But language is different. Consider Paige Arbeiter. She was a 2-pound 7-ounce preemie when she earned the nickname "Little Houdini" six years ago. A day and a half after delivery, she pulled the tube off her face to breathe on her own. And she dazzled her intensive-care nurses by inching across her incubator to hang a tiny foot out the door. When Paige went home after six weeks, her parents noticed that loud noises didn't faze her. Their pediatrician told them repeatedly not to worry, but when Paige was 10 months old they took her to New York's Long Island Jewish Speech and Hearing Center for tests. The verdict: she was nearly deaf in both ears. "Most people we told said, 'Oh, you caught it so early, she'll be just fine'," her mom recalls. "But we learned we'd missed a very important period in her speech and language development." Thanks to a cochlear implant and speech therapy, the spunky 6-year-old now proudly counts to 10. But her overall language proficiency remains that of a toddler.

Babies tackle grammar before they learn to wield a fork

Language is one of the most awesome tasks the human mind performs, and babies are uniquely poised to master it. They map meanings onto words while still sporting diapers, and they tackle grammatical analysis before learning to wield a fork. By the age of 3, most kids are generating sentences they've never heard spoken—and using them to alter the contents of other people's minds. Unfortunately, language doesn't always emerge without a hitch. As experts learn more about how kids learn to talk, they're also learning to spot disorders that can undermine the process. Impaired hearing is just one of them.

The journey to language begins in the womb. During the third trimester of pregnancy, many mothers notice that their babies kick and wiggle in response to music or loud noises. The sound of speech may draw a less spirited reaction, but there is little question that fetuses hear it. Researchers at New York's Columbia Presbyterian Medical Center have found that fetuses' heart rates drop predictably when their mothers speak a simple phrase ("Hello, baby"). And French scientists have gone a step further, showing that a fetus who's been hearing the same sound repeated ("babi, babi") will react to a sudden reversal of its elements ("biba, biba"). Within 96 hours of birth, babies distinguish their mother tongue from a foreign language, sucking more vigorously when they hear it spoken.

How does a child start to parse this river of sound into meaningful units? Simple conditioning is part of the story. Anyone bombarded by a particular language hears certain sound combinations more often than others, and babies are quick to home in on the most probable combinations. In one revealing study, a team led by University of Wisconsin psychologist Jenny Saffran familiarized 8-month-old infants with three-syllable nonsense words such as "bidaku" and "padoti" by playing them in random order on a voice synthesizer. Then the researchers reshuffled the syllables and tested the kids again. The babies easily distinguished bidaku and padoti not only from other nonwords like "dadobi" but also from hybrids like "kupado," a sequence they would have heard on the training tape whenever "bida-KU" bumped up against "PADO-ti." Long before they could attach meanings to words, these kids were processing them as discrete units—saying, in effect, "Call me 'pretty' or call me 'baby'. Just don't call me 'ty-ba'."

Conversing with a child of this age, you'd never guess she harbored such thoughts. Most kids are content to coo and scream for the first six months, but during the second half of the first year, they take up speaking in tongues. They'll go on endlessly about "ma-ma-da-da" without the slightest indication that they know what they're talking about. But as psychologists Roberta Michnick Golinkoff and Kathy Hirsh-Pasek observe in their new book, "How Babies Talk," such blather is a step on the road to articulate speech. "Babbling is analogous to putting a puzzle together over and over," they write. "Just as children learn a good deal about how puzzle pieces differ in small but significant ways, so do babies learn how to manipulate the pieces of sound that make up the puzzle of language." It's not just the syllables that make babbling so speechlike. It's the dead-on rhythms and the patterns of intonation. In one French study, laymen listening to recorded statements by babblers from various countries picked out the future Francophones with near-perfect accuracy.

Within months of their 1st birthday, most kids start attaching names to things. And whether they're learning Swahili or Swedish, they go about it in much the same way. Instead of proceeding by trial and error—unsure whether "doggie" refers to a part of a dog, to one dog in particular or to anything with four legs—children start with a set of innate biases. They assume that labels refer to wholes instead of parts (the creature, not the tail) and to classes instead of items (all dogs, not one dog). They also

Red Flags for Speech Problems

Sometimes a child's failure to put two words together by the time he is 24 months old means nothing. Sometimes it means there is a problem. According to the American Speech-Language-Hearing Association, there are some abnormalities that might reflect hearing loss, head injury or other conditions, and so call for a doctor's evaluation:

0–3 months: Does not listen to speech or does not make sounds repeatedly by cooing or gooing

4–6 months: Does not notice noisy toys, look for the source of sounds like the vacuum cleaner, or attend to parents' 'no'

7–12 months: Does not babble either long or short groups of sounds such as 'tata upup bibibibi' and does not say a word or two, even unclearly. Does not respond to her name.

1–2 years: Does not use one- or two-word questions ('Where kitty?'), put two words together ('mommy book') or listen to simple stories, songs and rhymes

2–3 years: Does not have a word for almost everything or use two- to three-word 'sentences' to talk about and ask for things. Can't understand differences in meaning ('go' and 'stop') or follow two requests ('Get the book and put it on the table'). Doesn't notice environmental sounds such as a doorbell.

3–4 years: Does not hear when you call from another room, or understand simple 'who?' 'what?' and 'where?' questions. Cannot be understood by people outside the family. If delays persist until kindergarten, most pediatricians recommend speech therapy.

TESSA NAMUTH

figure that one name is enough for any class of object (if it's a dog, it's not a cow). These assumptions are not always valid—there's only one Lassie, after all, and any dog qualifies as a mammal—but they enable kids to catalog new words with breathtaking efficiency. A typical child is socking away a dozen words a day by 18 months, and may command 2,000 of them by the age of 2.

This is when things get interesting. A chimp with a signboard can learn to asso-

ciate symbols with particular objects and actions, but toddlers do much more than that. Having acquired their words through mimicry, they start combining them—according to abstract rules that no one has taught them—to express their thoughts and feelings. Their first sentences may be crude utterances such as "Gonna cry!" or "Uppy me!" But between 24 and 30 months, kids who have never heard of syntax usually start marrying noun phrases to verb phrases to explain who did what to whom. If they happen to speak English, they know that "man bites dog" and "dog bites man" tell different stories, despite their identical words.

Some scholars have argued that kids learn to form sentences just as they learn to perceive word boundaries—by listening for statistical regularities in other people's speech. Grammatical analysis doesn't require specialized cognitive software, they say; it boils down to operant conditioning. According to this argument, a baby who encounters the sentences "the boy likes apples" and "the boy likes oranges" 50 times each will learn that the words "the," "boy" and "likes" are tightly correlated in certain circumstances, whereas apples and oranges show up only 50 percent of the time. As the baby encounters more sentences, the web of associations expands, providing more templates for original utterances.

But recent studies suggest there is much more to the story—that children actively seek out abstract grammatical rules. In one clever experiment, researchers led by New York University psychologist Gary Marcus presented 7-month-old infants with a language problem that couldn't be solved by operant conditioning alone. First the children spent two minutes listening to a series of three-word "sentences" such as "ga-ti-ga" and "li-na-li." The "words" varied from one sentence to the next, but the syntax didn't: any word appearing in the first position also appeared in the third. After familiarizing the children with these samples, the researchers played a different set of sentences—some obeying the A-B-A rule ("wo-fe-wo"), and some violating it ("wo-fe-fe"). The babies had never heard any of these new utterances, yet their attention patterns suggested that "wo-fe-wo" sounded familiar while the "nongrammatical" A-B-B sequences surprised them. The implication is that the kids weren't merely seeking out associations among "words" they'd already heard. They were spontaneously extracting the principles governing word order in general.

PARENTESE # Giving Children the Gift of Gab

Speaking to kids slowly and clearly aids language development

WHEN IT COMES TO VISION, newborns prefer simple sights like circles. But for sounds, they prefer complex stimuli like the highly intonated speech called parentese. The high pitch, slow pace and musicality of parentese may help children forge the brain circuits that let them identify the phonemes—distinct sounds—of their native language, a crucial step in understanding and producing speech. Parentese may also strengthen the neuronal circuits that tie together sounds and meanings in a child's brain. Some of its features:

Speaking **slowly** and with clear **enunciation** gives children a clean template on which to model their speech. More important, it literally trains neurons to specialize in hearing a particular phoneme, an ability crucial for learning to read. Emphasizing one word in a sentence ("Do you see that *bird*?") rivets the child's attention.

Repetition reinforces the neural pathways underlying language. Scientists have a mantra for this: "Cells that fire together, wire together."

In other words, the more a child hears "bed" and sees you point to it, the faster she'll get the connection. But don't turn it into a dreary drill. Children acquire language not by sitting passively while you talk and point but by taking turns in a **conversation.**

Four-month-olds are figuring out which mouth shapes go with which sounds, so chat with them **face to face.** And imitate what they say—babies love the **feedback.** Responding to "bot bot bot" with "yes,

here's your bottle" reinforces her halting attempts at words.

Don't dumb things down for toddlers. Those whose parents use many dependent clauses ("because…" and "which…") progress beyond simple sentences earlier than children of parents who do not. The more you **talk to your child,** the larger the vocabulary he will likely acquire. **Talking** *to* is the crucial part: merely hearing conversations, let alone TV, seems to have little positive influence on language development.

The language instinct runs so deep that even severely retarded children usually learn to talk. But this unique human propensity isn't foolproof. Any number of congenital or early-life problems—autism, hearing defects, brain lesions, social isolation—can derail language development. And an estimated 3 percent to 7 percent of children suffer from a selective, unexplained difficulty known as specific language impairment, or SLI. These kids exhibit normal hearing and intelligence, and have no other known handicaps. Yet they're late to talk, and even after they start, their facility and comprehension lag. They may say things like "I eating ice," even in grade school, and many go on to experience reading difficulties. Studies suggest the problem runs in families, but no one has identified culpable genes.

Unfortunately, there is no widely accepted treatment for SLI. Experts are even divided on the nature of the problem. Some suspect it's an auditory-processing disorder, in which the brain fails to distinguish properly among the brief blasts of sounds that encode language. In separate studies, neuroscientist Paula Tallal of Rutgers University and communication specialist Bev-

erly Wright of Northwestern University have found that SLI children are less adept than their peers at picking out brief tones amid other sounds of similar frequency. Both of these researchers believe that auditory-training programs, in which children hear exaggerated versions of the problematic sounds over and over, can ease SLI by heightening phonological awareness.

Other experts believe SLI is at root a grammatical disorder, and their findings are equally compelling. Working with MIT cognitive scientist Kenneth Wexler, Mabel Rice of the University of Kansas has shown repeatedly that affected children, though aware of grammatical categories, share problems with certain verb forms. Most English speakers learn by the age of 3 to mark regular verbs with "s" in the third person ("he walks"). SLI kids tend to stick with the infinitive, saying "he walk" and "she play." And auditory-processing problems are an unlikely explanation, because the same children effortlessly add "s" to nouns to form plurals. It's possible that SLI is a varied syndrome and that different researchers are charting different manifestations. But in assessing both auditory and grammatical deficits in SLI kids,

researchers led by Oxford University psychologist Dorothy Bishop have found the grammatical ones far more pervasive. "It seems as if we need to look beyond auditory processing," they conclude in a preliminary report.

SLI may never be preventable. By contrast, the more serious language problems facing little Paige Arbeiter can often be prevented today. If a newborn's hearing impairment is diagnosed and treated within six months, says Dr. Lynn Spivak of Long Island Jewish Medical Center, the child usually develops normal speech and language on schedule. But because the critical period for language development is so brief, any delay can have major consequences. Though Paige now thrills her parents by saying words like "butterfly," she may never have an intuitive feel for syntax. When she strings words together, the results tend toward "Go outside, Paige Mommy!" Thanks in part to the 1999 Newborn and Infant Hearing Screening and Intervention Act, 34 states now offer the $25 test for all babies before they leave the hospital. It's a small price to pay for so vast a wonder as language.

With TESSA NAMUTH

Approaching Families:
Facilitating Culturally/Linguistically Diverse Family Involvement

Howard P. Parette
Beverly Petch-Hogan

My classroom is much more diverse than in past years! I don't understand the backgrounds of many of the families of my children. So what do I do to get these parents involved in helping to make decisions about their children?

Special education classroom teachers often express concerns like these. Their classrooms increasingly include large proportions of students from culturally/linguistically diverse backgrounds (Kalyanpur & Harry, 1999). Communication with families is more and more important in schools today—and family involvement in special education team processes is mandated by the Individuals with Disabilities Education Act Amendments of 1997.

Parents of culturally/linguistically diverse students should be involved in

- Sharing their culture.
- Participating as assistants on field trips.
- Assisting in arts and crafts.
- Assisting with music and recreational activities.
- Participating actively in the special education planning process.

Such involvement is problematic for many families, given a variety of concerns, such as language difference, cultural expectations, and mistrust of or lack of experience with U.S. education systems.

Schools must make efforts to include family members in team decision making to an even greater extent than in the past. This article presents recommendations that may prove helpful to increase family involvement among culturally/linguistically diverse

families of children with disabilities (see box, "What Does the Literature Say?").

Communication with Families

Educators can use many forms of communicating with families of children with disabilities. Different communication approaches are needed with families from diverse cultures and linguistic backgrounds—approaches that may be strikingly different from typical strategies currently used by many teachers and related service personnel in public schools. In communicating with families from culturally/linguistically diverse backgrounds, remember that *one approach does not fit all.* Figure 1 presents a variety of questions that we might address to ensure such involvement during decision making.

Alternative routes to family involvement in disenfranchised communities may include community liaisons or family advisory councils.

As team members working with children and families, we should develop a range of strategies for use with families to facilitate greater participation in team decisionmaking. These strategies may be used in differing contexts and include contacts made with families, location of meetings and supports, and providing information/training.

Contacts with Families

Many school personnel have recognized that families from some culturally/linguistically diverse backgrounds will defer educational judgments to professionals who are perceived to be the "experts" in the education of children with disabilities. In such instances, it may be reasonable to anticipate limited family involvement in decision-making processes. Unfortunately, schools sometimes make the erroneous assumption that professionals *should* assume a lead role in providing information to or making contact with families in all instances.

Some families may have an inherent mistrust of school officials for many reasons (e.g., past negative experiences and fear of bureaucratic intervention in their lives or potential loss of services being received). In such instances, one alternative may be to identify *liaisons,* or entrees into the community in which the family resides. For example, some families might prefer to have a well-respected community leader, such as a physician or minister, to serve as the liaison between the school and the family. This would serve to facilitate accurate dissemination of information and to build trust by demonstrating that the school was sensitive to the cultural values of the family.

Mistrust may also exist in disenfranchised communities where family members feel that their issues will not be addressed in traditional educational forums. In such communities, alternative routes may be provided to family members to ensure that they have a voice in educational processes. One possibility is to create a Family Advisory

What Does the Literature Say About Diverse School-Family Communication?

Collaboration is an essential element in the successful development of partnerships between schools and parents. It enables people having diverse experiences to interact with the goal of reaching agreement on specific issues. Such interaction can result in

- Shared ownership of problem definitions and solutions.
- Shared knowledge and expertise.
- Increased cohesiveness and willingness to work together on future issues (Thousand, Villa, Paolucci-Whitcomb, & Nevin, 1996).

When family members collaborate with professionals, there is also a recognition that the family is the constant in the child's life, while services and professionals within the system are always in a state of flux (Shelton, Jeppson, & Johnson, 1987). Close working relationships between professionals and family members also ensures that service recommendations are flexible, accessible, and responsive to family needs (Angelo, 1997; Parette & Brotherson, 1996).

Unfortunately, some school communities still show an ongoing lack of respect for culturally/linguistically diverse families (Kalyanpur & Harry, 1999), even though many families want to be included in planning their children's education (Chavkin, 1989). The professional literature is replete with information about the characteristics of people from different cultures and linguistic backgrounds (Shea & Bauer, 1991, 1997). Professionals sometimes make the mistake of assuming that such characteristics may be generalized (e.g., assuming that a recent immigrant family from Ghana has the same cultural background as an African-American family whose Virginia heritage dates back 300 years) and approaches used with these families are thus similarly employed. Such insensitivity to "difference" may make family members feel angry, alienated, or undervalued.

Many educators recognize that family members from culturally/linguistically diverse backgrounds are less informed about and participate less in special education processes than family members from the dominant or mainstream culture (Bennett, 1988; Kalyanpur & Harry, 1999; Lynch & Stein, 1987). Conversations conducted with families across the United States (see e.g., Angelo, Jones, & Kokoska, 1995; Angelo, Kokoska, & Jones, 1996; VanBiervliet & Parette, 1999) suggest that families have many needs and expectations of professionals that often go unaddressed. If school personnel expect greater participation from culturally/linguistically diverse families, teams of educators must implement effective communication strategies.

Council or other forum for families to present their issues, concerns, and desires and be heard. Any forum that is created should be more than a token exercise for these families—what is communicated by participants *must* be considered in subsequent school decision making.

Interpreters can facilitate communication between school personnel and parents who have limited-English-proficiency skills. Families may have adequate language skills in their primary language but not in English. To facilitate communication, we should provide an interpreter who understands the needs of family members with these limited-English-proficiency skills. Conversely, we need to recognize the interpreter as a professional member of the team with consideration being given to the special characteristics of their job. For example, the interpreter needs adequate time to translate the information, as well as time for clarification, if the parent does not understand the information.

Sometimes interpreters may be needed when making contact with families. Many special educators and researchers have noted special considerations regarding the use of interpreters (e.g., Fradd & Whilen, 1990; Lynch, 1992). Use of interpreters often communicates sensitivity to the family's cultural background, though we should use caution to ensure that the wrong "message" is not communicated. For example, if we select a friend or relative of the family to be an interpreter, some family members may view this selection as invasive because some families may not want

others to have access to the information shared with school personnel. Also, interpreters sometimes may not have received adequate training and may translate, paraphrase, and add their opinions and interpretations when working with family members. When we consider using interpreters, we should ensure that the people we select have adequate skills in the languages used by families with whom they will be working.

Best Practice Tips—#1

- Some families will defer educational decision making to professionals.
- Consider using liaisons with families.
- Provide forums for families to be heard.
- Use *trained* interpreters.

Location of Meetings and Supports

Development of individualized education programs (IEPs), parent-teacher conferences, and other important meetings between family members and school personnel typically occur in school settings. Although this arrangement is generally convenient for school personnel, it may not be convenient for many families. When we invite families to participate in information-gathering or decision-making meetings, we need to be sensitive to the supports needed by many families. For example, families often have a need for transportation to and from meeting sites to

collaborate with school personnel (Judge & Parette, 1998). Whenever possible, we should provide alternatives to families for transportation to and from targeted meeting sites. While families are at the school, we should consider providing child care for families with young children who may need supervision.

Conversely, many families may prefer to have meetings at more "neutral" or comfortable, community-based sites (e.g., neighborhood churches or community centers). We need to offer this option to family members who may be hesitant to participate in team processes.

Best Practice Tips—#2

- Arrange for transportation to meetings, if needed.
- Provide child care, if necessary.
- Conduct meetings in family-friendly setting.

Providing Information/Training

As school personnel, we typically assume proactive roles in providing information and training to family members. For example, if a team is making a decision about a particular assistive technology device being considered for the child with a disability, responsibility for demonstrating the device or providing training in its use typically falls on professionals. Initial contacts with the family may be made by a counselor or social worker who may or may not speak the native language of the family. Such efforts, though well intentioned, may not be perceived favorably by families from diverse cultural/linguistic backgrounds.

In addition, we may often use more traditional approaches to providing information to families, such as using printed materials. We should keep in mind that the culture of educators is generally comfortable with information delivery and training approaches geared toward professional audiences (e.g., lectures coupled with the distribution of printed materials). Although such approaches may be effective with many professionals, they certainly are insensitive to the needs of families who may prefer more user-friendly strategies. For example, many schools use parent support groups as an alternative means of providing hands-on training and information to families. Seeing and hearing other family members who have children with disabilities is sometimes a much more powerful and effective means of working with families.

We should also consider that family members have not been trained to work with

---

Figure 1. Team Questions Designed to Enhance Family Participation in Decision Making

Assessment Design

- Have I individualized the team decision-making process for the family and the child?
- Have I taken the time to develop a trusting relationship with the family before starting the team decision-making procedures?
- Have I identified strategies for involving the family in the team decision-making process?
- Have I observed the child in a variety of naturalistic settings with and without caregivers?
- Have I included the extended family in the team decision-making process?
- Have I examined the team decision-making process for cultural biases?
- Do I know how or where to find cultural information that will help me during the team decision-making processes?

Professional Collaboration

- Have I made trained translators available to maintain communication with family members?
- Am I flexible when meeting with family members?
- Do I provide necessary assistance to the family members to ensure their participation in the team decision-making process?
- Is it possible to meet with the family members in their home before the team decision-making process?
- Have I informed family members of their rights in the decision-making process?
- Have I told family members about local support groups?
- Do I understand how the family feels about making direct contact with professionals involved in team decision making?
- Am I networking with other professionals to address cultural issues?

Cultural Issues

- Have I done a self-assessment of my own cultural background, experiences, values, and beliefs?
- Do my experiences, values, and beliefs allow me to interact with people from various cultures?
- Do I understand the family's values, beliefs, customs, and traditions?

- Have I modified the team decision-making process to ensure cultural competency?
- Do I try to achieve professional cultural competence?
- Can I train other staff members about cultural competence in the team decision-making process?
- Have I considered outreach organizations or individuals who can provide training?
- Do I communicate regularly with the cultural communities that I serve?
- Do I provide information and printed materials related to the team decision-making process in the language spoken by the family?
- Am I aware of the family's cultural rules regarding body language, eye contact, and proximity?
- Have I determined whether a community liaison would be the most appropriate contact through which to provide information to or receive information from the family?

Values

- Am I aware of the family's goals for the child and other family members?
- Am I aware of what the family expects out of me in the team decision-making process?
- Do I understand how family members may perceive a translator?
- Do I understand the family's attitude regarding disabilities?
- Do I know the key decision maker of the family?
- Do I understand the family's expectations of me as a professional?
- Do I understand the importance of the extended family?
- Am I aware of the family's approach to discipline?
- Do I understand the responsibilities of other siblings in the family setting?
- Does the family accept the idea of the team decision-making process as a tool to help their child?
- Does the family's religious affiliation influence their willingness to participate in or perceptions of the team decision-making process?

Family Factors

- Have I asked family members about their concerns for their child?

- Am I willing to pick up or arrange transportation for family members?
- Do I provide assistance to help family members when filling out forms necessary for the team decision-making process?
- Do I allow family members to share cultural information about their child?
- Have I identified the family's primary caregiver?
- Does the socioeconomic status of the family impact on the child for whom the team decision-making process is being considered?
- Have I examined the home setting and determined how it might facilitate or inhibit the team decision-making process?

Acculturation

- Do I understand how acculturation has influenced the family's perceived need for the team decision-making process?

Ethnicity

- Have I examined ethnic factors that might affect the child's or family's perception of the team decision-making process?

Social Influences

- Have I identified important social influences that might affect the child's or family's perception of the team decision-making process?

Past Experiences

- Have I identified past experiences of the child or family that could influence their current perception of the team decision-making process?

Developmental Expectations

Have I determined the family's expectations regarding developmental milestones for the child that might influence the perception of the team decision-making process?

Note: From *Cultural Competence in Screening and Assessment: Implications for Services to Young Children with Special Needs, Ages Birth Through Five* by M. Anderson & P. Goldberg, 1991, pp. 22–23. Chapel Hill, NC: National Early Childhood Technical Assistance System. Copyright 1991 by NECTAS. Adapted with permission.

their children with disabilities. We often assume that because a teacher or other team member shows parents how to implement a particular strategy with their child with a disability, that the parents, in turn, will be able to effectively teach the child the targeted skill. But family members may need more support and training than we thought initially. We may need to give thought to more family-centered approaches that truly support the family, such as including siblings and extended family members, who are often the ones who assume primary responsibility for taking care of or working with the child having a disability.

Understanding Family Priorities, Needs, and Resources

If we are to effectively include family members from diverse cultural/linguistic backgrounds in team processes, we must develop a greater understanding of and sensitivity to family priorities, needs, and resources. Families' perceptions of the needs for their children often differ from the perceptions of professionals (Judge & Parette, 1998).

Best Practice Tips—#3

- Use native-speaking individuals to make initial contact.
- Provide training and information in user-friendly formats.
- Don't assume that families know how to "teach" their children.

These perceptions are influenced by a range of factors, such as family life span issues, functions, and communication styles.

Family Life Span Issues

Teams must consider that families will have concerns regarding their children that change across the lifespan (Turnbull & Turnbull, 1990). When children are younger (0–5), family issues seem to concentrate on childrearing, obtaining needed services, understanding their child's disability, and setting expectations for their children. Once children reach school age (5–12 years), there is a shift in emphasis to establishing routines, clarifying issues related to mainstreaming, arranging for extracurricular activities, and participation in school-related planning activities. By adolescence (12–21 years), families begin to address different needs related to emerging sexuality of their children, the possibility of peer isolation of their children, planning

for career development, and dealing with the physical and emotional changes of puberty. In each of these stages, families must deal with varying levels of stress.

In communicating with families from culturally/linguistically diverse backgrounds, remember that one approach does not fit all.

Not surprisingly, families will vary markedly with regard to their abilities to deal with stressors associated with life issues. We should be aware of these changing family life issues and the stresses with which families must learn to cope because such concerns may have a marked effect on the degree to which families choose to be involved in planning for their children's education, as well as their perceptions of targeted goals identified by professionals.

Family Functions

We need to recognize that families have incredible demands placed on them in contemporary society. The demands faced by families from culturally diverse backgrounds may be difficult for team members to fully understand. For example, many families must make decisions regarding quality of life and implementing school-recommended interventions. When participating on teams, families may openly acknowledge the importance of certain prescribed interventions for their child, but recognize the difficulties inherent in implementing the recommendations in the home setting. When this "dissonance" occurs, families may simply choose quality of life (i.e., minimizing stressful situations and simplifying life at home) over being a "fully participating team member."

Time is also an issue related to the functioning of the family. Families from different cultural backgrounds will view time and its relationship/importance to team processes differently from many professionals. Families may not be on time for meetings, presenting a hurdle for teams who desire to adhere to rigorous timeliness necessary for planning IEPs and other school services. Team members must make adaptations in the way in which they conduct meetings, including more flexible scheduling of meeting times to accommodate the needs of families and capturing in-

formation (e.g., videotape and audiotape formats) and sharing with families.

Family Communication Styles

Team members who desire the participation of family members from culturally/linguistically diverse backgrounds should carefully consider who the "real" decision makers are in a particular family. In some instances, extended family members, such as grandmothers and aunts, assume primary responsibility for children with disabilities. If we can identify who these key players are, we can encourage and support their involvement in team processes.

Best Practice Tips—#4

- Identify what issues are important to the family.
- Consider whether interventions will result in family stress.
- Identify and give deference to key decision makers in family.

Final Thoughts

Many educators agree that the most effective integration of children with disabilities from diverse backgrounds occurs when families are more involved in team decision making. Including parents as volunteers, room parents, committee members, and in other ways ensures involvement (see "Resources for Team Members"). As mentioned previously, the questions in Figure 1 can help educators and other professionals develop strategies to increase family involvement in team decision-making processes. We need to carefully consider questions like these in our quest to communicate greater sensitivity to family issues, thus culminating in greater family involvement.

References

Angelo, D. H. (1997). AAC in the family and home. In S. Glennen & D. DeCoste (Eds.), *The handbook of augmentative communication* (pp. 523–545). San Diego: Singular.

Angelo, D. H., Jones, S. D., & Kokoska, S. M. (1995). Family perspective on augmentative and alterative communication: Families of young children. *Augmentative and Alternative Communication, 11,* 193–201.

Angelo, D. H., Kokoska, S. M., & Jones, S. D. (1996). Family perspective on augmentative and alternative communication: Families of adolescents and young adult children. *Augmentative and Alternative Communication, 12,* 13–22.

Bennett, A. T. (1988). Gateways to powerlessness: Incorporating Hispanic deaf children and families into formal schooling. *Disability, Handicap and Society, 3,* 119–151.

Chavkin, N. F. (1989). Debunking the myth about minority parents. *Educational Horizons, 67,* 119–123.

Fradd, S. H., & Whilen, D. K. (1990). *Using interpreters and translators to meet the needs of handicapped language minority students and their families.* Washington, DC: National Clearinghouse for Bilingual Education.

Individuals with Disabilities Act Amendments of 1997, P.L. 105-13. (1997, June 4). 20 U.S.C. 1400 et seq.

Judge, S. L., & Parette, H. P. (1998). Assistive technology decision-making strategies. In S. L. Judge & H. P. Parette (Eds), *Assistive technology for young children with disabilities. A guide to family-centered services* (pp. 127–147). Cambridge, MA: Brookline.

Kalyanpur, K., & Harry, B. (1999). *Culture in special education. Building reciprocal family-professional relationships.* Baltimore: Brookes.

Lynch, E. W. (1992). Developing cross-cultural competence. In E. W. Lynch & M. J. Hanson (Eds), *Developing cross-cultural competence. A guide for working with young children and their families* (pp. 35–62). Baltimore: Brookes.

Lynch, E. W., & Stein, R. (1987). Parent participation by ethnicity: A comparison of Hispanic, Black and Anglo families. *Exceptional Children, 54,* 105–111.

Parette, H. P., & Brotherson, M. J. (1996). Family participation in assistive technology assessment for young children with disabilities. *Education and Training in Mental Retardation and Developmental Disabilities, 31*(1), 29–43.

Shea, T. M., & Bauer, A. M. (1991). *Parents and teachers of children with exceptionalities: A handbook for collaboration.* Boston: Allyn & Bacon.

Shea, T. M., & Bauer, A. M. (1997). *An introduction to special education: A social systems perspective.* Madison, WI: Brown & Benchmark.

Shelton, T. L., Jeppson, E. S., & Johnson, B. H. (1987). *Family-centered care for children with special health care needs* (2nd ed.). Washington, DC: Association for the Care of Children's Health.

Thousand, J., Villa, R. A., Paolucci-Whitcomb, P. E., & Nevin, A. (1996). A rationale for collaborative consultation. In W. Stainback & S. Stainback (Eds), *Controversial issues confronting special education: Divergent perspectives* (2nd ed.). Boston: Allyn & Bacon.

Turnbull, A. P., & Turnbull, H. R. (1990). *Families, professionals, and exceptionality: A special partnership* (2nd ed.). Columbus, OH: Merrill.

VanBiervliet, A., & Parette, H. P. (1999). *Families, cultures, and AAC.* (CD-ROM). Little Rock, AR: Southeast Missouri State University and the University of Arkansas for Medical Sciences.

Resources for Team Members

CD-ROM

VanBiervliet, A., & Parette, H. P. (1999). *Families, cultures, and AAC.* (CD-ROM). Little Rock, AR: Southeast Missouri State University and the University of Arkansas for Medical Sciences. [Available from Program Development Associates, **http://www.pdassoc.com**]

Books

Barera, I., McPherson, D., & Kramer, L. (in press). *Cultural diversity and cultural competence: A handbook for early childhood practitioners.* Baltimore: Brookes.

Ford, A. L. (Ed.). (1999). *Multiple voices for ethnically diverse exceptional learners.* Reston, VA: The Council for Exceptional Children.

Gersten, R., Baker, S. K., & Marks, S. U. (1999). *Teaching English-language learners with learning difficulties: Guiding principles and examples from research-based practice.* Reston, VA: The Council for Exceptional Children.

Harry, B., Kalyanpur, M., & Day, M. (1999). *Building cultural reciprocity with families. Case studies in special education.* Baltimore: Brookes.

Kalyanpur, K., & Harry, B. (1999). *Culture in special education. Building reciprocal family-professional relationships.* Baltimore: Brookes.

Kroth, R. L., & Edge, D. (1997). *Strategies for communicating with parents and families of exceptional children* (3rd ed.). Denver: Love.

Lambie, R. (2000). *Family systems within educational contexts: Understanding at-risk and special-needs students.* Denver: Love.

Lynch, E. W., & Hanson, M. J. (Eds). (1998). *Developing cross-cultural competence. A guide for working with young children and their families* (2nd ed.). Baltimore: Brookes.

Roseberry-McKibbin, C. (1995). *Multicultural students with special language needs: Practical strategies for assessment and intervention.* Oceanside, CA: Academic Communication Associates.

Journal Articles

Coleman, M., & Churchill, S. (1997). Challenges to family involvement. *Childhood Education, 73*(3), 144–148.

Malloy, W. (1997). Responsible inclusion: Celebrating diversity and academic excellence. *NASSP Bulletin, 81*(585), 80–85.

McMackin, M. C., & Bukowiecki, E. M. (1997). A change in "focus": Teaching diverse learners within an inclusive elementary school classroom. *Equity & Excellence in Education, 30*(1), 32–39.

Reiff, J. C. (1997). Multiple intelligences, culture and equitable learning. *Childhood Education, 73*(5), 301–304.

World Wide Web

Family Village. (2000, March 24). [On-line]. Available: **http://www.familyvillage.edu.**

Federal for Children with Special Needs. (2000, June 15). [On-line]. Available: **http://fcsn.org/home.htm**

The National Information Center for Children and Youth with Disabilities (NICHCY). (2000). [On-line]. Available: **http://www.NICHCY.org/**

National Parent Information Network. (2000, March). [On-line]. Available: **http://www.npin.org/**

Parents Helping Parents. (no date). [On-line]. Available: **http://www.php.com**

The Special Needs Education (SNE) Project. (1999). [On-line]. Available: **http://www.education-world.com**

Howard P. Parette (*CEC Chapter #103), Professor; and **Beverly Petch-Hogan** (CEC Chapter #240), Professor, Elementary, Early, and Special Education, Southeast Missouri State University, Cape Girardeau.*

Address correspondence to Howard P. Parette, Graduate School, Southeast Missouri State University, One University Plaza, Cape Girardeau, MO 63701-4799.

Family AND CULTURAL ALERT!

Considerations in Assistive Technology Assessment

Jack J. Hourcade, Howard P. Parette, Jr., Mary Blake Huer

Imagine yourself as a special educator in San Francisco who comes across his student and her family in a restaurant. You are excited that your student has such a wonderful chance to use her new augmentative communication device, but you are disappointed to see that it is nowhere in sight, and that her father is speaking for her.

Or, imagine that you are a special educator teaching at the high school level in San Antonio. One day you learn to your dismay that your student with severe mental retardation, who in your opinion had been making excellent progress in using her electronic communication device, is no longer using the device. Her parents have apparently and suddenly become discouraged and disinterested in its ongoing use.

These and similar professional disappointments are inevitable if we as special educators are not sensitive to family and cultural issues in assessing technology needs of students with disabilities. In the first example, the girl's family is uncomfortable with the way the device draws attention to them, and so they prefer not to take it out and use it in public. In the second example, the teacher failed to realize that the Hispanic girl had just had her *quincancera*, a celebration of her 15th birthday. In the Hispanic culture, this frequently serves as a milestone to demonstrate the growing independence of the girl, and

marks a significant transition on the way to adulthood. Her failure to use the device has resulted from her parents' viewing her as an increasingly independent adult, and deciding to let her make her own decisions about whether to use the device.

Selecting Assistive Technology Devices

Assistive technology devices are pieces of equipment used to increase, maintain, or improve the functional capabilities of students with disabilities. Recommendations for these devices are often included in individualized education programs (IEPs) for students with disabilities.

Involving Families

While family participation in IEPs is theoretically mandated by law; in reality, the involvement of family members in team decision making is often limited. When we fail to involve the family in decisions about possible uses of assistive technology devices, assistive technology *abandonment* (Batavia & Hammer, 1989; Parette, in press), a failure/refusal to use the device, can result. Such an outcome represents a waste of increasingly scarce fiscal resources available to school systems.

Assessing Students' Skills

Assessment of student skills and abilities in special education has long relied on formal testing procedures, but over the past few years, less formal approaches to gathering information from families for decision making have become more common. Informal assessment strategies are particularly important in assistive technology decision making, because few standardized instruments are available.

Informal information-collection strategies require from special education teachers a high level of sensitivity to families and their needs. In particular, there are three specific needs reported by families as being especially important for professionals to understand in considering technology devices for students (Parette & VanBiervliet, 1995). Specifically, professionals should use the following guidelines:

- Understand family needs for *information* about assistive technology devices.
- Recognize the impact on, and changes in, *family routines* the assistive technology will cause.
- Consider the extent to which family members desire themselves or their children to be *accepted in community settings*.

Family Issues to Consider in Introducing Assistive Technology

• When we fail to involve the family in decisions about possible uses of assistive technology devices, assistive technology abandonment can result.

• Informal information-collection strategies require from special education teachers a high level of sensitivity to families and their needs.

• Parents need information, and how that information is provided can be as important as what is provided.

• The introduction of any technology device into a child's life is likely to have unanticipated effects on both the child and the family.

• Some families prefer to blend in, and feel that an assistive technology device makes the child (and the family) more noticeable.

• Families and teachers may have very different perceptions and values, based in part on the differing cultural backgrounds they bring to the IEP table.

• A family's values will affect the nature and extent of family participation in assistive technology decision making.

A research base incorporating data provided by families throughout the United States is now beginning to emerge (Parette & VanBiervliet, 1995). Using these data, we discuss specific and practical recommendations to help teachers become more sensitive to family needs during assistive technology decision making in each of these three areas.

Sensitivity to Family Need for Information

Parents need information, and *how* that information is provided can be as important as *what* is provided.

Researchers have frequently noted the importance of providing families with basic information regarding assistive technology devices (e.g., Angelo, Kokoska, & Jones, 1996). One particularly useful source of information on assistive devices is ABLEDATA. This U.S. Department of Education-sponsored database contains detailed descriptions on approximately 21,000 products from more than 3,000 manufacturers. ABLEDATA is accessed

through a low-cost CD-ROM, *Cooperative Database Distribution Network for Assistive Technology* (CO-NET), available through the Trace Center at the University of Wisconsin. This CD-ROM also contains 16 easy-to-use national directories of disability-related services that cover certain states, plus regional and nationwide data sources (CO-NET, 1996). Teachers and family members may use the CO-NET CD-ROM to learn of the range of assistive technology devices and to identify possible solutions for a particular child in the classroom setting.

Cultural sensitivity is an important issue to consider when proposing technological devices for children with disabilities.

While we can simply tell parents about some device, or even show it to them, it is often more helpful for parents to view another child actually using that device. This is especially useful if the child is similar culturally or ethnically to their child. Videotapes are a powerful format for this; they can help the family to see the use of the device in a real-life setting. Seeing an adaptive device being used successfully by another child is a convincing way to communicate the potential impact of assistive technology.

When a technological device is provided, a frequent though typically unasked question is who actually owns the device. When devices are purchased by the school system, families must understand that the school continues to own the device. If the child is to use the device off school grounds, families should understand the school's policies regarding such issues as responsibility for theft and damage. Some families will understandably be reluctant to use an expensive piece of equipment if they perceive that they will be held accountable for any damages. If teachers are involved in helping families obtain assis-

tive technology devices through funding mechanisms other than schools, the actual ownership of the device must be understood by all.

Sensitivity to Changes in Family Routines

The introduction of any technology device into a child's life is likely to have *unanticipated effects* on both the child and the family.

Often we as special educators do not adequately consider how a family's life can change when a child begins using some adaptive device. The overall high demands of caring for children with disabilities in general have been well documented (e.g., Miller & Hudson, 1994). These demands may be especially challenging with children with severe disabilities, the very children most likely to receive assistive technology devices.

Sometimes, in our professional excitement over the possibilities some device offers a child, we fail to consider the changes and stresses that the device can cause in the home. Computerized electronic assistive technology devices may require much training on the part of the child and family before they can be effectively used. Unfortunately, family members who participate in training sessions often report *information overload* during such experiences. More information is provided during intensive training than can possibly be used or remembered by the family. As a result, the device may be used incorrectly, inadequately, or not at all.

Special educators also must be aware that training can place a variety of stresses on families over and above those typically associated with having a child with a disability. For example, attendance at a remote site to receive training might require the parent to resolve such practical problems as obtaining time away from work, arranging for child care for other siblings, and managing transportation and related travel expenses (if the training is a multiple-day experience).

Certain devices may require family members to assume responsibilities for assistance in using or transporting the device. If the device is heavy, complex, or cumbersome, family members may quietly choose not to use it.

As special educators, before meeting with parents to discuss technology devices we must spend time identifying and considering these and other possible changes in family routines the device may require. When we do so, we significantly increase the likelihood the device will be used productively.

Sensitivity to Family Needs for Acceptance

Some families prefer to *blend in*, and feel that an assistive technology device makes the child (and the family) more noticeable.

When working with family members to identify appropriate assistive technology devices that may be used in community settings, special educators must first seek to learn if the family members are comfortable with, and are likely to use, an assistive technology device in the public settings the family frequents. It is understandable that some family members might feel uncomfortable using certain devices in public. For example, when the family attends church services, the child may not be able to *whisper quietly* using certain communication devices. Thus, family members may choose not to use the device in that setting.

If such reservations are widespread, the device may still have considerable usefulness at home. It may not help the child's overall inclusion, however, into the mainstream of society.

If the family feels that the device is too obtrusive, the special educator and the rest of the IEP team might brainstorm to identify other less conspicuous options. Perhaps a less expensive or lower technology solution would be less obtrusive and noticeable and would serve the overall purpose better. For example, a communication picture book might well be preferable in a church setting to a more sophisticated electronic device.

Cultural Sensitivity

In proposing technological devices for children with disabilities, we as special educators must be careful to be especially sensitive to important issues that are too frequently overlooked. A significant aspect of this is understanding that families and teachers may have very different perceptions and values, based in part on the *differing cultural backgrounds* they bring to the IEP table.

This issue is especially significant to us in special education, given the continuing overrepresentation of students from minority racial and cultural backgrounds (e.g., Ysseldyke, Algozzine, & Thurlow, 1992).

We sometimes forget that individuals from cultural backgrounds different from our own may see the world quite differently from us. In such cases, the quality of the special educational services provided both to students and family members will be impaired (Hetzroni & Harris, 1996; Parette, 1995; Trivelli, 1994; Soto, Huer, & Taylor, in press).

Parents need information, and how that information is provided can be as important as what is provided.

A variety of issues relevant to special education differ systematically across cultures in America. These include:

- Perceptions of disability held by family members.
- Attitudes toward the education system.
- Priorities regarding services deemed important for the child and family.
- Ideas regarding the importance and process of child care.
- Family perceptions of ability to collaborate with professionals.
- The extent to which life circumstances are viewed as being overwhelming.

When we as special educators consider the possible use of an assistive device for a child, we must recognize cultural-specific differences in how families might perceive these issues. Assistive technologies are playing an increasingly prominent role in the provision of services to children and youth with disabilities. In our excitement over the possibilities these technologies may offer to students with disabilities, we may fail to consider that our perceptions of the advantages and disadvantages of these devices may be quite different from the perceptions of the family of the student.

Teachers must realize that the Euro-American values of independence and self-sufficiency are not values shared by

family members from all cultures. Some cultures, for example Asian and Native American cultures, are more collectivist in nature. Often in these cultures children are viewed less as individuals in their own right, and more as parts of the family and the community. A certain degree of dependence on the family throughout life is expected and valued. Thus, the typical special education goal of increased independence that an assistive technology device might help with may not be seen as important to these families.

In addition, families having a collectivist orientation typically wish to fit in, and to avoid being perceived as being different from others. For example, some families in the African-American community may prefer not to have attention drawn to their children in social settings (Parette & Van-Biervliet, 1995). An assistive device that is obtrusive and does just this may be a poor choice.

In terms of other information we share with parents, special educators might be careful not to let their own cultural backgrounds filter the information they share with families. For example, many of us from Euro-American cultural backgrounds may automatically assume that mothers will wish information regarding how assistive technology devices may be used for socialization purposes and in community settings, while fathers are more interested in repair, maintenance, and programming (Angelo et al., 1996). However, as is the case with many generalizations, such an assumption may be invalid for family members from non-Euro-American backgrounds.

As educators, we should also consider the way we share information with family members from differing cultural backgrounds. Family members from certain cultural backgrounds may mistrust Euro-American school personnel. In such cases, having a representative from a community support system (e.g., a church or community action group) join the IEP meeting can help resolve this communication problem. It is often helpful to ask community resource or support personnel who are from the same cultural backgrounds of families to help us in providing information regarding assistive technology devices to families, and learning their needs.

Perhaps needless to say, having a language interpreter is necessary when English is not the primary language of the family. Even when parents do speak English, if it is not their first language, an interpreter can help in conveying subtleties

Figure 1. Family and Cultural Issues Questionnaire			
Question	**Yes**	**No**	**Notes**
1. Has the family clearly communicated concerns, needs, and goals about the child?			
2. Are the family's and child's daily routines identified?			
3. Would the family like a support group to convey information or training regarding assistive technology devices?			
4. Would the family prefer a community leader or liaison to convey information regarding assistive technology devices?			
5. Has a range of possible technology solutions for the child and family been explored?			
6. Do family members and the child want an assistive technology device?			
7. Are family expectations of the assistive technology assessment process clearly understood?			
8. Does the family understand issues related to funding and ownership of the assistive technology device?			
9. Do all family members understand how assistive technology devices may affect family routines?			
10. Have the various settings where the child might use assistive technology devices, and resulting demands/consequences of device usage there, been identified?			
11. Do families want to use devices in community settings?			
12. Are the family expectations of the assistive technology device clearly understood prior to purchase?			

Source: Copyright 1997 by Howard P. Parette. Used with permission.

and complexities that otherwise might not be understood.

Augmenting Our Perceptions

One way to think about family issues and cultural background is to see them as the air. Though air is crucial to our existence, we are so immersed that we seldom even notice or consider it. Some families with whom special educators will work in assistive technology assessment will demonstrate strong cultural identifications; others will not. Regardless of how strong or weak these values appear to be, they will nonetheless affect the nature and extent of family participation in assistive technology decision making.

A family's unique historical and cultural backgrounds influence factors such as the following:

- A family's willingness to seek help.
- The family's communication styles.
- The amount and type of participation family members choose.
- The goals the family selects.
- Which family members will be involved in school intervention efforts.

Special educators can become more effective in working with all families across cultures by recognizing their own cultural

ANNUAL EDITIONS

identities and values, and considering how these may be shaping their present professional beliefs (Hanson, Lynch, & Wayman, 1990).

Figure 1 offers some guidelines for special educators to consider as they work with families in assistive technology decision-making processes. In an era when diminishing fiscal resources for school services is the reality, sensitivity to family and cultural considerations will help to ensure that the most appropriate devices are selected for the children of all families.

References

Angelo, D. H., Kokoska, S. M., & Jones, S. D. (1996). Family perspective on augmentative and alternative communication: Families of adolescents and young adults. *Augmentative and Alternative Communication, 12*, 13–20.

Batavia, A. I., & Hammer, G. (1989). Consumer criteria for evaluating assistive devices: Implications for technology transfer. In J. J. Presperin (Ed.), *Proceedings of the 12th Annual Conference of the Rehabilitation Engineering Society of North America* (pp. 194–195). Washington, DC: RESNA Press.

CO-NET (Cooperative Assistive Technology Data Base Dissemination Network). (1996). *Hyper-ABLEDATA Database,* CO-NET CD ROM version (8th ed.). Madison, WI: Trace Research and Development Center.

Hanson, M. J., Lynch, E. W., & Wayman, K. (1990). Honoring the cultural diversity of families when gathering data. *Topics in Early Childhood Special Education, 10,* 112–131.

Hetzroni, O. E., & Harris, O. L. (1996). Cultural aspects in the development of AAC users. *Augmentative and Alternative Communication, 12,* 52–58.

Miller, S. P., & Hudson, P. (1994). Using structured parent groups to provide parental support. *Intervention in School and Clinic, 29*(3), 151–155.

Parette, H. P. (1995, November). *Culturally sensitive family-focused assistive technology assessment strategies.* Paper presented at the 11th Annual International Early Childhood Conference on Children with Special Needs, Orlando, FL. (ERIC Document Reproduction Service No. ED 387 996)

Parette, H. P. (in press). Effective and promising assistive technology practices for students with mental retardation and developmental disabilities. In A. Hilton & R. Ringlaben (Eds.), *Effective and promising practices in developmental disabilities.* Austin, TX: PRO-ED.

Parette, H. P., & VanBiervliet, A. (1995). *Culture, families, and augmentative and alternative communication (AAC) impact: A multimedia instructional program for related services personnel and family members.* Grant funded by the U.S. Department of Education, Office of Special Education and Rehabilitative Services, Office of Special Education Programs Special Projects (No. H029K50072).

Soto, G., Huer, M. B., & Taylor, O. (in press). Multicultural issues in augmentative and alternative communication. In L. Lloyd, D. H. Fuller, & H. H. Arvidson (Eds.), Augmentative and alternative communication. Boston: Allyn & Bacon.

Trivelli, L. U. (1994). The impact of human and multicultural diversity on assistive technology outreach and services. NARIC Quarterly, 4(3), 1, 6–8.

Ysseldyke, J. E., Algozzine, B., & Thurlow, M. L. (1992). Critical issues in special education (2nd ed.). Boston: Houghton-Mifflin.

Jack J. Hourcade *(CEC Chapter #225), Professor, Elementary Education and Specialized Studies, Boise State University, Idaho;* **Howard P. Parette, Jr.** *(CEC Missouri Federation), Professor, Department of Elementary, Early, and Special Education, Southeast Missouri State University, Cape Girardeau;* **Mary Blake Huer**, *Professor, Department of Speech Communication, California State University, Fullerton.*

This article is supported in part by Grant No. H029K50072 from the U.S. Department of Education to the first author. Opinions expressed herein are those of the authors alone and should not be interpreted to have agency endorsement.

Address correspondence to H. P. Parette, Jr., Elementary and Special Education, Southeast Missouri State University, One University Plaza, Cape Girardeau, MO 63701.

UNIT 5
Developmental Disabilities

Unit Selections

Key Points to Consider

- What strategies can make transition from special education in primary school to regularized education in middle school easier for a child who is developmentally disabled?

- How can unit organizer routines keep high school students with DD motivated to achieve and improve their performance in regular education classes?

- What is diagnostic overshadowing and how does it affect the diagnosis of depression in students with developmental disabilities and/or traumatic brain injuries?

 **Links: www.dushkin.com/online/**
These sites are annotated in the World Wide Web pages.

Arc of the United States
http://www.thearc.org
Autism Society Early Interventions Package
http://www.autism-society.org/packages/early_intervention.pdf
Disability-Related Sources on the Web
http://www.arcofarizona.org/dislnkin.html
Gentle Teaching
http://www.gentleteaching.nl

In our efforts to be more "politically correct" and not to inflict pain, we now avoid labels such as "mentally retarded." We always put the individual first and add the condition of disability second (when and if it is necessary). Students and adults who have cognitive skills falling two standard deviations below the norm for their age are now considered cognitively developmentally disabled. Children who have sustained brain damage through traumatic brain injury even if they score two standard deviations below the intellectual norm for age are traumatically brain injured, not developmentally disabled. Children and adults with autism or variants of autism (for example, Asperger disorder) are subsumed under a separate disability category by IDEA as well. Three out of four individuals with classic autism do score two standard deviations below the IQ mean. Nevertheless, cognitive developmental disorders, traumatic brain injuries, and autism are each recognized as separate disability categories by IDEA.

Children with significantly subnormal intelligence were once classified as "educable," "trainable," or "custodial" for purposes of placement. These terms are strongly discouraged today. Even severely developmentally disabled children are educable and can benefit from some schooling. The current preferred categorical terms for children who are developmentally challenged are "intermittent," "limited," "extensive," and "pervasive." These terms refer to how much support the individuals need to function as capably as possible.

The U.S. Individuals with Disabilities Education Act (IDEA) mandates free and appropriate public school education for every child, regardless of mentation. While the legal windows on education are from ages 6 to 16 in the United States, individuals with developmental disabilities are entitled to a free and appropriate education from age of assessment (birth, early childhood) to age 21. This encompasses parent-child education programs and preschool programs early in life and transitional services into the community and world of work after the public school education is completed.

The inclusion of children with disabilities in regular education classes has been controversial (see Unit 1) throughout the 25 years since the first version of IDEA was signed into law. Some school systems have succeeded brilliantly in integrating students with cognitive developmental disabilities into their regular classes. Other schools have fought the law every step of the way. Their histories are full of law suits brought by parents to try to obtain the services to which the law entitles them. These less-than-stellar school systems, and some U.S. states that have been notorious laggards, complain that the law is too cumbersome. They lament that it interferes with their abilities to meet budgets and to educate their nondisabled student population. There have been few negative consequences for school systems and/or whole state education departments who have resisted placing cognitively disabled students in regular classrooms. Therefore some parents still invoke formal complaint procedures against schools to get their children out of full-time special classes or special schools. Parents who request due process hearings are often labeled "problem parents."

A child with cognitive developmental disabilities who is in the mildest "intermittent" classification needs support at school at times when special needs arise and at times of life transitions. This terminology is generally used for children whose disabilities

do not create an obvious and continual problem. These children have slower mentation but also have many abilities.

The next level of support, classified as "limited," is usually used for children whose disabilities create daily limitations on their abilities, but who can achieve a degree of self-sufficiency after an appropriate education in the least restrictive environment. Limited refers to the period of time from diagnosis until adulthood (age 21). The "extensive" support classification extends the support throughout the life span for individuals whose developmental disabilities prohibit them from living independently. The "pervasive" support classification is used infrequently. It is only for those individuals whose disabilities prevent them from most activities of self-help. Pervasive support is intensive and life-sustaining in nature. These more severe classifications are seldom seen in public schools.

The majority of children with developmental disabilities can be placed in the intermittent support classification. To casual observers, they often do not appear to have any disabilities. However, their ability to process, store, and retrieve information is limited. In the past, this group of children was given IQ measurements between two and three standard deviations below the mean (usually an IQ below 70 but above 55). Intelligence testing is an inexact science with problems of both validity and reliability. The current definition of developmental disability endorsed by the American Association on Mental Deficiency (AAMD) does not include any IQ scoring results other than to use the phrase "subaverage intellectual functioning." It emphasizes the problems that individuals with developmental disabilities have with adaptive skills such as communication, self-care, home living, social skills, community use, self-direction, health and safety, functional academics, leisure, and work.

The causes of developmental disabilities (DD) are unclear. About one-half of all individuals with DD are suspected of having sustained some brain damage prenatally, neonatally, or in childhood. Among the better-known factors that damage brain tissue are early birth and/or low birth weight, anoxia, malnutrition, drugs, viruses, radiation, trauma, and tumors.

The first article in this unit depicts the transition of a boy with developmental disabilities from special education in primary school to regular education in middle school. The authors emphasize the collaborative efforts of the school staff, how they shared leadership roles, and how they attended to due process. The problems encountered by the school, the student, and the family and also the factors that contributed to the inclusive education success are presented.

The second selection depicts the problems faced by high school teachers who struggle to give appropriate educational challenges to students with a vast range of mental abilities. The authors argue that students with developmental disabilities should not be allowed to slip through the cracks. It is possible to improve their performance using unit organizer routines. The authors describe how to do this.

Unit 5 ends with an article that addresses the problem of melancholy in students with developmental disabilities. Depression is a common syndrome in such students. It is difficult to recognize due to the coexisting symptoms of intellectual deficits. The problem of diagnostic overshadowing is discussed.

Collaborative Planning for Inclusion of a Student with Developmental Disabilities

Jane E. Doelling, Suzanne Bryde, Judy Brunner & Barbara Martin

It appears that many education professionals in both general and special education are experiencing confusion regarding the concept of inclusion. There is a misconception regarding corresponding legal mandates pertaining to provision of services to students with disabilities. In a recent position statement, The Council for Exceptional Children (1993) cites the need for increased collaboration and greater emphasis on inclusive practices. Inclusion in itself is not a legal mandate; however, implementing the Individual Educational Plan (IEP) in the least restrictive environment is a component of the Individuals with Disabilities Education Act (IDEA) of 1990. Full inclusion programs typically offer students with disabilities services in the general education classroom with little or no time in special education settings. IDEA mandates that placement decisions be made by a multidisciplinary team and that a continuum of service delivery options be maintained.

The setting in which educational services for students with disabilities are provided remains a major issue, particularly in middle level and secondary education where students are expected to spend a great deal of time in content classes. Nolet and Tindal (1993) suggest that demands for response in content classes may directly affect students' ability to use content information and that low performing students benefit from accommodative instruction that includes modeling of problem solving solutions and rich contextual clues. Most general educators agree that inclusion is a positive practice, but do not feel prepared to serve students with disabilities. A support system with shared involvement is necessary for successful inclusion (Simpson, & Myles, 1993).

The current paradigm shift to less restrictive models for educating students with disabilities requires collaborative planning, routine modification of instructional materials, and the inclusion of parents and peers as important components of the educational process (Bradley & Fisher 1995). The following discussion will focus on clarifying issues surrounding inclusion, as well as a description of specific action taken to implement an appropriate educational program for Matt, an 11-year-old student with autism, entering a middle school program. Emphasis is placed on the collaborative efforts of school staff, the importance of shared leadership roles, adherence to appropriate due process, and analysis of the instructional environment in planning and implementing an inclusive educational program appropriate to individual needs.

History

Matt had previously received educational services in a self-contained language development classroom with limited integration in general education classes at the elementary level. The greatest concerns expressed by Matt's family and the school team were social interaction and severely delayed communication. Matt was functioning at approximately an eight-year-old level with the exception of expressive language which fell below other areas. He rarely initiated interaction with peers and had developed limited interest in age-appropriate leisure activities. Previous success with implementing behavioral change was credited with determining the reasons for Matt's behavior through an analysis of environmental variables and planning intervention accordingly. (See Figure 1)

The middle school Matt was to attend had implemented a collaborative teaching model that involved core teams of three content teachers in general education with one special services consultant/teacher assigned to each team. The district had no autism specialist and the middle school teachers were apprehensive about working with a student that presented such unique challenges. The family requested that the next IEP include age-appropriate tasks and specific plans for including Matt with typical peers. They expressed long range goals for Matt that included independent living and employment in a competitive or semi-supported setting; however, they noted their concern that this did not seem possible without exposure to typical language and social models. A systematic plan of transition was developed in order to ease the movement to middle school for Matt, his family and school personnel.

Figure 1

Functional Behavioral Analysis and Interventions

A. Setting/Task	Antecedent	Intervention	Implementor
Hall transition to music	Student transition to music with limited supervision from teachers posted at each end of the hall.	Modeling and guided practice of appropriate hall behavior and increased adult proximity to Matt. Fade proximity with practice.	All educators collaborate.
Behavior(s) Matt followed behind peer in line. Touched peer on shoulder 5 times in 2 minutes.	**Consequence(s)** Peer tolerant of first two touches. Turns to Matt and shouts "stop" for the last three touches. Matt smiles.	Direct instruction in appropriate interaction skills. Generalization sessions implemented in natural contexts (luncheon, hall, classroom).	Special educators
	Function Request for interaction/attention. Difficulty with self monitoring.	Develop monitoring/cueing system. (Card that reads "Hands down" and "Act like a teenager.")	Special educators
		Monitoring and check for appropriate behavior.	All educators collaborate

B. Setting/Task	Antecedent	Intervention	Implementor
	Teacher asked student to open social studies text, survey the passage, and brainstorm information gleaned from survey.	Develop prior knowledge for lesson through vocabulary lessons, survey of pictures, participation in hands-on activities.	Special educators
Behavior(s) Walked to the back of the room. Repeatedly stacked and unstacked library books for duration of 15-minute discussion. Did not comply to verbal directive to return to seat.	**Consequence** Matt told to return to seat. Teacher ignored behavior since Matt's activity was not disruptive.	Include structured, parallel lesson to be implemented independently on a visual schedule.	Special educators
	Function Escape/avoidance. Protest of non-meaningful activity. Confusion.	Structure cooperative group activity appropriate to diverse abilities (e.g. recycling school materials, identifying community resources and how to care for them).	All educators collaborate

Phase One: Planning the Transition

The special education director and middle school principal assumed leadership roles for initial transition planning. A meeting was arranged with the family and included elementary team members as well as the team from the receiving middle school. Due to questions regarding Matt's placement and the content of his IEP, it was essential to set an agenda for the meeting that reflected sensitivity to the family's requests and adherence to due process. Figure 2 includes the agenda for the transition team.

By reviewing major instructional goals for the district and comparing them to Matt's Present Level of Performance (PLP), the team addressed the family's wishes regarding inclusion of Matt in age-appropriate academic activities. For example, the team related district curriculum goals such as listening and reading comprehension skill development to the needs identified in Matt's diagnostic report and corresponding IEP. For the benefit of general education professionals, as well as Matt's family, it was noted in the IEP that Matt would not be expected to master all district curriculum goals presented at his chronological age level and that modification was fair and appropriate based on diagnostic data documenting the effects of Matt's disability.

> Figure 2
> ## Agenda for the Transition Team
>
> 1. Review the IEP and all available diagnostic and programming data in the following areas: social, behavioral, academic, health, adaptive, and cognitive to determine Present Level of Performance (PLP).
> 2. Determine IEP goals and objectives appropriate to meeting needs identified in the PLP.
> 3. Determine placement and services appropriate to implementing goals and objectives.
> 4. Determine accommodations necessary for implementation of goals and objectives across settings (i.e. grading alternatives, curricular and material modifications, physical arrangements, teaching and student response modes).
> 5. Assign a liaison/case manager to coordinate the collaborative process and implementation of the IEP.

It was the decision of the team that full inclusion would not meet all specified IEP goals and objectives at that time. Matt needed specialized language, occupational therapy, and special education services to meet individual needs. However, it was also determined that many of the goals and objectives of Matt's IEP could be attained in both special and general educational settings.

In an effort to alleviate confusion regarding the district's policy on inclusion, a brief explanation had been added to both the student and faculty handbooks. A portion of the district policy is provided here:

- Decisions regarding services and educational placement will be based on a multidisciplinary evaluation and a detailed IEP developed by the family and educational team.
- Regardless of disability, students will be fully included in general education programs, when deemed appropriate by the IEP team. A full continuum of service delivery options should be maintained by the school district as full inclusion may not meet the needs of all students.
- Those students whose IEP does not include full inclusion requirements should be placed in the

least restrictive environment possible based on the student's needs and the continuum of available services.

Finally, it was determined that Mr. Brown, the special education teacher assigned to one of the established middle school teams would serve as liaison, case manager, and integration specialist for Matt's program. This determination was based on the team's record of success in regard to meeting educational goals and Mr. Brown's experience with developmental disabilities.

Phase Two: Preparing for the Transition

In an effort to address programmatic barriers to collaboration, district administrators agreed to provide transitional support by providing an additional plan hour for Matt's team leader, Mr. Brown. A commitment was also made to provide an instructional aide for Matt. It was noted the support of the individual aide would be phased out as Matt progressed since the ultimate family and school goal was developing his independence. Further, Mr. Brown received specialized training in autism to serve as a consultant for the middle school, thus enhancing a site-based approach to program management. Conceptual barriers to inclusion were addressed through district supported staff development and team planning coordinated by Mr. Brown. Other team members attended various staff development activities supported by the district. To facilitate transition to the middle school setting, several ecological variables affecting Matt's performance were analyzed. Examples from the functional behavioral analysis that assisted the team in program planning are noted in Figure 1. The provision of contextual cues within a structured environment had been noted as important to behavioral control and supported in data collected and the professional literature on autism. Based on this analysis of behaviors, the team implemented a plan that included a visual schedule with clear criteria for assigned tasks and a physical arrangement that reduced frustration.

Phase Three: Implementing the Program

The majority of the goals and objectives on Matt's IEP were to be implemented across settings. Because several different implementors were involved, it was necessary to establish a system for effective collaborative planning and systematic communication. An agenda for planning sessions was established by the team with a focus on five areas: (a) instructional content, (b) methods of presentation, (c) participant roles, (d) evaluation procedures, and (e) lesson accommodations. In an effort to further improve communication and consistency of programming, Matt carried his individual schedule across settings. Mr. Brown followed a rotating instructional schedule, alternating days in inclusive settings while still providing direct instruction to students in special education settings. This system allowed him to work with students on IEP objectives as well as assist the general education teacher with inclusive programming.

Providing services in inclusive settings required each team member to share leadership roles and all team members to be consultants in their varied areas of expertise. A primary barrier expressed by general educators on Matt's team was time involved in development of an alternate curriculum for Matt as well as concern with the appropriateness of the academic curriculum. Mr. Brown took the lead in designing a curriculum that included prevocational skills crucial to independent adult functioning yet, when possible, parallel to the general education curriculum. General educators typically took lead roles in collaborative planning sessions involving the discussion of content for future instructional units. Alternative lessons plans were maintained on disk by Mr. Brown and other building specialists to be disseminated among instructional teams so that they could be modified and appropriately implemented for diverse learners.

Providing Matt with a means to more readily communicate with individuals across settings was imperative to successful integration, socialization, and behavioral control; therefore, speech and language therapy was provided in individualized sessions, as well as the general education settings, hall transitions, and luncheon. To ensure that language programming goals were clear, each team member was provided with a data collection form containing five communication skills specific to Matt's IEP. In addition, each member kept brief records regarding progress to share in collaborative planning sessions.

Due to Matt's expressive communication problems, a small photograph album with line drawing illustrations was employed. Sight words and phrases were attached to each picture; therefore, the system could be used to enhance reading and vocabulary skills. The low technology system was chosen for its flexibility and its potential for promoting communication between Matt and his peers and adults.

With desks arranged in a format that promoted face-to-face interaction, Matt was assigned to cooperative learning groups. An additional peer mediated strategy found to contribute to positive outcomes for Matt and his peers was peer tutoring (Dettmer, Thurston, & Dyck, 1993). Mr. Brown and the general education team members discussed cooperative roles appropriate to various curricular assignments and Matt's role in these assignments. Teachers analyzed cooperative lessons and structured them to provide rich contextual cues including schedules, material organizers, and self-monitoring forms. Specific cooperative group behaviors were targeted for direct instruction in language therapy and in the special education setting. These included passing papers, making eye contact, requesting assistance, taking turns, and listening. Peers were selected as cooperative group partners on the basis of their expressed interest in working with Matt and because they were noted to be appropriate social and academic models.

It was apparent that positive behavioral intervention could not be separated from academic and communication instruction. Priorities identified in the team planning process included expanding Matt's repertoire of leisure activities, replacing socially inappropriate behaviors with appropriate skills, and developing friendships. It was determined that serving as an office worker would provide opportunity to apply social and academic skills. Matt was paired with a peer for some office activities and conducted other jobs independently. Opportunities were structured for Matt to interact, take direction, and request assistance from secretaries, administrators, or other adults in the building in an effort to generalize targeted social behaviors.

Peer networks were expanded from the original cooperative group members by rotating a peer in and out of the cooperative group on a periodic basis. In addition, Matt was assigned to a home room group that met twenty minutes daily. Each home room group in the building chose a theme or area of interest to pursue and Matt's group met in the gymnasium due to their interest in weight lifting and physical development. Matt's occupational therapist designed a program to be implemented in daily sessions and appropriate to Matt's physical ability and sensory integration needs. In addition to meeting social and motor development goals, mathematics goals were implemented by having Matt and a peer monitor physical progress.

Summary

Support for collaborative efforts to provide services to students with disabilities in inclusive settings became a district priority. Some faculty meetings and district inservice days were reserved for team meetings as educators' schedules were organized to promote collaborative planning. District policies and philosophy clearly reflected inclusive educational practices; however, programming decisions continued to be based on individual student needs, attributes of the school, and the expertise of building professionals.

It is important to note that variables and processes noted to contribute to success for Matt may not generalize to all students with disabilities; and, of course, problems with implementation did occur. Although there is a need for further research that validates effective collaborative and inclusive practices, the existing literature does support many of the practices implemented in Matt's educational program. These include the use of cooperative learning techniques; analysis of the instructional environment to determine variables affecting learning; problem solving strategies; and the shared leadership and consultative roles demonstrated by administrators, instructional team members, and ancillary staff (Dettmer,

Thurston, & Dyck, 1993; Ysseldyke, Christenson, & Kovaleski, 1994). Matt did not master all district curricular goals; however, partial inclusion in the general education setting did contribute to the increased success with language, social, and academic goals of Matt's IEP.

Programmatic collaborative barriers noted in the literature (Johnson, Pugach, & Hammitte, 1988 [as cited in Heron & Harris, 1993]; Dettmer, Thurston, & Dyck, 1993) included scheduling problems, lack of resources, and lack of shared planning time and lack of role clarification. These were primarily addressed through administrative support and as a part of district reorganization. Conceptual barriers to collaboration and inclusion also corresponded to those noted in the literature and these included philosophical differences and lack of knowledge regarding diverse populations. In Matt's case, administrative support was essential, particularly for establishing a school climate that reflected the shared responsibility of educating all students. Therefore, professional credibility and the resolve of all team members are required to alleviate any conceptual barriers that may exist.

Educators want instructionally relevant strategies for teaching students with special needs and brainstorming alone may not lead to effective intervention (Ysseldyke, Christenson, & Kovaleski, 1994). Previously, emphasis was placed on the special educator as an outside or impromptu consultant and on the operation of parallel, segregated service delivery systems. It is essential that instructional models stress collaborative planning and problem solving that address the needs of education professionals, as well as a diverse student population.

As noted in Matt's program, decisions evolved from analysis of the learning environment along with assessment of learner characteristics. This emphasis on environmental analysis may include consideration of instructional presentation, physical accommodations, teacher expectations, academic engaged time, and adaptive instruction as recommended by Ysseldyke and others (1994). In summary, the following guidelines are offered to middle level educators planning collaboratively for inclusion of children with disabilities:

1. Conduct data review and planning sessions (IEP meetings) prior to placement in inclusive settings. These team sessions should include a consideration of family, professional, and peer needs along with a review of all present-level information for the particular child to be included. Long term goals (including post graduation goals) and corresponding short term objectives must be developed with clear delineation of settings for implementation, acceptable standards of performance, evaluation procedures, accommodations, and roles of various professionals.

2. Determine training, support service, and organizational needs as deemed appropriate from review of IEPs and general instructional goals. A focus on strengthening site-based management, collaborative opportunities, and the reallocation of available resources to meet the needs of diverse learners is essential to successful inclusion. Professional development needs may include enhancement of expertise in academic or behavioral strategies while organizational restructuring may call for reassignment of personnel or the reorganization of teams, planning times, or instructional schedules.

3. At collaborative planning sessions conduct ongoing evaluation of student performance and modify classroom instruction and IEPs accordingly. Collaborative sessions should include analysis of the effectiveness of instructional content, teaching methods, classroom organization, evaluation procedures, and professional roles. Analysis must be based on measurable outcomes for *all* students in the setting and IEPs may need to be revised prior to the expected annual review.

4. In collaborative planning sessions, determine how district curriculum goals and instructional methods can be modified to meet the needs of individuals with IEPs. Partial participation, alternative grading systems, peer coaching, and reduced assignments may all be appropriate. Inclusion in general education may not mean that students with IEPs are expected to master all objectives of the inclusive setting.

5. Delineation of professional roles should be based on analysis of the needs of all students within the setting. Although the general educator is basically responsible for presentation of content, and the special educator responsible for accommodation, roles may change. In collaborative instructional partnerships, flexibility, respect for individual expertise, and equal participation are stressed.

Educators demonstrate a wide range of skills and training; therefore, no single collaborative model is likely to be successful. General education teachers must clearly identify concept and principles they view as critical and special education teachers must support this process by providing expertise in formatting content information (Nolet & Tindal, 1993). Further, a continuum of services to meet the needs of individuals with varied needs must be maintained. Placement in collaborative, integrated settings remains an individualized decision based on the specific goals and objectives targeted in the IEP by a multidisciplinary team.

References

Bradley, D. F., & Fisher, J. F. (1995). The inclusion process: Role changes at the middle level. *Middle School Journal, 26*(3), 13–19.

The Council for Exceptional Children (1993). CEC policy on inclusive schools and community settings. *Supplement to Teaching Exceptional Children, 25*(4)

Dettmer, P., Thurston, L. P., & Dyck, N. (1993). *Consultation, collaboration, and teamwork for students with special needs.* Needham Heights, MA: Allyn & Bacon.

Heron, T. E., & Harris, K. C. (1993). *The educational consultant.* Austin, TX: Pro-ed.

Nolet, V., & Tindal, G. (1993). Special education in content area classes: Development of a model and practical procedures. *Remedial and Special Education, 14*(1), 36–48.

Simpson, R. L., & Myles, B. S. (1993). General education collaboration: A model for successful mainstreaming. In E. L. Meyen, G. A. Vergason, & R. J. Whelan (Eds.), *Challenges facing special education* (pp. 63–78). Denver, CO: Love.

Ysseldyke, J. E., Christenson, S., & Kovaleski, J. F. (1994). Identifying students' instructional needs in the context of classroom and home environments. *Teaching Exceptional Children, 26*(3), 37–41.

Jane E. Doelling, Suzanne Bryde, and Barbara Martin teach at Southwest Missouri State University in Springfield. Judy Brunner is a middle school principal in the Springfield Public Schools in Missouri.

From *Middle School Journal*, January 1998, pp. 34-39. © 1998 by the National Middle School Association (NMSA). Reprinted by permission.

Don't Water Down!
ENHANCE

Content Learning Through the Unit Organizer Routine

If it weren't for students impeding our progress in our race to the end of the term, we could certainly be sure of covering the material. The question, however, is not whether we as teachers can get to the end of the text or the end of the term, but whether our students are with us on that journey.

(P. Cross, personal communication, 1994)

Daniel J. Boudah • B. Keith Lenz • Janis A. Bulgren • Jean B. Schumaker • Donald D. Deshler

These remarks are an accurate and thoughtful response to some of the greatest challenges facing secondary teachers today as they attempt to meet their students' needs.

- The volume of information teachers are expected to teach is expanding dramatically, while the amount of instructional time remains constant.
- The community's expectations for improved student performance on local, state, and national competency exams are constantly increasing.
- Much of the information teachers are expected to teach is extremely complex, abstract, and often of little interest to students.
- Today's classes are becoming increasingly diverse and frequently include students who are high, average, and low achieving, as well as students who are considered gifted, students with disabilities, and those who are at risk for school failure. Thus, meeting the

varying needs of students from each of these groups while fulfilling the other demands related to content coverage poses an enormous task for the secondary classroom teacher.

To meet these challenges, we need instructional techniques that do not simply water down content learning, but are effective—and also acceptable to both teachers and students. This article translates one research-based teaching technique into practice. We describe and illustrate the instructional procedures, offer practical tips, and cite additional resources to support teachers.

Content Enhancement and the Unit Organizer Routine

Content Enhancement is a strategic approach to planning for and teaching content to academically diverse groups of students. It involves making decisions

about what content to emphasize in teaching, transforming that content into learner-friendly formats, and presenting this content in memorable ways. In short, through application of sound instructional principles and techniques, teachers can enrich the learning of all students without sacrificing important content. Moreover, teachers carry out instruction in an engaging partnership with students.

We have developed and validated several Content Enhancement instructional techniques, or "routines," in cooperation with teachers (e.g., Bulgren, Schumaker, & Deshler, 1993; Lenz, Marrs, Schumaker, & Deshler, 1993). These routines are commercially available with training (see "Additional Resources"). One Content Enhancement routine is called the Unit Organizer Routine. This routine focuses on how a teacher introduces, builds, and gains closure on the critical ideas and information in a content area unit. A unit is any "chunk" of content that a teacher selects to organize information into lessons and that ends in some type of test or closure activity. Typically, a content area course (e.g., science, history, math, English) is divided into several such units that may or may not conform to the organization of a textbook. Teachers and students often benefit from use of a routine designed to organize and enhance understanding of these chunks of content information.

The Unit Organizer Routine can help teachers plan for, introduce, and build a unit so that *all* students can do the following:

- Understand how the unit is part of bigger course ideas or a sequence of units.
- Understand the "gist" or central idea regarding the unit through a meaningful paraphrase of the unit title.
- See a structure or organization of the critical unit information.
- Define the relationships associated with critical information.
- Generate and answer questions regarding key unit information.
- Monitor their progress and accomplishments in learning.
- Keeping the "big ideas" and structure of the unit in mind as they learn the unit content.

In general, teachers can use the Unit Organizer to help students understand where they have been, where they are, and where they are going on their journey through the content.

> ## The Unit Organizer enables teachers to present the content of a unit in an interactive way to students.

To introduce and teach the information in a unit, teachers use a visual device, called the *Unit Organizer*. During the interactive presentation of the Unit Organizer, teachers follow a set of instructional steps, called *Linking Steps*, that are imbedded within an instructional sequence—the *Cue-Do-Review Sequence*. Thus, successful use of the Unit Organizer Routine is based on three critical components: the Unit Organizer device, the instructional Linking Steps, and the Cue-Do-Review Sequence.

The Unit Organizer Device

To help teachers present their "vision" of a unit's information, they can use a visual device, called the Unit Organizer. Serving as the "centerpiece" of the Unit Organizer Routine, the Unit Organizer graphically organizes and depicts the content of the unit and related information.

The Unit Organizer consists of two pages:

- Page 1 presents an overall organization for the unit information, relationships, questions, and tasks.
- Page 2 provides an ongoing structure for effective note-taking.

Typically, the teacher and students construct Page 1 together at the introduction of a unit, when they simultaneously construct information on blank Unit Organizer forms. Figures 1 and 2 show templates for Pages 1 and 2, respectively; Figures 3 and 4 show examples of the completed pages. As the teacher and the students progress through the unit, they co-construct Page 2 as they add and connect relevant and important details that support the key information presented on Page 1.

The completed examples in Figure 3 and 4 show what the teacher and students created for a unit on the causes of the Civil War in a high school U.S. history class. As illustrated, a Unit Organizer does not depend on a textbook. Teachers and students can use the device to tie together information in a unit for which there is no textbook or to pull multiple textbook sections, chapters, or sources together to create a unit.

The Unit Organizer Sections

Each section of the Unit Organizer contains a specific type of information related to the unit.

1. *Current Unit.* In this section, students write the title of the new unit. This may be the name of the section of a textbook on which you are basing the unit or the name you give the unit. In Figure 3, the name of the current unit is "Causes of the Civil War."

2. *Last Unit/Experience.* The information in this space includes the name of the last unit that was covered or the last experience the students had relating to the current unit. In Figure 3, the name of the last unit was "Growth of the Nation."

3. *Next Unit/Experience.* In this section, students write the name of the unit or experience that will follow the current unit. In Figure 3, the name of the next unit is "The Civil War."

4. *The Bigger Picture.* This section contains the name of the theme of larger category that holds several units together. In general, the name of this section, "The Bigger Picture," helps students understand how multiple units are related. In Figure 3, for example, the theme or larger category into which the last, current, and next units fit is "The Roots and Consequences of Civil Unrest."

5. *Unit Map.* The unit map—the heart of the Unit Organizer—includes two sources of information, as follows:

Unit Paraphrase—a "gist" statement, written in the oval at the top of the map, along with the page numbers of the text related to it. The unit paraphrase captures the central point or meaning of the current unit. Students write this paraphrase in words that they can easily understand and relate to, or as in the Figure 3 example, in words that reveal the central meaning of the unit title. Students can use a horizontal dotted line to separate the paraphrase from the text page numbers where they can find relevant information. In Figure 3, the unit paraphrase translates the name of the current unit, "Causes of the Civil War," into the central idea of "Sectionalism."

Graphic Organizer—a type of flow chart or "semantic" map showing the organization of the unit content. Students write key words within geometric shapes, such as ovals, to indicate the parts of the unit to be learned. In Figure 3, the unit map illustrates the four parts of the unit on the Civil War; "Areas of the U.S.," "Differences Between the Areas," "Events in the U.S.," and "Leaders Across the U.S." As a rule, the unit map should include no more than seven parts.

Within the unit map, students should draw lines between the geometric shapes and the unit paraphrase and include "line labels" on each line to indicate the relationships between the parts and the main idea of the unit. Students write the line labels in such a way that the words in the unit paraphrase, the line label, and the words in a connected geometric shape then form a complete sentence. The lines and line labels are critical elements in the map that help students understand how the parts of the unit are connected or related. When you include lines and line labels, you enable students to remember substantially more about unit information (Novak & Gowin, 1984).

Figure 1. First Page of a Blank Template for the Unit Organizer Device

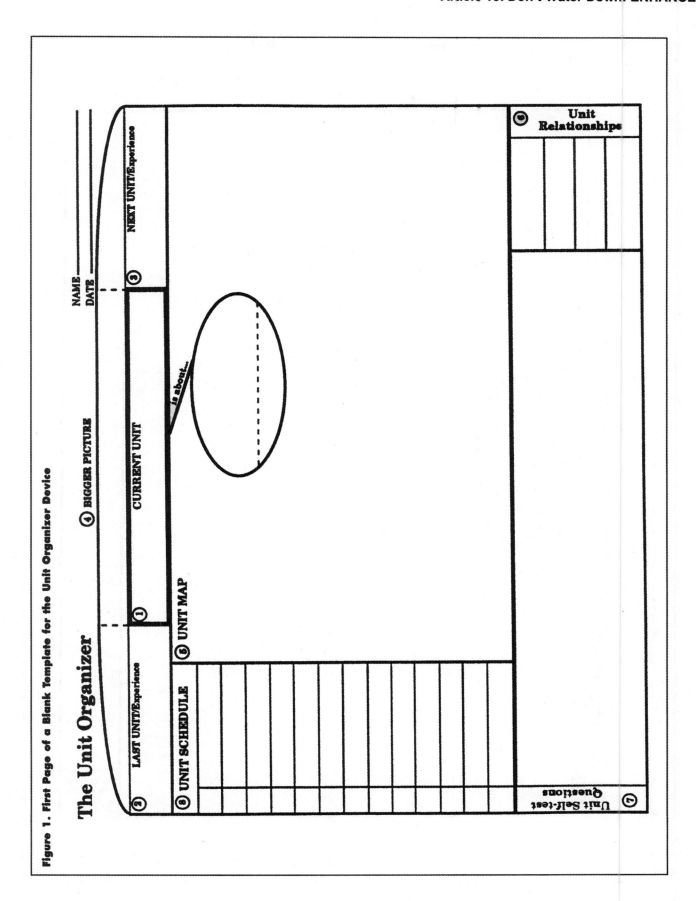

The Unit Organizer

NAME_____
DATE_____

② LAST UNIT/Experience

④ BIGGER PICTURE

① CURRENT UNIT

is about...

③ NEXT UNIT/Experience

⑧ UNIT MAP

⑨ UNIT SCHEDULE

⑥ Unit Relationships

⑦ Unit Self-test Questions

Figure 2. Second Page of a Blank Template for the Unit Organizer Device

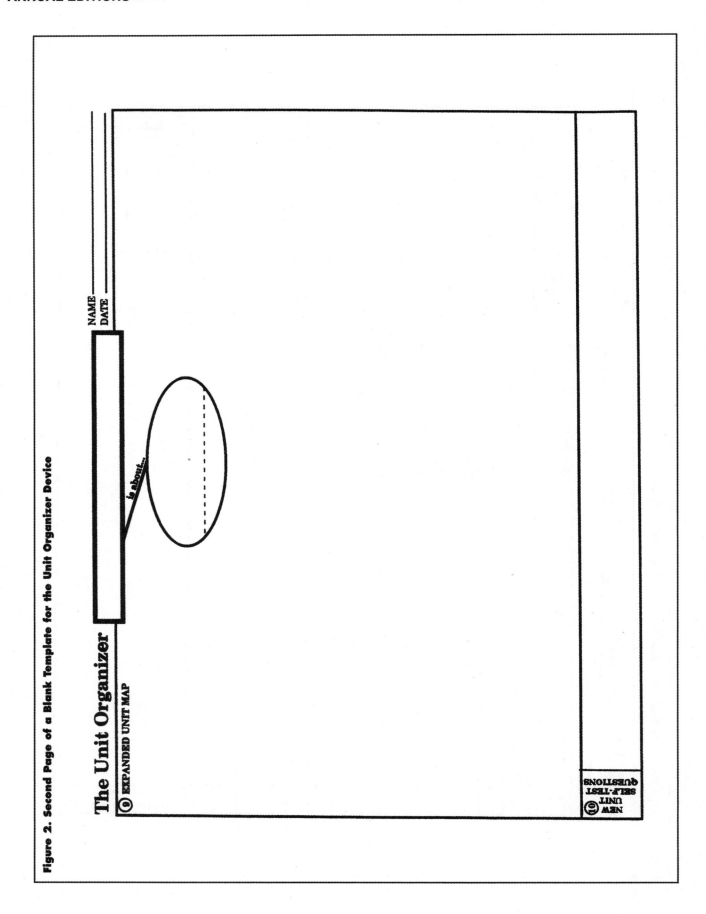

Figure 3. First Page of a Completed Unit Organizer Device

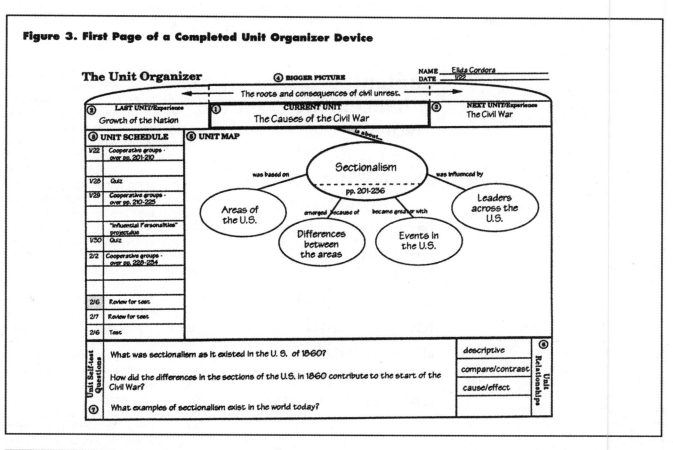

Figure 4. Second Page of a Completed Unit Organizer Device

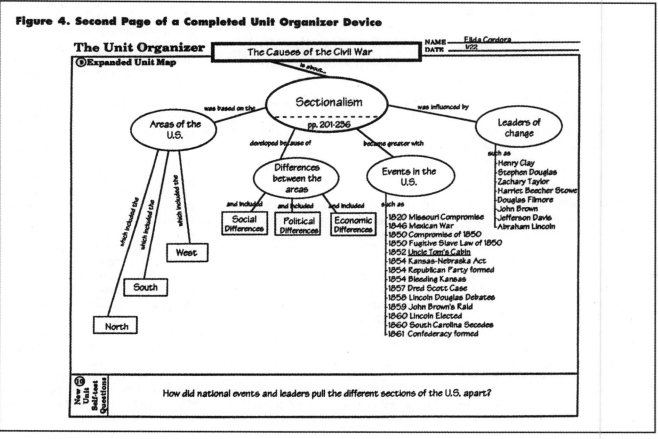

6. *Unit Relationships*. Students use this section to write the names of relationships that might be important to look for and the kinds of thinking required to learn the unit information. In Figure 3, for example, the teacher and students noted that the various areas of the nation must be described and then compared and contrasted to understand how their differences led to the Civil War.

7. *Unit Self-Test Questions*. Students use this section to generate and write questions related to different parts of the unit that they should be able to answer when the unit is complete. Later, when preparing for the unit test, students can ask themselves these questions to review the content of the unit. Figure 3 shows one of the questions that students generated about the Civil War: "What was sectionalism as it existed in the U.S. of 1860?"

8. *Unit Schedule*. The information in this section summarizes the schedule of required tasks, activities, or assignments that students must complete during the course of the unit. In this section, students write down their list of projects, homework assignments, and tests, rather than lesson topics for the unit. Figure 3, for example, shows dates in the square boxes and associated tasks and assignments in the adjacent rectangular boxes. Students should leave spaces in the schedule for items you or the students decide to add later during the unit.

9. *Expanded Unit Map*. After you introduce the unit, and you and your students complete the first page of the Unit Organizer, you can use the second page throughout and at the end of the unit to expand the unit map by adding critical subtopics, details, and key vocabulary in note form. Together, you and your students can identify and add these details daily to the expanded unit map as extensions of the original parts of the map. Students can use the expanded map as a note-taking device during daily lessons or during review at the end of each lesson. Figure 4 shows the expanded unit map for the unit on the "Causes of the Civil War."

10. *New Unit Self-Test Questions*. Use the space below the expanded unit map to write questions that you and your students identify as you explore the unit. For example, Figure 4 shows a question the teacher and students added to the expanded unit map: "How did national

events and leaders pull the different sections of the U.S. apart?"

> # Content Enhancement involves making decisions about what content to emphasize in teaching, transforming that content into learner-friendly formats, and presenting this content in memorable ways.

An Abbreviated Example of How to Use the Unit Organizer Routine

Using the Cue-Do-Review sequence (see box, above), lead students through the content of the unit by engaging them in the Unit Organizer Routine.

Cue

Hand out blank copies of the Unit Organizer device and explain that the class will be beginning a new unit, using the Unit Organizer. Show a blank Unit Organizer on an overhead projector and explain that you will complete that one as students complete their own. This should take only a few minutes. In addition, the first time the Unit Organizer is used, spend a few minutes talking about what it means to be organized at home, organized with school-work in a binder, and then talk about the value of the Unit Organizer for organizing class information. Each subsequent time that a Unit Organizer is used, it would still be valuable to review the benefits of using

the device and your expectations for student participation.

Do

Engage students in completing the Unit Organizer, using a set of Linking Steps. Linking Steps refer to the procedures a teacher uses to present the content of a unit in an interactive way to students. Linking Steps guide the way the Unit Organizer is used when introducing the unit (using Page 1 of the Unit Organizer), expanding the unit (using the Expanded Unit Organizer), and gaining closure on the unit. Although it would take less time to simply tell students what to write in each of the sections of the Unit Organizer, prompt student responses with questions that will enable them to actively use the device and will enhance their learning at each step.

First, help students to see the overall context of the unit and how the new unit is related to previous and future learning. Ask students to recall the name of the previous unit, prompt them to look at a text for the name of the current unit, and hypothesize the name of the next unit. Then ask them how the three units fit together, what they have in common, or the name of a larger category to which they might belong. Students seldom may be asked to think and respond to questions at that level, but even upper elementary students are able to provide reasonable responses when asked. With any group of students, it may be necessary to paraphrase a student's response to clarify the bigger picture. Complete Sections 1–4 of the Unit Organizer at this step when introducing the unit, and review the information in these sections at unit closure.

Second, discuss and complete information in the Unit Map in order to help students identify and see the structure of main ideas or parts of the unit. If a major part of the unit includes a textbook chapter, ask students to survey the chapter for major headings, discuss probable main ideas, and then write them on the Unit Map in Section 5 of the Unit Organizer. For younger students and for the benefit of those with poor motor skills, help students by showing them how to map out (i.e., draw) the total number of ovals or shapes that correspond to the number of main ideas that will be present on the completed Unit Map. Do so before discussing and writing the names of the main ideas in the ovals. Also, don't forget to include the lines and line labels! Throughout daily lessons in the unit, connect critical details and information to the

Cue It! Do It! Review It!

A Cue-Do-Review sequence is a simple formula for making the most of the Unit Organizer Routine (or any instructional strategy). You can use it to focus students' attention on the Unit Organizer device, implement the device, and check student understanding. Mark Twain might have referred to this as "You tell 'em what you're gonna tell 'em. You tell 'em. And you tell 'em what you told 'em." Here's how it works:

1. Provide a "Cue." As with any instructional device (e.g., globe, video, role play activity, graphic organizer), you will enhance students' understanding by (a) directing their attention to the device and explaining what it is (if it is not already obvious), (b) explaining your expectations, and (c) showing how using the device will help students succeed.
2. In the "Do" step, use a set of Linking Steps for (a) introducing, (b) using and expanding, and (c) gaining closure on a unit with the Unit Organizer.
3. In the "Review" step, use a simple review to check and clarify student understanding of information discussed, as well as the process for using the Unit Organizer.

main ideas on the Expanded Unit Map in Section 9. Review the information in both sections at unit closure.

> **Within the unit map, you should draw lines between the geometric shapes and the unit paraphrase and include "line labels" on each line to indicate the relationships between the parts and the main idea of the unit.**

Third, after students see how the critical parts of the unit are structured, ask them to discuss and identify possible relationships or kinds of thinking required to understand the information in the main parts of the unit. Prompt students to analyze the Unit Map, the main ideas contained in it, and the relationships among the main ideas, and their relation to the Unit Paraphrase. Using the completed example in Figure 3,

ask questions such as "We have one main idea regarding the sections of the country. On a test, what might you be asked to do? How might you be asked to think about that information?" Write these unit relationships in Section 6 of the Unit Organizer when the unit is introduced, and be sure to review them at the end of the unit.

Fourth, prompt students to create some good questions that correspond to the different parts of the unit map and unit context. For a moment, students can pretend that they are the teacher and select test questions. Work with students to make sure that critical questions related to mastery of the content are included and recorded in Section 7 of the device. The Unit Relationships also may be clarified at this step as students recognize the kinds of thinking that are required (e.g., listing, explaining, comparing, predicting) to address the questions that they write.

As an alternative, some teachers have found it beneficial to write the Unit Self-Test Questions in Section 7 before analyzing the Unit Relationships in Section 6 because the latter step is less difficult for many students if the self-test questions can be identified first. For example, after writing the questions, some teachers prompt students to identify whether certain questions would require students to compare, explain, name, or problem-solve, or use other thinking skills, and then write students' responses into the Unit Relationships section.

As the unit progresses, record new questions in Section 10. Review the questions from Section 7 of the Unit Organizer and, later, from Section 10 of the Expanded Unit Organizer throughout the unit and at the end of the unit, before any test.

Finally, describe and create the list of assignments and due dates to assist stu-

dents in planning for, managing, and completing tasks and assignments related to the current unit. Prompt students to write these assignments in Section 8 of the Unit Organizer when the unit is introduced. Be sure to review the list throughout the unit.

> **Using the Unit Organizer, teachers ask students to discuss and identify possible relationships or kinds of thinking required to understand the information in the main parts of the unit.**

When co-constructing the first page of the Unit Organizer device at the beginning of a new unit, the "Do" step may take an entire class period (i.e., 45–55 minutes) or more depending on student discussion and content difficulty.

Review

After introducing the unit, after adding daily information in the Expanded Unit

Organizer, and at the closure of a unit, it is important to check student understanding. After co-constructing the Unit Organizer at the beginning of a unit, take a few minutes to review the information contained in all eight parts of the device. Ask questions like these:

- What's the name of the new unit?
- What's another way of writing the name of the unit?
- How many main parts are there in the unit?
- What questions should we be able to answer by the time we finish the unit?
- What process did we go through to really understand this unit?
- When is your test?

Also, ask students to describe how the Unit Organizer helped them to learn.

> **The Unit Organizer Routine can provide a powerful and effective way for teachers to plan for and teach students with and without disabilities, in content area classes.**

Tips, Suggestions, and Modifications

Planning Tips

First, when you are ready to use The Unit Organizer Routine, begin by selecting one class in which to try it out—perhaps your least demanding class in terms of diversity or classroom management. Also consider beginning with a unit that is fairly uncomplicated or one that includes more concrete information rather than more abstract information. For instance, a unit on mammals might be a better place to start than a unit on photosynthesis.

Second, collect the materials you plan to use in your unit, such as slides and textbooks.

Third, always construct a draft of the Unit Organizer device before introducing it to the class. The Unit Organizer truly does work well as a planning routine as well as a teaching routine. In fact, the first time you plan while using the Unit Organizer, you may find that it takes some extra time because you might realize ways to better organize unit information that you may have presented many times before.

Logistical Suggestions

When you are ready to introduce a new unit with the Unit Organizer, consider these suggestions:

- Copy and distribute to students two-sided copies of the Unit Organizer device with the main Unit Organizer on one side and the Expanded Unit Organizer on the second side.
- Cue students to take notes on the Unit Organizer.
- Use fine- or extra-fine-tip overhead transparency pens to add information to the Unit Organizer during presentations.
- Construct the Expanded Unit Map using different geometric shapes (e.g., ovals for main ideas, squares for first level details, and triangles for less important details).
- Vary the colors in construction of the Expanded Unit Map to reflect different levels of information of detail.
- When co-constructing the Expanded Unit Map with students, use "Inspiration" software, from Inspiration Software, Inc., to quickly and neatly lay out the critical and connected details with the use of technology.

Ideas for Modifications

In addition, consider these modifications for students with disabilities and others who are low achieving:

- Rather than constructing a Unit Organizer on an overhead projector, enlarge the device and create a laminated copy to post on the wall and construct it there.
- Create a blank Unit Organizer on a bulletin board, cut out geometric shapes from construction paper, and tack them up on the bulletin board to display unit information.
- Draw empty geometric shapes on a Unit Organizer or partially complete the Unit Organizer before copying for students.

- Enlarge the Unit Organizer onto legal size (8"x14") paper for students to complete.
- As a review activity before a test, hand out 3"x5" index cards or colored Post-Its or "sticky notes" to small groups of students and prompt them to reconstruct the organization of unit main ideas and details on poster paper, as well as draw in the lines and line labels.

> **Students can pretend that they are the teacher for a moment and select test questions.**

Assessment Considerations

When you are ready to assess student learning at the end of a unit, be sure that your test reflects the emphasis of your Unit Organizer and its sections. In other words, if you have previously used a particular unit test with the same unit in previous school years, evaluate the test to see whether the big ideas are emphasized over the smaller ones. Construct and weight test items that assess understanding of big ideas rather than rote recall of details. More specifically, consider including questions that relate to explaining the unit map and the relationships among critical pieces of information.

Final Thoughts

Research on the Unit Organizer Routine (Lenz, Schumaker, et al., 1993) has shown that teacher planning was enhanced and the performance of low-achieving students, students with learning disabilities, and average-achieving students improved substantially in regard to understanding and retaining information. In fact, the students of teachers who use the routine regularly and consistently scored an average of 15 percentage points higher on unit tests than did students of teachers who used it only irregularly (see box, "Research Supporting the Unit Organizer Routine").

Research Supporting the Unit Organizer Routine

Researchers conducted a study of the Unit Organizer Routine (Lenz, Schumaker, et al., 1993) in the U.S. Midwest across three high school and three middle school general education classrooms identified as being inclusive by the school district. The researchers collected data intensively through the use of single-subject, multiple-baseline designs on two high-achieving, two average-achieving, two low-achieving, and two students classified as having a learning disability. The researchers collected student performance data over a 7-month period.

Research has shown that use of the Unit Organizer Routine enhanced teacher planning and the performance of low-achieving students, students with learning disabilities, and average-achieving students. These students substantially improved their understanding and retention of information. In fact, among these groups, the students of teachers who used the routine *regularly* and consistently scored an average of 15 percentage points higher on unit tests than did students of teachers who used it only *irregularly*.

Teachers also reported that the Unit Organizer Routine helped those students with language problems and whose first language was not English acquire secondary content. Although the overall performance of high-achieving students did not substantially increase in these studies, the researchers observed increases in performance when the content became more difficult and abstract for individual students. Since the original study was conducted, teachers in many culturally and geographically diverse communities throughout the United States have replicated the results.

Teachers and students who achieve these kinds of results are truly winners. This winning attitude was expressed by one teacher who said, "Focusing on the 'big idea' questions enables me to think more clearly about what are the tools or things I can give students to have them see the patterns" (V. Arndt Helgesen, personal communication, 1993). Thus, the Unit Organizer Routine can provide a powerful and effective way for teachers to plan for and teach students with and without disabilities in content area classes because it focuses on quality rather than simply on quantity. Together, teachers and students can more successfully navigate each unit journey from beginning to end without watering down the learning outcomes.

References

Bulgren, J. A., Schumaker, J. B., & Deshler, D. D. (1993). *The concept mastery routine*. Lawrence, KS: Edge Enterprises.

Lenz, B. K., Marrs, R. W., Schumaker, J. B., & Deshler, D. D. (1993). *The lesson organizer routine*. Lawrence, KS: Edge Enterprises.

Lenz, B. K., Schumaker, J. B., Deshler, D. D., Boudah, D. J., Vance, M., Kissam, B., Bulgren, J. A., & Roth, J. (1993). *The unit planning routine: A guide for inclusive planning* (Research Report). Lawrence, KS: University of Kansas Center for Research on Learning.

Novak, J. D., & Gowin, D. B. (1984). *Learning how to learn*. New York: Cambridge University Press.

Daniel J. Boudah (*CEC Texas Federation*), *Assistant Professor, Department of Educational Psychology, Special Education Programs, Texas A&M University, College Station.* **B. Keith Lenz** (*CEC Chapter #665*), *Senior Research Scientist;* **Janis A. Bulgren** (*CEC Chapter #665*), *Senior Research Scientist;* **Jean B. Schumaker** (*CEC Chapter #665*), *Associate Director; and* **Donald D. Deshler** (*CEC Chapter #436*), *Director, Center for Research on Learning, University of Kansas, Lawrence.*

Address correspondence to Daniel J. Boudah, Department of Educational Psychology, Special Education Programs, Texas A&M University, 704 Harrington Education Center, College Station, TX 77843-4225 (e-mail: boudah@acs. tamu.edu).

Additional Resources

Lenz, B. K., Bulgren, J. A., Schumaker, J. B., Deshler, D. D., & Boudah, D. J. (1994). *The unit organizer routine*. Lawrence, KS: Edge Enterprises.

This teacher manual, as well as others in the Content Enhancement Series, are available with training. For more information, contact Janet Roth at The University of Kansas, Center for Research on Learning, 3061 Dole Building, Lawrence, KS 66045. Phone: 785-864-4790; e-mail: JRoth@quest.sped.ukans.edu

Identifying Depression
in Students with Mental Retardation

Laura M. Stough
Lynn Baker

The belief that people with mental retardation are always happy, carefree, and content is a misconception. In reality, students with mental retardation are at risk for the same types of psychological disorders as are students without cognitive deficits (Crews, Bonaventura, & Rowe, 1994; Johnson, Handen, Lubetsky, & Sacco, 1995; Sovner & Hurley, 1983).

As many as 10% of children with mental retardation suffer from depression, in contrast to the lower prevalence rate of 1%–5% in children without mental retardation

---

Many researchers have actually found a *higher* rate of depressive disorders in people with mental retardation (e.g., Borthwick-Duffy & Eyman, 1990; Menolascino, 1990; Reiss, 1990). Teachers should be aware of this increased risk for depression so that they can appropriately refer their students for diagnosis and treatment. In this article, we present suggestions for detecting and treating childhood depression.

Prevalence and Symptoms of Depression

Although little research has investigated the precise prevalence of depression in children with mental retardation, special education teachers will likely encounter students with depression. Several studies have suggested that these children exhibit symptoms of sadness, loneliness, and worry at a much higher rate than do their peers without disabilities (e.g., Matson & Frame, 1986; Reiss, 1985). These studies estimated that as many as 10% of children with mental retardation suffer from depression, in contrast to the lower prevalence rate of 1%–5% in children without mental retardation (Cantwell, 1990).

Clinical depression is usually determined by a psychologist or psychiatrist, who uses the *Diagnostic and Statistical Manual of Mental Disorders, Fourth Edition* (DSM-IV; American Psychiatric Association, 1994) to make the diagnosis. To be formally diagnosed as "depressed," a child must experience *five different clinical signs of depression* over a 2-week period. The primary symptom is that the student exhibits either an overall depressed mood or a loss of interest in daily activities (also called *anhedonia*). Some students may express this depressed mood in the form of persistent irritability, rather than by sadness or withdrawal.

Figure 1.
Signs of Major Depression

Look for five or more of these symptoms in the same 2-week period. These symptoms should represent a *change* from the person's previous typical level of functioning:

- Depressed or irritable mood most of the day, nearly every day.
- Decreased interest in pleasurable activities.
- Significant weight loss or weight gain.
- Sleeping problems.
- Activity level has increased or decreased.
- Fatigue or energy loss.
- Feelings of worthlessness or guilt.
- Loss of concentration.
- Thoughts of death.

Source: Adapted from the *Diagnostic and Statistical Manual of Mental Disorders-Fourth Edition*, by the American Psychiatric Association, 1994, Washington, DC: Author.

The remaining four symptoms are expressed as *changes* in a student's usual functioning. These changes may be expressed as either an increase or decrease in any of the following areas: (a) appetite or weight;

(b) sleep habits; (c) activity level; (d) energy level; (e) feelings of worthlessness or guilt; (f) difficulty thinking, concentrating, or making decisions; or (g) recurrent thoughts of death or suicidal ideations, plans, or attempts (see Figure 1).

Students with *mild* mental retardation seem to be at risk for depression because they often can perceive that their peers without disabilities are able to accomplish tasks that they themselves cannot

---

Causes of Depression

Students may experience depression as a result of a negative life event, such as the loss of a parent, stresses at home, or adjustment to a new environment. This type of reactive depression is normal and is not a cause for concern unless the depressive symptoms linger and significantly interfere with a student's typical level of functioning. In other cases, there may not be a clear precursor for the depression, yet the student consistently is in a depressed mood. It is when this mood persists over a 2-week period that a teacher should observe the child for other signs of depression.

Students with *mild* mental retardation seem to be at risk for depression because they often can perceive that their peers without disabilities are able to accomplish tasks that they themselves cannot (Eaton & Menolascino, 1982). They may also be aware, via negative peer experiences, that they are different and viewed negatively by society. These observations can then lead to a higher risk for depression and low self-esteem. Conversely, people with *severe* mental retardation are not as likely to be diagnosed with depres-

sion as those with mild retardation, but this may be because of their limited ability to verbally express feelings of sadness or hopelessness, rather than an actual decreased risk for depression (Charlot, Doucette, & Mezzacappa, 1993; Pawlarcyzk & Beckwith, 1987). As a result, depression may be easily overlooked in people with severe mental retardation.

Difficulty of Detection and Diagnosis in Students with Mental Retardation

Teachers, parents, and direct care workers are usually the first to notice that a child with mental retardation is having a problem; however, they often find it hard to determine if the problem is behavioral or emotional (Borthwick-Duffy, 1994). Often, diagnosticians and psychologists tend to attribute symptoms of depression to a student's limited cognitive functioning, rather than to the depression that the student is experiencing. This underdiagnosis of depression is called *diagnostic overshadowing*, in that the depression is deemphasized because the student additionally is labeled as mentally retarded (Crews et al., 1994; White et al., 1995).

The lack of understanding that most psychologists have about students with mental retardation usually results from the lack of exposure that psychologists have had with this population. Phelps and Hammer estimated that fewer than 25% of professionals in the area of psychology receive information about mental retardation in their graduate programs (as cited by Nezu, 1994). As a result, the teacher's input to the psychologist about a student's emotional well-being is extremely important.

The classroom teacher continually monitors the cognitive, social, and emotional well-being of students. Although many students with mild mental retardation can verbalize their feelings of depression, those with more severe limitations tend to

express their depression primarily through changes in their behavior. The teacher can help detect these changes in students' behavior by being sensitive to variations in their overall mood or activity level. Teachers can help identify when a student's behavior has changed in its frequency, intensity, or duration.

For example, some students with mental retardation who are experiencing depression become more aggressive (Reiss & Rojahn, 1993). In these cases, the teacher can give valuable input about how typical the aggressive behavior is and when the behavior first was exhibited by the student. Such input can offset the previously mentioned "overshadowing" in correctly diagnosing depression in students with mental retardation.

Detecting Symptoms in the Classroom

Behavioral Markers

It is most common for a person who is depressed to exhibit an overall mood of sadness. Children with mental retardation, however, may express their sadness through withdrawing and decreasing their social interactions with their peers. Alternatively, they may change the way in which they interact with their peers, becoming irritable or even aggressive toward them. Also, teachers should pay attention when students exhibit new, inappropriate behavior, such as noncompliance or distractibility. In some cases, students may even begin to express their depression through self-injurious behavior. Although behavioral markers such as these may stand out, they may also be quite subtle: A depressed student may simply not seem to take pleasure in activities that he or she previously enjoyed.

Figure 2.
Ideas for Treating Students' Depression Across Life Settings

Skill Building

- Develop the student's communication skills.
- Try a social skills unit to develop interpersonal skills.
- Focus on problem-solving.
- Teach conflict resolution.

Resource Networking

- Work with the family to find needed community resources.
- Start a parent support group in your school.
- Obtain literature from a mental health center about depression.

Expression Opportunities

- Develop nonverbal means for student expression: music, dance, art.
- Role-play potentially stressful situations and appropriate solutions.
- Use films and stories to teach problem-solving.

Relationship Opportunities

- Have pets in class.
- Have students write or draw to pen pals.
- Provide appropriate peer-group opportunities.
- Invite volunteers from the community to develop supportive friendships.
- Find group activities outside the school setting appropriate for the student.

Physical Markers

People with depression usually experience changes in their *vegetative functioning*, or eating and sleeping patterns. Students with mental retardation may also exhibit these signs. Teachers should be aware of changes in overall activity level (either a decrease or an increase) in their students. A student who usually is calm and methodical may show signs of hyperactivity, whereas a student who usually maintains a high level of activity may become withdrawn and slow to respond to stimuli. Changes in weight or interest in food can also be markers of depression. Again, the teacher should look for changes in usual student patterns: the formerly thin student who puts on a substantial amount of weight quickly or the voracious eater who suddenly has no appetite.

Sleep behavior can also be a sign of depression, either increased sleeping or a decrease in the hours the student sleeps. A common occurrence for someone who is depressed is to have little difficulty going to sleep but then awaken in the early morning. Teachers should be aware that sleepy or lethargic students may be suffering from these sleep disturbances during the night.

Treatment of Depression in Children with Mental Retardation

The Individuals with Disabilities Education Act (IDEA) not only ensures the right to free and appropriate educational services, but also to related services, such as psychological assessment and counseling. Many times the school district has programs or staff that can help a student diagnosed as depressed. Once the student has been assessed, the teacher can work closely with the school psychologist or counselor to provide supportive therapy for the student.

The teacher can also discuss with the family any additional support needs that they might have as these needs may contribute to the stress that the student is experiencing. Loss of employment, death of a family member, or economic hardships can all affect the student's level of depression. Teachers should be aware of changes in their students' home environments to help determine if a student is depressed—as opposed to, for example, simple being oppositional. These support needs often occur across settings, for example, at family outings or at recreational activities (see Figure 2).

Examining the settings in which a student functions on a regular basis can help pinpoint obstacles or difficulties that the student is experiencing in these areas, for example, appropriately talking to peers at the community pool. Knowledge of these difficulties thus can help the teacher target instructional objectives for the student in the classroom, such as learning social skills training.

Psychological Services

Psychological services in the mental health community are limited for people with mental retardation. One reason for this may be the bureaucratic structure of these services. Typically, services for people with mental retardation and services for people with mental health needs are provided separately. This separation of services often results in a quandary between agencies as to who should provide services and, often, in a lack of services for the person who is "dually diagnosed."

The most popular forms of psychological services used for children without cognitive limitations experiencing depression may also be used with children with mental retardation. The most popular forms of therapy for children with depression are behavioral therapy, social and adaptive skills training, psychotherapy, and the use of psychiatric medications. These and additional treatment modalities are listed in Figure 3.

Because children with mental retardation are a heterogeneous group, the mental health provider must make modifications in these approaches and techniques. Rubin (1983) suggested that providers should consider the following characteristics of a child when providing psychological services to a student with mental retardation:

Figure 3. Possible Types of Therapy Appropriate for Use with Students with Depression

Individual psychotherapy: The student discusses issues with a counselor or psychologist on an individual basis. The focus is on the student's perceptions and behaviors. The student is usually guided to make his or her own interpretations and goals for change.

Group psychotherapy: Usually a group is formed around a common problem that each member of the group shares to some degree. Groups are usually facilitated by a professional counselor or psychologist. The involvement and support of the other group members are part of the therapeutic treatment.

Family therapy: The family meets with a psychologist or counselor who moderates while problems and solutions are generated by the family members. Family interactions, perceptions, and roles are the areas of focus and change.

Skills training: Building social skills allows the student to engage in social situations while he or she receives modeling and coaching from a therapist or teacher. These social situations allow the student to practice skills in particular deficit areas.

Psychodrama: Guided by a psychologist or counselor, the student acts out themes or roles that represent areas of concern and unresolved conflict. The drama provides emotional release and insight into these areas of concern.

Art therapy: A nonverbal therapy, usually directed by a psychologist, counselor, or art therapist, art therapy uses art as the milieu in which emotions and thoughts can be expressed freely.

Music therapy: A nonverbal therapy, usually directed by a psychologist, counselor, or music therapist, music therapy uses music to help students express and release emotions.

Play therapy: A psychologist or counselor works with the student as he or she plays with toys or other materials that permit expression of conflict issues.

Psychopharmacology: This type of therapy uses prescription drugs to treat medical problems associated with mental disorders.

- Intellectual aptitude.
- Capacity for relationships.
- Neurological functioning.
- Communication skills.

In addition, the mental health provider should always be apprised of the student's current medication intake and medical history.

When we ignore signs of depression in children with mental retardation, these children become at risk for being misunderstood, underestimated, and untreated.

Final Thoughts

Intellectual functioning does not seem to offset depression; in fact, those with mild mental retardation seem to be at an even greater risk for depression. We say, "seem to be," because of the paucity of recent research in this important area. In addition, many treatment techniques for depression that have proven successful in persons without retardation remain untested in those with mental retardation (Sevin & Matson, 1994).

Children with mental retardation experience pain, loss, and depression as do other people. When we ignore signs of depression in children with mental retardation, these children become at risk for being misunderstood, underestimated, and untreated.

References

American Psychiatric Association. (1994). *Diagnostic and statistical manual of mental disorders* (4th ed.). Washington, DC: Author.

Borthwick-Duffy, S. A. (1994). Epidemiology and prevalence of psychopathology in individuals with mental retardation. *Journal of Consulting and Clinical Psychology, 62,* 17–27.

Borthwick-Duffy, S. A., & Eyman, R. K. (1990). Who are the dually diagnosed? *American Journal on Mental Retardation, 94,* 586–595.

Cantwell, D. P. (1990). Depression across the early life span. In M. Lewis & S. M. Miller (Eds.), *Handbook of developmental psychopathology* (pp. 293–310). New York: Plenum.

Charlot, L. R., Doucette, A. C., & Mezzacappa, E. (1993). Affective symptoms of institutionalized adults with mental retardation. *American Journal on Mental Retardation, 98,* 408–416.

Crews, W. D., Bonaventura, S., & Rowe, F. (1994). Dual diagnosis: Prevalence of psychiatric disorders in a large state residential facility for individuals with mental retardation. *American Journal on Mental Retardation, 98,* 688–731.

Eaton, L. F., & Menolascino, F. J. (1982). Psychiatric disorders in the mentally retarded: Types, problems, and challenges. *American Journal of Psychiatry, 139,* 1297–1303.

Johnson, C. R., Handen, B. L., Lubetsky, M. J., & Sacco, K. A. (1995). Affective disorders in hospitalized children and adolescents with mental retardation: A retrospective study. *Research in Developmental Disabilities, 16,* 221–231.

Matson, J. L., & Frame, C. L. (1986). *Psychopathology among mentally retarded children and adolescents* (Vol. 6). Beverly Hills: Sage.

Menolascino, F. J. (1990). The nature and types of mental illness in the mentally retarded. In M. Lewis & S. M. Miller (Eds.), *Handbook of developmental psychology* (pp. 397–408). New York: Plenum.

Nezu, A. M. (1994). Introduction to special section: Mental retardation and mental illness. *Journal of Consulting and Clinical Psychology, 62*(1), 4–5.

Pawlarcyzk, D., & Beckwith, B. E. (1987). Depressive symptoms displayed by persons with mental retardation: A review. *Mental Retardation, 25,* 325–530.

Reiss, S. A. (1985). The mentally retarded, emotionally disturbed adult. In M. Sigman (Ed.), *Children with emotional disorders and developmental disabilities: Assessment and treatment* (pp. 171–193). Orlando, FL: Grune & Stratton.

Reiss, S. A. (1990). Prevalence of dual diagnosis in community-based day programs in the Chicago metropolitan area. *American Journal on Mental Retardation 94,* 578–585.

Reiss, S. A., & Rojahn, J. (1993). Joint occurrence of depression and aggression in children and adults with mental retardation. *Journal of Intellectual Disability Research, 37,* 287–294.

Rubin, R. L. (1983). Bridging the gap through individual counseling and psychotherapy with mentally retarded people. In F. J. Menolascino (Ed.), *Mental health and mental retardation: Bridging the gap* (pp. 119–128). Baltimore: University Park Press.

Sevin, J. A., & Matson, J. L. (1994). An overview of psychopathology. In D. C. Strohmer & H. T. Prout (Eds.), *Counseling and psychotherapy with persons with mental retardation and borderline intelligence* (pp. 21–78). Brandon, VT: Clinical Psychology Publishing.

Sovner, R., & Hurley, A. (1983). Do the mentally retarded suffer from affective illness? *Archives of General Psychiatry 40,* 61–70.

White, M. J., Nicholas, C. N., Cook, R. S., Spengler, P. M., Walker, B. S., & Look, K. K. (1995). Diagnostic overshadowing and mental retardation: A meta-analysis. *American Journal on Mental Retardation, 100,* 293–298.

Read More About It

General Information on Depression and Mental Retardation

Borthwick-Duffy, S. A., & Eyman, R. K. (1990). Who are the dually diagnosed? *American Journal on Mental Retardation, 94,* 586–595.

Charlot, L. R., Doucette, A. C., & Mezzacappa, E. (1993). Affective symptoms of institutionalized adults with mental retardation. *American Journal on Mental Retardation, 98,* 408–416.

Matson, J. L., & Barrett, R. P. (1990). Affective disorders. In J. L. Matson & R. P. Barrett (Eds.) *Psychopathology in the mentally retarded* (pp. 121–146). New York: Grune & Straton.

Menolascino, F. J. (1990). The nature and types of mental illness in the mentally retarded. In M. Lewis & S. M. Miller (Eds.), *Handbook of developmental psychology* (pp. 397–408). New York: Plenum.

Treatment and Counseling

Hurley, A. D. (1989). Individual psychotherapy with mentally retarded individuals: A review and call for research. *Research in Developmental Disabilities, 10,* 261–275.

Nezu, C. M., Nezu, A. M., & Gill-Weiss, M. J. (1992). *Psychopathology in persons with mental retardation: Guidelines for assessment and treatment.* Champaign, IL: Research Press.

Petronko, M. R., Harris, S., & Kormann, R. J. (1994). Community-based behavioral training approaches for people with mental retardation and mental illness. *Journal of Consulting and Clinical Psychology, 62,* 49–54.

Schroeder, S. R., Schroeder, C. S., & Landesman, S. (1987). Psychological services in educational settings to persons with mental retardation. *American Psychologist, 42,* 805–808.

Laura M. Stough (*CEC Texas Federation*), *Senior Lecturer; and* **Lynn Baker**, *Doctoral Candidate, Department of Educational Psychology, Texas A&M University, College Station.*

Address correspondence to Laura M. Stough, Department of Educational Psychology, Texas A&M University, 704 Harrington Tower, College Station, TX 77843–4225 (e-mail: stough@acs.tamu.edu).

UNIT 6

Emotional and Behavioral Disorders

Unit Selections

Key Points to Consider

- If a teacher suspects that a student with EBD is being abused, must he or she notify the parents? Must the teacher prove that abuse is occurring?

- How does the wraparound system work? What are some tips for teachers using the system?

- What are the five integral processes involved with mentorship? What is their importance?

 **Links: www.dushkin.com/online/**
These sites are annotated in the World Wide Web pages.

Resources in Emotional or Behavioral Disorders (EBD)
http://www.gwu.edu/~ebdweb/index.html

The definition of a student with emotional behavioral disorder (EBD) usually conjures up visions of the violence perpetrated by a few students who have vented their frustrations by taking guns to school. One of the hot topics in special education today is whether or not students with emotional and behavioral disorders are too dangerous to be included in regular education classes. The statistics show that students with EBDs are as likely to be the victims of violence or bullying by nondisabled classmates as to be the troublemakers. The definition of EBDs broadly includes all emotionally disordered students with subjective feelings such as sadness, fear, anger, guilt, or anxiety that give rise to altered behaviors that are outside the range of normal. Some, but not all, may be potentially dangerous.

Should children with chronic and severe anger, already convicted of problem behaviors such as violent acts or threats of violence, be re-enrolled in inclusive regular education classes with individualized education plans (IEPs)? Although teachers, other pupils, and school staff may be greatly inconvenienced by the presence of one or more behaviorally disordered students in every classroom, the law is clear. The school must "show cause" if a child with EBD is to be permanently moved from the regular classroom to a more restrictive environment.

The 1994 Gun-Free Schools Act in the United States requires the expulsion of a student who brings a firearm to school. The Individuals with Disabilities Education Act (IDEA) in its 1997 reauthorization made a compromise for students with EBDs or other conditions of disability. If bringing a gun to school is related to their disability (teasing, being bullied) they are exempt from the Gun-Free Schools Act legislation. They can be expelled, but only for 10 days while the school determines their degree of danger to others. If they are judged to be really dangerous, they can temporarily be given an alternate educational placement for 45 days, subject to reassessment. Their IEPs should not be rewritten to place them in a permanent restrictive setting unless their acts were clearly unrelated to their disabilities (which would be hard to prove). This double standard is very controversial. Students without disabilities are expelled with no educational provisions for a full year.

The identification and assessment of students with emotional and behavioral disturbances is controversial. Labels are discouraged because of their effects on self-concept and self-esteem. A student can benefit more from an unlabeled IEP giving strengths, aptitudes, and achievements, plus a characterization of the dimensions of altered behavior in which he or she has specific needs, which is updated frequently as progress is made and/or as new behaviors arise.

For educational purposes, children with behavior disorders are usually divided into two main behavioral classifications: (1) withdrawn, shy, or anxious behaviors, and (2) aggressive, acting-out behaviors. The debate about what constitutes a behavior disorder, or an emotional disorder, is not fully resolved. *The Diagnostic and Statistical Manual of Mental Disorders* (4th edition) (*DSM-IV*) sees serious behavioral disorders as a category first diagnosed in infancy, childhood, or adolescence. Among the *DSM-IV* disorders of childhood are disruptive behaviors, eating disorders, tic disorders, elimination disorders, separation anxiety disorders, and reactive attachment disorders.

The numbers of students identified as having disorders of emotions and behaviors (EBDs) helps determine a state's eligibility for federal funding of special education each year. This categorization for statistical and monetary purposes does not describe the severity of the emotional or behavioral disorder. This category encompasses about 9 percent of the students served by special education in the United States each year.

An alliance of educators and psychologists proposed that IDEA remove the term "serious emotional disturbances" and instead focus on disordered behaviors that adversely affect educational performance. Conduct usually considered a sign of emotional disorder, such as anxiety, depression, or failure of attachment, can be seen as behaviorally disordered if it interferes with academic, social, vocational, and personal accomplishment. So, also, can eating, elimination, or tic disorders, and any other responses outside the range of "acceptable" for school or other settings. Such a focus on behavior can link the individualized educational plan curriculum activities to children's behavioral response styles.

Inclusive education does not translate into acceptance of disordered behaviors in the regular education classroom. Two rules of thumb for the behavior of all children, however capable or incapable, are that they conform to minimum standards of acceptable conduct and that disruptive behaviors be subject to fair and consistent disciplinary action.

What causes students to act out in hostile, aggressive behaviors directed against school personnel or other students? An easy, often-cited reason is that they are barraged with images of violence on the news, in music, on videos, on TV programs, and in movies. It is too facile: The barrage is aimed at everyone, yet only a few decide that they want to become violent and harm others. Aggressive, acting-out children commonly come from homes where they see real violence, anger, and insults. They often feel disconnected, rejected, and afraid. They do not know how to communicate their distress. They may appear to be narcissistic, even as they seek attention in negative, hurtful ways. They usually have fairly easy access to weapons, alcohol, and other substances of abuse. They usually do not know any techniques of conflict management other than acting out.

The first article in this unit addresses the violence of child abuse, which is often a forerunner of students' problems with EBD. The authors provide physical and emotional indicators for which teachers should watch. They also discuss preventing, reporting, and support networking after the fact.

The second article addresses the need to identify children with EBDs as early as possible and to institute primary prevention. Bronfenbrenner's systems theory was the basis for the research program. The authors suggest support services involving many team members and many components of intervention: "An ounce of prevention is worth a pound of cure." Parents, children, and other team members work together at conflict management and social skills development in wraparound ways.

The third article about EBDs describes support services for older students that teaches conflict resolution by pairing adolescent mentors and proteges. Such programs, when monitored carefully, can have innumerable benefits.

Anger, Dismay, Guilt, Anxiety—The Realities and Roles in Reporting Child Abuse

Jeanette C. Nunnelley and Teesue Fields

In 1997 more than three million children were reported to child protective services (CPS) for child abuse and neglect, and 1,054,000 cases were confirmed by authorities (Prevent Child Abuse America 1998). This number represents 15 out of every 1,000 children in the United States. Approximately 8% of all cases of confirmed victims of maltreatment were child sexual abuse. Since 1985 the fatalities rate as a result of abuse has increased by 34% (Wang & Daro 1998).

Every human emotion is experienced when the statistics above become reality for the early childhood educator. As the examples (see "Unfortunate Realities") depict, there is anger at the parents or perpetrator and utter dismay that anyone could deliberately inflict suffering on an innocent child.

When abuse is reported, a certain amount of guilt for making the accusation is present along with anxiety and stress associated with the re-quired procedures and possible court experiences. There is always empathy and grave concern for the child, who often exhibits frustrating behavior patterns that are hard to understand. In some cases an adult's own early childhood experiences are rekindled with overwhelming feelings. Also flaws in the reporting system and in individual schools and centers can stifle a teacher's best attempts at helping a child.

Many caregivers and teachers who try to report instances of suspected child abuse are thwarted by administrators who don't want trouble and squelch the case. The teacher is made to understand that she is expected to drop the matter.

Because of these conflicting emotions, lack of training, and so few support systems for the persons reporting child abuse, individuals may want to ignore suspected abuse. However, it is often the early childhood educator in a child care setting, Head Start, preschool, kindergarten, or other similar program who first encounters abusive situations. Therefore, it is imperative that every teacher, assistant, counselor, and administrator be knowledgeable about child abuse in general. They must also understand reporting procedures, recognize the various emotions associated with them, and seek support as needed.

Get training in reporting child abuse and neglect

In 1974 the U.S. Congress passed the Child Abuse Prevention and Treatment Act, which requires states receiving federal funds for combating child abuse to adopt mandatory reporting. Today, in every state in the United States as well as the District of Columbia and the Virgin Islands, certain professionals (including early childhood educators) are required to report suspicions of child abuse and neglect to proper authorities. Exact procedures and wordings may vary, but the bottom line is that failure to report is illegal.

Unfortunately, studies show that among professionals substantial gaps exist on what is required for the reporting procedures (Reiniger, Robinson, & McHugh 1995). In research conducted for the National Center on Child Abuse and Neglect, almost 40% of the professionals mandated to report abuse admitted that at some time in their careers they had suspected abuse but decided not to report it (Zellman & Bell 1990). Approximately one-fourth of the health care professionals and one-half of all child care providers in the sample had no reporting experience.

Misconceptions, such as the belief that parents are to be notified first and the person reporting must *prove* the abuse, are very common, particularly among child care providers (Wurtele & Schmitt 1992). Workplace characteristics, levels of knowledge and training concerning maltreatment, and positive beliefs about protective service agencies also influence reporting practices (Zellman & Bell 1990).

Results from a national teacher survey reveal that approximately two-thirds of the respondents believe that training on child abuse by their schools is insufficient (Abrahams, Casey & Daro 1992). One imperative, therefore, is that professionals receive training relevant to the reporting procedures in their state. Such professional development must be comprehensive and not limited simply to recognizing signs of abuse and neglect. Reporting procedures, the role of protective service workers, and information on immunity to liability need to be covered (Reiniger, Robinson, & McHugh 1995).

Another major variable about reporting maltreatment is the actual

Unfortunate Realities

Chindwin, a new employee in a child care facility, discovered what appeared to be cigarette burns on a toddler assigned to her room. She showed them to the director, who informed her that she didn't want to hear about such incidences. The director said she had spent too much time away from the center on another occasion when she had reported a case of child abuse. Chindwin felt bewildered an confused. She knew she should report the problem, but she wanted to keep her job.

Tarrissa was concerned about one of the girls in her first-grade class. The child was somewhat obsessed with keeping her hands clean and was reluctant to ever go to the bathroom with other children. Following the established procedure in her school, Tarrissa discussed her concerns with the school counselor. Unfortunately the information became buried on the counselor's desk, and Tarrissa's suspicions of sexual abuse never were reported.

Renaldo, a teaching assistant in a special program for children with profound disabilities, discovered multiple bruises all over one child's back. Renaldo became physically ill at the sight and enraged that anyone would do such a thing to someone so vulnerable. The abuse was reported, and the child was immediately removed from the home. Renaldo never saw the boy again, and he often wondered what had happened to him.

Margaret, the owner of a family child care home, had worked for months with a family experiencing domestic violence. After a particularly bad incident, the mother sought refuge in a shelter and, fearing for her children's lives, sent the police to retrieve her daughters from Margaret's care. The girls were terribly frightened to go with the officers and cried and clung to Margaret. The experience was traumatic for everyone.

definition of *abuse*. Cultural groups, family rights issues, religious doctrines, and assumptions about children influence a state's definition (Tower 1992). An individual's own

beliefs and feelings about discipline also affect attitudes toward reporting abusive situations. Teachers seem particularly reluctant to be bound by specific definitions that may infringe on discipline strategies of the school or the home (Tite 1993). However, whatever a teacher's personal belief system might be, early childhood professionals should know the legal definition of *abuse* in their state and also realize their own emotional biases.

Misconceptions such as the beliefs that parents are to be notified first and that the person reporting must prove the abuse are very common. Knowledge and training about maltreatment and reporting procedures help.

For instance, a family child care provider becomes concerned when a three-year-old has marks on his legs from "being spanked by Daddy." When the provider discusses it with the father, he explains that he believes in strict discipline and thinks hitting his son with a switch is the best way to help him learn good behavior. The provider knows that the boy and his father have a good relationship, so she is reluctant to make a report. Although it is a very stressful and confusing situation, the provider must report the problem.

Be aware of school or program policies

How early childhood programs, school districts, family child care, or child care centers specifically report suspected cases of child abuse and neglect may vary according to their policies. Tower (1992) suggests that it is important for each setting to have procedures that assist teachers and other personnel in making reports. These policies should clearly state who is responsible for calling in

Four Types of Child Abuse

Type/definition	Physical indicators	Emotional indicators
Physical abuse: adult inflicts or allows infliction of physical injury by other than accidental means	bruises lacerations welts, lumps, bumps unexplained fractures burns--cigarette, scalding water,	verbalizes abuse shows fear of going home or of punishment acts severely withdrawn
Neglect: adult deprives a child of conditions necessary for appropriate development (food, shelter, medical care, and so forth)	severely underweight dark circles under eyes inappropriate dress gross uncleanliness immature physical development	continual fatigue continual hunger with voracious appetite chronic absenteeism begging for or hiding food
Sexual abuse: adult (or older child in a position of power) uses a child for sexual gratification or permits another person to use a child for sexual gratification	foreign matter in genitals bruised or dilated genitals recurrent urinary tract infections difficulty/pain in walking	seductive behavior artwork depicting sexual themes self-destructive behavior sleep disorders running away prostitution
Emotional abuse: adult inflicts mental/emotional harm using verbal harassment, threats,, and systematic destruction of a child's self-esteem,	obesity self-abusive behaviors (head banging, hair pulling, rocking)	severely withdrawn overly submissive or apathetic verbalizes self-hate

the report and any follow-up activities, such as court appearances, that may be needed.

Even when policies for reporting child abuse are in place, those responsible often feel their action is a betrayal of the family and they themselves become victims. For example, school counselors often must perform a multitude of conflicting roles associated with a child abuse report (Remley & Fry 1993). The counselor becomes the liaison between the victim and investigators and frequently must testify in court. In child care centers or other preschool programs, these roles are often filled by the director. In many public schools, the principal takes on these duties. Educators feel that valuable work time is lost; teachers have concern about further repercussions toward the child; families are angry and threats

are made; the school or center gets bad publicity—the list goes on. Even in the face of these realities, the report must be made.

Other issues that may need to be addressed are family counseling and possible medical attention for the child (Wolverton 1987). Additionally, ongoing contact with child protective services, leading to mutual training, the creation of task forces and various multidisciplinary teams, and joint public advocacy efforts, strengthens relationships and avoids misunderstandings.

Know the specific signs of child abuse

It is extremely traumatic for those working with children to encounter child abuse in any form, and educators often avoid preparing them-

selves with the necessary knowledge about the identification. The cruel reality is that most educators will face that role. The chart titled "Four Types of Child Abuse" highlights major categories of child abuse with accompanying indicators as identified by the National Center on Child Abuse and Neglect (1986).

Many abusing behaviors could signify other problems; thus interpretations must be cautious. It is important for educators to note the pattern for behavior as much as the behavior itself. For instance, are there recurring injuries or does a usually happy child suddenly become extremely withdrawn and fearful when touched?

Children *do* fall and *do* have accidents on the knees, elbows, shins, and forehead. However, bruises in the softer areas of the body, such as the back, genital areas, thighs, buttocks, face, or back of the legs, are cause for suspicion. Children *do* have sexual curiosities, but a preoccupation with or extreme protectiveness about the genital areas is not normal. Repetition of injuries can also be significant. A final reality is that some children are much more likely to be abused, such as those with disabilities or from communities plagued with social problems of drug abuse and violence (Cates, Markell, & Bettenhausen 1995).

Understand the causes of child abuse

Because recognition of abuse is so emotionally charged, it is important to know why it occurs. Anger and dismay are dealt with more easily when teachers understand why abuse happens. Many child abusers were abused themselves and had poor parenting models. Iverson and Segal (1990) found that many child abusers have low self-esteem or experience depression and other mental health problems. Many face societal issues such as economic stress, lack of social supports, and substance abuse problems (Tower 1992). Often, one adult in the home may be the abuser, and the other is unaware of the behavior. In some cases one parent may be financially or emotionally dependent on the other parent or someone else living in the household who is the abuser. Teenage mothers also are more at risk for abusing their children due to their own lack of maturity (Iverson & Segal 1990).

Regardless of the situations, perpetrators must not be excused. However, simply to punish the abuser without addressing underlying issues is not effective in eliminating the problem in early childhood settings or society. Early childhood professionals must recognize the realities of the broader issues associated with child abuse.

Report suspicions of abuse!

A knowledge of the state's definition of child abuse, policies of the child care program, and the issues surrounding child abuse will assist a teacher in reporting suspected cases. Generally, reports are made to the proper authorities 24 hours a day, 365 days a year, via a published hotline. Agencies are usually listed in the phone book under Child Protection Services or other similar names. The caller may remain anonymous, but being available as a resource may prove valuable to the investigation. The reporter of child abuse is protected under law if the call has been made in good faith.

Usually, the person reporting child abuse will need to give the following information:

- child's name, age, and address;
- parent's name and address; and
- a description of the problem observed.

In some states, additional information is needed. The childhood educator may be asked about other occasions of injuries to the child or details that may assist the state agency receiving the report (Tower 1992). It is not up to the teacher to investigate or prove the suspected case, but to report it. The child protective services agency will do the investigation.

Reporting the suspicion of abuse is not a choice—it's a legal obligation.

If the CPS agency determines that action should be taken, a caseworker is sent to the home or setting, and the child may be removed temporarily. If further investigation reveals serious abuse, sometimes it is necessary to remove the child from the home and place him or her in foster care. This decision is never made lightly by either the social service agency or the courts. The action is taken to protect the child.

As difficult as it is for a young child to be placed with strangers, even more difficult is coping with a seriously battered child. In less serious cases, most states provide abusers with access to family counselling and other services. Even if action by CPS does not seem immediate, a report may be confirmed by future ones; it also may be useful in substantiating previous indications. Teachers should always report their suspicions.

A Fortunate Reality

Kim was a new teacher in a kindergarten program and discovered a number of bruises on the soft part of Eric's thighs. He was a very shy child who seldom interacted with anyone. Because of her training related to child abuse, she recognized the distinct outline of a strap mark in the bruises.

Following school policy, Kim showed the bruises to the school counselor, who immediately reported the concerns to child protective services. Other reports had been made from a child care center the year before, and now a full investigation was implemented.

Knowing that the school had reported the incident, the family made threats to the school's principal and other personnel. Kim, the counselor, and the principal attended a district-sponsored support group for those reporting child abuse.

Even though the case dragged on for months and the counselor had to make several court appearances, the family was participating in court-ordered counseling. A number of substance abuse issues were being addressed, and the family appeared to be functioning more appropriately.

Eric was becoming a good student and seemed much more outgoing in class. Because child abuse was reported, the child and the family found help.

Once the decision has been made to report the abuse, the child should not be questioned by anyone until the appropriate agency is present. To prevent trauma to the child and to preserve the integrity of the case, the child should be asked to tell the story as few times as possible.

Seek emotional support

Reporting a case of child abuse can be very traumatic for the teacher/caregiver. Individuals worry, "Will I break up the family? Have I done the right thing? Will the parents be angry? Will I see the child again? Will I have to go to court? Will I lose my job?" If a report is made and nothing happens, the teacher also may feel frustrated by the system. If a parent confronts the caregiver in anger or removes the child from the program, guilt and a deep sense of loss may also occur.

First, it is important for teachers to recognize that these feelings are normal. Some steps that could help include the following:

- Talk to someone who has also reported cases of child abuse, such as the director of the program, another family child care provider, a school counselor, the principal, or the school nurse.

- Start a support group in the school district or area for those who generally make abuse reports and court appearances.

- Set up meetings within local professional organizations to address the issue of child abuse and its effect on those who report it.

The state affiliates of Prevent Child Abuse America (PCAA), formerly the National Committee to Prevent Child Abuse, may have local child abuse councils that resources and a friendly listening ear. It is important to note that many child abuse survivors have revealed that the silence of adults who must have known of the abuse was as hard to take as the abuse itself (Calao & Hosansky 1983). Finally, teachers must remember that reporting the suspicion of abuse is *not* a choice—it is a legal obligation.

Become familiar with resources for preventing child abuse

Just as early childhood professionals must report child abuse, they also must concern themselves with prevention. If a teacher believes that abuse is a possibility, a referral to an appropriate organization or agency is also in order. Some churches and state agencies offer counseling. Parents Anonymous is an organization that exists nationwide to assist parents who think they might be in danger of abusing a child. Parents can discuss their fears and anger in an atmosphere that is nonjudgmental. In doing so, they find ways to confront their anger and their problems.

PCAA and its state affiliates have brochures, other literature, and various programs that educate parents and others on effective interactions with children. Teachers may also read and become familiar with the "NAEYC Position Statement on the Prevention of Child Abuse in Early Childhood Programs and the Responsibilities of Early Childhood Professionals to Prevent Child Abuse" (NAEYC 1997). Finally, early childhood educators can be advocates for programs that confront social issues such as teen pregnancy, violence in the home, drug abuse, and economic difficulties.

Help the child

The focus of this article is on the realities of reporting child abuse and efforts to help the child. However, it is also important to mention that early childhood professionals should be aware of existing programs in the community that assist children in recognizing and reporting abusive situations. Additionally, there are educational materials beyond the scope of this article that inform teachers and others in understanding the abused child. Appropriate children's literature can also aid the individual child who may be dealing with child abuse.

The primary goal of understanding, reporting, and coping with the realities of child abuse is to ultimately help children and families. With all early childhood professionals working together in the new millennium, perhaps these realities will no longer exist.

References

Abrahams, N., K. Casey, & D. Daro. 1992. Teachers' knowledge, attitudes, and beliefs about child abuse and its prevention. *Child Abuse and Neglect* 16: 229–38.

Calao, F., & T. Hosansky. 1983. *Young children should know.* New York: Berkley.

Cates, D. L., M. A. Markell, & S. Bettenhausen. 1995. At risk for abuse: A teacher's guide for recognizing and reporting child abuse and neglect. *Preventing School Failure* 39(2): 6–9.

Iverson, T. J., & M. Segal. 1990. *Child abuse and neglect: An information and reference guide.* New York: Garland.

NAEYC. 1997. NAEYC position statement on the prevention of child abuse in early childhood programs and the responsibilities of early childhood professionals to prevent child abuse. *Young Children* 52(3): 42–46.

National Center on Child Abuse and Neglect. 1986. *Child abuse and neglect: An informed approach to a shared concern.* No. 20-01016. Washington, DC: Author.

Prevent Child Abuse America. 1998. *Child abuse and neglect statistics.* Chicago, IL: Author. (http://www.childabuse.org/facts97.html)

Reiniger, A., E. Robinson, & M. McHugh. 1995. Mandated training of professionals: A means for improving reporting of suspected child abuse. *Child Abuse and Neglect* 19: 63–70.

Remley, T. P., & L. J. Fry. 1993. Reporting suspected child abuse: Conflicting roles for the counselor. *The School Counselor* 40: 253–59.

Tite, R. 1993. How teachers define and respond to child abuse: The distinction between theoretical and reportable cases. *Child Abuse and Neglect* 17: 591–603.

Tower, C. 1992. *The role of educators in the protection and treatment of child abuse and neglect.* DHHS publication no. ACF 92-30172. Washington, DC: U.S. Department of Health and Human

Services, Administration for Children and Families, Administration on Children, Youth and Families National Center on Child Abuse and Neglect.

Wang, C. T., & D. Daro. 1998. *Current trends in child abuse reporting and fatalities: The results of the 1997 annual fifty state survey.* Chicago, IL: Prevent Child Abuse America.

Wolverton, L. 1987. *What's a teacher to do? Child abuse education for the classroom.* Albany: New York State Education Department.

Wurtele, S., & A. Schmitt. 1992. Child care workers' knowledge about reporting suspected child abuse. *Child Abuse and Neglect* 16: 385–90.

Zellman, G. L. & R. M. Bell. 1990. *The role of professional background, case characteristics, and protective agency response in mandate child abuse reporting.* R-3825-HHS. Washington, DC: U.S. Department of Health and Human Services.

Additional resources

National Child Abuse Hotline
800-422-4453

Parents Anonymous
800-421-0353

Prevent Child Abuse America (formerly National Committee to Prevent Child Abuse) 200 South Michigan Ave., 127th Fl. Chicago, IL 60604-2404
312-663-3520
http://www.childabuse.org

Jeanette C. Nunnelley, Ed.D., is assistant professor and coordinator for elementary and early childhood education at Indiana University Southeast in New Albany. She is a board member of Prevent Child Abuse Kentucky and has worked in a variety of early childhood settings.

Teesue H. Fields, Ph.D., is associate professor and program coordinator of counselor education at Indiana University Southeast in New Albany. Her research interests include group work in schools and prevention strategies for children at risk.

An earlier version of this article (Fall 1998) was published in Kaleidoscope, *Journal of the Kentucky Association for the Education of Young Children,* and is revised and printed with permission.

Wraparound Services for Young Schoolchildren with Emotional and Behavioral Disorders

Susanna Duckworth • Sue Smith-Rex • Suzanne Okey • Mary Ann Brookshire • David Rawlinson
Regenia Rawlinson • Sara Castillo • Jessie Little

- *Suspension cut in half.*
- *Almost one-half fewer absences.*
- *Referrals to the office reduced by two-thirds.*
- *Parent conferences increased four-fold.*

Would you like to see results like these for your students with emotional and behavioral disorders? This article shows how.

In communities across the United States, educators, mental health practitioners, parents, and students have come face to face with the fact that even young elementary schoolchildren can become a threat to society and to themselves. The reauthorization of the Individuals with Disabilities Education Act (Public Law 105-17, IDEA Amendments of 1997, P.L. 105-17, 300.520, 64 Stat. 12412 [199]) makes it less difficult to expel dangerous or violent students with special needs from general and special education class-rooms. In addition, IDEA provides suggestions regarding alternative settings as a means for delivering appropriate educational interventions. Being removed from school, however, should be a last resort; and educators should explore every avenue before a child is either expelled or placed in an alternative setting.

This article describes a project we conducted in a suburban location in the southeastern United States and suggests ways other educators might develop such supports for children and their families.

A dynamic process involves establishing trust, relationship building, and continuous assessment.

Meeting the Needs of Children and Their Families

We designed this project to meet the needs of young elementary schoolchildren with severe and complex emotional and behavioral disorders (EBD). These were children who were often angry, violent, and vulnerable to abuse. The intervention project for this self-contained class of children with EBD began in January 1999 and continued until May 2000. At the beginning of the project, the class contained 8 male students, who had been identified as early as kindergarten or first grade. During the project, class enrollment ranged from 8 to 12 students, 11 males and 1 female, whose ages ranged from 6 to 9 years. A behavioral support team determined that the children should remain in school.

To increase the chances for these children to be included in a general education setting, we implemented a family-centered system using "wraparound" services for the children and their parents (see Clark & Clarke, 1996; Eber, Nelson, & Miles, 1997; Eber, Osuch, & Redditt, 1996; VanDenBerg & Grealish, 1996). A wraparound system is "a needs-driven process for creating and providing services for individual children and their families" (Eber et al., 1997). We used this definition to direct our project. To better under-stand how to use a wraparound system, we studied the application of systems theory (see box, "Systems Theory").

Our review of the literature led us to develop the following guiding questions, which then provided the impetus for our project:

- What are the features of a hands-on wraparound system of services to serve young children with EBD?

- How can we increase parents' participation in their child's educational program?

- What can we learn from parental needs and concerns that will help us to better serve children with EBD?

- How can we better prepare our future teachers to meet the behavioral challenges of the 21st century?

We then created a behavioral support team to plan and address the guiding questions. Figure 1 shows our conceptualization of a wraparound system. Note the integration of school, team, and community services "wrapping around" the group of children and parents involved in our 18-month intervention project.

Systems Theory and a Wraparound System

The most common framework for understanding family assets, needs, resources, and perceptions is systems theory. This theory spotlights family values, priorities, and needs within a responsive, hierarchical, and methodical environment (von Bertalanffy, 1968). As early as 1970, Hobbs applied systems theory concepts to "ecological strategies" in his program for children with emotional disturbance, Project Re-Ed. Bronfenbrenner's (1977; Bronfenbrenner & Nevill, 1994) systems theory model focuses on human development and renewing support for children and families.

Systems theory, using Bronfenbrenner's research, has been put into practice by Bailey, who has written extensively about preschool children with special needs (Bailey & Wolery, 1992). It is from Bailey's interpretation of Bronfenbrenner's work, as well as Brooks-Gunn (1995), that we took our ideas and developed a wraparound system of services for helping children with EBD and their parents.

Role of the Behavioral Support Team

Members of the behavioral support team were people who expressed an interest in working with one another to support young children with EBD and their parents. The team, which consisted of professionals from a local university, a public school district, and a mental health agency (see Figure 2), met monthly to plan, problem-solve, and determine answers to the guiding questions. Parents were considered members of the behavioral support team because of their knowledge of their own needs, as well as the needs of their children. Parents were also recipients of wraparound services.

We developed several components to achieve the goal of implementing successful interventions for young children with EBD:

- *Data-based behavioral instruction* was directed by data collected in an observation booth by university students, teachers, and other professionals. The observation booth was available to parents, who were invited to observe their children at any time during the school day.

Figure 2. Behavioral Support Team Members

- University Special Education Professors (2)
- University Education Majors Serving as Mentors (12)
- Special Education Teacher
- Teaching Assistant
- Guidance Counselor
- Principal
- Clinical Child Psychologist from Local Mental Health Agency
- Director of the Local Alternative School Program
- Parents of the Children with Emotional and Behavioral Disorders

---

- *An innovative suspension program,* provided by the school's principal, was called "The Therapeutic Day" (see box). This program reduced full-day suspensions.

- *Cost-free, direct services* in the classroom provided by a clinical child psychologist from the local mental health agency. In addition, free individual family counseling was available at the agency site.

- *A mentoring program* conducted by university education majors. Each mentor was assigned a student from the class. Mentoring options included having lunch, tutoring, and participating in outdoor activities such as touch football, basketball, and miniature golf.

- *The use of the research-based social skills curriculum, Second Step* (Committee for Children, 1999).

Figure 1. A Wraparound System

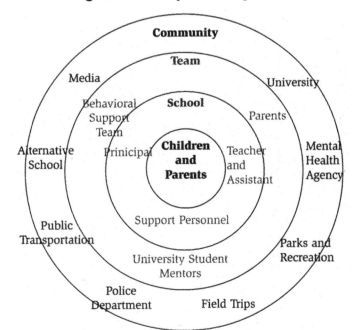

- *Monthly evening parent meetings,* scheduled with parental input, were held in the school library, with transportation provided as needed by the members of the behavioral support team. These meetings turned out to be the most important component of the program.

TO INCREASE THE CHANCES FOR THESE CHILDREN TO BE INCLUDED IN A GENERAL EDUCATION SETTING, WE IMPLEMENTED A FAMILY-CENTERED SYSTEM USING "WRAPAROUND" SERVICES

In addition, we visited consenting families in their homes so that the team could further clarify questions about the purposes of the project and of wraparound services.

We were enthusiastic with the process from the beginning, but we had to continuously remind ourselves to review and revise what we were doing with the children and their parents. We felt that if the project were to be successful, parents must be able to enhance their child-rearing skills and must be able to establish levels of trust with all members of the behavioral support team.

"The Therapeutic Day"

The purpose of "The Therapeutic Day" was to *increase* the amount of time a child would stay in school rather than to *increase* referrals to the principal and out-of-school suspensions. To these ends, the teacher used a cell phone programmed with the phone numbers of each child's parents so that phone calls could be immediate and, through conferencing and problem-solving, could increase parental participation for taking responsibility to help their children stay in school. The principal was a positive support, rather than symbolizing punishment.

Also, the principal coordinated with the university special education professors in providing opportunities for the education majors to serve as mentors—tutoring students, having lunch with them, and sponsoring a monthly "Fabulous Friday" event. Students earned points from a classroom behavior plan to participate in special events. As noted in Table 1, the discipline actions taken brought results.

The Participating Children and Their Parents

As the behavioral support team attempted to address our original guiding questions, which focused on parental needs and concerns about children with EBD and parental participation in educational programs, we reviewed some statistical data: 92% of the parents were single, and 92% of the students qualified for participation in the federal free lunch program. These data gave insight into parents' financial needs and their family structures. We asked ourselves how we could address the needs of parents who

were single-handedly juggling employment issues and parental responsibilities while they were confronting pressures brought about by raising children with EBD.

We decided to have monthly parent meetings during which various behavioral support team members would present topics, such as effective discipline (Rawlinson, 1997), character building, behavior modification, mental health issues, and medications. We hoped that the topics would provide parents with an array of options to use at home that would support the educational program offered at school. We knew we could not conduct the parent meetings, however, without input from the parents themselves.

THE WRAPAROUND SYSTEM HELPED ANSWER THE PERENNIAL QUESTION, HOW CAN WE INCREASE PARENTS' PARTICIPATION IN THEIR CHILD'S EDUCATIONAL PROGRAM?

To that end, the first monthly meeting session began with a parental needs assessment. Outcomes from the assessment determined the topics selected for the subsequent meetings (see box, "Who Says My Child Has Behavior Problems in School?"). All participating members of the behavioral support team reviewed the needs-assessment findings, which demonstrated to all how parental requests for help were being honored. The following monthly discussion topics came out of the parental needs assessment:

- Feelings and attitudes.
- Who says my child has behavior problems in school?
- Family issues.
- How to handle stress.
- Losing a job.
- Finances.
- How to handle failure.
- Transportation problems.
- Dealing with unacceptable behavior.
- Trust-building and communication.
- Available community resources.
- How values are learned in life.
- How to communicate encouragement to your child.

During the sessions that followed, we began talking about feelings, attitudes, and character building. We also discussed situations arising at home, which cause children to behave inappropriately. We presented strategies to help parents with their children's problem behaviors; one source of strategies was *Second Step,* which uses a simple step-by-step method to modify behavior.

Behavioral support team members learned that parental needs, just as the students', were concrete. Issues of transportation, jobs, recreation, mental health, and childhood psychotropic medications were stresses in parents' lives. They had real survival needs that had to be addressed. Over 6 months, the parents listened to community representatives, as well as members of the behavioral support team, who could answer questions and facilitate meetings.

Who Says My Child Has Behavior Problems in School?

Steps that take place:

1. The *teacher* is usually the first to notice that a behavior problem interferes with a child's progress in the classroom. Some examples of behavior problems:

hitting	showing signs of depression
having tantrums	refusing to obey
being too quiet or withdrawn	using bad language
yelling	demonstrating uncontrolled anger

2. The *teacher* tells the *principal* or *school psychologist* about the child and the problem. This is called "referral."
3. The *school psychologist* observes the child in the classroom for several days.
4. The *school psychologist* gives the child several tests. Some examples of tests are behavior checklists, social/interaction tests, intelligence tests.
5. The *school psychologist* uses test results to see if the child's behavior fits the label "emotional disturbance," a category determined by the state education agency and used by the local school district.
6. If the child's behavior fits the label, the *school psychologist* sets up an individualized education program (IEP) meeting with the *parent, general education teacher, special education teacher, principal,* and others.
7. If all parties agree, *special education* services are provided for the child.

All behavioral support team members—including the parents—began to see one another as people with similar problems, hopes, and dreams. Trust was established. Many parents admitted that they, themselves, had experienced adjustment problems in school and that they continued to have little control over their own anger. They also admitted that there were serious problems at home with their children. The parents began to ask for help from people they now trusted. It became apparent that parents, as well as children, would not be open to learning unless it was relevant to their lives, presented in a meaningful way, and facilitated by someone who has taken the time to form a relationship of trust with them.

CELL PHONES AND AN OBSERVATION BOOTH WERE ESSENTIAL PARTS OF THE WRAPAROUND SERVICE

The Principal as a Major Key to Success

The school principal was a member of our behavioral support team. He was pivotal in getting the program off the ground. He had an in-depth knowledge of the students, their families, and the school's and communities' needs. Because of his associations and good communication with the school district office, he was able to obtain funds for the construction of the observation booth that helped us answer some of the wraparound systems' guiding questions dealing with parental participation and teacher preparation. The observation booth provided

- Opportunities for parents and professionals to observe children in their daily school setting.
- A specific milieu for university education majors to use observational recording techniques and to reflect on effective teaching practices.

10 Tips for Teachers

1. Use frequent positive reinforcement. Research says five positive reinforcements for *each* negative, (Beck & Williamston, 1993).
2. Ignore negative behavior that does not interfere with others' learning or influence others' behavior.
3. Tell children specifically what you want them *to do,* rather than what you want them *to stop doing.* For example, if a child is swinging his arms around and bothering another child, tell him to put his hands in his pockets or fold his arms instead of telling him to stop swinging his arms.
4. Use lots of humor.
5. Once you have stated that a certain consequence will follow a specific action, you *must* follow through with the consequence.
6. Give students the choice of two options, *both* of which are acceptable to you.
7. Change the physical environment, that is, rearrange the desks, and so forth.
8. Elicit support from parents in the form of "pep talks" before behavior is out of control.
9. Use masking tape on the floor to delineate personal space.
10. Spend plenty of time teaching procedures, and review them frequently during the year.

The principal provided essential leadership in finding alternative methods of support for the classroom teacher when the students' behaviors were violent and unacceptable. As the project progressed, he no longer viewed full-day suspension as the preferred option. Through the use of "The Therapeutic Day" (see box), students were able to remain in school or the classroom for at least a half-day and often for the entire day, instead of being suspended (see Table 1).

Table 1. Discipline Report from the Osiris Database

Discipline Actions Taken	1998–1999	1999–2000	% Decrease or Increase
Referrals to the office	128	46	- 64
Absences—partial day	78	18	- 230
Absences—full day	182	102	- 44
Suspensions	84	41	- 49
Parent Conferences	19	79	+ 415

As noted in Table 1, there was a significant decrease in referrals to the office, school absences, and suspensions. "The Therapeutic Day" technique was used in building cultural competence. For students to be culturally competent, they must have appropriate adaptive behavior and academic skills.

The Teacher as the Creator of Cultural Competence

Another member of the behavioral support team was the special education teacher in the self-contained class. Her role was to provide daily academic and behavioral instruction that would build *cultural competence* in the students (see box, "10 Tips for Teachers").

Academic Instruction

Academic instruction was based on each student's IEP. The teacher individualized all work and used a variety of instructional formats, including direct instruction. The students closely followed the general education curriculum, with allowances for their strengths and weaknesses. As well, the teacher used state curricular standards and a variety of instructional materials.

Behavior Management and Social Skills Development

Use of behavior management strategies, such as those found in "10 Tips for Teachers," and the administration of the *Second Step* program allowed the teacher to devote more class time to academic instruction, thereby enhancing the development of cultural competence. The teacher obtained documentation of student adaptive and academic behavior outcomes by means of a point-based behavior plan. Students and parents were able to monitor performance by reviewing total daily points that students earned for appropriate behaviors demonstrated in school.

The *Second Step* curriculum is a research-based program that teaches strategies for behavior management and appropriate social interaction. Mastery of the *Second Step* strategies leads children toward cultural competence. Topics in the curriculum include

- Developing empathy.
- Controlling impulses.
- Managing anger.

Instruction is teacher directed, based on posters, activities, and scripts provided by the publisher. Students with EBD are encouraged to generalize and transfer strategies learned in the *Second Step* program to other situations. For example, in our project, the teacher encouraged students to use *Second Step* role-playing activities to demonstrate empathy after reading a story about a student who had lost her home in a fire. Students who displayed appropriate social skills were allowed to participate in art, music, and physical education classes with their general education peers. To be effective with children with EBD, the teacher was committed to addressing academic, social, and behavioral needs.

What We Learned

In search of answers to the wraparound system's guiding questions, we gained insight and drew the following conclusions:

- The features of an ideal wraparound system of services for young children with EBD should include
  –A systems theory framework.
  –A continuing pledge by a behavioral support team to improve the lives of children and their parents.
  –A data-based program design that includes planning, problem-solving, and implementing interventions.
  –Creative and positive administrative leadership
  –Use of preferred practice based on research ("*OSEP Provides Solutions*,", 2000).

OUR BEHAVIORAL SUPPORT TEAM CONSISTED OF PROFESSIONALS FROM A LOCAL UNIVERSITY, A PUBLIC SCHOOL DISTRICT, AND A MENTAL HEALTH AGENCY—AND PARENTS OF THE CHILDREN IN THE CLASS.

- To increase parent participation in a child's educational program,
  –Trust must be established.

–Parent meetings must be perceived as meaningful and enjoyable.

–The school must project a supportive tone for children and their families.

- We can learn from parents that they have as many needs as their children do, and that parents must trust the school before change can occur.

- To better prepare teachers to address the challenging behaviors of children in the 21st century, teacher education programs must include

–Access to data-collection opportunities.

–Preferred practices that are research based.

–Instruction in trust-building skills.

–A long-term commitment to intervention programs.

We must overcome other obstacles if we are going to educate children with EBD in their least restrictive environment. Students' success will be significantly increased if schools consider using a wraparound system of services, attempt to build programs that increase parental trust and support, and identify alternatives to the expulsion of students with severe and complex emotional and behavioral disorders. As school districts continue to examine means of helping children with EBD and their parents, we must create systems of services that are supportive, are family-centered, and address the needs of educators.

References

Bailey, D. B., & Wolery, M. (1992). *Teaching infants and pre-schoolers with disabilities* (2nd ed., p. 66). Englewood Cliffs, NJ: Prentice-Hall.

Beck, R., & Williamston, R. (1993). *Project Ride for preschoolers: Responding to individual differences in education.* Longmont, CA: Sopris West.

Bronfenbrenner, U. (1977). Toward an experimental ecology of human development. *American Psychologist, 32,* 513–531.

Bronfenbrenner, U., & Nevill, P. R. (1994). America's children and families: An international perspective. In S. L. Kagan & B. Weissbourd (Eds), *Putting families first: America's family support movement and the challenge of change* (pp. 3–27). San Francisco: Jossey-Bass.

Brooks-Gunn, J. (1995). Children in families in communities: Risk and intervention in the Bronfenbrenner tradition. In P. Moen, G. H. Elder, Jr., K. Luscher, & H. E. Quick (Eds.), *Examining lives in context: Perspectives on the ecology of human development* (pp. 467–519). Washington, DC: American Psychological Association.

Clark, H. B., & Clarke, R. T. (1996). Research on the wraparound process and individualized services for children with multiple-system needs. *Journal of Child and Family Studies, 5*(1), 1–5.

Committee for Children. (1999). *Second Step Program,* Seattle, WA: Author.

Eber, L., Nelson, C. M., & Miles, P. (1997). School-based wraparound for students with emotional and behavioral challenges. *Exceptional Children, 63,* 539–555.

Eber, L., Osuch, R., & Redditt, C. A. (1996). School-based applications of the wraparound process: Early results on service provision and student outcomes. *Journal of Child and Family Studies, 5*(1), 83–99.

Hobbs, N. (1970). Project Re-Ed: New ways of helping emotionally disturbed children. In Joint Commission on Mental Health of Children (Ed.), *Crisis in child mental health: Challenge for the 1970s.* New York: Harper & Row.

IDEA Amendments of 1997, Public Law 105-17, 300.520, 64 Stat. 12412 (199). [ERIC document Reproduction Service]

OSEP provides solutions to improve student behavior. (2000, March). *CEC Today, 6*(6), 1–15.

Rawlinson, R. M. (1997). *From discipline to responsibility: Principles for raising children today.* Minneapolis, MN: Educational Media Corporation.

VanDenBerg, J. E., & Grealish, E. M. (1996). Individualized services and support through the wraparound process: Philosophy and procedures. *Journal of Child and Family Studies, 5*(1), 7–21.

von Bertanlanffy, L. V. (1968). *General systems theory.* New York: George Brazilles.

Student Mentors and Protegés Learning Together

Brenda Burrell • Susan J. Wood • Theodore Pikes • Connie Holliday

Mentorship programs that pair students with emotional disturbances/behavioral disorders (EBD) as mentors and protégés can be an effective school-based intervention. Adolescents with EBD who have demonstrated gains toward eliminating problematic behaviors and exercising self-control can make positive contributions in a mentoring relationship with young children with EBD. Structured, supervised, and sustained interactions between secondary student mentors and elementary student protégés can be designed to produce specific academic and behavioral outcomes—for both protegés and mentors.

> *MENTOR-PROTEGÉ RELATIONSHIPS ARE POWERFUL OPPORTUNITIES FOR PERSONAL DEVELOPMENT THAT REQUIRE PEOPLE TO GIVE AND RECEIVE AT THE MOST BASIC LEVELS OF HUMAN CARING.*

This article provides a general description of mentorship, a justification for mentoring relationships between students with EBD, guidelines for establishing a mentorship program, and an account of the actual implementation of a mentorship project. According to Nash and Treffinger (1993), the mentorship concept receives high accolades from a wide range of participants. Mentorship has global appeal and praise because it works.

What Is Mentoring?

Mentorship is a dynamic and reciprocal relationship that can be beneficial for both the protegé and the mentor. Gehrke (1988) viewed the mentor-protegé relationship as a powerful and unique opportunity for personal development that requires individuals to give and receive at the most basic levels of human caring. According to Anderson and Shannon (1988), mentorship is a set of five distinct but integral processes:

1. *An intentional process*—the mentor intentionally carries out his or her responsibilities.
2. *A nurturing process*—the protegé's growth and development toward greater maturity is fostered by the mentor.
3. *An insightful process*—the protegé acquires and applies the wisdom of the mentor.
4. *A protegéective and supportive process*—the mentor safeguards and advises the protegé.
5. *A role modeling process*—the mentor provides a standard and a style of behavior that the protegé can understand and follow.

> *ADOLESCENTS WITH EBD WHO HAVE BENEFITED FROM EFFECTIVE EDUCATIONAL INTERVENTIONS SHOULD BE EXPECTED TO HAVE ACQUIRED SOME POSITIVE ATTRIBUTES, INFORMATION, AND SKILLS THEY CAN USE FOR THE BENEFIT OF OTHERS.*

Mentorship can contribute to growth in all areas of a person's life, in part because mentorship is a combination of multiple processes. Processes involve investments of thought, time, and effort that elicit a vast mixture of developments and changes that allow people to continue to expand their capabilities.

Justification of Mentorship Between Students with EBD

The notion that the mentor is a role model for the protegé provides a basis for one of the strongest arguments *against* and one of the strongest arguments *for* the use of students with EBD as mentors. Having a student with EBD as a mentor could be detrimental if the mentor models inappropriate and undesirable behaviors. However, a major purpose of education is to promote academic and social development and to facilitate positive change. Consequently, adolescents with EBD who have benefited from effective educational interventions should be expected to have acquired some positive attributes, information, and skills they can use for the benefit of others. Their prior experiences as elementary students with EBD and the fact that they acquired targeted academic and behavioral skills in the context of those EBD experiences suggest that they may be the most helpful in assisting current elementary students with EBD to also acquire desirable academic and behavioral skills.

Students with EBD may be the most practical and beneficial mentors because they may provide a role model that the protegé finds understandable and attainable—perhaps because of the commonalty of their classification, which affects each participant's most significant life events (e.g., self-concept formation, socialization, education).

Both academic and social/behavioral problems are characteristic of students with EBD (Mathur, Kavale, Quinn, Forness, & Rutherford, 1998; Smith, 1998). The protegé may evidence positive changes in response to a model with whom they can closely identify, such as a person with whom the protegé shares the collective history of EBD. Similarly, mentoring can be a potent part of an adolescent's program of intervention for fostering skills in establishing and maintaining interpersonal relationships.

STUDENT MENTORS ALSO MUST HAVE OPPORTUNITIES TO EXPERIENCE LEADERSHIP AND DECISION-MAKING ROLES.

Researchers have identified several qualities mentors should possess that would be both appealing and beneficial to the protegé (Burrell, Fernandes, & Holliday, 1998; Nash & Treffinger, 1993; Newcombe, 1988; Wildman, Magliaro, Niles, & Niles, 1992). Secondary students with EBD who have experienced success in their educational programs can be expected to exhibit basic qualities associated with successful mentors, or these qualities can be targeted for development for the benefit of the student as a person, as well as a mentor. Mentors need to be

1. *Knowledgeable*—the mentor should know more than the protegé, but he or she does not need to know everything.

2. *Credible*—the mentor should have successful academic and behavioral experiences; the protegé should be able to witness the success.

3. *Supportive*—the mentor should be able to encourage, use praise, and give constructive criticism; the mentor provides specific and formative feedback to the protegé.

4. *Facilitatory*—the mentor should be a guide or coach, not a dictator; the protegé should be able to have his or her own experiences, while being guided.

5. *Available*—the mentor should be accessible to the protegé; time spent together is a crucial element in the relationship.

6. *Empathetic*—the mentor should be able to identify and understand the protegé's situation, feelings, and motives; the shared experience of being students with EBD should contribute to the mentor's ability to empathize; he or she actually has walked in the shoes of the protegé.

General Guidelines for Constructing Mentorship Programs

Effective mentorship programs can be constructed only if participants establish a strong and clear conceptual foundation (Anderson & Shannon, 1988). Purpose, creativity, and personal investment are critical elements for effective mentoring relationships. Participants need a clear vision in conjunction with a structured mentoring program. Participants should have a functional understanding of what their specific mentoring relationship will entail. This understanding is essential if the participants are to commit to the mentoring program willingly, execute it with sincere dedication to its success, and recognize and embrace its outcomes with a confidence that promotes introspection and growth.

Forming a conceptual foundation requires that *all* participants, particularly the mentors, help develop the program. In a student mentoring program, the teacher would need to maintain the role of supervisor; but student mentors also must have opportunities to experience leadership and decision-making roles. This promotes some of the most prized possible outcomes of mentoring. Having students act as collaborative decision makers in matters affecting them promotes feelings of control and independence. If students are to learn to self-regulate their behavior, they must have opportunities to make and follow through on decisions regarding behavior (Johnson, Johnson, Dudley, & Burnett, 1992). Educators can find many ways to provide opportunities for mentor leadership during the planning and implementation of a mentorship program.

Ideally, a mentorship program should be participant-specific; that is, the program should be designed to match the needs, interests, and objectives of the actual mentors and protegés. Nevertheless, following some general guidelines to construct specific mentorship programs is advisable.

Anderson and Shannon (1988), the National Institute of Mental Health (1993), and The Council for Exceptional Children (1997) have generated guidelines for different purposes and for different target populations (e.g., new teachers). These guidelines have many commonalities, however, and they can be used with many mentoring programs because they allow sufficient room for program individualization.

We have provided two sets of guidelines: one for teachers whose students

would be mentors and one for teachers whose students would be protegés (see boxes), along with a list of sources for additional guidelines (see Table 1).

Mentorship Between Students with EBD in Action

Let's look at an actual school-based mentorship program. All student participants were African-American males with EBD who attended public schools in low-income urban areas. The four mentors were 13–15 years old, and the five protegés were 9–11 years old. The program was initiated because the protegés' teacher asked the mentors' teacher for help. The mentors' teacher provided tips and suggestions to the protegés' teacher and also suggested that her secondary students act as "older brothers" for the elementary students, because all the students were males and most of the protegés did not have older brothers or fathers who could provide a positive influence.

Before the teachers began the project, the student mentors had demonstrated exemplary academic and behavioral gains and needed social enrichment *more* than teacher-oriented management related to problem behaviors. They had demonstrated their abilities to engage in critical thinking, exercise self-control, and act in a responsible and respectful manner. The mentors followed explicit and implicit guidelines of appropriate conduct and they excelled in academics. Concurrently, the student protegés had exhibited extremely problematic behaviors and a lack of academic success.

Participation in the mentorship program was voluntary and was supported by parents and principals. Each student mentor was paired with one or two student protegés by the teachers (based on impressions of temperament). The teachers explained the purpose, scope, and expected outcomes of the project to each group of students separately and, on a second occasion, to the collective group. Student input provided the basis for developing several activities that involved the protegés' visiting the mentors' middle school, the mentors' visiting the protegés' elementary school, and joint field trip experiences.

In addition, there were written and telephone communications and frequent discussion within each group regarding the progress and outcomes of the project. Commentaries were informal and verbal and exclusively positive.

EACH PROGRAM SHOULD BE TAILORED TO THE INDIVIDUAL NEEDS OF THE STUDENTS INVOLVED, BUT FOLLOWING SOME GENERAL GUIDELINES IS ADVISABLE.

The mentoring program appeared to be effective in decreasing some of the most problematic behaviors of the elementary students while increasing their positive social interaction skills and self-perceptions. Also, the student protegés spent more time engaged in academic tasks. Positive outcomes Schrader and Valus (1990) identified as benefits of cross-age tutoring and outcomes other scholars have associated with mentorship (Dalton, 1996; Ellis, 1997; Nash & Treffinger, 1993; Pringle, Anderson, Rubenstein, & Russo, 1993; Roberge, 1995) matched the outcomes for student mentors.

The student mentors demonstrated enhanced self-esteem and self-confidence; increased levels of tolerance and caring about others; and skillful teaching and application of academics and prosocial skills. The only negative aspect of the program was that a formal evaluation was not included. For a "snapshot" of what one mentor learned, see box "Mentorship Snapshot."

Evaluation Guidelines

Evaluation is an important component of any program. Careful monitoring of the program and assessment of its outcomes can enhance motivation and facilitate communications that interest others in replications of the program. Also, ongoing evaluation, assessment, and refinement of the program as it grows, expands, or changes to meet future needs of the participants are crucial (CEC, 1997). The evaluation of mentorship programs, however, is definitely not simple. The effect of the program may not be apparent for years (Struchen & Porta, 1997).

As Struchen and Porta (1997) have noted, educators should devise evaluation programs with established notions of the type and degree of change anticipated, when they are likely to be evident, and the method and means for conducting the evaluation. The evaluation of a mentorship program should

- Be from multiple perspectives (e.g., students, school staff, parents).
- Involve the collection and analyses of both quantitative and qualitative data.

- Result in constructive feedback that is used to refine and improve the mentorship program.

THE MENTORING PROGRAM APPEARED TO BE EFFECTIVE IN DECREASING SOME OF THE MOST PROBLEMATIC BEHAVIORS OF THE ELEMENTARY STUDENTS WHILE INCREASING THEIR POSITIVE SOCIAL INTERACTION SKILLS AND SELF-PERCEPTIONS.

Final Thoughts

Finding ways to harness major resources and expertise to enhance outcomes for students at risk of educational failure is one of the most pressing challenges to educators (Wang & Reynolds, 1995). A school-based mentorship program between students with EBD, with mentors who have lived the experience of EBD, is a promising intervention for meeting the need. Teachers can collaborate to provide opportunities for students with EBD to serve as protegés and mentors in carefully crafted and monitored programs that can yield unmatched and innumerable benefits.

SPONSOR A CULMINATING EVENT TO THANK THE MENTORS AND FOR EVERYONE TO EXPRESS THEIR THOUGHTS AND FEELINGS ABOUT THE MENTORSHIP PROGRAM.

References

Anderson, E., & Shannon, A. (1988). Toward a conceptualization of mentoring. *Journal of Teacher Education, 39*, 38–42.

Burrell, B., Fernandes, R., & Holliday, C. (1998, March). *Implementing a parent mentoring program to help prevent child abuse and neglect.* Paper presented at the Louisiana Council on Child Abuse 12th annual "Kids are Worth It" conference, Baton Rouge.

Council for Exceptional Children (CEC) Professional Standards and Practice Standing Committee. (1997). CEC guidelines for developing a mentorship program for beginning special education

Table 1. Mentoring Resources by Description and Contact Information

Resource	Description	Contact Information
The Mentoring Partnership	A mentoring program for students 8-18 years of age	www.mentoringworks.org
Peer Resources	Source for peer, mentor, and coach resources	www.peer.ca/peer.html
Rotary Reader	A progressive mentoring program for grades K-5	www.rotaryreader.org
Bibliographies and Books, Guidebooks, & Manuals on Mentoring	Mentoring and peer coaching resources	www.teachermentors.com
National Mentoring Center	Assisting schools and communities in improving local mentoring programs	www.nwrel.org
Mentors	Peer mentoring	www.nesu
Mentoring Works	Reproducible fact sheet on mentoring	(202) 729-4345; Free
The National Mentoring Partnership	Report describing the characteristics of mentoring models in various settings	The National Mentoring Partnership, 1600 Duke Street, Alexandria, VA 22314, (703) 224-2200
One-on-One	A guide for establishing local mentoring programs	U.S. Department of Education, 400 Maryland Avenue, S.W., Washington, DC 20022
A Youth Mentoring Directory	Information on established mentoring programs	United Way of America, 701 N. Fairfax Street, Alexandria, VA 22314
Big Brothers Big Sisters of America	Mentoring opportunities nationwide	www.bbbsa.org

teachers. *TEACHING Exceptional Children, 29*(6), 19–21.

Dalton, H. F. (1996). Minority male after-school program. *Plan for social excellence*. Mt. Kisco, NY: Plan for Social Excellence (ERIC Document Reproduction Service No. ED 405 409)

Ellis, J. (1997). Volunteer mentorship programs to prevent and respond to troubled behavior. *Alberta Journal of Educational Research, 43*(1), 53–56.

Gehrke, N. (1988). On preserving the essence of mentoring as one form of teacher leadership. *Journal of Teacher Education, 39*(1), 43–45.

Johnson, D., Johnson, R., Dudley, B., & Burnett, R. (1992). Teaching students to be peer mediators. *Educational Leadership, 50*(1), 10–13.

Mathur, S.R., Kavale, K. A., Quinn, M. M., Forness, S. R., & Rutherford, R. B. (1998). Social skills interventions with students' emotional and behavioral problems: A quantitative synthesis of single-subject research. *Behavioral Disorders, 23*(3), 193–201.

Nash, D., & Treffinger, D. (1993). *The mentor kit.* Waco, TX: Prufrock Press.

National Institute of Mental Health. (1993). *From the lab bench to the classroom: A program planner's guide to developing summer fellowship for classroom science teachers.* Rockville, MD: Author. (ERIC Document Reproduction Service No. ED 402 201)

Newcombe, E. (1988). *Mentoring programs for new teachers.* Philadelphia: Research for Better Schools.

Newton, A. (1993). Students as mediators. *Project seed.* Auburn, ME: Maine Center for Educational Services. (ERIC Document Reproduction Service No. ED 361 631)

Pringle, B., Anderson, L. M., Rubenstein, M. C., & Russo, A. W. (1993). *Tutoring and mentoring services for disadvantaged secondary school students: An evaluation of the secondary schools basic skills demonstration assistance program.* Washington DC.: Policy Study Associates. (ERIC Document Reproduction Service No. ED 363 686)

Roberge, R. (1995). *Project P.O.D.S.: Providing opportunities for developing success.* Greensboro, NC: Canadian Guidance and Counseling Foundation. (ERIC Document Reproduction Service No. ED 401 499)

Schrader, B., & Valus, A. (1990) Disabled learners as able teachers: A cross-age tutoring project. *Academic Therapy, 25*, 589–597.

Smith, D. D. (1998). *Introduction to special education: Teaching in an age of challenge* (3rd. ed.). Needham Heights, MA: Allyn & Bacon.

Struchen, W., & Porta, M. (1997). From role-modeling to mentoring for African American youth: Ingredients for successful relationships. *Preventing School Failure, 41*, 119–123.

Wang, M. C., & Reynolds, M. C. (Eds.). (1995). *Making a difference for students at risk.* Thousand Oaks, CA: Corwin.

Wildman, T. M., Magliaro, S. G., Niles, R. A., & Niles, J. A. (1992). Teacher mentoring: An analysis of roles, activities, and conditions. *Journal of Teacher Education, 43*, 205–213.

Brenda Burrell, *Associate Professor, Department of Special Education and Habilitative Services, University of New Orleans, Louisiana.* **Susan J. Wood**, *Administrator, Boston Public Schools, Massachusetts.* **Theodore Pikes**, *Associate Professor, Department of Special Education and Habilitative Services, University of New Orleans, Louisiana.* **Connie Holliday**, *Principal, New Orleans Public Schools, Louisiana.*

Address correspondence to Brenda Burrell, Department of Special Education and Habilitative Services, University of New Orleans–ED 246, New Orleans, LA 70148-2530 (e-mail: bburrell@uno.edu).

From *Teaching Exceptional Children*, January/February 2001, pp. 24-29. © 2001 by The Council for Exceptional Children. Reprinted with permission.

UNIT 7
Vision and Hearing Impairments

Unit Selections

Key Points to Consider

- Are schools for the visually disabled dinosaurs or mainstays? Defend your answer.

- What important lessons can teachers and students with good vision learn from a student who is blind and participating in an inclusive classroom?

- How can visual materials be used to enhance learning environment?

 **Links: www.dushkin.com/online/**
These sites are annotated in the World Wide Web pages.

Info to Go: Laurent Clerc National Deaf Education Center
http://clerccenter.gallaudet.edu/InfoToGo/index.html
The New York Institute for Special Education
http://www.nyise.org/index.html

Earlier, more adequate prenatal care, preventive medicine, health maintenance, and medical technology have reduced the number of children born either blind or deaf. In the future, with knowledge of the human genome and with the possibility of genetic manipulation, all genetic causes of blindness and deafness may be extinct. However, now and in the future, environmental factors will probably still leave many children with vision and hearing impairments.

Children with visual disabilities that cannot be corrected are the smallest group of children who qualify for special educational services through the Individuals with Disabilities Education Act (IDEA). Legally, a child is considered to have low vision if acuity in the best eye, after correction, is between 20/70 and 20/180 and if the visual field extends from 20 to 180 degrees. Legally, a child is considered blind if visual acuity in the best eye, after correction, is 20/200 or less and/or if the field of vision is restricted to an area of less than 20 degrees (tunnel vision). These terms do not accurately reflect a child's ability to see or read print.

The educational definition of visual impairment focuses on what experiences a child needs in order to be able to learn. One must consider the amount of visual acuity in the worst eye, the perception of light and movement, the field of vision (a person "blinded" by tunnel vision may have good visual acuity in a very small field of vision), and the efficiency with which a person uses any residual vision.

Public Law 99-457, fully enacted by 1991, mandated early education for children with disabilities between ages 3 and 5 in the least restrictive environment. It also required individualized family service plans outlining what services would be provided for parents and children, by whom, and where. These family service plans (IFSPs) are updated every 6 months. This early childhood extension of IDEA was especially important for babies born with low vision or blindness. When the Congress reauthorized IDEA in 1997 they extended these early services from birth through 3 for children with special needs such as babies born with blindness.

In infancy and early childhood, many children with low vision or blindness are given instruction in using the long cane as soon as they become mobile. Although controversial for many years, the long cane is increasingly being accepted. A long cane improves orientation and mobility and alerts persons with visual acuity that the user has a visual disability. This warning is very important for the protection of persons with blindness/low vision.

Children with visual impairments that prevent reading print are usually taught to read braille. Braille is a form of writing using raised dots that are "read" with the fingers. In addition to braille, children who are blind are usually taught with Optacon scanners, talking books, talking handheld calculators, closed-circuit televisions, typewriters, and special computer software.

Hearing impairments are rare, and the extreme form, legal deafness, is rarer still. In order to be assessed as hard-of-hearing for purposes of receiving special educational services, a child needs some form of sound amplification to comprehend oral language. In order to be assessed as deaf a child cannot benefit from amplification. Children who are deaf are dependent on vision for language and communication.

When children are born with impaired auditory sensations, they are put into a classification of children with congenital (at or dating from birth) hearing impairments. When children acquire problems with their hearing after birth, they are put into a classification of children with adventitious hearing impairments. If the loss of hearing occurs before the child has learned speech and language, it is called a prelinguistic hearing impairment. If the loss occurs after the child has learned language, it is called a postlinguistic hearing impairment.

Children whose hearing losses involve the outer or middle ear structures are said to have conductive hearing losses. Conductive losses involve defects or impairments of the external auditory canal, the tympanic membrane, or the ossicles. Children whose hearing losses involve the inner ear are said to have sensorineural hearing impairments.

In 1999 The Newborn and Infant Hearing Screening and Intervention Act in the United States provided incentives for states to test the hearing of newborns before hospital discharge. Thirty-four states now offer this test for a small fee. When an infant is diagnosed with deafness or hearing loss, appropriate early education can begin immediately under the auspices of IDEA.

Students with vision or hearing impairments whose disabilities can be ameliorated with assistive devices can usually have their individualized needs met appropriately in inclusive classrooms. However, students with visual and/or hearing disorders whose problems cannot be resolved with technological aids need the procedural protections afforded by law. They should receive special services from age of diagnosis through age 21, in the least restrictive environment, free of charge, with semiannually updated individualized family service plans (IFSPs) until age 6, and annually updated individualized education plans (IEPs) and eventually individualized transition plans (ITPs) through age 21. The number of children and youth who qualify for these intensive specialized educational programs is small.

Many professionals working with individuals who are deaf feel that a community of other people who are deaf and who use sign language is less restrictive than a community of people who hear and who use oral speech. The debate about what has come to be known as the deaf culture has not been resolved.

The first article in this unit deals with the pros and cons of inclusion in general education classes for students with visual disabilities. In this informative article the author argues that special schools or special classes may be less restrictive for children with severe visual disorders.

The second article is the story of a girl who, blind from infancy, was warmly welcomed into an inclusive classroom. Gathary gave lessons on hope and wonder as she received lessons in academics. Two support staff aides helped her classroom teacher, and some modifications of the classroom were necessary, but the efforts were small compared to the enormous benefits experienced by all.

The unit's third selection is concerned with the education of students who are deaf or hearing impaired. The promise of the authors is that communication and instruction are best enhanced with visually stimulating environments. The article describes how to use visual strategies as graphic organizers of information.

Schools for the Visually Disabled: Dinosaurs or Mainstays?

In an age of inclusion, specialized schools for the visually disabled play an integral part of the continuum of placements offered for students with disabilities.

Michael J. Bina

Schools for blind or visually disabled children have existed in the United States for more than 169 years. Some ask, Why have they survived this long? Has not inclusion made these placement options obsolete? If federal and state laws mandate education in the least restrictive environment, why do local school districts still send children to segregated settings? Are the high per capita costs justifiable? Should not the resources for these schools be redirected to local education agencies to improve services in students' home communities?

These are fair and not uncommon questions asked by the general public, legislators, and even many educators. For answers, we must listen carefully to current students, former students, local school leaders, and parents whose children attend or have attended these schools. Schools

for blind children may seem an outdated service delivery model, but as Jim Durst, principal of the Indiana School for the Blind, recognizes, the educational outcomes of students prove that these placement options are justifiable, legitimate, and critically essential "for some children all of the time and for all children some of the time."

Obsolete and Unnecessary?

The inclusion movement has not eliminated the need for specialized schools for blind children. In fact, to a large extent it has increased the need for specialized services to enable children with visual disabilities to succeed in regular classrooms.

For students with visual disabilities to be meaningfully and successfully included in regular programs and to keep up with their classmates, they must have educational support

services, reading and writing skills, and materials in accessible formats. To expect a child without skills to be successful in a regular education setting without supports would be as ill-advised as immersing a nonswimmer in the deep end of a pool with a sink-or-swim expectation. Although students might survive the experience, they certainly wouldn't enjoy it or thrive to their full potential.

Today, local directors of special education schools refer blind children to schools for the blind to help them thrive rather than just survive—so that they can better integrate themselves into their local schools. Often, these referrals are for short-term placements in the school's on-campus program, summer school enrichment or compensatory skill training, or consultative outreach services that support children remaining in their local districts.

In 1900, the blindness field was the first disability group to integrate or mainstream students in public schools. Even before the advent of the Education for All Handicapped Children Act, approximately 93 percent of students with visual disabilities were already placed in their local school districts, with 7 percent in specialized schools. Although this ratio has remained the same, many specialized schools report increasing referrals for outreach services and summer and regular on-campus enrollment. The U.S. trend shows not a diminishing need but rather a legitimate placement option in response to the steadily increasing demands from local districts. Schools for the blind are not a substitute for public school programs but are an important complementary option.

Least Restrictive Environment

Educators in local schools are committed to fulfilling the spirit and letter of the federal and state legislation that mandates that all children with disabilities be educated with their nondisabled peers to the maximum extent possible. However, some school districts find its implementation impossible owing to circumstances over which they have no control.

For example, Mr. Adams, a rural area director of special education, has been unable for the past five years to recruit qualified staff to meet the needs of visually disabled students in his district because of a national specialized-teacher shortage. Only 33 U.S. universities offer preservice training programs for teachers of the visually disabled. Unfortunately, these 33 programs graduate fewer than 200 students each year. The demand throughout the United States far outweighs the supply of graduates from each program. This is compounded by the very high yearly attrition rate of specialists. Mr. Adams, therefore, must refer many of his district's visually disabled students to the school for blind children.

In another scenario, Mr. Sands, a director of special education in a large Indiana community, is fortunate to have recruited and retained qualified teachers for visually disabled students. Even though his district has qualified staff, he makes occasional referrals for placements to the school for blind children. He refers students who have difficulty achieving academically in the regular classroom and who need more intensive and individualized instruction than what is locally available. In these cases, the individualized education program team has determined that a school for blind children is the least restrictive environment—or the most productive setting. Many students benefit from immersion in a learning environment where all the staff in every class and dormitory can instruct and reinforce critical blindness-specific skills, such as Braille reading and writing, orientation and mobility (independent travel) and daily-living skills.

Rebecca, a high school sophomore from Mr. Sands's district, attended her first five grades at a school for the blind, returning to her neighborhood school for junior high. Her family, Mr. Sands, and his staff determined that Rebecca would benefit from returning to the school for the blind for at least the first two years of high school. Rebecca, who also attends a nearby local high school part-time, has taken advantage of the school's revolving door policy, in which students can come and go depending on their changing needs. Rebecca's parents and the staff from both schools agree that placement cannot be a one-size-fits-all solution: The question is not which option is best—they both are.

In another situation, Ms. Dare, a director of special education in the state's largest city, utilizes a school for the blind on a daily basis for students in her district who are having difficulty in large school settings. Often, these students can attend both schools, taking academic courses at the school for the blind, for example,

and vocational courses at the local high school. These children can go home every evening, but frequently they stay overnight in the dormitory to take advantage of recreational programs, such as swimming, dances, Boy Scouts or Girl Scouts, or Special Olympics; on- or off-campus jobs; extracurricular competitive sports, such as track and field, swimming, or wrestling; or band, choral, speech, or debate activities.

Real-World Connections

Shawn, who was born blind, has a twin sister who is fully sighted. Although he attended a school for the blind for his entire school career, he was able to have the best of both worlds by attending a nearby local high school part-time. Now an alumnus of the school, Shawn told me,

> I knew when I was in high school that I was getting a good education because I could compare it to what my twin sister was getting from our public school. But until I got to college, I really didn't recognize how very well prepared I was.

Shawn described how the premed students in his fraternity house frequently sought his assistance with English themes, research papers, and math assignments. He knew that his abilities to match subjects with verbs, to organize his thoughts on paper, and to calculate numbers were superior in many cases to his fraternity brothers' abilities. He also felt more mature than his fraternity brothers because of his early dormitory experience dealing with, and adapting to, others.

Shawn's dormitory experience also helped him work independently. When he went home on weekends, he taught his parents, who tended to be overprotective, how he could do things for himself and why they needed to let him. His parents struggled with his living away from home, particularly in the early grades. However, when they saw his progress—his strong "can do" attitude, his confidence, his happiness, and his many friends—they realized that this sacrifice was necessary for his current and future independence and success.

Shawn just earned his college degree and is currently employed as a social worker. He lives in an apartment and does his own cooking, shopping, and other household chores. He travels in the community independently, using skills he learned in orientation and mobility, a related service that was not available in his home school.

Not all students are exactly like Shawn. Blind and developmentally delayed, Megan just graduated from a school for the blind. Unlike Shawn, she will not go to college or live independently in an apartment. But with the assistance of a job coach, she is employed, and she lives in a supervised group home. Megan, too, was not sheltered from "real world" realities or segregated from the community.

Shawn's and Megan's career experiences began in their early grades, and later both had on- and off-campus jobs. Shawn attended the local high school for academic enrichment and social experiences; Megan went off campus to gain experience working in a community adult workshop. Both Shawn and Megan moved from their dormitories into three-bedroom houses while in high school, and both were expected to shop for groceries, prepare food, clean the house, and meet other responsibilities. Shawn lived in one of the school's independent living houses without a live-in supervisor; Megan lived in a semi-independent living program with ongoing staff supervision. Shawn earned a pass to travel off campus independently to any location; Megan went many places in the community with adult supervision. Megan was required to open and maintain a checking account at a local bank where she deposited her check each week and conducted financial transactions.

Both Shawn and Megan also distinguished themselves in extracurricular activities. Shawn was a wrestler, competing with other blind athletes on the national level and with public school opponents in state competitions. He also developed powerful speaking skills, which led to participation in state and national oratory contests, and had challenging roles in school plays. His parents, proud of his extensive involvement, often asked Shawn if he ever had time to sleep! Megan was widely recognized for her singing. Twice she sang the national anthem at the state Special Olympics competition, and she sang in the school's chorus that traveled around the state and country.

The Cost of Value

These are impressive achievements. A state government official, after attending graduation at a school for the blind, commented on how well prepared the graduates appeared and how much progress they had made at the school. A school administrator replied, "Yes, but you are well aware of the criticism our school receives for the high per pupil cost and perceived 'expensiveness.'" The state official responded,

> How can they place a value on what these children were provided, what they have clearly gained, and what we know they are going to accomplish because of our investment in them? Look at the value rather than the cost.

In a similar conversation, Mrs. Botkin, whose teenage son is visually disabled and autistic, said,

> They can either pay now to make my son independent or *he* will pay in the future if he does not get the services he needs. We must decide whether we are going to socialize our children in less expensive programs that do not have all the essential services or we are going to instruct them and make sure they get skills. My son's success is only possible in a program that costs more.

The per capita cost statistics are often misleading. If all the services provided at a school for the blind could be replicated in the local district, the cost per capita would be the same in both settings. However, because blindness is a low-incidence condition and each district does not have large numbers of visually disabled students, the local services would likely be less economical than those in a centralized setting where the ratio of staff to students is higher and therefore the cost is less per pupil.

A colleague employed in a large Illinois public school reported that the per capita costs of students in her district were comparable to the instructional costs at a school for blind children. She indicated that because her district provided comprehensive and intensive full services, costs were higher than those in a local district that provided only the bare essentials, such as an itinerant teacher working with a student only one or two times a month. She defined full services as highly adapted technology; a full complement of specialized itinerant and resource teachers; and such related services as orientation and mobility, physical and occupational therapy, and special transportation. In her district, transportation costs were high because of the need to bus children extensively throughout the large metropolitan area.

Another factor is that the specialized school's costs include not only the educational expenses but also the provisions for food, housing, supervision, utilities, and other expenses over a 24-hour day. These costs are not included in public school expenditure figures. When comparing costs in both settings, we must match services for services. To say that one option with fewer services is less expensive is unfair. The more expensive options provide more services.

But shouldn't the resources be redirected to local education agencies to improve services in students' home communities? This appears to be a logical strategy given the least restrictive language in the law. However, because qualified specialists are typically not available, local districts are not likely to fill all the positions needed and would have to regionalize programs to consolidate services. Therefore, students would still be unable to attend their neighborhood schools, and some students would end up without any services. Specialized services would lose their effectiveness if they were scattered throughout the state. The state would also lose a major resource center and would no longer be able to provide outreach services.

Least Restrictive or Most Productive?

Are schools for the visually disabled dinosaurs on the verge of extinction or credible placements of distinction? Consider the impact that blindness has on learning for such students as Megan and Shawn, the role that specialized schools play in overcoming their potentially devastating disabilities, and the ever-increasing demands for these services from local districts.

All these examples illustrate the value and necessity of providing a continuum of service options when students need alternatives to their local school programs. Schools for visually disabled students are an integral part of this continuum of options. A district may call upon the specialized school when it is unable to recruit specialized staff and provide services locally. Whenever a particular student is not achieving to his or her potential, school leaders can turn to this "more restrictive"—or potentially more productive—setting.

Michael J. Bina is Superintendent of the Indiana School for the Blind, 7725 N. College Ave., Indianapolis, IN 46240 (e-mail: binami@speced.doe.state.in.us).

Seeking the Light:
Welcoming a Visually Impaired Student

Anita Meyer Meinbach

Every once in a while, if you are lucky, you will have a student in your classroom who reaches into your heart, touches your soul, and stays with you a lifetime. Once in a while, if you are lucky, you will have a student whose wisdom and *joie de vivre* are a constant reminder of the choices we have to make every day, the perspectives we choose to take, and how we choose to see the proverbial glass. I was one of the lucky ones—a teacher with a very special student whose determination, outlook, and indomitable spirit provided special lessons in living. Gathary sees the beauty in what is invisible to the eye. She takes delight in everything around her and celebrates life. Her mind is filled with images; her heart is filled with joy. Those of us fortunate enough to know Gathary have gained in countless ways. She has forced us to reassess what we perceive to be our own limitations and has made us aware that each of us is responsible for determining what limits we reach. Gathary is blind, and has been from infancy; but, in a sense, Gathary has opened our eyes by sharing her visions of hope and wonder.

Gathary joined our sixth grade class, a language arts and geography block, in January 1997. For most of us, it was our first opportunity to interact with someone who is blind. While every day did not go smoothly, the journey was worth every bump; and in the end, we all gained in kindness, understanding, and empathy. What follows is based on a conversation that took place at the end of the school year. Gathary, her mother Leslie (an art teacher at our school), Beth Gordon (the visual itinerant teacher), three friends, and I met to discuss many issues that affected Gathary, her classmates, and teachers and to evaluate the ways in which the classroom atmosphere and curriculum met the needs of the visually impaired. As the classroom teacher, I was especially anxious to know what changes and adaptation were most worthwhile and what I might have done differently to contribute to an even more successful experience.

With the growing popularity of inclusion, more and more teachers will be concerned with mainstreaming and its ramifications. Teaching middle school adds to the challenge simply because of the very nature of middle school students who are experiencing dramatic physical, social, and emotional changes. It is sometimes difficult for middle school students, who are coping with their own lives, to empathize and reach out to others. Often, their own lack of confidence and lowered self-esteem cause them to appear heartless and unfeeling. Their need for peer-acceptance makes inclusion not only difficult for the special needs students who so desperately want to fit in, but also for the regular classroom students who desire conformity and wish to find their own place in which to fit.

Since the conversation shed light on many important issues affecting the visually impaired in the mainstreamed setting of a middle school, a synthesis of the responses to specific questions pertinent to teachers are being shared in the hope that it will provide ideas and inspiration for those working with middle school students who face special challenges.

> **Gathary has made wonderful friends this year; and, according to Gathary, these are the first strong friendships she has made with peers who are sighted.**

Issue: Mainstreaming

Question: What considerations were most important in determining whether or not to fully mainstream Gathary into Southwood Middle School?

A close working relationship among the teachers in a school is critical for a blind student. Since Southwood Middle has an extremely close knit faculty, both Gathary's parents and the support staff, provided by Dade County schools, who have worked with Gathary over the years, believed this would be the best setting to allow Gathary to "spread her wings." Gathary was first mainstreamed in the second grade, but it was a more sheltered atmosphere, which was appropriate at the time. For part of the day she was in a class with eight other visually impaired students (K–4), all functioning at different levels. She was only mainstreamed for a short time each day (45 minutes, two times a day). This was not enough time to develop friendships. It also made it hard for her to gain a perspective on peers. This year, except for math class, Gathary has been completely mainstreamed. She has learned how to cope and deal with situations she probably would not confront in a more protective environment. She also has been more challenged academically and has risen to this challenge. Gathary has made wonderful friends this year; and, according to Gathary, these are the first strong friendships she has made with peers who are sighted.

Question: What qualities are most important for teachers with students who have special needs?

Perhaps the most important quality for teachers working with special needs students is attitude. There needs to be a willingness to work with the itinerant vision teacher and other members of the support staff. Teachers working with special students must realize that they are part of a team. While the support staff tries not to pull Gathary out of content area classes, there have been times when this was necessary, and it was important that the classroom teacher make allowances. While every teacher tends to believe that his or her subject is the most important and can not be missed, in reality there are other important skills such as assistive technology and life skills instruction that students like Gathary must master. Therefore, there are times that the training for this must take precedence over subject matter curriculum. The support of mainstream teachers is imperative.

Additionally, because there is a need for special equipment and materials, teachers have to be quite flexible and adapt these materials into lessons. The flip side is also true; sometimes there may not be materials in braille, for example, to support the lesson. The teacher must then attempt to find ways in which the material can best be taught. In science lab, for example, much of the learning is empirical. In Gathary's case, the teacher found ways for Gathary to become involved through the use of senses other than sight.

Finally, teachers of students with special needs must be especially organized and able to plan well in advance. Supplementary materials and resources need to be gathered and there needs to be sufficient time for worksheets, notes, and tests to be transcribed in braille and available in time for the lessons.

Issue: Use of paraprofessionals

Question: Often students with physical disabilities are provided with a paraprofessional. Did Gathary have this option?

In some situations, the use of a paraprofessional is advisable to aid the visually impaired with mobility and assist with classroom adaptations. However, in Gathary's case, her itinerant vision teacher felt it was not necessary. She seems to be functioning well under the guidance of two support staff members who work directly with Gathary and indirectly with the classroom teacher. The two support staff members include Beth, the itinerant vision teacher, and an orientation and mobility (O&M) instructor. Acting as a liaison with her classroom teachers, Beth sees Gathary on a daily basis to provide instruction in the use of her assistive technology compensatory academic skills including Nemeth code (mathematical braille code), social interaction skills, and other life skills. This curriculum is provided to facilitate her full integration into the mainstream classroom environment.

> **At the beginning of each school year, a team meeting is set up with all of Gathary's teachers. The support staff is introduced and suggestions are offered to help the classroom teachers fully integrate her into their class routines.**

Another factor in deciding against the use of a paraprofessional was the fact that Gathary needed to be more independent. Knowing how middle school students are beginning to assert their independence from adults, we were confident that she would have more of an opportunity to make friends without a paraprofessional by her side. Additionally, as Leslie explained, "If there were a paraprofessional, I was concerned that there might not be the direct relationship between student and teacher, but rather between the teacher and paraprofessional." As it was, there were many opportunities to discuss Gathary's progress with support staff and to ask questions and get advice on materials and techniques to help Gathary become successful in learning specific subject matter. Sometimes, we met during a planning period, other times during lunch, or sometimes in the few minutes between classes.

Question: How was Gathary able to maneuver about the school; what special training did she receive?

Before Gathary goes to a new school, she is usually given extensive mobility training. In addition, the O&M

instructor works with Gathary for thirty minutes, two times a week. This instruction is ongoing, throughout the school year, and will be maintained each year she is in mainstreamed situations.

Figure 1

Organizations

American Foundation for the Blind
15 W. 16th St. NY, NY 10011
(212)620-2000 (800)232-5463

American Printing House for the Blind
1839 Frankfort Ave., Louisville, KY 40206
(502)895-2405

Association for Education and Rehabilitation of the Blind and Visually Impaired (AER)
206 N. Washington St., Suite 320
Alexandria, VA 22314-2528 (703)548-1884

Council for Exceptional Children, Division for the Visually Handicapped
1920 Association Dr., Reston, VA 22091 (703)620-3660

Howe Press of the Perkins Schools for the Blind
175 North Beacon St., Watertown, MA 02171
(617)924-3400

Library of Congress National Library Service for the Blind and Physically Handicapped/Talking Book Library
1291 Taylor St., NW, Washington, DC 20542
(202)707-5100 (800)424-9100
www.loc.gov/nls/nls.html

National Braille Press
88 St. Stephen Street, Boston, MA 02115 (800)548-7323

National Federation of the Blind
1800 Johnson St., Baltimore, MD 21230 (410)659-9314
http://www.nfb.org

Recording for the Blind and Dyslexic
20 Roszel Road, Princeton, NJ 08540 (609)452-0606
http://www.rfbd.org/

Seedlings Braille Books for Children
P.O. Box 51924, Livonia, MI 48151-5924 (800)777-8552

Before Gathary would attempt to maneuver the halls of Southwood Middle, the O&M instructor first created a three dimensional layout of the school for Gathary to study. This layout is like a raised map that allowed Gathary to mentally conceptualize the space. The second part

of the instruction involved mobility skills so that Gathary could move about the space safely.

Gathary also learned about sighted guide techniques (how to safely use a sighted person as a guide), how to use auditory clues to maneuver and find her way, and how to use her cane. I selected several students to assist Gathary when she needed help. These students walked to class with Gathary to make sure she arrived safely and Gathary taught them the correct way for guiding her. While this was successful the majority of the time, Gathary often felt the need for more independence. Her guides, however, were afraid to let go, afraid Gathary would fall. Gathary, however, anticipated the falls, knowing they were necessary if she were to become more self-sufficient.

Question: What special training is usually given to teachers?

Generally, at the beginning of each school year, a team meeting is set up with all of Gathary's teachers. At this time, the support staff is introduced and suggestions are offered to help the classroom teachers fully integrate her into their class routines. Additionally, a full day, county-wide inservice is provided in the fall for classroom teachers and administrators to provide more comprehensive curriculum and background information on mainstreaming our visually impaired students.

While it is important that teachers be prepared and trained to work with special needs students, teachers must also be prepared to deal with the attitudes of a classroom of students—each with their own problems who do not always empathize or even attempt to understand the specific needs, problems, or concerns of those around them. If mainstreaming is to be successful, students and teachers must work together as a team.

Gathary came to our school in the middle of the school year, and unfortunately, none of her teachers were given the chance to take advantage of this special training opportunity. However, teachers working with special needs students should be well versed in the exceptionality and explore the different classroom dynamics that may occur as the result of mainstreaming.

Issue: Classroom curriculum and classroom modifications

Questions: What modifications needed to be made in the classroom to accommodate Gathary?

Gathary needed to be seated in a desk that facilitated her entering and leaving the classroom easily. Her work area also needed to be situated close to the shelves in which the braille books were stored so that she could reach them independently.

Because it is important that the visually impaired be able to safely move around the room and feel comfortable doing so, students in the class had to be very aware of where they put their own materials such as bookbags and lunch boxes so that Gathary would not trip over anything. Care was given to ensure that cabinet doors were closed. Special procedures for fire drills and other emergencies had to be established to ensure Gathary's safety and specific students were selected to guide Gathary in the event of an emergency. However, regarding emergencies, some authorities suggest that the blind child "be instructed to take hold of the nearest moving child or adult and quickly and quietly follow others" (Torres & Corn, 1990, p. 25).

The other students resented her going to lunch early and felt that Gathary got special treatment.

Another area of concern is in the use of the restroom. It is extremely important that blind students have someone of the same sex accompany them to the restroom so stalls can be checked to make sure that they are reasonably sanitary and to ensure that no one is hiding in one. Additionally, several students were selected to take turns being Gathary's sighted guide on the way to lunch and other classes. Southwood Middle is two stories high and even for a sighted person the stairways are not always easily maneuvered. Consequently, we allowed Gathary and one other student to leave class five minutes before the bell so that she could get to her next class without having to "fight" the crowds. We also allowed her to leave for lunch a few minutes earlier so that she could get through the line more easily. The other students, however, resented this and felt that Gathary got special treatment. To them, Gathary is lucky—she gets to go to lunch early. "Why should she get special privileges?" they asked. This problem reflects the importance of involving students, especially at the middle school level, in sensitivity training which is paramount to a successful mainstreaming effort.

During a biography unit, we read about Louis Braille. This gave Gathary the springboard for talking about her experiences learning braille.

Another area of modification is in the realm of discipline. Children with special needs must be held accountable to the same code of conduct as the other students in the classroom. I sometimes bent the rules for Gathary and this actually was a tremendous disservice to her. It angered the other students who tended to see issues only in

black and white, not shades of gray. This characteristic of the middle school students leads to their strong sense of justice and they were incapable of understanding why I would allow Gathary to do something they were not allowed to do.

Finally, as with all students, special students need positive feedback and acknowledgment that they have done a good job. It is important that the teacher remember that non-verbal communication—a smile, body language, etc. needs to be transformed for the visually impaired into a pat on the back or a quiet, "Good job."

Question: What modifications needed to be made in the curriculum to accommodate Gathary?

Opportunities for tactual and auditory learning need to be considered. In some cases, for example, Gathary was "walked" through an activity area to get a feeling for the environment before the class participated in a specific activity. It is also important to provide concrete experiences and suggest ways that parents can supplement these at home.

Curriculum should include issues that related to the visually handicapped. For example, during a biography unit, we read about Louis Braille. This gave Gathary the springboard for talking about her experiences learning braille. It is, however, important to remember that these modifications to the curriculum be subtle.

During class, I involve students in a great deal of oral reading, writing, discussion, and cooperative learning. Gathary was not only able to take part in these, but students were consistently amazed at her fluency in reading braille. I did find that I minimized my use of the chalkboard and overhead transparencies, although there were times I needed to use these to illustrate a point or to model writing. If teachers find, however, that the modifications for a specific activity are so great that they significantly change the focus or objective of the activity, than perhaps a parallel activity designed for the special needs student should be considered. While the goal of mainstreaming is to make adaptations so that all students can be involved, this may occasionally prove difficult. In some content areas, for some lessons, alternative teaching methods should be considered.

Specific materials for the visually impaired can help advance the lessons. Special measurement tools are available to teach math skills such as braille clocks and rulers. Special maps with raised borders can be ordered to augment geography lessons. A variety of trade books and text books are available on audio tape as well as in braille (see Figure 1). When our class read specific literary works, Gathary not only had a copy of the book in braille, but also listened to the words read aloud on auditory tapes. The best lessons, I discovered, included the use of both braille text and audio tapes. The braille allows the student to better understand the structure of language and revisit certain sections.

According to Beth, "The most successful of the blind are those who have been readers of braille." Many textbooks are available in braille but usually have to be ordered well in advance, in June if possible. We are able to get most of our textbooks on loan from the Florida Instructional Materials Center.

The key, as with working with any student, is to find and encourage the strengths and talents that will allow the student to "shine" in any type of learning environment.

In order to make communication between the classroom teachers and the support staff more efficient, a special mailbox in the teacher's workroom was set aside. Any worksheets, class notes, tests, or other instructional materials that needed to be written in braille were placed in this box. Beth then either transcribed the material herself, or if time allowed, sent the material to a transcriber in the county office. The transcribed braille worksheets were placed in another specially labeled box and a note was placed in our mailbox to advise us that the material was ready. The mailbox also afforded us an opportunity to ask questions, present concerns, and make special requests for help.

Question: How was Gathary provided with specific information that could not be put into braille?

This question was at the heart of my biggest concern when I learned Gathary was joining our class. It is not uncommon for me, as I am sure it is for most teachers, to change my lesson plans at the last minute. When it was impossible to have the material I needed for a revised lesson transcribed into braille, Gathary worked with another student who read the material aloud. Often, Gathary took a copy of the material home so that she could "reread" it with her family. Each week, for example, our class received a copy of a special current events magazine. Students took turns describing different pictures and features in the magazine and others read articles aloud. When videos were shown, a student was selected to sit next to Gathary and quietly describe what Gathary could not see. I realized that not only was this helpful to Gathary, but it was also extremely beneficial to the other students because they became aware of the power of words to bring pictures to life and create mental images. In their own way, they enabled Gathary to "see." Descriptive videos are available in which a narrator describes much of the action. Companies such as Descriptive Video Service (DVS) provide narration for certain shows that air on public television as well as commercially produced vid-

eos. The videos are excellent and rich in language and vocabulary. They are also the perfect tool for training students in this type of narration.

Question: What group configurations worked best?

While Gathary worked well independently, she seemed to truly enjoy working in a cooperative group. Gathary brought many talents to group settings. Her group project on the pyramids of Egypt resulted in the creation of a video in which Gathary used her ear for languages and accents to play the part of an English archaeologist. On a mythology project, she and her team created a mythological crossword puzzle using special tiles with raised letters that could be felt. Having her work with others in her group not only helped them create unique products but also allowed other members of the group to know Gathary in a new context. This, in turn, led to tremendous social growth and friendships.

The key, as with working with any student, is to find and encourage the strengths and talents that will allow the student to "shine" in any type of learning environment. As students such as Gathary become acknowledged for their abilities, they become more confident, more secure of their place in the classroom, more accepted, and more accepting.

Issue: Technology equipment

Question: What special equipment is needed to help the visually impaired progress successfully?

One of the biggest concerns facing a parent of a special needs student in the mainstreamed environment is that their child be able to compete academically in the classroom. In addition, Gathary's parents were especially determined that Gathary "not be a burden to the classroom teacher." As a consequence, Gathary's parents made every effort to equip Gathary with special equipment that would enable her to function more independently and more efficiently in the classroom. Some of the equipment was provided by the county but certain other devices were purchased by her parents. Gathary uses a Braille Lite which is a computerized braille note taker. It is quite small and easy to manipulate. Her Braille Lite fits into her book bag and takes up little room on her desk. It has many of the features of a computer which allow her to edit her work and then print it on a printer or emboss it for her own use. Additionally, it has a raised braille display so that Gathary can tactually read what she has typed in. Before she received her Braille Lite, everything Gathary brailled had to be transcribed. Now, she can plug the Braille Lite into a regular printer and a printed copy is generated for the sighted teacher. As a result, she is much less dependent on a sighted transcriber to complete assignments. This equipment enabled Gathary to take almost the same exams and tests as did her classmates, typing the answers into her Braille Lite and then printing them so they could be graded. Once in a while, certain questions were eliminated from a test when it was not possible to create an appropriate tactual equivalent. For example, some questions used maps and graphs which could not easily be transcribed into braille.

Question: Did the special equipment needed ever present a problem?

The students in the class were naturally very curious about the equipment and wanted to experiment with it. Since Gathary's equipment allows her to function more self-sufficiently and experience added success and independence, she is extremely protective of her things. During the year, she was quite apprehensive that something would be broken and, in a sense, cut her connection to the visual world—a very frightening and real possibility. As a result, it is vital that students be taught to understand the importance of these devices and how they assist Gathary. When Gathary first entered Southwood, Beth Gordon came to the classroom and, with Gathary's assistance, demonstrated the use of each piece of equipment. Students were especially impressed with the fluency with which Gathary read braille when they could not even "feel" the raised dots. However, while a majority of students understood the need to respect Gathary's equipment, there was still a handful of students, who despite the repeated demonstrations and explanations, continued to "tease" Gathary by touching her equipment—another reminder of the importance of sensitivity training. Others continued to touch the equipment out of curiosity. "The challenge," as Leslie aptly put it, "is to make the equipment interesting to others but, at the same time, make sure they understand its importance to Gathary and learn to respect it."

Question: What equipment is most important for the visually impaired to have in the classroom?

There were two different perspectives in regard to this question. According to Gathary," As far as academics are concerned, the computer (Braille Lite) is most important to me. As far as mobility, my cane is the most important." Beth, however says that, "Actually, it's not the equipment but rather the braille proficiency and listening skills that our visually impaired students have learned that allow them to be successful in the classroom. However, the braille note takers have certainly enhanced our students' abilities to be competitive with their mainstream peers."

Issue: Socialization

Question: In terms of friendships, what has Gathary experienced at Southwood?

When asked this question, Gathary's face lights up—and so does her mom's! "I've made great friends—for the first time!" Gathary explained. Her mom added, "This is the first time Gathary has fostered strong friendships with sighted peers. It's the first time she's been to 'sleepovers' at someone's home other than a relative." On Mondays, Gathary would come to class regaling us with all the new and wonderful experiences she had had over the weekend with her friends.

Question: From the first time you met Gathary, how has your impression changed?

It did not take any of us long to change any preconceptions we might have had about the blind. We soon realized that Gathary is much more like the other students than she is different. We began to see her simply as someone who must do some things a bit differently. Her friends both responded similarly, saying," We see her as a person, just like us. She just doesn't have the ability to see. She uses her hands to read."

However, while mainstreaming has taken away the veil of mystery surrounding the blind, it has changed Gathary's perception of herself. Leslie explained, "For the first time in her life, Gathary is beginning to realize that she doesn't have something others have." Yet, she is dealing with this and makes the most of the gifts she does have—a lesson all of us need to learn.

Question: While Gathary made many friends at Southwood, she also seemed to have difficulty with some students. What problems occurred and what do you think could be done to improve the situation?

"Sometimes students poked me and screamed in my ear. They frightened me," Gathary explained. One of her friends responded to this, "being blind is hard. I wish they could understand what it's like. I get frustrated seeing others tease her. It almost makes me cry inside."

I am terribly troubled when I reflect on the way in which some of my students treated Gathary. While so many were kind, caring, and went out of their way to help Gathary whenever possible, there were others who went out of their way to inflict added pain. I found that just talking to students about this issue was not always sufficient. Many could not see beyond their own problems and did not have the capacity to empathize. "Most who tease Gathary," Leslie acknowledged, "never gave much thought to what it would be like to suddenly approach a person who is in darkness."

Leslie, however, expressed optimism in terms of our ability to affect the way in which students react to one another, "I think sensitivity can be developed—maybe not to the same level in each person, however. People need to become sensitive not only to the challenges a blind person must face, but also sensitive to the issue of how hard a blind person must work to make accomplishments appear effortless." Again, the need for sensitivity training is evident.

Figure 2

Print Resources for Teachers

Hazekamp, J. and Huebner, K.M. (Eds.). (1989). *Program planning and evaluation for the blind and visually impaired students: National guidelines for educational excellence.* New York: American Foundation for the Blind.

Mangold, S.S. (Ed.). (1982). *A teacher's guide to the special educational needs of blind and visually handicapped children.* New York: American Foundation for the Blind.

Torres, I. and Corn, A.L. (1990). *When you have a visually handicapped child in your classroom: Suggestions for teachers.* New York: American Foundation for the Blind.

Unfortunately, as mentioned earlier, because Gathary entered our school in the middle of the year, our students did not receive any type of sensitivity training. "In the past though," Beth explained, "we had a workshop for teachers and put devices on their eyes to simulate different eye problems. This was very successful and helped teachers gain an appreciation for what visually impaired students experience. I believe this type of simulation could benefit not only teachers but students as well. However, because of the seriousness of this exercise, students should be exposed to the situations in small group counseling situations with a counselor to follow up the simulation with discussion that allows students to freely discuss their experience and how it will determine or affect their behavior.

Question: Why is it important that students with disabilities be in the regular classroom?

We have all seen tremendous growth in Gathary not only academically but socially. As Leslie explained, "I know how much better she's doing and how much more 'normal' she's acting in social situations outside of school. This is critical so that she can function in the world as an adult. The things she's grappling with now are things all of us deal with. Frustrations are part of the growth pattern."

Being in this school and being successful have given Gathary the confidence she needs to deal with new situations. Students with disabilities need to have the opportunities to interact with all kinds of children. This promotes their social and emotional growth and affords the other students an opportunity to see how proficient students with disabilities can be.

However, mainstreaming does not just benefit the special needs student. It benefits us all, as the responses to the final questions suggest. Because of the nature of these questions, I would like the reader to "hear" the answers just as they were spoken—from the heart:

Question: How has knowing Gathary changed you?

Lauren: I think I've become a better person. She helps me know how to treat all people better.

Amanda F: She's taught me that I can help others and she's shown me how. I respect what Gathary does for herself and I have also become more sensitive.

Amanda A: Having her as a friend makes me look at life from a different point of view. I learned what it means to have a true friend, how to treat friends, and what it's like to be blind. Knowing Gathary has made me respect people more, those with other problems, not just the blind.

Question: In 10 years, where do you see Gathary?

Beth: I can't wait to see where Gathary is in years to come. I see her as a journalist, traveling the world. She has a zest for life, an ability with languages, and she has a way with people and with words.

Leslie: I anticipate she'll have a full education and travel. I see opportunities for her to use her love for different cultures, especially the Hispanic culture. She becomes completely absorbed in every culture she is introduced to.

Gathary: I would like to be a translator. I want to speak to people in their language

Question: What is one word that best describes Gathary?

Lauren R and Amanda F: Amazing
Amanda A: *So* amazing there's no word
Anita: Joyful
Beth: A gift

A Final Note

The 1997–98 school year was one of tremendous growth and awareness of the various considerations and adaptations that must be addressed to insure successful mainstreaming of the visually impaired in the middle school. But beyond that, and far more critical, is the way Gathary helped illuminate that which is important. From her we all gained a deeper appreciation for life, and a sense that "nothing is impossible." These were the lessons Gathary taught us—her gifts to those lucky enough to embrace them. As teachers we must remember that all our students are gifts. We must remember to nurture their dreams and encourage their visions for tomorrow. And if we are smart, the lessons we learn from students such as Gathary will become part of us as we consistently seek the light of understanding.

Anita Meyer Meinbach is a teacher at Southwood Middle School, Miami, Florida.

Originally appeared in the November 1999 issue of *Middle School Journal*, pp. 10-17. © 1999 by the National Middle School Association. Reprinted by permission.

Visual Teaching Strategies for Students Who Are Deaf or Hard of Hearing

John Luckner • Sandra Bowen •Kathy Carter

How do we enhance communication and instruction with students who are deaf or hard of hearing? Many educators and researchers suggest that we establish visually rich learning environments. In such environments, teachers would use the following instructional aids:

- Sign, fingerspelling, and speech reading.
- Equipment such as overhead projectors, bulletin boards, computers, and televisions.
- Materials including pictures, illustrations, artifacts, slides, computer graphics, and films with captions.

Why use these methods and materials? Given the auditory limitations that accompany a hearing loss, most students who are deaf are primarily visual learners (e.g., Nover & Andrews, 1998; Reeves, Wollenhaupt & Caccamise, 1995). Lane, Hoffmeister, and Bahan (1996) used the term "visual people" to describe the deaf population (p. 116).

In recent years, we have witnessed a strong push for greater use of sign and American Sign Language (ASL) features in educational settings (e.g., Mahshie, 1995). Though using sign for communication and instruction has many benefits for students, signing, like speech, provides a *transient* signal. The signal moves—it is there, and then it is gone. Consequently, we need to find more visual strategies to help students focus on important information, see how concepts are connected, and integrate prior knowledge with new knowledge.

PEOPLE WHO ARE DEAF OR HARD OF HEARING ARE "VISUAL PEOPLE."

This article describes some general visual teaching strategies, discusses how to develop and use graphic organizers, provides a sample unit and lesson using graphic organizers, and furnishes many examples of visual materials to use with *all* students.

VARIETY IS IMPORTANT: USE WRITTEN WORDS, LINE DRAWING PICTURES, DETAILED DRAWINGS, COMPUTER-GENERATED PICTURES, PHOTOGRAPHS, PHOTOCOPIED PICTURES, CUTOUTS FROM MAGAZINES, ACTUAL LABELS AND WRAPPERS, SIGNS AND LOGOS, AND COUPONS AND REAL OBJECTS.

General Visual Teaching Techniques

We have found it essential to adapt learning environments and use teaching strategies that help students maximize their learning time—essential, that is, if we want students who are deaf or hard of hearing to succeed in school. Here are some general suggestions for choosing visual materials (Hodgdon, 1995):

- Choose visuals students will easily recognize.
- Use larger-size pictures or photographs (5 x 7 or 8 x 10 inches) with younger students.
- Use a variety of visual materials, including written words, line drawing pictures, detailed drawings, computer-generated pictures, photographs, photocopied pictures, cutouts from magazines, actual labels and wrappers, signs and logos, and coupons and real objects.

Combinations of words and some form of graphics is usually the best choice. Learn to draw simple pictures yourself—uncomplicated shapes and stick figures can be helpful.

Table 1: Examples of Web Sites and Addresses with Valuable Visual Information	
Site Name	**Address**
National Geographic	http://www.nationalgeographic.com
The Smithsonian Institute	http://www.si.edu
The History Channel	http://www.historychannel.com
Nova Online	http://www.pbs.org/wgbh/nova
American Museum of Natural History	http://www.amnh.org
Windows to the Universe	http://www.windows.umich.edu
Archiving Early America	http://www.earlyamerica.com
Britannica Online	http://www.eb.com
Science A Gogo	http://www.scienceagogo.com
How Stuff Works	http://www.howstuffworks.com
National Air and Space Museum	http://www.nasm.si.edu

Examples of visual aids that teachers can use in the classroom to enhance the communication and learning process include the use of a classroom rules chart, job and choice menus, transition time cards and charts, task organizers, daily schedules, and the Internet.

Classroom Rules Chart

An important element of effective classroom management is establishing, teaching, and enforcing classroom rules. Rules that are posted and referred to often help students function in the complex social and emotional environment of the classroom and provide a framework for the teacher to reinforce appropriate behaviors. You can develop a chart with classroom rules, and pictures, photographs, or clip art can accompany the written rules on the chart to help students learn to manage themselves more independently. Whenever possible, students should assist in developing the rules. Examples of rules for elementary age students might include:

- Always try your best.
- Raise your hand when you need help.
- Keep your work and work area neat.
- Respect one another.
- Pay attention when others are communicating.

Job and Choice Menus

Involve students in the daily chores of making a classroom an organized and comfortable environment for learning and socializing. For the teacher, student participation reduces the number of tasks that you need to complete each day. Students experience personal responsibility, decision making, and contributing to a common cause. Classroom jobs can be posted with words and pictures or photographs, and the person responsible for completing the task can be rotated on a daily or weekly basis. Choice menus can be established using words, photographs, pictures, or logos for things such as the areas of the room to work in, who to work or play with, activities to do when work is finished, enrichment activities to be completed, or books that can be read related to the unit of study.

Transition Time Cards/Charts

Transition time refers to the time it takes to change from one activity to another. You and your students can develop a set of cards or a chart with the specific tasks that need to be accomplished during transition times. Use written words and accompanying pictures or photographs. Examples include: Put your materials away, get your lunch, line up, and walk to the cafeteria quietly.

Task Organizers

Some students experience difficulty completing an activity or job because they are distracted easily or they can't remember the order of steps needed for completion. Such students would benefit from a set of pictures in a pocket-size photo album or a chart that lists all the steps to be done with accompanying pictures or photographs. Examples include listing the steps for starting the computer, completing a science experiment, reader and writer workshops, or taking care of a class pet.

Daily Schedules

The daily schedule can be used as a guide for structuring the classroom environment, as well as a way to stimulate conversation and language development. Hodgdon (1995) suggested the following steps for creating and using a daily schedule:

- Divide the day into segments reflecting the major activities of the day.
- Give each segment a name that you will refer to consistently.
- Choose a representation system, such as words and pictures or words and photographs, that will be understood easily.
- Determine what the schedule will look like—size and location—and whether it will be a chart, written on the blackboard, or photocopied and given to students individually.
- Decide how the students will use the schedule at the beginning of the day.

Table 2. Creation and Use of Graphic Organizers

Created by	When Created	Purpose of Creation
Teacher	Before students read the materials in the textbook	To preview reading material, assess prior knowledge, and to provide an advanced organizer for content.
Teacher	After students have read the material in the textbook	To review the reading material, highlighting key points from the chapter. To use as a review or for assessment.
Teacher and students	During reading of the material	To highlight main ideas. To provide assistance for difficult reading passages or concepts.
Teacher and students	After students have read the material in the textbook.	To assess comprehension and to outline key points. To use as a review or for assessment.
Students	After students have read the material in the textbook.	To enhance or assess reading comprehension and content information or to review for an examination.

- Decide how the schedule will be referred to throughout the day.
- Establish ways to use the schedule to communicate with other professionals and family members.

The Internet

The technology of the World Wide Web (WWW) can be used to access an enormous electronic library of pictures, photographs, graphics, and videos. These resources can be integrated across the curriculum to help develop background knowledge, to provide specific examples, or to develop media-rich lessons. Table 1 lists examples of Web sites that have valuable visual information.

Using Graphic Organizers

Visual representations of knowledge are referred to by a variety of names including semantic maps, webs, semantic organizers, story maps, or Venn diagrams. We use the general term *graphic organizers* to refer to representations used to assist in making organizational patterns of text visual (Bromley, Irwin-DeVitis, & Modlo, 1995). When used with students, graphic organizers provide a framework to make thought and organization processes visible (Tarquin & Walker, 1997). This framework provides a foundation for learning by linking background knowledge with the major concepts and facts of new learning.

A TEACHER AND STUDENTS CAN USE DIALOGUE AND GRAPHIC ORGANIZERS TO REVIEW TEXT MATERIAL.

Graphic organizers allow teachers to omit extraneous information while emphasizing important concepts and demonstrating their connection to each other. This visual representation of information is easier for students to remember than extended text (Bromley et al., 1995; Dye, 2000). Most important, the use of graphic organizers allows

students to be actively involved in the processes of listening, speaking, signing, reading, writing, and thinking. And, as Table 2 summarizes, teachers can create graphic organizers and use them in a variety of ways. A valuable software program that can be used for developing graphic organizers has been created by Inspiration Software, Inc. They allow you to try the software for a 30-day trial period by accessing their Web site: http://www.inspiration.com.

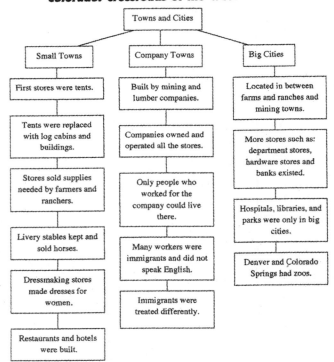

Figure 1. Example of a Hierarchical Graphic Organizer from *Colorado: Crossroads of the West*

Figure 2. Example of a Conceptual Graphic Organizer from the First Chapter of *Bridge to Terabithia*

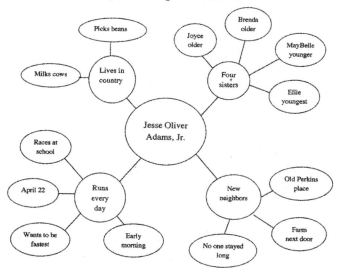

Figure 4. Example of a Cyclical Graphic Organizer from *Biology: An Everyday Experience*

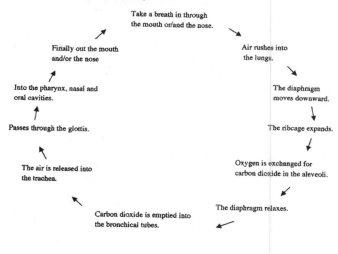

The following are examples of four basic patterns of graphic organizers, identify by Bromley et al. (1995). Each graphic organizer can be simplified or made more complex by deleting or adding "branches." This flexibility allows students with different levels of knowledge and skill to participate in the same activity.

Hierarchical Patterns

If information includes a main concept and subconcepts, you can organize it in a linear manner, using a hierarchical pattern. Figure 1 shows a hierarchical pattern that provides an outline of the material found in a chapter from *Colorado: Crossroads of the West* (Downey & Metcalf, 1999, Chapter 11, pp. 161–178). This chapter describes the history of towns and cities in the state of Colorado.

Conceptual Patterns

If information has a central idea, category, or class with supporting facts such as characteristics, examples, or descriptors, you can use a conceptual pattern. Figure 2 shows the use of a complex conceptual pattern to organize the events that occurred in Chapter 1 of the book *A Bridge to Terabithia* (Paterson, 1977). This chapter centers around the main character, Jesse Oliver Adams, Jr., and his family.

Sequential Patterns

Displaying the chronological order of events, particularly those having a specific beginning and an end, can be done by using a sequential pattern. The most common sequential pattern is a timeline. These patterns also can be used to

Figure 3. Example of a Sequential Graphic Organizer Using the Events of *The Very Hungry Caterpillar*

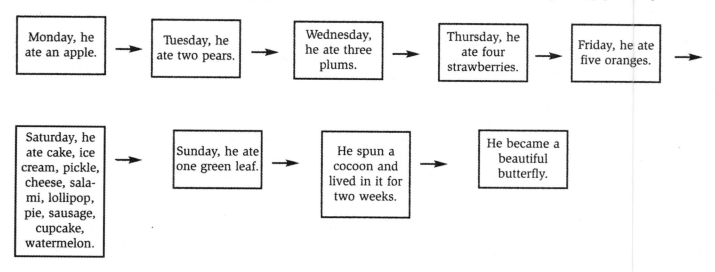

Figure 6. Example of a Lesson for Teaching with a Graphic Organizer

Create graphic organizer (Figure 5) with the students as they answer questions and discuss economy, from the chapter in the book.

Teacher (T): Yesterday we read section 2 from the social studies book. Let's review what you read. (Call on individual students to review main topics and ideas from the reading.)

Student (S): Slavery.

T: Yes. What is slavery?

S: When white people owned black people to help them work on their farms.

T: What were the large farms called?

S: Plantations.

T: Were the plantations important to the southern colonies?

S: Yes

T: Why?

S: That's how they earned money.

T: That's right. The term used to discuss how people earn money to live in an area is called the economy. Let's write a definition for economy on the map. (Write economy and a definition on the map. Definition: The way people use resources to make a living).

T: Great. Let's take a look at the plantations in the southern colonies and figure out why the plantation owners needed slaves. You have already mentioned that farming and plantations as part of the southern colonies so let's add that to the map too. (Write in farming and plantations.) What was special about the land of the southern colonies that helped the economy?

S: The soil was good for growing crops.

T: That's right. The southern colonies were able to grow specific crops that the other regions of the states could not grow. One of the reasons was the soil. What was another reason they could grow the crops?

S: The warm weather.

T: Exactly. What crops did they grow?

S: Tobacco and rice. (List the crops on the map as the students mention them.)

T: Yes, anything else?

S: I remember the book also talked about something used in blue jeans.

T: That's correct. The plantation owners also grew a plant used for blue dye. Who remembers what that plant is called?

S: Indigo.

T: Do manufactures still use indigo to dye your blue jeans?

S: No, today they use chemicals.

T: All right, so we have listed tobacco, rice, and indigo. Tell me about growing rice? What is required to grow rice?

S: The rice was grown in the swamps. So they had to drain the swamps and build dikes, before they could plant. Then the rice had to be irrigated and harvested.

T: Good explanation! So why did the plantation owners need slaves?

S: The plantation owners wanted slaves who knew how to grow rice because they had grown rice in Africa before they were brought to America.

T: What did rice have to do with the economy in the southern colonies?

S: They sold rice to other colonies.

T: That's right! They sold or exported the rice to the other colonies. Growing the crops was important to the economy because the southern colonies exported their crops to other colonies. Was it easy to grow rice in the southern colonies?

S: No, it was hard work. That's why they wanted the slaves to do it.

T: The hard work was one of the reasons the plantation owners wanted slaves to help them. As the plantations grew, more slaves were needed to complete all the work. What do you remember from the reading was another reason slaves were needed to grow rice?

T: Another important factor that relates to the economy and to the plantations is trade. (Add trade to the map.) How did they send the crops out and bring the slaves in?

S: By boat.

T: Exactly. Let's look at the map in your book on page 133. Notice all the rivers and waterways which ran through the southern colonies. Why were these rivers the key to the success of the southern economy?

S: They could export the crops and bring in the slaves on boats.

T: Right. Crops were exported and slaves were imported. Let's write a definition for these two terms: export and import. (Write the words and the definitions on the map.)

T: How do exports and imports influence an economy?

S: (Accept all reasonable answers)

T: What resources or products does the United States export now?

S: (Accept all reasonable answers)

T: What resources or products does the United States import now?

S: (Accept all reasonable answers)

T: What do you think would have happened in the southern colonies if they would not have had slaves?

S: (Accept all reasonable answers)

T: Today we have discussed the economy of the southern colonies. Looking at our map, we see there were two important aspects of the economy: farming and trade. The warm climate and the rich soil grew a variety of crops, which generally could not be grown in the other colonies. These farms were called plantations. The plantation owners made a living growing and selling the crops. However, as their plantations became larger, they needed help to work on the plantations. That is the main reason slaves were brought into the southern colonies. The vast waterways of the southern colonies made it relatively easy to transport resources and people. So crops were exported and slaves were imported, and the southern economy grew. Are there questions or comments?

S: Respond to all questions and comments.

T: Today we have discussed the economy of the southern colonies and talked about the importance of slaves to that economy. Tomorrow we will look at the culture of the southern colonies and discuss plantation owners' treatment of slaves.

represent cause/effect, process/product, or problem/solution-type situations. Figure 3 shows a simple sequential pattern used to identify the specific events that happen to the caterpillar in *The Very Hungry Caterpillar* (Carle, 1969). The caterpillar spends 1 week eating more and more food until finally he becomes a fat caterpillar and builds a cocoon. By ordering each event, a student can easily understand the process of how a caterpillar transforms into a beautiful butterfly.

Cyclical Patterns

You can use a circular formation to display a series of events that occur within a process. There is no beginning or end, just a continuous sequence of events. Figure 4 shows a cyclical pattern that could be used to summarize the cycle of respiration that has been presented in *Biology: An Everyday Experience* (Kaskel, Hummer, & Daniel, 1992, Chapter 13, pp. 267–277).

Figure 5. Graphic Organizer of *America's Past and Promise* Created with Students

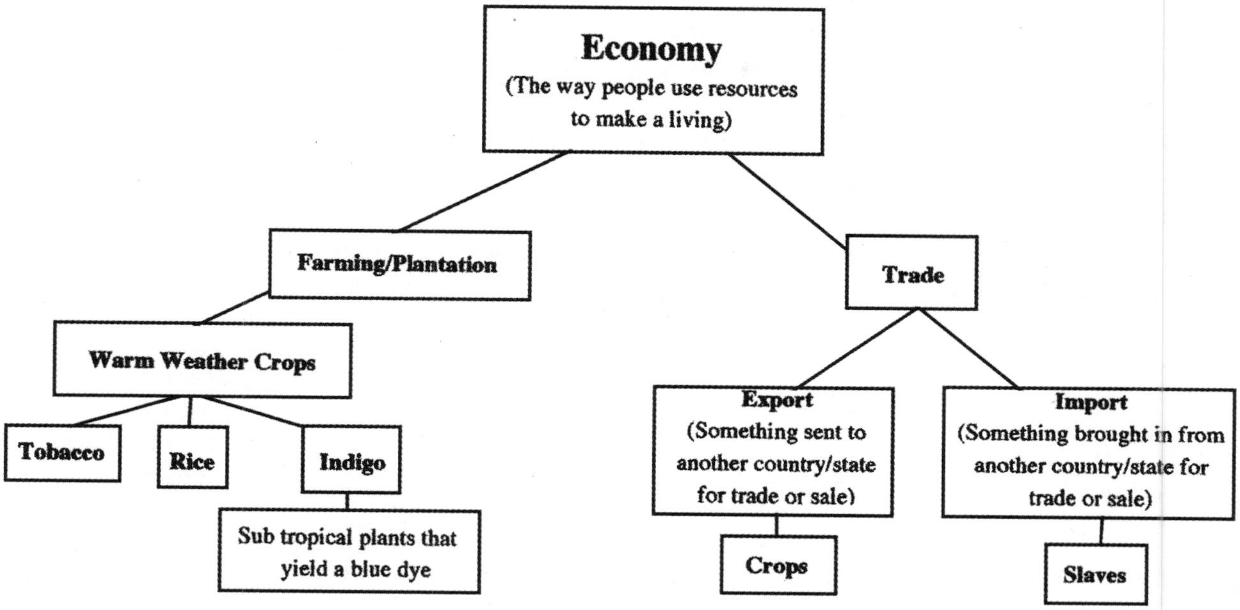

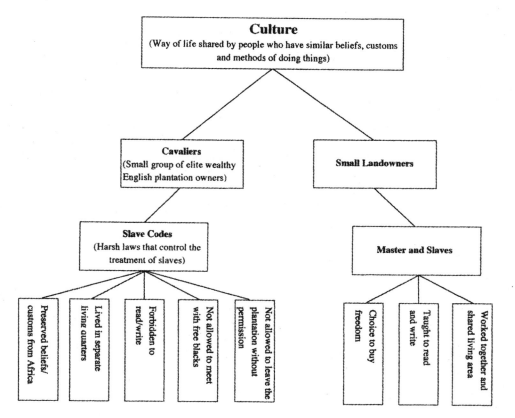

Figure 7. An Explicit Graphic Organizer Created by Teacher and Students of Materials from *America's Past and Present*

Sample Unit and Lesson Using A Graphic Organizer

Here we have provided an outline of a sample unit of study that uses a variety of graphic organizers. We prepared this unit for middle school students, Grades 6–8. We took the content material for this unit from *America's Past and Promise* (Mason, Garcia, Powell, & Risinger, 1998, Unit 1, Chapter 7, Section 2, pp. 132–135). The main concepts discussed in this section are the economy and culture of the southern colonies of the United States. The teacher and students will create the graphic organizer, shown in Figure 5, after the students have read the assigned section. Figure 6 provides an example of the dialogue that may occur as the teacher and students create the graphic organizer.

VISUAL AIDS INCLUDE CLASSROOM RULES CHART, JOB AND CHOICE MENUS, TRANSITION TIME CARDS AND CHARTS, TASKS ORGANIZERS DAILY SCHEDULES, AND THE INTERNET.

Figures 5 and 6 show how a teacher and students can use dialogue and graphic organizers to review text material. The graphic organizer shown in Figure 7 may also be created in a similar manner.

Final Thoughts

Teaching students how to access the information provided on visual supports can improve student participation and understanding, as well as prepare them to better use the visual supports found in our daily lives, such as packages, menus, logos, maps, and assembly instructions. In addition, teachers and students can use visual strategies to illustrate the organization of ideas and information and provide background information for topics of study or discussion. Visual teaching strategies provide nontransient signals that can be used for prereading, postreading, writing, content subjects, assessment, improving social interactions, and behavior management. These strategies build on the strengths of students who are deaf or hard of hearing.

References

Bromley, K., Irwin-DeVitis, K., & Modlo, M. (1995). *Graphic organizers: Visual strategies for active learning.* New York: Scholastic Professional Books.

Carle, E. (1969). *The very hungry caterpillar.* New York: Philomel Books.

Downey, M. T., & Metcalf, F. D. (1999). *Colorado: Crossroads of the West* (3rd ed.). Boulder, CO: Pruett.

Dye, G. A. (2000). Graphic organizers to the rescue: Helping students link—and remember—information. *TEACHING Exceptional Children, 32*(3), 72–76.

Hodgdon, L. (1995). *Visual strategies for improving communication. Vol. 1. Practical support for school and home.* Troy, MI: Quirk Roberts.

Kaskel, A., Hummer, P. J., & Daniel L. (1992). *Biology: An everyday experience.* Lake Forest, IL: Glencoe.

Lane, H., Hoffmeister, R., & Bahan, B. (1996). *A journey into the deaf-world.* San Diego, CA: Dawn Sign Press.

Mahshie, S. N. (1995). *Educating deaf children bilingually.* Washington, DC: Gallaudet University Pre-College Programs.

Mason, L. C., Garcia, J., Powell, F., & Risinger, C. F. (1998). *America's past and promise.* Evanston, IL: McDougal and Littell.

Nover, S. M., & Andrews, J. F. (1998). *Critical pedagogy in deaf education: Bilingual methodology and staff development.* Santa Fe: New Mexico School for the Deaf.

Paterson, K. (1977). *A Bridge to Terabithia.* New York: Harper Trophy.

Reeves, J. B., Wollenhaupt, P., & Caccamise, F. (1995). *Deaf students as visual learners: Power for improving literacy and communication.* Paper presented at the International Congress on Education of the Deaf, Tel Aviv, Israel. (ERIC Document Reproduction Service No. ED 390 209)

Tarquin, P., & Walker, S. (1997). *Creating success in the classroom: Visual organizers and how to use them.* Englewood, CO: Teacher Ideas Press

John Luckner (CEC Chapter #381), Professor; **Sandra** Bowen (CEC Chapter #382), Assistant Professor; and **Kathy Carter**, Doctoral Student, Division of Special Education, University of Northern Colorado, Greeley.

UNIT 8
Multiple Disabilities

Unit Selections

Key Points to Consider

- Can paraeducators make a difference in the education of students with multiple disabilities? How can paraeducators be taught specialized skills quickly?

- How many people benefit from a high school peer tutoring program? Who are they? Why do each of them reap benefits?

- Can teachers access state-of-the-art technology to assist in their education of students with multiple disabilities? How?

 **Links: www.dushkin.com/online/**
These sites are annotated in the World Wide Web pages.

Activity Ideas for Students With Severe, Profound, or Multiple Disabilities
http://www.palaestra.com/featurestory.html

For most of the twentieth century, children with multiple disabilities (MD) were kept hidden in their parents' homes or put into institutions. Any father or mother presenting such a child at a public school for admission was ridiculed and turned away. The Individuals with Disabilities Education Act (IDEA) in the United States has turned this around. Such children may now be enrolled in general education classes if that is appropriate. They are entitled to a free education in the least restrictive environment that serves their needs. IDEA, in its 25 years of existence, has allowed millions of students, who once would have been written off as "uneducable," to be given some form of schooling.

A child placed in the category of multiple disabilities may have cognitive developmental disabilities, and/or speech and language impairments, and/or autism, and/or traumatic brain injuries, and/or emotional and behavioral disorders, and/or visual impairments, and/or hearing impairments, orthopedic impairments, health impairments, or any combinations of these. While a child with multiple disabilities (MD) does not need to be disabled in every category set forth by the IDEA in order to be so labeled, each child with MD is very special and very needy. Most of them have more than two co-occurring areas of exceptionality. The practice of deinstitutionalization (removing individuals from hospitals and large residential institutions and keeping them in their own homes), and the legal initiatives requiring free and appropriate public education in the least restrictive environment, has closed some of the cracks through which these children once fell. However, the needs of many children with multiple disabilities are not yet being adequately met.

The success of IDEA (bringing children with MD out of their hidden abodes and into the light of our consciousness), has been counterbalanced by the failure of schools to adequately educate children with MD. Their school dropout rate is unjustifiably high. Some of the reasons for the educational mismanagement of children with MD are shortages of qualified special educators, underfunding of programs, lack of knowledge about which methods and materials would work best for each individual child, frustration with accountability, reams of paperwork, less than perfect assessment tools, and a general resistance to implementing the provisions of the IDEA.

One of the problems that looms largest in the collection of enigmas that hinder appropriate education for children with MD is lack of acceptance and preparation by the school system for their inclusion. Advocates for the rights of disabled individuals have used the term "handicapism" to describe a similar prejudice and discrimination directed at disabled students. The greater the disability, the greater the evinced prejudice. A disability (not able) does not translate the same as a handicap (hindrance, not at an advantage). The words should not be used interchangeably. A person who is not able to do something (walk, see, hear) has a disability but does not have to be handicapped. Schools impose handicaps (hindrances) by preventing the student with the disability from functioning in an alternative way. Thus, if a student who cannot walk can instead locomote in a wheelchair, he or she is not handicapped. However, if a building or classroom has no ramps, and is inaccessible to a wheelchair user, then the school has imposed a handicap by preventing access to that particular property of the environment. There are millions of ways in which properties of our school environments and characteristics of our behavior prevent children with multiple disabilities from functioning up to their potentialities.

Public schools have resisted the regular education initiative (REI) that calls for general education classes rather than special education classes to be primarily responsible for the education of students with more severe and multiple disabilities. The inclusive school movement, which supports the REI, would have special education teachers become consultants, resource specialists, collaborative teachers, or itinerant teachers rather than full-time special education teachers. While arguments for and against the REI have not been resolved, most educators agree that an appropriate education for each child with a disability may require a continuum of services. Some children, especially those with multiple disabilities, may require an environment more restrictive than a general education classroom in which to have the types of assistance they need to function up to their potentialities. Teacher education typically does not offer comprehensive preparation for working with children with MD who require extensive special educational services. In addition, children with MD often require related services (for example, chemotherapy, physical therapy, psychotherapy, transportation) to enable them to learn in a classroom environment.

Many children and youth with MD suffer from a lack of understanding, a lack of empathy, and handicapist attitudes that are directed at them. They present very special problems that few teachers are equipped to solve. Often the message they hear is, "Just go away." The challenge of writing an appropriate individualized education plan (IEP) is enormous. Updating the IEP each year and preparing an individualized transition plan (ITP), which will allow the student with MD to function as independently as possible after age 21, is mandated by law. These students must be served. Excuses such as no time, no money, and no personnel to provide appropriate services are unacceptable.

The first article in unit 8 suggests that paraeducators can play a very important role in giving one-on-one services to students with MD in inclusive education settings. A major need is to provide inservice training for paraeducators. This selection describes a one-day workshop that gives paraeducators an overview of effective methods of teaching adaptive skills to students with MD.

The second article of the unit reports on the unexpected benefits of high school peer tutoring. The authors describe a peer tutoring program that has achieved phenomenal success in Danville, Kentucky, since its initiation in 1983. They describe how to set up a program and how to evaluate its usefulness, citing research that documents its effectiveness as a learning tool and as a social tool.

The unit's final article discusses the uses of new technology to construct alternate portfolios for students with multiple disabilities. Four students with physical, cognitive, and behavioral characteristics of disability, none of whom could learn on a standard computer, were taught to use the assistive Intellikeys instead. They had a smorgasbord of other technological aides and customized Intellikeys overlays. All four students showed increased achievement and independence.

Article 23

Training Basic Teaching Skills to Paraeducators of Students with Severe Disabilities

A One-Day Program

Lakeisha beams at the teacher as she demonstrates her new skills at setting the table with plates, cups, forks, an napkins.

The new paraeducator can't wait to report that he successfully taught Jon to put on his coat independently.

Finally conquering the copy machine at her workplace, Susan proudly delivered 30 copies of the newsletter to her co-workers.

Marsha B. Parsons
Dennis H. Reid

Since the early 1970s, a technology for teaching students with severe disabilities has been evolving. Research behind the development of this teaching technology has indicated that the strategies for teaching students with severe disabilities are somewhat different from strategies used with students who have mild or moderate disabilities. Whereas the latter students may benefit substantially from teaching strategies based on verbal instruction, students with severe disabilities often require more individual instruction, using a high degree of physical guidance.

This article shows that when teachers and other staff members proficiently use physical guidance in conjunction with other teaching strategies, such as task analysis, prompting, reinforcement, and error correction, students with severe disabilities can learn useful skills (Parsons, Reid, & Green, 1993). And paraeducators can

quickly learn to assist students with their learning.

The role of paraeducators is becoming even more important as greater numbers of students with severe disabilities receive their education in inclusive settings.

Paraeducators in Inclusive Settings

The valuable role paraeducators can play in teaching students with severe disabilities is currently well recognized and is becoming even more important as greater

numbers of students with severe disabilities receive their education in inclusive settings. Whereas special education teachers often learn appropriate teaching strategies during their preservice training, paraeducators rarely have specific preservice training in how to use the teaching strategies that constitute "best practice" for these students. Hence, a major need in special education is to provide inservice training for paraeducators in effective methods of teaching adaptive skills to students with severe disabilities.

TSTP is efficient because the program can be conducted in one 8-hour workday.

149

Characteristics of Successful Staff Training Programs

Research has delineated four characteristics of successful staff training programs (Reid, Parsons, & Green, 1989). Each of these characteristics is particularly relevant in selecting a program for training paraeducators to teach students with severe disabilities.

1. Training focuses on *performance-based skills:* The training emphasizes what staff *do* when teaching their students. Although many programs provide interesting and *potentially* useful knowledge regarding teaching processes, such programs rarely train staff specifically how to apply the knowledge in actual teaching situations. How well paraeducators translate knowledge about the teaching process into the action of teaching directly affects the quality of education students receive.

2. Training is conducted *efficiently:* When paraeducators attend training away from the students' classrooms, schools and districts often must hire substitute personnel to assist with instruction, as well as with other essential routines, such as transportation and lunch. For school systems to have the resources to maintain well-trained paraeducators, cost factors must be contained by providing staff training as quickly as possible.

3. Training must be *effective:* In one sense, declaring that staff training should be effective seems to be asserting the obvious. School systems, however, frequently invest large sums of money in a staff training program with little, if any, verification of the program's effectiveness. Educators must examine the effectiveness of a training program from two perspectives:

- The program should result in staff mastery of the skills taught by the program. Staff should not complete the training until they achieve a criterion of satisfactory, hands-on teaching performance.
- The program is truly effective only if students learn when staff use their newly acquired teaching skills.

4. For long-term success of staff training programs, the training must be *acceptable* to staff. When staff dislike the training process, they are less willing to be involved in the training. Staff's negative reactions to training also result in unpleasantness for the staff trainer, which can cause the individual charged with staff training duties to become reluctant to conduct the training.

Teaching-Skills Training Program

We developed the Teaching-Skills Training Program (TSTP) to ensure that human service personnel are adequately prepared to teach people with severe disabilities. We conducted research over a 5-year period to meet each of four criteria for successful staff training (see box, "Characteristics of Successful Staff Training Programs"; Jensen, Parsons, & Reid, 1997; Parsons et al., 1993; Parsons, Reid, & Green, 1996; Reid & Parsons, 1996).

In initial research conducted to validate the program's effectiveness, we taught 9 direct-support staff and 4 supervisors in a residential program for people with severe disabilities to apply basic teaching strategies, with at least 80% proficiency (Parsons et al., 1993). In subsequent research, we trained 24 staff members, including group home personnel, paraeducators, and undergraduate teaching interns, to teach with 80% proficiency using TSTP (Parsons et al., 1996). Acceptability research has indicated that staff respond favorably to the training procedures (Parsons et al., 1993; Reid & Parsons, 1996). Finally, TSTP is efficient because the program can be conducted in one 8-hour workday (Parsons et al., 1996).

Since the initial validation research, educators have used TSTP to successfully train more than 300 paraeducators and other support personnel. Equally important, students with severe disabilities have made progress toward acquiring adaptive skills when their paraeducators have used the skills they learned during the program (Parsons et al., 1993).

To illustrate, graduates of TSTP have taught children with severe disabilities in an inclusive preschool program the following skills:

- Wash hands.
- Recognize numbers and letters of the alphabet.
- Operate a cassette player.
- Eat with a spoon.
- Respond to one-step directions.

In a school classroom for students with severe multiple disabilities, other graduates have taught students the following skills:

- Drink from a cup.
- Press a switch to activate a radio or TV.
- Use augmentative communication devices.

Other graduates have used the teaching strategies developed through TSTP to teach job skills to adults with severe disabilities—at the workplace.

Figure 1. Sample Activity Illustrating the Rationale for Using Task Analyses

Why Is a Task Analysis Important When Teaching a New Skill?

1. If you were asked to teach someone to prepare a place setting incorporating a plate, cup, napkin, knife, fork, and spoon, draw the placement of the items on a placemat. Assume that the placemat is already on the table in the appropriate place.

2. Compare what you have drawn to the drawings of others in the group. How many place settings among the group were exactly like yours?

3. Draw a place setting following the task analysis provided by the instructor.

4. Compare what you have drawn by following the task analysis to the drawings of others in the group. How many place settings were exactly like yours?

Task Analysis for Place Setting

1. Place the plate in the center of the placemat.
2. Place the napkin directly beside and to the left of the plate.
3. Place the fork on the napkin.
4. Place the knife directly beside and to the right of the plate.
5. Place the spoon directly beside and to the right of the knife.
6. Place the cup directly above the tip of the knife.

Teaching Skills

TSTP focuses on four basic teaching competencies: task analysis, least-to-most assistive prompting, reinforcement, and error correction.

Types of prompts range from mild forms of assistance, such as gesturing to the student, to more directive prompts, such as physically guiding the student through a skill.

Task Analysis

We teach staff that to use task analysis, they should list each specific behavior in performing a targeted skill sequentially, in the order the behavior should occur for the skill to be performed correctly. They teach the kinds of behavior, or steps, in the order specified in the task analysis to facilitate learning so that each step becomes a signal for the performance of each subsequent step in the task analysis. Figure 1 illustrates a task analysis for teaching students how to set a table for lunch or dinner.

Using the Least-to-Most Assistive Prompting Strategy

When teaching a student to put on her coat, the first step of the task analysis is to pick up the coat. If the student does not pick up the coat independently, the paraeducator might begin by saying to the student, "Pick up your coat."

If the verbal prompt does not result in the student's picking up the coat, the paraeducator might tell her to pick up the coat while simultaneously pointing to the coat.

Subsequently, if the combined verbal and gestural prompt as just described does not evoke the student's picking up the coat, the paraeducator might tell the student to pick up the coat while guiding her hand toward the coat (verbal and partial physical prompts).

Least-to-Most Assistive Prompting

Providing assistance on a continuum of least-to-most prompting involves giving a student only the assistance necessary to correctly complete each step of the task analysis. Types of prompts range from mild forms of assistance, such as gesturing to the student, to more directive prompts, such as physically guiding the student through a skill.

We teach staff that if the level of assistance they provide at first does not enable the student to correctly complete a step in the task analysis, they should gradually increase assistance—level of prompting—until the student successfully performs the step (see box, "Using the Least-to-Most Assistive Prompting Strategy").

Reinforcement and Error Correction

The third and fourth teaching competencies work together. *Reinforcement* is the means by which a paraeducator can increase the likelihood across successive teaching sessions that a student will perform the skill that the paraeducator is attempting to teach. We teach staff that a reinforcing consequence is more than a reward or provision of a preferred item. A consequence provided in the context of a teaching program can be regarded as a reinforcer only if student performance of the skill improves over time. Hence, one of the most important skills of paraeducators who teach people with severe disabilities is determining what constitutes reinforcement for a given student, and effectively providing that reinforcement to encourage student learning. Praise and attention are effective reinforcers for many students. Also, engaging in preferred activities following teaching sessions can function as a reinforcer.

TSTP focuses on four basic teaching competencies: task analysis, least-to-most assistive prompting, reinforcement, and error correction

---

When a student incorrectly performs a step within a skill, a staff member must deal with the *error* in a manner that promotes student learning. In essence, errors are opportunities for students to practice the wrong way of completing a skill and should be prevented whenever possible.

We teach paraeducators to prevent errors by increasing the assistance provided on a given step when they see that the student is about to make an error. When the staff member cannot prevent an error, he or she immediately stops the student and has the student repeat the step of the task while providing enough assistance to prevent the error from occurring a second time. For example, when a student who is learning to use a copier loads the paper incorrectly, the paraeducator should stop the student, remove the paper, and provide more assistance so that the student loads the paper a second time with no mistake.

Training Format

For paraeducators in our program, we use a training format consisting of classroom-based instruction, on-the-job monitoring and feedback, and follow-up supervision.

Classroom-Based Component

The primary purpose of the classroom-based training is to familiarize paraeducators with the *rationale* for each teaching competency (task analysis, prompting, and so forth) and the terminology used in describing the teaching process.

For example, using the activity shown in Figure 1, we show the rationale for using a *task analysis* to ensure that staff members teach students a skill in a consistent way. When several staff trainees draw a place setting without the task analysis, almost invariably the placement of cups, plates, and other items will differ across the staff trainees. Thus, if each trainee were teaching a student the task, the task would differ each time it was taught, so that a student with severe disabilities would find it difficult to learn to perform the task. If all trainees follow the task analysis when drawing the place setting, however, the completed drawings should look the same.

A second purpose of the classroom-based training is to begin training staff in the *performance skills* necessary to teach students with severe disabilities by having trainees practice the skills in a role-play situation. We limit the group size of classroom-based training to six trainees. Working with a small group allows the instructor sufficient time for the instruction, observation, and feedback necessary to ensure that each trainee acquires the teaching competencies.

During classroom-based training, we teach prospective paraeducators the skills of task analysis, prompting, reinforcement, and error correction, one at a time. We provide a rationale for using each skill to teach people with severe disabilities, and we demonstrate both correct and incorrect applications of each skill. Trainees practice and receive feedback about their performance from the instructor until each trainee can perform each respective teaching skill proficiently in a role-play situation (see box, "Modeling, Practice, and Feedback").

On-the-Job Monitoring and Feedback

The primary purpose of on-the-job monitoring and feedback is to ensure that trainees can apply the teaching skills learned during the classroom-based component in an actual teaching situation with their students. The instructor observes the trainee's teaching in the classroom and provides feedback regarding the trainee's application of the teaching skills. Through monitoring, the instructor determines the trainee's proficiency in applying each of the teaching competencies.

Modeling, Practice, and Feedback

Instructor demonstration of a teaching skill, followed by trainee practice of the skill with subsequent feedback from the instructor, is the most important aspect of classroom-based training.

Modeling. When training paraeducators how to use a least-to-most assistive prompting strategy, the instructor first demonstrates a prompting sequence in a teaching program with a staff trainee who plays the role of a student.

Practice. Each trainee practices implementing the prompting strategy, with another trainee playing the role of the student.

Feedback. After the trainee practices the prompting strategy, the instructor provides the paraeducator feedback regarding the accuracy of his or her prompting.

Using an Observation Form. To facilitate the instructor's job in this respect, we use the form shown in Figure 2, in conjunction with the criteria listed in Table 1. The form in Figure 2 guides the instructor in focusing on whether or not the trainee performs each of the teaching skills proficiently.

To use the observation form, the observing instructor lists steps of the task analysis (e.g., steps for setting a table) in the appropriate order along the left side of the form. As illustrated in Figure 2, the observer scores each teaching skill under the column labeled for the respective skill on the line corresponding to the designated step of the task analysis. The observer scores each performed skill as being either correct (+) or incorrect (-). Nonapplicable (NA) is scored if there is no opportunity to perform one of the teaching skills for a given step of the task analysis. Table 1 shows the specific criteria for scoring a teaching skill as correct.

In small groups, para-educators role-play effective teaching strategies.

Providing Feedback. Following observation of the student-teaching session, the instructor provides the trainee with feedback by explaining the teaching skills that were correctly and incorrectly performed. For those teaching skills that the trainee performed incorrectly, the instructor describes or demonstrates how the skill should have been performed.

The trainee's teaching proficiency is calculated by dividing the total number of *correctly* implemented teaching skills across all program steps by the *total* number of all skills taught, and multiplying by 100%. This calculation results in a percentage of correct teaching skill application, as illustrated in Figure 2. We consider a staff trainee *proficient* when he or she scores at least 80% correct during two separate observations of student teaching.

Follow-up Supervision

We designed the final component of TSTP, follow-up supervision, to ensure that paraeducators maintain their teaching skills at the 80% proficiency level. Establishing maintenance procedures is essential for the long-term success of staff training programs (Reid et al., 1989, Chapter 4). This part of the program, of course, lasts longer than 1 day!

Follow-up supervision entails implementing a schedule for continued observation of staff teaching and provision of feedback. The frequency of follow-up sessions is determined by how proficiently a given paraeducator continues to teach—the more proficient the teaching skills, the less frequently observations with feedback are needed, and vice versa.

Role of Special Education Teachers and Administrators

We have successfully implemented TSTP using two different staff training models: direct training and pyramid training.

Direct Training

A model that works well in settings where fewer than 10 staff require training involves having one instructor directly train all staff. The instructor is responsible for the classroom-based training, on-the-job observations, and follow-up supervision for all staff in a school or agency. The instructor may be a principal, supervising teacher, or educational consultant—essentially, anyone with experience using the teaching strategies, observing staff performance, and providing feedback. The *Teaching-Skills Training Program Instructor's Manual*, available from the authors, serves as a guide in implementing the program (Reid & Parsons, 1994).

Pyramid Training

In school systems where a large number of staff require training, other researchers have successfully used the *pyramid* staff training model (Demchak & Browder, 1990). Using the pyramidal model, one instructor initially trains all *supervising teachers*, who, in turn, directly train the paraeducators whom they supervise. The type of training teachers should receive is twofold:

- Teachers may need to complete TSTP to ensure that the teachers themselves are proficient in the skills they will be training to paraeducators.

- Teachers should be trained in the supervisory skills of systematically observing the teaching skills of others and providing feedback to improve the teaching process. This focused supervisory training for teachers is often essential to the successful training of paraeducators because, although teachers are expected to supervise paraeducators, few teachers have had training in effective strategies for supervision.

Figure 2. Sample of a Completed Form for Observing Teaching Proficiency

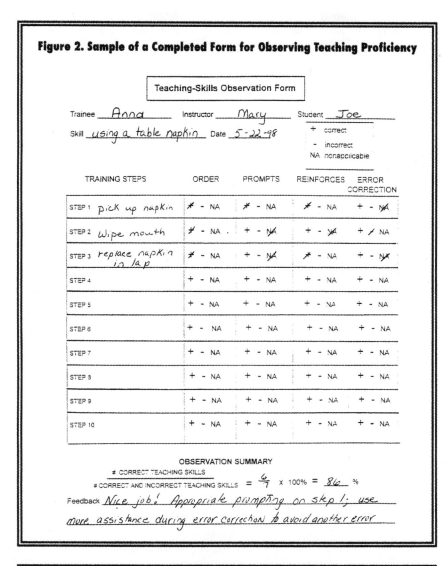

Table 1. Definitions for Correct Application of the Basic Teaching Skills

Teaching Skill	Definition for Correct Application
Order	The steps of the task analysis are taught in sequence so that each step taught is preceded by the specific step listed in the task analysis.
Prompt	Each successive prompt (if more than 1 prompt is used) provided for a given step in the task analysis involves more assistance than the previous prompt.
Reinforcement	A positive consequence is provided following the last correct step of the task analysis and is not provided following any incorrectly performed step. Reinforcement could be provided following any correctly performed step but must be provided following the last correctly performed step.
Error Correction	When the student incorrectly performs a step of the task analysis (i.e., a behavior incompatible with the step), the student is required to repeat the step; and a more assistive prompt is provided on the second trial. The prompt on the second trial should provide sufficient assistance so the student completes the step without another error.

Focused supervisory training (in observation and feedback methods) for teachers contributes to the successful training of paraeducators

Supervisory training for teachers should include practice in observing another staff member teach, completing the observation form, and giving feedback in a role-play situation. A protocol for teachers to use as a guide for giving diagnostic feedback is presented in Figure 3. Once a teacher is competent in observing and providing feedback in a role-play situation, the instructor observes the teacher on the job as the teacher observes the paraeducator conduct a teaching session. When the teacher can provide accurate feedback to the paraeducator regarding the latter's teaching skills, then the teacher independently observes and provides feedback to the paraeducator several times each week until the paraeducator can perform the basic teaching skills.

Research has indicated that when teachers complete TSTP, as well as the additional supervisory training, they can train paraeducators to implement the basic teaching skills through observation and feedback in the classroom and *without the paraeducators participating in the classroom-based component* (Jensen et al., 1997). Moreover, these researchers found that the supervisory training improved the teacher's *own teaching skills* when those skills were below the 80% proficiency criterion prior to training. The supervising teacher provides follow-up supervision for paraeducators through intermittent observations and feedback.

Figure 3 shows a checklist that supervising teachers can use to guide their feedback sessions. This form actually constitutes a "task analysis" for providing feedback, beginning with setting a positive tone and ending with making a positive statement.

Figure 3. Protocol for Giving Diagnostic Feedback to a Staff Member Following the Observation of a Teaching Session

Supervisor's Feedback Checklist

Staff Trainee ____________ **Student** ____________ **Skill** ____________

Supervisor __________ **Location** __________ **Time** _____ **Date** _____

Feedback Components

Check each component included in your feedback to the trainee. Check NA (nonapplicable) for components 4 and 5 if no teaching errors were made.

	Yes	No	NA
1. Set a positive tone for feedback session			
2. Began diagnostic feedback with positive feedback			
3. Gave appropriate positive feedback.			
4. Identified each skill category with teaching errors			
5. For each category with teaching errors, described how the teaching skill should have been performed correctly			
6. Solicited questions for feedback from trainee			
7. Referenced current training status			
8. Ended feedback session with a positive statement			

Student and Parent Input

The highly effective teaching strategies espoused by the Teaching-Skills Training Program require brief teaching sessions involving one student at a time. Individual instruction, however, is only one component of a quality educational experience for students with severe disabilities. Students and family members should have significant input into which skills warrant teaching in this manner and how much time should be directed to individual teaching services versus other valuable educational supports.

When individualized teaching, embedded within the daily routine, is deemed necessary, the TSTP provides paraeducators with the requisite teaching skills to improve student achievement.

References

Demchak, M., & Browder, D. M. (1990). An evaluation of the pyramid model of staff training in group homes for adults with severe handicaps. *Education and Training in Mental Retardation, 25*, 150–163.

Jensen, J. E., Parsons, M. B., & Reid, D. H. (1997). *Multiple effects of training teachers to improve the data recording of teacher aides*. Manuscript submitted for publication.

Parsons, M. B., Reid, D. H., & Green, C. W. (1993). Preparing direct service staff to teach people with severe disabilities: A comprehensive evaluation of an effective and acceptable training program. *Behavioral Residential Treatment, 8, 163–185.*

Parsons, M. B., Reid, D. H., & Green, C. W. (1996). Training basic teaching skills to community and institutional support staff for people with severe disabilities: A one-day program. *Research In Developmental Disabilities, 17*, 467–485.

Reid, D. H., & Parsons, M. B. (1994). *Training to teach in a day: The teaching skills training program instructor's manual.* Morganton, NC: Carolina Behavior Analysis and Support Center, Ltd.

Reid, D. H., & Parsons, M. B. (1996). A comparison of staff acceptability of immediate versus delayed verbal feedback in staff training. *Journal of Organizational Behavior Management, 16*(2), 35–48.

Reid, D. H., Parsons, M. B., & Green, C. W. (1989). *Staff management in human services: Behavioral research and application.* Springfield, IL: Charles C Thomas.

Marsha B. Parsons, *Associate Director, Carolina Behavior Analysis and Support Center, Ltd., Morganton, North Carolina.* **Dennis H. Reid**, *Associate Professor, Louisiana State University Medical Center, New Orleans.*

Address correspondence to Marsha B. Parsons, Carolina Behavior Analysis and Support Center, Ltd., P.O. Box 425, Morganton, NC 28680.

From *Teaching Exceptional Children*, March/April 1999, pp. 48-54.

The Unexpected Benefits of High School Peer Tutoring

Amy Wildman Longwill
Harold L. Kleinert

Flexible scheduling, course credits, and alternative assessments are some characteristics of an innovative peer tutoring program in Danville, Kentucky. And students with disabilities, who receive the tutoring, are not the only beneficiaries.

This article describes how high school peer tutoring programs can enhance educational outcomes, including increased academic performance, for students both with and without moderate and severe disabilities. Moreover, we describe how peer tutoring programs can play an important role for all participants as high schools increasingly undergo fundamental educational restructuring. Finally, we note how peer tutoring programs can promote greater levels of general education class participation and community inclusion for students with significant disabilities.

Fundamental Changes in High School Programs

Over the past decade, significant changes in best practices have oc-curred at the high school level in both general and special education services for students with moderate and severe disabilities. In general education, restructuring has resulted in the following strategies:

Interdisciplinary projects
Block scheduling
Alternate portfolios
Reciprocal teaching and learning
Course credit for peer tutoring
Student-produced adaptations
Cooperative learning
Natural supports
Community links
Developing career interests
Genuine friendships

- *Block scheduling*, for example, students attending four classes per semester, with each class lasting 90 minutes instead of 60, to allow for greater in-depth exploration of specific topics.
- *Increased interdisciplinary learning opportunities*, for example, an ecol-ogy assignment in which students are required to integrate writing, mathematics, and biology skills into a single, applied project on recycling and its impact on pollution in their own community.
- *Performance-based assessment*, in which students are evaluated more by the solutions they develop to address actual problems rather than the knowledge they can feed back on more traditional pen-and-pencil tests (Brandt, 1992; Falvey, Gage, & Eshilian, 1995).

Best practices for high-school age students with moderate and severe disabilities have likewise undergone a significant shift during this time. Following a renewed focus on essential life outcomes (Hardman, McDonnell, & Welch, 1997) teachers have placed greater emphasis on the development of social interaction skills, genuine friendships, and support networks for students with significant disabilities at the high school level, and the importance of learning *along with* (and not always *from*) their peers without disabilities (Coots,

Bishop, Grenot-Scheyer, & Falvey, 1995; Giangreco, Cloninger, & Iverson, 1993). Moreover, reflected in the newly enacted 1997 Amendments to the Individuals with Disabilities Education Act (IDEA) is the requirement that the learning results of students with significant disabilities be included in general state and district student assessment measures—that these students' educational outcomes are a part of school accountability, too.

These fundamental changes in school practice at the national level have had their counterpart in Kentucky. As a result of the Kentucky Education Reform Act of 1990 (KERA), educators have established a set of 57 learner outcomes, or academic expectations. These outcomes are meant for *all* students, including students with moderate and severe disabilities. Thus *all* students, including those with severe disabilities, take part in the state's performance-based assessment and accountability system (Steffy, 1993; Ysseldyke, Thurlow, & Shriner, 1992). While students with and without *mild* disabilities are collecting their best work for their required math and writing accountability portfolios, students with *moderate and severe* cognitive disabilities are participating in the state's assessment system through the Alternate Portfolio (Kleinert, Kearns, & Kennedy, 1997).

High school peer tutoring programs can enhance educational outcomes, including increased academic performance, for students both with and without moderate and severe disabilities.

Finally, these national and state reforms have had a significant impact at the local level. For example, Danville, Kentucky, High School (DHS) incorporated block schedul-

ing for all students at the start of the 1995–96 school year. To emphasize a more interdisciplinary curricular approach, the principal implemented a school-wide policy that students must complete one entry for their required writing portfolio from *every* class, including electives. At the same time, students with moderate and severe disabilities had begun developing their own Alternate Portfolios, as an integral part of the school's score in Kentucky's mandatory assessment and accountability system.

All these changes—for students with moderate and severe disabilities and for general education students—have prompted educators in Kentucky to take a new look at high school peer tutoring. Specifically, we needed to ask how peer tutoring can focus on these essential outcomes for all students, with activities designed so that students are learning with and from each other.

Peer Tutoring in Danville

Peer tutoring is not a new program at Danville High. In fact, peer tutoring, as a formal credit elective, originated in Kentucky at DHS in 1983. As was typical in many such programs, peer tutoring at DHS was initially set up to provide social interactions between students with and without disabilities. Students without disabilities enrolled in peer tutoring to receive academic course credit. The course required students to complete a series of self-study modules in such areas as beliefs and attitudes, legal rights of people with disabilities, educational programming needs, and family issues; take multiple choice type tests on their readings; and do class projects (Guiltinan & Kleinert, 1987; Kleinert et al., 1991). Students also received grades for their daily work and their interactions with the students with moderate and severe disabilities for whom they acted as tutors. The instructors hoped that, from these more formally structured interactions, friendships would develop

(and, sometimes, real friendships did occur).

With the emergence of both general and special education reforms, however, it was time to make changes in peer tutoring, as well. What has evolved at DHS is a series of activities and assignments that allow peer tutors to learn about issues of concern to people with disabilities, to learn with students with disabilities as they work on projects together, and to develop deeper insights into the nature of human relationships and social policy (e.g., inclusion, full community participation). These activities have allowed peer tutors to develop an awareness of significant life issues and to develop their own opinions and beliefs about these issues. (See box "Setting Up a Peer Tutoring Program.")

What the Research Says About Peer Tutoring

Extensive research on peer tutoring can be viewed in three categories:

- Peer tutoring is a well-recognized strategy for increasing instructional effectiveness in programs for students with moderate and severe cognitive disabilities and enhancing interactions with peers without disabilities (Haring, 1991; Haring, Breen, Pitts-Conway, Lee, & Gaylord-Ross, 1987; Helmstetter, Peck, & Giangreco, 1994; Salisbury, Gallucci, Palombaro, & Peck, 1995; Sprague & McDonnell, 1984; Thousand & Villa, 1990).
- Peer tutoring offers many benefits to students both with and without disabilities, as well as to their parents and teachers (see Figure 1), as noted extensively throughout the literature.
- Much of the research has focused on social and educational outcomes for the *tutee* (Helmstetter, Peck, & Giangreco, 1994; Kishi & Meyer, 1994).

Some of the peer tutor topics for both reading and writing assign-

Figure 1
Benefits of Peer Tutoring

For Students with Moderate and Severe Disabilities:
- Opportunities for sustained, positive interactions and friendships (Haring, 1991; Stainback, Stainback, & Wilkinson, 1992)
- Increased opportunities to practice needed skills (Sprague & McDonnell, 1984)
- Age-appropriate role models (Kleinert, Guiltinan, & Farmer, 1991)
- Development of prosocial behaviors and communication skills (Staub & Hunt, 1993)
- Promotion of equity among students and the discovery of hidden strengths of students with significant disabilities (Salisbury, Gallucci, Palombaro, & Peck, 1995)

For Peers without Disabilities:
- Increased acceptance of individual differences (Helmstetter, Peck, & Giangreco, 1994)
- A deeper sense of social justice and advocacy for others (Falvey, Gage, & Eshilian, 1995)
- Increased self-esteem and knowledge of self (Peck, Donaldson, & Pezzoli, 1990; Helmstetter et al., 1994)
- Better understanding of how to communicate with and provide assistance to people with moderate and severe disabilities (Clayton, 1993; Staub & Hunt, 1993)

For Special Education Teachers:
- Increased instructional time for students in school and community settings (Sprague & McDonnell, 1984)
- More age-appropriate expectations for their students (Kleinert et al., 1991)
- Opportunities to become more personally and professionally integrated into the school's general education programs (Clayton, 1993)

For Parents of Students with Moderate and Severe Disabilities:
- Increased skill gains for their son or daughter
- Enhanced opportunities for the development of friendships for their son or daughter (Kleinert et al., 1991)

For Parents of General Education Students:
- An interest in pursuing a career in the helping professions on the part of their son or daughter
- Increased enthusiasm for school on the part of their son or daughter (Kleinert et al., 1991)

ments have included the desirability, benefits, and potential drawbacks of including students with severe disabilities in general education classes at the high school level; opportunities for peer tutors to develop their *own* strategies for adapting and modifying general education class activities to meet the needs of a student with a moderate or severe disability; the meaning and importance of friendships in all of our lives; and the pros (or cons) of the Americans with Disabilities Act as an instrument of social justice and basic human rights. The new peer tutoring assignments relate closely to the academic expectations that have been identified for all Kentucky students (Steffy, 1993). For example, here are two of these outcomes:

- Students recognize issues of justice, equality, responsibility, choice, and freedom, and apply these democratic principles to real-life situations.
- Students use critical thinking skills in a variety of situations that will be encountered in life.

Each activity requires peer tutors to develop a written product, usually from a reading assignment and always from a writing prompt. Students are required to relate the topics to their own experiences and to their activities in peer tutoring; they are graded on both the quality and logic of their ideas, as well as the clarity of their writing.

Indeed, one of the most valuable aspects of peer tutoring in Kentucky today is that peer tutors are often providing assistance to students with moderate and severe disabilities in the development of Alternate Portfolio entries, while the students without disabilities are simultaneously able to complete requirements for their *own* portfolios. Peer tutoring has thus evolved more into a context of learning *together*, helping one another and supporting each other's efforts. Such a context provides a more fertile ground for the development of genuine friendships, and lessens the potentially negative impact of peer tutors seeing themselves as extensions of the teacher, as

opposed to participating as true learning partners of students with significant disabilities (Kleinert, 1996).

For example, all students at DHS are required to take a Writing Workshop Class as a part of developing their school accountability portfolios. Together, peer tutors and students with significant disabilities work on their "Letters to the Reviewer" (a state requirement for both general writing portfolios and Alternate Portfolios). They also work together to compile their own Table of Contents, design their own Cover Page, and assemble their portfolio entries. For a student with a significant disability whose primary mode of communication is a picture communication system, a peer may help that student to develop a written description of what the student has communicated through pictures.

For many of the same reasons, peer tutoring also provides an excellent framework for increasing the meaningful participation of students with moderate and severe disabili-

Setting Up a Peer Tutoring Program

1. Create with your school administration and other interested faculty a framework for a high school peer tutoring course. Develop a course syllabus, including course overview, learning objectives, and required activities and assignments, and decide who may enroll in the class (at DHS enrollment is usually limited to 11th and 12th graders).

2. Include the new course in your high school's description of course offerings. Make sure that eligible students, faculty, and guidance counselors are all aware of the new elective.

3. Ensure that students can enroll in the peer tutoring course through the same process that they register for their other courses. (Some teachers have also found it helpful to personally interview prospective peer tutors.)

4. Do not accept more peer tutors than you can actively engage in learning activities with students with disabilities, and limit the number of peers who may sign up for the course during each scheduled period of the day.

5. On the first day of class, give peer tutors the essential information they need about the course (e.g., grading, assignments, behavioral expectations). Stress the importance of learning together and that students are expected to support each other.

6. Schedule writing assignments (based on required readings and school and community learning experiences) approximately every 2 weeks. Initial assignments are due weekly; toward the end of the course, more in-depth projects are due at approximately 3-week intervals.

7. Make writing assignments reflective and insist on the student's best work. You may want to coordinate the development and grading of these assignments with members of your school's English faculty.

8. Ensure that students with significant disabilities and peer tutors are given a range of opportunities throughout the course to engage in cooperative learning activities in both school and community settings, as well as the opportunities to develop friendships.

9. For students who have completed the peer tutoring course but who wish to continue their learning, consider offering a more advanced course on an independent study basis (this should be developed as an individualized learning contract between the student, teacher, and school principal).

10. Frequently evaluate the impact of your peer tutoring program; seek the input of students (with and without disabilities), parents, and other teachers, as well as your own observations and data on student learning.

---

ties in general education classes. If a peer tutor is enrolled in the same class as a student with a disability, that peer tutor can be an excellent source of natural support for the student with a disability. Indeed, one of the required peer tutor assignments (identifying potential adaptations in general education class activities) provides a wealth of ideas for both special and general education teachers. In the context of that assignment, students read an article about curricular modifications to enhance general education class participation for students with significant disabilities (see Tashie et al., 1993). Students must then develop ways, through the use of a general education class activity analysis (Roger, Gorevin, Fellows, & Kelly, 1992), to adapt one of their *own* classes for an individual student with a significant disability. Peers have developed a number of practical and innovative strategies for adapting course content and instruction across a variety of classes (e.g., English, art, history, and music). Here are some of their ideas:

- In art class, instead of having Richard, who has severe disabilities, draw a picture, he could paste pictures from magazines.
- When completing research papers, Tony could work with picture symbols on a topic or theme of his choice. He could use the pictures, arranged or copied from his communication system, for a research report.
- When a large reading assignment is required, peers could write summaries of each reading for Karla. This would help the student who was developing the summary learn the material and help Karla understand the basic themes or ideas.
- In typing class, when there are longer assignments, Tom could type his personal identification information or what he did in the community that day.
- As a part of the yearbook class, Lauren could classify photographs into activity categories such as school classes, clubs, and sports.

- In biology, for an oral research presentation to the class, Derrick could develop a collage of local fruits and vegetables, and the best places to purchase the seeds for those plants.

Besides providing an essential link to academic classes, peer tutors can also provide a natural link to the community for students with significant disabilities. Many peer tutors work in the community on a part-time basis and introduce students with disabilities to their co-workers in their own jobs. Peers also may provide support to students with disabilities in their respective job searches. For example, one of the requirements of the peer tutoring class is that both peer tutors and students with disabilities develop their own job resumés; of course, they work on this together.

Yet it is important to remember that this community-linking goes both ways. Because students with significant disabilities usually participate in community-based instruction (CBI) extensively at the secondary

---

Reflections of a Peer Tutor

This is my second semester as a peer tutor. That in itself says a lot about my feelings toward the class. You don't see me signing up for plant physiology for a second semester! I have learned more about my true identity and aspirations in this class than I ever dreamed to. The values and experiences that I have gained will be important to me for years to come. It is easy to express my growth as a person through writing about peer tutoring. Several pieces that I have written will be included in my senior writing portfolio.

The particular prompt I am writing from instructs me to write an introduction to peer tutoring for future peer tutors. It will include advice, suggestions, and examples of what it takes to be a successful peer tutor.

Day one. I know what you are thinking, unless you have had a personal encounter with students with disabilities prior to now, you feel the same way that everyone else does. You are somewhat nervous, intrigued, and even frightened. Don't be–sit back, take a deep breath, and get over it!

It will take time and patience to become a good peer tutor. It will not happen overnight. The students will not magically adjust to you, or fall in love with you, neither you with them, but it won't take long....

I can honestly say that I know I have gained just as much from being a peer tutor as the students have from me. I have grown immensely as a peer tutor, and filled an empty place in my heart....

Soon I will be moving on to college, and few classes have prepared me for the next phase of my life like peer tutoring. I have learned about happiness, diversity, patience, strength, determination, and above all, life in its true essence.

Katie Corcoran
Danville High School

---

level, many of them are already familiar with their community. For example, when a new discount store opened in Danville, students with moderate and severe disabilities often chose that new store as a site to work on their purchasing skills. Two of the peer tutors, assigned to provide assistance with shopping and budgeting skills, commented what a help the students (with disabilities) were to them in learning their way around the new store.

Peer tutors love to go on community-based instruction themselves, and the longer class periods facilitated by block scheduling has increased opportunities for their participation. In addition to providing carefully planned assistance on targeted CBI skills to students with moderate and severe disabilities, peer tutors continue to gain skills in budgeting, nutrition, banking, and overall shopping. Peers continue to comment about how much they learn when they go on CBI with students with disabilities.

Evidence of Learning Together

As noted previously, students with moderate and severe disabilities in Kentucky must complete Alternate Portfolios as the students in the general assessment system simultaneously complete writing and math portfolios. For students in the Alternate Portfolio assessment, the special education teacher must enable these students to show evidence of extensive interactions with peers and reliance on natural supports, as well as clear documentation of students' performance of learned skills across a wide range of school and community settings. This evidence is presented through a series of portfolio entries (see Kleinert et al., 1997).

Peer tutors are valued resources in documenting each of these Alternate Portfolio assessment requirements. Peer tutors frequently develop friendships with students with disabilities that go well beyond the classroom. Peers collaborate with students with disabilities within and outside of the school, in such activities as going to youth group, out for pizza on Saturday night, or to the movies; researching topics at the school and public libraries; and going Christmas shopping together. Peers collaborate on community instruction while shopping, banking, eating at a fast food restaurant, and participating in community recreation and leisure activities. Each of these instances can provide an appropriate context for showcasing both learned skills and valued social relations at an exemplary performance level for students in Kentucky's alternate assessment system (Kleinert et al., 1997). This documentation can take the form of written or photographic entries (e.g., a portfolio entry centered on community recreation/leisure activities in which the student engages), course projects developed together, or examples of instructional programming and student self-evaluation data across school and community settings. Finally, peer tutors may assist students with moderate and severe disabilities in completing their entries and assembling the entries into a finished portfolio.

As peer tutors provide this support, they also are developing their own portfolio entries. Essays on the meaning and purpose of friendship, the essential need for all students to be an integral part of their community, or what they have learned from their peer tutoring experience have provided the context for outstanding writing entries. Students have even used their peer tutoring assignments as a part of their college admission application, as evidence of their best writing.

Encouraging Self-Evaluation

As a culminating activity for their peer tutoring experience, tutors are required to complete a self-evaluation matrix during the latter part of the semester. For this assignment, each peer determines five characteristics they believe essential for a peer tutor. They then must describe that characteristic, as it would be shown at four different performance levels (novice, apprentice, proficient, and distinguished—the four levels that are used to score students' work in Kentucky's overall assessment and accountability system). Finally, using their own rubric, peers must evaluate their performance. They must also complete a written explanation for their score. Here are some of their final comments on the course and on their own performance:

- "This class will have more meaning than *any* other classes on your schedule…. Expect the class to be one you will remember for a lifetime."

- "You are there for support, not to do students' work, a job they are supposed to be doing…. You will have learned that students with disabilities are capable of doing anything you are."

Peer tutoring continues to evolve at DHS in a way that reflects rapidly changing educational practices and paradigms for students both with and without moderate and severe disabilities. The teachers have experienced a renewed excitement and challenge related to peer tutoring, as they attempt to integrate the learning experiences of their students into a curriculum reflecting high expectations for all.

References

Brandt, R. (1992). On performance assessment: A conversation with Grant Wiggins. *Educational Leadership, 49*(8), 35–37.

Clayton, J. (1993). *Peer power manual for middle school students*. Lexington: Kentucky Statewide Systems Change Project, Human Development Institute, University of Kentucky.

Coots, J., Bishop, K., Grenot-Scheyer, M., & Falvey, M. (1995). Practices in general education: Past and present. In Falvey, M. (Ed.), *Inclusive and heterogeneous schooling: Assessment, curriculum, and instruction* (p. 18). Baltimore: Paul Brookes.

Falvey, M., Gage, S., & Eshilian, L. (1995). Secondary curriculum and instruction. In Falvey, M. (Ed.) *Inclusive and heterogeneous schooling: Assessment, curriculum, and instruction* (p. 355). Baltimore: Paul Brookes.

Giangreco, M., Cloninger, C., & Iverson, V. (1993). *Choosing options and accommodations for children*. Baltimore: Paul Brookes.

Guiltinan, S., & Kleinert, H. (1987). *High school peer tutoring manual*. Frankfort: Division of Exceptional Children Services, Kentucky Department of Education.

Hardman, M., McDonnell, J., & Welch, M. (1997). Perspectives on the future of IDEA. *Journal of the Association for Persons with Severe Handicaps, 22*, 61–76.

Haring, T. (1991). Social relationships. In Meyer, L., Peck, C., & Brown, L. (Eds.), *Critical issues in the lives of people with severe disabilities* (p. 204). Baltimore: Paul Brookes.

Haring, T., Breen, C., Pitts-Conway, V., Lee, M., & Gaylord-Ross, R. (1987). Adolescent peer tutoring and special friend experiences. *Journal of the Association for Persons with Severe Handicaps, 12*, 280–286.

Helmstetter, E., Peck, C., & Giangreco, M. (1994). Outcomes of interactions with peers with moderate or severe disabilities: A statewide survey of high school students. *Journal of the Association for Persons with Severe Handicaps, 19*, 263–276.

Kishi, G., & Meyer, L. (1994). What children report and remember: A six-year follow-up of the effects of social contact between peers with and without severe disabilities. *Journal of the Association for Persons with Severe Handicaps, 19*, 277–289.

Kleinert, H. (1996). *Kentucky classrooms—Everyone's welcome: A practical guide to learning and living together*. Lexington: Human Development Institute, University of Kentucky.

Kleinert, H., Guiltinan, S., & Farmer, J. (1991). *High school peer tutoring manual—revised edition*. Frankfort: Division of Exceptional Children Services, Kentucky Department of Education.

Kleinert, H., Kearns, J., & Kennedy, S. (1997). Accountability for *all* students: Kentucky's Alternate Portfolio assessment for students with moderate and severe cognitive disabilities. *Journal of the Association for Persons with Severe Handicaps, 22*, 88–101.

Peck, C., Donaldson, J., & Pezzoli, M. (1990). Some benefits nonhandicapped adolescents perceive for themselves from their social relationships with peers who have severe handicaps. *Journal of the Association for Persons with Severe Handicaps, 15*, 241–249.

Roger, B., Gorevin, R., Fellows, M., & Kelly, D. (1992). *Schools are for all kids: School site implementation level II training*. San Francisco: California Research Institute, San Francisco State University. (ERIC Document Reproduction Service No. ED 365 052)

Salisbury, C., Gallucci, C., Palombaro, M., & Peck, C. (1995). Strategies that promote social relations among elementary students with and without severe disabilities in inclusive schools. *Exceptional Children, 62*, 125–137.

Sprague, J., & McDonnell, J. (1984). *Effective use of secondary age peer tutors: A resource manual for high school teachers*. Eugene: Center on Human Development, University of Oregon.

Stainback, W., Stainback, S., & Wilkinson, A. (1992). Encouraging peer supports and friendships. *TEACHING Exceptional Children, 24*(2), 6–11.

Staub, D., & Hunt, P. (1993). The effects of social interaction training on high school peer tutors of schoolmates with severe disabilities. *Exceptional Children, 60*, 41–57.

Steffy, B. (1993). Top-down—bottom-up: Systemic change in Kentucky. *Educational Leadership, 51*(1), 42–44.

Tashie, C., Shapiro-Barnard, S., Schuh, M., Jorgensen, C., Dillon, A., Dixon, B., & Nisbet, J. (1993). *From special to regular, from ordinary to extraordinary*. Concord: Institute on Disability/University Affiliated Program, University of New Hampshire. (ERIC Document Reproduction Service No. ED 387 963).

Thousand, J., & Villa, R. (1990). Sharing expertise and responsibilities through teaching teams. In Stainback, W., & Stainback, S. (Eds), *Support networks for inclusive schooling: Interdependent, integrated education.* (p. 162). Baltimore: Paul Brookes.

Ysseldyke, J., Thurlow, M., & Shriner, J. (1992). Outcomes are for special educators too. *TEACHING Exceptional Children, 25*(1), 36–50.

Amy Wildman Longwill, *Teacher, Danville High School, Kentucky.* **Harold L. Kleinert**, *Training Director, Human Development Institute, University of Kentucky, Lexington.*

Address correspondence to Harold L. Kleinert, Human Development Institute, University of Kentucky, 126 Mineral Industries Bldg, Lexington, KY 40506-0051 (e-mail: haroldk@ihdi.uky.edu).

Authors' Note: As of this writing, Kentucky is the only state in which all students, including students with moderate and severe cognitive disabilities, are fully represented in school and district accountability indexes (Kleinert et al., 1997). Yet the 1997 Amendments to the Individuals with Disabilities Education Act (IDEA) require that all states develop alternate assessments for those students who cannot participate in general state and district educational assessments, and that these alternate assessments be in place no later than July 1, 2000.

Preparation of this article was supported, in part, by the U.S. Department of Education Office of Special Education and Rehabilitation Services (Grant No. H086J20007). However, the opinions expressed do not necessarily reflect the position or policy of the U.S. Department of Education, and no official endorsement should be inferred.

Using Technology to Construct Alternate Portfolios of Students with Moderate and Severe Disabilities

Anne Denham

Elizabeth A. Lahm

The 1997 Amendments to the Individuals with Disabilities Education Act (IDEA '97) require that all states include students with disabilities in their measures of accountability. Such measures may be part of the statewide and districtwide general education assessment programs through appropriate accommodations or through alternate assessments for those who cannot complete the general education assessment (Kleinert & Kearns, 1999).

Inclusion in Statewide Assessments

Since 1992, Kentucky has been including all students in the statewide assessment and going beyond federal regulations by including all students in the accountability system. Students receiving special education services are assessed in one of three ways:
- Through participation in the general education assessment program.
- Through participation in the general assessment program with accommodations.
- Through participation in the alternate portfolio system.

This article shares how the students in one classroom achieved "Distinguished" ratings, the highest of ratings, on their alternate portfolios, using assistive technology (see box, "What Is an Alternate Portfolio?").

Student Profiles

We conducted multiple case studies in one Kentucky classroom for students with moderate to severe cognitive disabilities to explore the process of using the IntelliKeys keyboard as an alternative computer input device for the production of the alternate portfolio. The classroom is located in a small elementary school (430 fourth- and fifth-grade students) in rural Kentucky. The students receive instruction in the general education classroom, the community, and a special class. The teacher has 12 years' experience servicing students in both the general and special education environment, is a recent graduate of an assistive technology educational specialist degree program, and holds an Assistive Technology Practitioner certificate. The students use a selection of assistive technology devices commensurate with their needs, to include single communication aids; a variety of switches to access tape recorders, electric kitchen mixer, and television through an environmental control; and an adaptive keyboard with custom overlays to access the computer.

> **How do we provide alternate assessments for those who cannot complete the general education assessment?**

Four of the seven students in the class were in the age groups of students in the fourth and eighth grades and were thus required to participate in the Kentucky assessment program. Three were 9-year-old females, and one was a 13-year-old male. Two students were classified as having severe cognitive disabilities and two as having multiple disabilities. Table 1 describes these students further, according to physical, cognitive, and behavioral domains. The teacher determined that they qualified to participate in the assessment by completing an alternate portfolio.

What Is an Alternate Portfolio?

The alternate portfolio showcases student work where educators can assess learning across life domain activities in a comprehensive way. It represents performance-based evaluation, using a multidisciplinary approach, and models the use of holistic scoring. As with the general education portfolio scoring system, educators score alternate portfolios on four different levels: novice, apprentice, proficient, and distinguished. To qualify for a distinguished score, the highest level, the student must show the following:

• Progress on specifically targeted skills that are meaningful in current and future environments.
• Planning, monitoring, and evaluating self progress.
• Evaluation used to extend performance.
• Extensive evidence of Kentucky Academic Expectations in all entries.
• Natural supports.
• Use of adaptations, modifications, and/or assistive technology to evidence independence.
• Performance occurring in a variety of integrated settings, within and across all entries.
• Clearly established mutual friendship(s) with peers without disabilities.
• Choice and control in age-appropriate portfolio products within and across all entries.

The alternate portfolio assessment was designed by Kentucky educators specifically for those students whose limitations in cognitive function prevented completion of the standard assessment program (see below "Alternate Portfolios in Kentucky"). Eligibility is determined by the IEP committee, by considering cognitive function, adaptive behavior, cause of limited function, application skill level, use of community-based instruction, and level of performance with supports. Kleinert, Kearns, and Kennedy (1997) stated that between 0.5% and 1.0% of the public school students meet such requirements.

In addition to becoming part of the school's accountability indexes, alternate portfolios serve as "an 'instructional organizer' to give clarity and focus to the student's daily educational program, and as a teaching tool for students to learn higher order self-management, planning, and self-evaluation skills" (Kleinert, Haigh, Kearns, & Kennedy, 2000, p. 24). Such organizers provide teachers with a solid framework from which to work.

Alternate Portfolios in Kentucky

For more information about alternate portfolios, as implemented in Kentucky, visit the following Web sites:
Kentucky Alternate Portfolio Online
http://www.ihdi.uky.edu/projects/KAP/
Kentucky Alternate Portfolio Assessment Teacher's Guide (PDF format)
http://www.ihdi.uky.edu/projects/KAP/downloads/ap%20book99.pdf

Each of the four students was required to produce five entries for their alternate portfolio, in addition to demonstrating their use of a daily schedule and writing a letter to the reviewers. Table 2 shows the activities selected for these students to illustrate Kentucky's academic expectations within four content areas. Statements in black are target skills, and statements in italic are questions they had to respond to in order to demonstrate that skill. For example, Amanda demonstrated her computation skills by responding to the question "Did I count the cans?" on her activity sheet for loading the soda machine. One curricular area entry for each student was the focus of the study and is used to demonstrate the assessment process.

> **Students used a smorgasbord of assistive technology: single communication aids; a variety of switches to access tape recorders, electric kitchen mixer, and television through an environmental control; and an adaptive keyboard with custom overlays to access the computer.**

All four students were unable to use the standard computer keyboard effectively. The teacher determined that the IntelliKeys keyboard was an appropriate adaptation for each. Three of the students used switches plugged into the IntelliKeys, in addition to the IntelliKeys keyboard itself. The switches were used to highlight and read text on the activity sheet with the use of text reading software.

The teacher constructed a custom overlay for each student, using Overlay Maker (IntelliTools, 1996) to support each student's individual needs. The overlay provided response choices to be used in the completion of a data sheet that was displayed on the computer (see Figure 1). By pressing a response choice on the overlay, the student caused the text programmed into that cell to be entered into the data sheet. The amount of text in the response depended on the student's level of functioning. For example, one student was able to record a complete sentence by sequencing three response choices, whereas another had only "yes" or "no" programmed as response choices. Color and location were used on the overlays to provide visual cues as to which response choices should be used for each of the assessment questions. Figure 2 is an example of one student's overlay.

The teacher provided a short training session for each student and one peer buddy on all components of the assessment process. For each student, the IntelliKeys with a custom overlay was used to respond to the assessment

Table 1. Profile of the Students in the Study

Subject	Physical Characteristics	Cognitive Characteristics	Behavioral Characteristics	Disability
Sandra: Age 9	Hearing impaired; hyperactive; impaired speech	Exceedingly low academic ability compared with typical peers	Noncompliant; resists authority	Multiple: hearing impaired and severe cognitive disability
Christine: Age 9	Low to fluctuating tone; nonambulatory; verbal though not clearly understood by anyone other than parent	Exceedingly low academic ability compared with typical peers	Friendly but demanding; persistent presence	Multiple: physical and severe cognitive disability
Amanda: Age 9	Small, ample stamina to function well with peers	Very low academic ability; beginning academics; delayed language skills	Friendly, predominantly smiling; enjoys being the center of attention; loud; silly behaviors	Severe cognitive disability
Brent: Age 13	Very small and thin; exhibits self-stimulatory behaviors; nonverbal; ambulatory but resistant	Nonparticipatory	Self-stimulatory behaviors; little response to peers or adults; very little interaction with others	Severe cognitive disability

questions. The teacher created an activity data sheet using a word processor with table capabilities (Microsoft, 1997). Figure 1 shows one of these activity data sheets. The text-to-speech feature of the software (textHELP! 1999) was used to read each assessment question to the student. The student responded using the custom overlay, and their answer was read back to them so they could confirm the correctness of the answer.

The teacher provided a short training session for each student and one peer buddy on all components of the assessment process.

Each student had content area tasks for which they were responsible. One student was in charge of filling the soda machine; another, shopping for ingredients for a cooking activity. After the activities were completed, they rated and commented on their performance using the activity data sheet. With a peer, they sat at the computer workstation. They responded to the assessment questions that were read aloud by the computer, using the activity-specific IntelliKeys overlay to "type" their response to each question. The peer provided prompts and assistance when needed. On the activity sheet, independent responses were recorded in blue and assisted responses

were recorded in red. Based on that record, each student's level of independence was determined across four trials. Table 3 (page 14) shows the increase in independence across the trials for each student.

Examples of Student Use of Portfolio Entries

Amanda

We used Amanda's math entry for this study with the following activities: (a) filling the soda machine with a peer, (b) taking cans to the recycling center, and (c) purchasing items at the store. Targeting improvement in computation and money skills, Amanda planned, monitored, and evaluated her activities by using the IntelliKeys and the custom overlay to respond to the questions on the activity sheet. The activity sheets and overlays were designed to allow Amanda to read the text with the text-reading software and construct a variety of sentences in response to the questions posed on the activity sheet. The response keys on the custom overlay were grouped according to color and use to facilitate correct choice (Figure 3).

On the first trial activity sheet, 48% of Amanda's responses were made independently. By the fourth trial, Amanda had increased her independence to 88%. Figure 4 illustrates how on one response item, the quality of her responses also improved. Before using the IntelliKeys, Amanda was limited to handwriting her response, which was painstakingly slow. The IntelliKeys system allowed her to write 56 words in 20 minutes, a feat she could not have accomplished without it. Amanda's reaction to the IntelliKeys system was, "This is neat."

Table 2. Student Evidence of Performing Each of the Nine Criteria for a "Distinguished" Rating

Assessment Dimension and Requirements of the Alternate Portfolio	Amanda-Math • Loading soda machine • Recycling cans • Shopping at the store	Christine-Lang.Arts • Cooking • Purchasing items for cooking	Sandra-Soc.Studies • Art activity • Shoping for art supplies	Brent-Science • Pet care • Purchase items at the store
Performance:				
Progress on specifically targeted skills which are meaningful in current and future environments	Increased accuracy by 20% or more in computation and coin values Did I count the cans?	Increased accuracy by 20% or more in visual scanning ability Did I scan my pictures?	Increased frequency of requesting assistance in an appropriate manner by 20% or more Did I follow directions?	Increased accuracy by 20% or more in selecting the correct object Did I touch the correct object?
Planning, monitoring, and evaluating self progress	Evaluating performance Did I say I am ready?	Reporting and following a sequence of tasks What will I do first?	Following a sequence of tasks Do I know what to do?	Following a sequence of tasks Did I wash my hands when I finished?
Evaluation used to extend performance	Developing a goal for the next session Next time I will try harder with...	Making a quality choice using visual scanning Did I try harder with...	Making a quality choice related to a targeted skill Next time I will try harder with...	Making a quality choice related to a targeted skill Did I try harder with...
Extensive evidence of Kentucky Academic Expectations in all entries	E.G. Quantifying, How many cans did we need? Classifying, Did I put the soad in the right space?	E.g. Reading, Did I use pictures to read the recipe? Production, What am I making	E.g. Accessing information, Did I ask for help if I needed it? Democratic principles, Did I have good manners in class?	E.g. Constancy, Did I follow my schedule? What do I plan to do first? Speaking, Did I use my switch to ask for food?
Supports:				
Natural support	Peers working on estimation and mental math skills Who worked with me today?	Peers working on math skills wihtin the cooking activity What friend cooked with me today?	Peers exploring a variety of media within the art activity Who did I sit with today?	Peers learning about domestic animals within the pet care activity Which friend helped me today?
Use of adaptations, modifications, and/or assistive technology to evidence independence	Big key calculator; IntelliKeys to record performance on the computer	Switch controlled electric mixer; IntelliKeys to record performance on the computer	Modified goals; IntelliKeys to record performance on the computer	Auditory switch device; IntelliKeys to record performance on the computer
Settings:				
Performance occurring in a variety of integrated settings, within and across all entries	Teacher's lounge, office, stockroom, recycle center, store Where did I go?	Classroom, kitchen, store, office, other classrooms Where did I go?	Art room, classroom, cafeteria, store Where did I go?	Classroom, kitchen, restroom, store, recycle center Where did I go?
Social Relationships:				
Clearly established mutual friendship(s) with non-disabled peers	Time spent in activities with peers to facilitate friendships Who helped me today?	Time spent in activities with peers to facilitate friendships What friend cooked with me today?	Time spent in activites with peers to facilitate friendships Who did I sit with today?	Time spent in activities with peers to facilitate friendships Which friend helped me today?
Context:				
Choice and control in age-appropriate portfolio products within and across all entries	Multiple opportunities for choice and decision making Did I make a choice?	Multiple opportunities for choice and decision making Did I say I was ready?	Assuming personal responsibility Did I ask for help correctly?	Multiple opportunities for choice and decision making What do I plan to do first?

Table 3. Level of Independent Performance During Completion of Activity Sheets

		Percentage of Responses Made Independently				
Student	Activity	Trial 1	Trial 2	Trial 3	Trial 4	Overall Gain
Amanda	Soda	48	56	72	88	25%
	Recycle	55	66	82	71	
	Store	62	72	85	82	
Christine	Cooking	25	54	60	75	43%
	Store	35	53	71	--	
Sandra	Art class	4	24	16	35	22%
	Store	18	22	31	30	
Brent	Pet care	7	25	44	56	32%
	Store	40	40	50	56	

Figure 1. Soda Machine Activity Sheet

Prompt	Response			
Date				
Did I use my schedule?				
Did I say I am ready?				
What will I do first?				
Did I use my sheet so I know what to do next?				
Where did I go?	Office Lounge	Office Lounge	Office Lounge	Office Lounge
Did I write what sodas were needed?				
Did I use my list to say what sodas were needed?				
Did I count the cans?				
Did I make a choice?				
How many cans did we need?				
Did I put the can in the right place?				
Did I do a good job?				
Did I try harder?				
Next time I will do better at ...				
Who helped me today?				
What did my friend do?				

Christine

Christine's alternate portfolio activities targeted her language arts objectives. She engaged in two activities to demonstrate her achievements: cooking and buying items from the store. Before using the IntelliKeys for recording responses. Christine was limited to using a rubber stamp to indicate a yes/no response to questions on the activity sheets. That was accomplished with physical assistance from a peer or adult to assist in stamping and reading the questions. The overlay was designed to be simple, with large keys outlined in black. The keys were arranged by color and location to facilitate correct responses. The overlay keys also directly addressed her individualized education program (IEP) objectives—to visually scan pictures or objects from left to right or from top to bottom. Christine also used two color-coded single switches plugged into the IntelliKeys, to highlight activity sheet cells on the computer and to have it read each question.

> Sandra's initial trial with the art class activity showed that 4% of her responses were made independently. By the fourth trial she increased her independence to 35%.

As with Amanda, by the fourth trial Christine had increased her performance level substantially, achieving 75% of her responses independently with the cooking activity sheet. Christine attended well to the reporting activity and appeared to enjoy the print output. She asked to take it home with her.

Sandra

Sandra's portfolio demonstrated her achievements in social studies. She participated in two activities: shopping for art supplies, and participating in a general education art class. Sandra's overlays were simple, using color coding and

Figure 2. Amanda's IntelliKeys Overlay

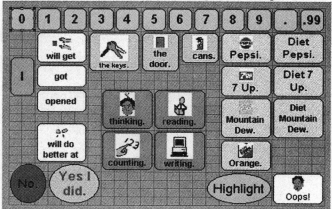

Figure 3. Amanda's Additional IntelliKeys Overlay

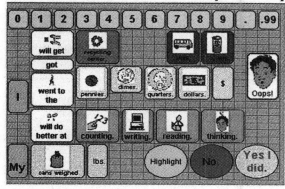

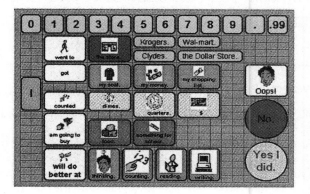

location, to facilitate correct responses. When using the IntelliKeys, Sandra listened to the peer who cued her verbally and with gestures, as necessary. She also used switches to highlight and read the text. Sandra responded well to peer cues, tolerating their guidance, following their directions, and remaining seated during the activity. Sandra's initial trial with the art class activity showed that 4% of her responses were made independently. By the fourth trial she increased her independence to 35%. A similar gain was found in the shopping activity. She apparently enjoyed working on the computer with the IntelliKeys. She grinned and clapped as each entry was keyed into the cell, and read with the text reader as it was typed. She anxiously waited for the printed output so she could take it from the printer's paper tray.

> # The design of the custom overlay is an important consideration in the success of student use of the IntelliKeys.

Brent

Brent's example is for his science entry. Two custom overlays were used—one overlay was restricted to two cells demonstrating a yes/no response to the activity sheet questions, and the other with five keys giving Brent the opportunity to document a high-quality independent choice over his area of improvement (Figure 5). Two

switches were used to highlight and read the text as with the other students.

Brent averaged a 32% gain in independent performance. Brent's responses were more erratic than the others, but this is typical for Brent. He requires consistent cueing and often hand-over-hand instruction with physical cues. Brent is nonverbal and at present has an inconsistent system of communication. He required physical guidance to be seated and consistent cueing to remain seated. Brent's response to the question regarding improved performance was generated through activation of two out of five keys linked to his IEP goals and targeted skills. He consistently chose either the "choose the right one" or "look" key, both located at the bottom of the overlay toward the left (Figure 6 on page 16). It is not clear if the location of the activated keys on the overlay was a factor.

Figure 4. Example of Amanda's Responses to One Activity Question

Prompt	Student Response			
	Day 1	Day 2	Day 3	Day 4
Did I use my money?	Yes I did.	Yes I did. I $	Yes I did.	Yes I did. I counted $ 1.

External Review

Each alternate portfolio in this study was scored at the regional level by trained teams of scorers using a double-blind method. Table 4 presents the two scores awarded each portfolio. Out of a total of 40 possible scores when including each dimension, the portfolios carried 36 distinguished ratings and 4 proficient ratings. This results in a 90% distinguished rating when considering each dimension separately. The alternate portfolio is scored holistically, however, assigning one score to each complete portfolio. These four students received a rating of "distinguished."

> # The design of the custom overlay is an important consideration in the success of student use of the IntelliKeys.

Overlay Design

The design of the custom overlay is an important consideration in the success of student use of the IntelliKeys. Thorough knowledge of student need and capabilities of the device is essential to use the customizing features and maximize student potential. As a result of this study, we can share several design tips (see box "Design Tips for Customizing IntelliKeys Overlays"). Experimentation based on observation, however, is the most important element.

First, overlay design must be student centered. Motor and cognitive abilities guide the spatial arrangement of the overlay. Range of motion and reach are considerations for the placement of buttons. Items that will be needed more frequently should be easily within reach to avoid fatigue and frustration. Fine motor abilities are factored into button size. For students with cognitive impairments, color and clustering can facilitate use. Buttons in close proximity should be related to a single task and may be highlighted in a specific color to provide cues to the student for their use.

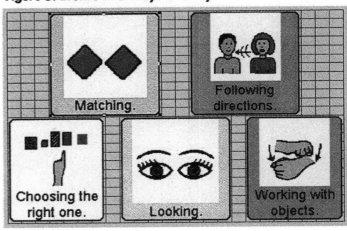

Figure 5. Brent's IntelliKeys Overlay

These design considerations are especially useful with more complex overlays.

Cognitive abilities play a role in the number of buttons or response options, and the design of the button depends on the student's cognitive level (for example, contrast Amanda's overlay in Figure 2 with Brent's in Figure 5). Type of graphic representation of a response option is critical. Pairing the written word with the picture will be beneficial for some students, but detrimental to others.

If using different layouts for different tasks, it is important to maintain as much consistency across the layouts as possible. For example, you may always put program commands (e.g., enter, space, delete) in the upper left quadrant and task-specific content keys in the lower right. In doing so, you reduce the cognitive load on the students as they complete each response. Taking both cognitive and motor abilities into account, you facilitate increased accuracy and reduction of time, which both contribute to fatigue.

Table 4. Scores Received from Two Reviewers on the Alternate Portfolio Dimensions

Student	Amanda	Christine	Sandra	Brent
Performance	Distinguished Distinguished	Distinguished Distinguished	Distinguished Distinguished	Distinguished Distinguished
Support	Distinguished Distinguished	Distinguished Distinguished	Proficient Distinguished	Distinguished Distinguished
Settings	Distinguished Distinguished	Distinguished Distinguished	Distinguished Distinguished	Distinguished Distinguished
Social relationships	Proficient Distinguished	Distinguished Distinguished	Distinguished Proficient	Proficient Distinguished
Contexts	Distinguished Distinguished	Distinguished Distinguished	Distinguished Distinguished	Distinguished Distinguished

Figure 6. Example of Brent's Responses to One Science Activity Question

Prompt	Student Response			
	Day 1	Day 2	Day 3	Day 4
Next time I will try harder with ...	Choose the right one.	Choose the right one.	Look.	Look.

Design Tips for Customizing IntelliKeys Overlays

• Student needs and functioning level must drive the content and format.

• Use voice output to read the prompt and read the response back to the user.

• Group keys according to color to facilitate correct responses.

• Enable the "nonrepeat" function to ensure only one entry per response.

• Use left-to-right formats to naturally facilitate sentence construction.

• Size the text and the keys to match the visual abilities of the user.

• Program whole words and phrases into the keys to speed responses.

• Match the programmed responses to the student's cognitive ability (e.g., single-word responses limit the construction of complete sentences).

• Outline keys in black to improve contrast.

• Place frequently used keys on the user's dominant side of the keyboard.

• Include graphics on the keys with the text for the nonreader.

• Consider the complexity of training issues when choosing keys (e.g., arrow keys for directional movement are very difficult to teach).

• Place keys that are common across overlays in a consistent location on each.

Sample Peer Responses to Interview Questions

Six general education peers helped the students use the IntelliKeys during recording sessions. The overwhelming consensus was that the peers liked using the IntelliKeys with the students, primarily because it enhanced the student level of performance and increased their independence. The following are some of their responses:

• One peer appeared quite shocked at Amanda's performance within her math entry, and remarked that he did not know "she could do all that."

• Most peers were surprised with work that the students were able to produce with the IntelliKeys, and admitted that it elevated their opinion of the students' ability.

• Observations indicated that the peers enjoyed the process of working with the students, though this was in the form of a peer-tutor relationship.

• Each peer reported that working with a student helped him or her to get to know the student better, since they spent more time together. Spending time with one another provided the opportunity for relationships to develop, an important element within the social relationships dimension of the alternative portfolio.

Sample Student Responses Recorded in Observation Notes

• "Amanda appears to enjoy the technical aspects of the program; perhaps it gives her a sense of independence that she cannot get from other methods of reading and writing."

• "Amanda appears pleased with her work. At no time does she appear hurried or anxious to get finished. The teacher does not have to remind her to remain on task."

• "Christine was compliant in coming to the computer. She appears to enjoy computer tasks since it does give her an avenue for written expression and she likes to take things home."

• "Christine's mother came into the classroom when she was completing the activity sheets and Christine became animated and demanded that her mother watch what she was doing."

• On her first trial with the IntelliKeys, Sandra "grinned and clapped as each entry was keyed into the cell and read with the text-to-speech software as she typed."

• During Brent's first trial completing the science activity sheet, "Brent voiced and resisted being seated in the chair by the computer. He looked upwards at all times and avoided contact with the IntelliKeys and the monitor."

• Brent "does better on the computer than he does with the stamps since he is selecting the key and is the cause of the entered text."

Final Thoughts

In addition to the data showing the achievements of the students with disabilities, observations of the students working with their peers on these tasks confirmed other benefits of the program. Overall, the peers gained a better perspective on the students' abilities, and the students responded positively to their accomplishments and interactions with their peers (see boxes, "Sample Student Responses," for student observations and peer interviews).

This series of case studies denotes a beginning level of research, and is an indication for further definitive research at a critical time when states are looking to include students with moderate and severe disabilities in their accountability indexes. Studies of a more rigorous method of inquiry and more reliable data collection in the area of student support and assistive technology and assessment are essential. Kentucky is the only state fully including the assessment of this population in their school accountability indexes, and thus provides an excellent base for research.

Another area of focus for future research is on overlay design issues, because it is apparent that they influence output. Researchers and practitioners might look at overlay design and attempt guidelines to facilitate increased independence, increase output, and minimize the potential for student error.

References

IntelliTools. (1996). Overlay maker. [Computer software]. Novato, CA: Author.

Kleinert, H., Haigh, J., Kearns, J., & Kennedy, S. (2000). Alternate assessment. Lessons learned and roads not taken. *Exceptional Children, 67,* 51–66.

Kleinert, H., & Kearns, J. (1999). A validation study of the performance indicators and learner outcomes for Kentucky's alternate assessment for students with significant disabilities. *Journal of the Association for Persons with Severe Handicaps, 24*(2), 100–110.

Kleinert, H., Kearns, J., & Kennedy, S. (1997). Accountability for all students: Kentucky's alternate portfolio assessment for students with moderate and severe cognitive disabilities. *Journal of the Association for Persons with Severe Handicaps, 22*(2), 88–101.

Microsoft Corporation. (1997). WORD 97. [Computer software]. Redmond, WA: Author.

textHELP! (1999). Read & write. [Computer software]. Antrim, N. Ireland: Author.

Anne Denham *(CEC Chapter #5), Teacher, Mason County Public Schools, Maysville, Kentucky.* **Elizabeth A. Lahm** *(CEC Chapter #180), Assistant Professor, Department of Special Education and Rehabilitation Counseling, University of Kentucky, Lexington.*

Address correspondence to Elizabeth A. Lahm, Department of Special Education and Rehabilitation Counseling, University of Kentucky, 229 Taylor Education Building, Lexington, KY 40506-0001 (e-mail: ealahm1@pop.uky.edu).

From *Teaching Exceptional Children,* May/June 2001, pp. 10-17. © 2001 by The Council for Exceptional Children. Reprinted with permission.

UNIT 9

Orthopedic and Health Impairments

Unit Selections

Key Points to Consider

- What is the most important thing for children with orthopedic and health impairments to learn in kindergarten?

- What kinds of accommodations are appropriate for students with health impairments (e.g. cancer, asthma, epilepsy)?

- Why do browsers make it more difficult for people with orthopedic impairments to access the Web? How can Web sites be made more accessible?

 **Links: www.dushkin.com/online/**
These sites are annotated in the World Wide Web pages.

Association to Benefit Children (ABC)
http://www.a-b-c.org
Introduction: Community Travel
http://isd.saginaw.k12.mi.us/~mobility/ctpintro.htm
Resources for VE Teachers
http://cpt.fsu.edu/tree/ve/tofc.html

Try using the word "handicapped" on a computer with a spell check. The twenty-first century computers are programmed to advise you that this is a derogatory term when applied to any individual. Older dictionaries defined "handicapped" as inferior and in need of an artificial advantage. People were described as handicapped if they were encumbered by physical limitations. Today, handicapped means limited by something in the environment. Handicap is synonymous with hindrance. If a property of the environment prevents a person with an orthopedic or health impairment from functioning to the best of his or her abilities, then the environment has imposed a handicap.

Children and youth with orthopedic and health impairments can be divided into classifications of mild, moderate, and profound. Within most impairments, the same diagnosis may not produce the same degree of disability. For example, children with cerebral palsy may be mildly, moderately, or profoundly impaired.

Orthopedic impairments are usually defined as those that hinder physical mobility and/or the ability to use one or more parts of the skeletomuscular system of the body. Orthopedic problems may be neurological (brain or spinal cord) or skeletomuscular (muscles or skeletal bones). Regardless of etiology, the child with an orthopedic impairment usually has a problem with mobility. He or she may need crutches or other aids in order to walk or may be in a wheelchair.

Health impairments are usually defined as those that affect stamina and predominantly one or more systems of the body: cardiovascular, respiratory, gastrointestinal, endocrine, lymphatic, urinary, reproductive, sensory, or nervous systems. Children with health impairments usually have to take medicine or follow a medical regimen in order to attend school. The degree of impairment (mild, moderate, profound) is usually based on limitations to activity, duration of problem, and extent of other problems.

Orthopedic and health impairments are not always mutually exclusive. Many times a child with an orthopedic impairment also has a concurrent or contributing health impairment, and vice versa. In addition, children with orthopedic and health impairments may also have concurrent conditions of educational exceptionality.

Some children with orthopedic and health impairments have only transitory impairments; some have permanent but nonworsening impairments; and some have progressive impairments that make their education more complicated as the years pass and may even result in death before the end of the developmental/educational period.

Each of the dimensions defined in the preceding paragraphs makes educational planning for children with orthopedic and health impairments very complicated.

The reauthorized IDEA mandates that schools must pay for all medical services required to allow orthopedically or health-impaired students to attend regular education classes. The only exceptions are the actual fees for the physician who provides the health services. Thus, if children need ambulances to transport them to and from school, the schools must pay the tab. Federal appropriations for special educational services only pay about 10 percent of the bills. High-cost special needs students can, therefore, quickly drain the funds of state and local education departments.

Teachers may resent the need to spend teacher time giving medications or providing quasi-medical services (eg. suctioning, changing diapers) for students with health impairments in the many schools which no longer have school nurses.

Resentment is common in parents of nondisabled students who feel that the education of high-cost disabled students robs their children of teacher time, curriculum, and supplies to which they should be entitled. More than 95 percent of special needs students attend regular schools today. About 3 percent attend separate schools and about 2 percent are served at home, in hospitals, or in residential facilities.

When orthopedic or health impairments are diagnosed in infancy or early childhood, an interdisciplinary team usually helps plan an individualized family service plan (IFSP) that includes working with parents, medical and/or surgical personnel, and preschool special education providers.

When the orthopedic or health impairment is diagnosed in the school years, the schoolteachers collaborate with outside agencies, but more of the individualized educational planning (IEP) is in their hands. Children who have orthopedic and/or health impairments need psychological as well as academic support. Teachers need to help them in their peer interactions. Teachers should also work closely with parents to ensure a smooth transition toward a lifestyle that fosters independence and self-reliance. By middle school individualized transition plans (ITPs) should be developed. They should be implemented throughout highschool and until age 21 when the students move to adult living. The ITPs must be updated every year. Schools are held accountable for their success in helping students with orthopedic and health impairments to make smooth transitions to maturity.

The first article emphasizes the importance of allowing young children with orthopedic and/or health impairments to interact with children without such disabilities as early as possible (preschool). Assistive technology, especially computers, can make their full participation possible. The social skills learned in preschool (such as how to take turns) are important for all children, abled and disabled.

The second selection for this unit suggests some of the accommodations that school systems must make to ensure that students with orthopedic and health impairments receive an appropriate education. It explains the 504 plans required under the Americans with Disabilities Act. MaryAnn Byrnes points out that the teaching profession is about allowing students to learn. Removing barriers will do that.

The last selection in this unit considers the benefits of computer technology in eliminating obstacles faced by elementary, middle, and high school students with physical disabilities. Educators may need to help students with disabilities use computers. They need to find out whether Web sites are accessible to students with unique disabilities. They also need to alert the Web site designers if their information is not accessible to some students, and why.

I LEARNED How to Take Turns
And Other Important Early Childhood Lessons
Helped Along by Computers

Cynthia Lau

We know that computers are like magnets to young children and educators are finding many benefits of their use with young children with disabilities—particularly the enhancement of these children's social skills. "What I learned in kindergarten" is indeed important—taking turns, paying attention, focusing, following instructions, and working with other people.

Preschool is a place for young children to master social skills and develop self-esteem from social interaction with peers. For successful inclusion of young children, the opportunity must exist for young children with physical disabilities to interact with their peers. Assistive technology has the potential to increase the full participation of young children with physical disabilities in the preschool setting. Computer activities can promote the much-needed social interaction among children with and without disabilities. There are specific methods the teacher can use to facilitate social interaction for a child with physical disabilities.

This article shows how even children with significant physical disabilities can use the computer independently—if given the correct positioning, appropriate computer peripherals and software, groupings, and instructional strategies.

Positioning

Teachers should first consider principles of positioning and seating when the focus is on technology and social interaction of children with physical disabilities (Wright & Bigge, 1991). Proper positioning will enable the child to be physically ready to perform activities and access computer activities, promote a positive self-image, and allow the child to interact with others more

easily (Trefler, 1992). For children with limited movement, success at accessing a single switch for computer activities varies depending on optimal seating, positioning, and control of the individual's movement (Behrmann, Jones, & Wilds, 1989; Everson & Goodwyn, 1987; see Figures 1a and 1b).

The child in Figure 1a is improperly positioned in a standard preschool chair and is having a difficult time attending to the computer task. In Figure 1b, the child is properly positioned in a Rifton chair with his pelvis, back, and feet supported. The checklist shown in Table 1 can assist teachers in optimally positioning a child with physical disabilities for computer activities and to interact socially with peers.

A cooperative learning group is an essential strategy for promoting positive social interaction among children with severe physical disabilities.

Figure 1a. Improper Positioning

Figure 1b. Proper Positioning

Table 1.
Classroom Checklist for Proper Positioning at the Computer for Social Interaction

Criterion	Met	Not Met
1. Is the child's head at midline? (e.g., ears are directly over shoulders and face is facing forward)		
2. Is the child's pelvis at midline? (e.g., hips are in the back of the seat and are not tilted to one side)		
3. Is the child's trunk at midline? (e.g., trunk is not tilted to one side)		
4. Are the child's shoulders at midline? (e.g., shoulders are not hunched forward)		
5. Are the child's forearms supported? (e.g., elbows are flexed at 90 degrees and supported by the table, arm rest, or tray)		
6. Are the child's legs in a neutral position? (e.g., thighs are slightly apart; knees and ankles are bent at 90 degrees)		
7. Are the child's feet in a neutral position and supported? (e.g., feet are directly under the knees and facing forward; feet are supported by the floor or feet rest)		
8. Is the child seated at the same height as other children at the computer (e.g., eye contact and verbal exchange can easily be achieved among children in the group)		
9. Is the computer monitor at the child's eye level (e.g., the child can easily see the monitor without tilting his or her head)		
10. Is the computer table accessible to the child? (e.g., the child can easily reach the computer peripherals)		

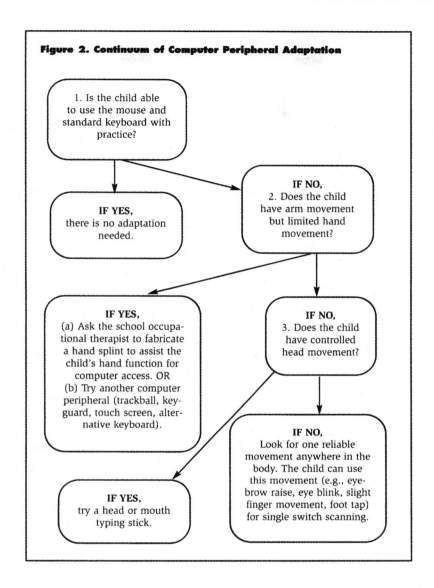

Figure 2. Continuum of Computer Peripheral Adaptation

1. Is the child able to use the mouse and standard keyboard with practice?

IF YES, there is no adaptation needed.

IF NO, 2. Does the child have arm movement but limited hand movement?

IF YES, (a) Ask the school occupational therapist to fabricate a hand splint to assist the child's hand function for computer access. OR (b) Try another computer peripheral (trackball, keyguard, touch screen, alternative keyboard).

IF NO, 3. Does the child have controlled head movement?

IF NO, Look for one reliable movement anywhere in the body. The child can use this movement (e.g., eyebrow raise, eye blink, slight finger movement, foot tap) for single switch scanning.

IF YES, try a head or mouth typing stick.

Computer Peripherals

When working with young children with disabilities, there needs to be a match between the child's sensorimotor abilities and the appropriate computer peripherals (Behrmann et al., 1989). There are varieties of computer peripherals that can make the computer more accessible to children with a wide range of physical disabilities. These peripherals may include mouse, keyboard, touch screen, or a wide range of single switchers. In addition, King and Alloway (1992) showed that young children used various computer peripherals at different input rates. Close evaluation of computer peripherals for children with physical disabilities is needed to determine the fastest and least tiring input method.

Proper positioning will enable the child to be physically ready to perform activities and access computer activities, promote a positive self-image, and allow the child to interact with others more easily.

Ideally, the educational team of the teacher and related service providers (e.g., speech and occupational therapists) can collaborate on decisions regarding the most appropriate computer peripheral. Figure 2 shows the continuum of adapta-

tion of computer peripherals to meet the needs of children with a range of physical limitations. This continuum helps teachers make decisions about the type of computer peripheral adaptation that each child needs. Minimal adaptation and specialized peripherals would be the easiest for the teaching staff to implement and maintain throughout the school year.

Software

With the abundance of new software programs introduced each year, selecting appropriate software is a critical decision for teachers (Shade, 1996). Problems in software were identified as a major challenge in implementing assistive technology (Hutinger,

Johanson, & Stoneburner, 1996). In response to the software problem, the *Children's Software Revue* (1998) is a newsletter that has detailed reviews on the latest software. This newsletter has a list of top-rated software programs for children, a software review instrument for teachers to use, and an informative Web page at http://:www2. childrenssoftware.com. Table 2 shows a list of preschool software programs teaching social skills to young children. These software programs teach listening, sharing, and interpersonal skills.

> *Preschool is a place for young children to master social skills and develop self-esteem from social interaction with peers.*

Most software programs used in early childhood classrooms are often poorly suited to the needs of the children (Haugland & Shade, 1994). For example, some software programs require too quick of a response time for a child with physical limitations; and other programs address only cause and effect and therefore are not developmentally appropriate (Hutinger et al., 1996). Not only does software need to meet the physical and cognitive needs of the children in the classroom, but also there must also be a variety of soft-

ware available to keep children motivated to learn and be socially interactive at the computer throughout the school year. In one study, in an integrated preschool classroom, software programs were changed daily to maintain the children's interest; subsequently children with and without disabilities showed more socially directed behavior while at the computer (Spiegel-McGill, Zippiroli, & Mistrett, 1989).

Shade (1996) offered three major areas of consideration when choosing software: the child, the teacher, and technical features. To increase social interaction, some of the components are especially important.

- The software should allow the child to make independent decisions about what he or she wants to do, with minor help from adults (Shade, 1996).

- The software should be developmentally appropriate. For example, if the program is too cognitively demanding, the child will have difficulty balancing academic and social demands (Clements, Nastasi, & Swaminathan, 1993).

- Independence from adult instruction on how to use the software will allow more opportunities for interaction with other children at the computer in a playing mode.

- The software must be intrinsically motivating and allow experimentation, as

in open-ended programs (Shade, 1996).

These characteristics will maintain the interest of the students and give them a topic about which to communicate.

Grouping Strategies

To have successful inclusion, teachers need to group children with disabilities together with children without disabilities in activities throughout the day. Children need actual adult intervention and instruction to build social interaction. In integrated environments, young children without disabilities tend to play with children without disabilities or with children with mild disabilities more than peers with moderate to severe disabilities (Guralnick, Connor, Hammond, Gottman, & Kinnish, 1995). Research completed in integrated environments shows that there are specific grouping strategies to facilitate social interaction among all children while they play and work at the computer (Clements & Nastasi, 1998; Clements et al., 1993; Evans, Salisbury, Palombaro, & Peck, 1995). Teachers can use small groups of two to three children seated in front of the computer and select children for the group who already play together in other situations. Further, the children with disabilities may be mixed with the older children in the class without disabilities who are more socially skilled, cooperative, and patient.

Table 2. Software Resources

Title	Publisher	Teaches	Rating
Build a Book with Roberto (1996)	Theatrix Interactive	stories, social skills	3.7
Elmo's Preschool Deluxe (1997)	Creative Wonders (Learning Company)	letters, numbers, shapes, listening, social skills	4.5
Captain Kangaroo Life's First Lessons—Adventure #1	Knowledge Adventure	social skills	3.8
My Little Pony	Hasbro Interactive	social skills, animals	3.9
Sesame Street Reading Is Fun! Toddler Edition	Creative Wonders	early reading and social skills	3.8
Wimzie's House: A Surprise for Horace	Micro-Intel	social skills	4.0
Wimzie's House: Play Along	Micro-Intel	social skills	3.8

Note: These software programs have been rated by Children's Software Review on a scale of 1 (low) to 5 (high). Please refer to their Web site at www.2childrenssoftware.com for more information on these programs.

Table 3. Sequence of Verbal and Nonverbal Behavior to Teach at the Computer

What to Do	What to Say
1. Look at Johnny.	1. Say his or her name.
2. Sit closer to Johnny.	2. Ask, "What game do you want to play on the computer?"
3. Touch Johnny's arm.	3. Ask, "What are you doing on the computer now?"
4. Point to the screen.	4. Say, "Show me what you are doing on the computer."
5. Give the mouse to Johnny.	5. Ask, "May I have the mouse?"
6. Take turns.	6. Ask, "Whose turn is it?"

Note: From *Play and Imagination in Children with Autism*, 1999 (p. 99), by P. J. Wolfberg, New York: Teachers College Press, Columbia University. Adapted with permission.

Instructional Strategies

A qualitative study of elementary school teachers teaching in an inclusive classroom with students with physical disabilities identified the need for actively facilitating social exchanges between children (Salisbury et al., 1995). Lipinski, Nida, Shade, and Watson (1986) showed that social interaction behaviors at the computer include cooperating, helping/sharing, praising, and initiating social interaction. Instructional strategies to increase social interaction behavior at the computer include modeling and praise of social behaviors, structuring cooperative activities, peer tutoring, using less invasive assistance, and using social-communication guidance. Increasing the level of teacher direction for social skills at the computer minimizes behavior such as aggression and competition (Clements et al., 1993). In addition to adult modeling of appropriate helping, sharing, and praising behavior, teachers can give positive feedback to students exhibiting other positive social interactions at the computer, such as initiating a social interaction. For example, children need feedback, such as, "I like the way you (smiled at, looked at, or talked to) Johnny."

A cooperative learning group is an essential strategy for promoting positive social interaction among children with severe physical disabilities (Salisbury et al., 1995). The teacher can facilitate cooperation by placing two chairs in front of one computer, suggesting that children work in pairs, and encouraging cooperative goals or encouraging children to communicate as they work on individual projects (Clements et al., 1993). To in-crease cooperation among children at the computer, the teacher can pick a software program that has an end goal. An example of such a program is Mr. Potato Head (Hasbro Interactive, 1997). This open-ended program allows children to build a picture of Mr. Potato Head and then print the creation. The teacher may structure this activity as a cooperative task for the students to take turns building and sharing the final product.

Given that some children are able to operate the software programs independently or with minimal assistance from adults, the children can then spontaneously and effectively teach and help each other in computer activities. Peer tutoring is helpful because it allows advanced students to help and socially interact with other students at computer activities. Peer assistance is sometimes more welcome than assistance from adults when using the computer (Clements & Nastasi, 1992; Salisbury et al., 1995). Young children often emulate their teachers' behavior when helping their peers; therefore, teachers should pay special attention to their instructional techniques at the computer (Clements & Nastasi, 1992).

Teachers should also take care to use the least invasive assistance that will allow the child with physical disabilities to participate as fully as possible. Young children with physical disabilities are at high risk for learned helplessness (Basil, 1992; Brinker, 1984). The teacher can first ask if the child needs help, and then give minimal amount of verbal or physical prompts needed for successful task completion. Physical prompts are generally more invasive than verbal cues and therefore should be used last. In this manner, children with-out a disability will model appropriate helping behavior, rather than physically taking the activity over for the child with physical disabilities. The child with physical disabilities will be expected to participate as fully as possible in the social exchange and computer activity.

Social-communication guidance is a strategy used as a part of guided participation in integrated play group intervention (Wolfberg, 1999). Social-communication guidance strategies focus on recognizing and responding to both verbal and nonverbal communication behavior, such as initiating and maintaining an interaction with a peer (Wolfberg). These strategies are adapted to increase social interaction at the computer. See Table 3 for the sequence of behavior the child can use to initiate and maintain interaction at the computer. The teacher can systematically teach these cues to the student. The intent is for children to naturally incorporate these sociocommunicative strategies into their repertoire and no longer need adult guidance.

Final Thoughts

Proper positioning in front of the computer can facilitate better physical access to the computer and social interaction among a small group of children. The variety of computer peripherals available makes the computer accessible to children who do not have the skills to operate a standard mouse or keyboard. Teachers can select the developmentally appropriate and open-ended software that has been reviewed by colleagues. Specific grouping and instructional strategies can optimize the social skills and subsequent social interaction

What Does the Literature Say About Technology and Young Children's Social Skills?

Positive social relations influence the intellectual, communicative, interpersonal, and emotional development of young children (Parker & Asher, 1987). Some children with disabilities have been shown to exhibit significant social skill deficits (Guralnick, 1990). Social skill deficits may result in peer rejection, disproportionate placement in special classes, and poor self-esteem (Strain, 1981).

There has been some preliminary evidence of the positive effects of technology on your children's social skills (Clements et al., 1993; Howard, Greyrose, Kehr, Espinosa, & Beckwith, 1996; Spiegel-McGill et al., 1989). Parents and staff working with young children with physical disabilities reported that the greatest impact of assistive technology was on emotional outcomes, including enhanced self-concept, social interaction, cooperation, and exploratory play (Behrmann et al., 1989; Hutinger et al., 1996). In addition, according to the National Association for the Education of Young Children (NAEYC, 1996), early childhood educators should promote access to appropriate technology for young children with special needs for whom assistive technologies may be essential for successful inclusion (NAEYC). Using assistive technology may enhance young children's cognitive and social abilities (NAEYC).

Teachers need more methods to incorporate assistive technology into the ongoing curriculum for children with physical disabilities (Hutinger et al., 1996). The computer in the preschool classroom is becoming more pervasive, and computer-based activities can be used to facilitate more positive social interactions, such as initiating and terminating interactions, turn taking, attending to an object or person, and following instructions (Wilds, 1988).

among children with and without disabilities. Teachers can fade physical and verbal prompts over time and have children socially interact at the computer independently over time.

Given that computers are becoming commonplace in the early childhood school settings, we should use them to teach skills that will help all children live productively and harmoniously.

References

Basil, C. (1992). Social interaction and learned helplessness in severely disabled children. *Augmentative and Alternative Communication, 8*, 188–197.

Behrmann, M. M., Jones, J. K., & Wilds, M. L. (1989). Technology intervention for very young children with disabilities. *Infants and Young Children, 1*(4), 66–77.

Brinker, R. P. (1984). The microcomputer as a perceptual tool: Searching for systematic learning strategies with handicapped infants. In R. E. Bennett & C. A. Maher (Eds.), Microcomputers and exceptional children (pp. 21–36). New York: Haworth.

Children's Software Revue. (1998). Children's Software Evaluation Instrument. *Children's Software Revue, 3*, 4.

Clements, D. H., & Nastasi, B. K. (1988). Social and cognitive interactions in educational computer environments. *American Educational Research Journal, 25*, 87–106.

Clements, D. H., & Nastasi, B. K. (1992). Computers and early childhood education. In M. Gettinger, S. N. Elliott, & T. R. Kratochwill (Eds.), *Advances in school psychology: Preschool and early childhood treatment directions* (pp. 186–246). Hillsdale, NJ: Lawrence Erlbaum.

Clements, D. H., Nastasi, B. K., & Swaminathan, S. (1993). Young children and computers: Crossroads and directions from research. *Young Children, 48*(2), 56–64.

Evans, I. M., Salisbury, C. L., Palombaro, M. M., Berryman, J., & Hollowood, T. M. (1992). Peer interaction and social acceptance of elementary-age children with severe disabilities in an inclusive school. *Journal of the Association for Persons with Severe Disabilities, 17*, 205–212.

Everson, J. M., & Goodwyn, R. (1987). A comparison of the use of adaptive microswitches by students with cerebral palsy. *American Journal of Occupational Therapy, 41*, 739–744.

Guralnick, M. J. (1990). Social competence and early intervention. *Journal of Early Intervention, 14*(1), 3–14.

Guralnick, M. F., Connor, R. T., Hammond, M., Gottman, J. M., & Kinnish, K. (1995). Immediate effects of mainstreamed settings on the social interactions and social integration of preschool children. *American Journal on Mental Retardation, 10*, 357–377.

Hasbro Interactive. (1997). Mr. Potato Head saves Veggie Land. [Computer software]. Playskool Children's Educational Software.

Haugland, S. W., & Shade, D. D. (1994). Software evaluation for young children. In J. L. Wright & D. D. Shade (Eds.), *Young children: Active learners in a technological age* (pp. 63–76). Washington, DC: National Association for the Education of Young Children.

Howard, J., Greyrose, E., Kehr, K., Espinosa, M., & Beckwith, L. (1996). Teacher facilitated microcomputer activities: Enhancing social play and affect in young children with disabilities. *Journal of Special Education Technology, 13* (1), 36–47.

Hutinger, P., Johanson, J., & Stoneburner, R. (1996). Assistive technology applications in educational program of children with multiple disabilities. A case study report on the state of practice. *Journal of Special Education Technology, 13*(1), 16–35.

King, J. A., & Alloway, N. (1992). Preschooler's use of microcomputer and input devices. *Journal of Educational Computing Research, 8*, 451–468.

Lipinski, J. A., Nida, R. E., Shade, D. D., & Watson, J. A. (1986). The effect of microcomputers on young children: An examination of free-play choices, sex differences, and social interactions. *Journal of Educational Computing Research, 2*, 147–168.

NAEYC. (1996). NAEYC position statement: Technology and young children—ages three through eight. *Young Children, 51*(6), 11–16.

Parker, J. G., & Asher, S. R. (1987). Peer relations and later personal adjustment: Are low-accepting children at risk? *Psychological Bulletin, 102*, 357–389.

Salisbury, C. L., Galluci, C., Palombaro, M. M., & Peck, C. A. (1995). Strategies that promote social relations among elementary students with and without severe disabilities in inclusive schools. *Exceptional Children, 62*, 12, 125–137.

Shade, D. D. (1996). Software evaluation. *Young Children, 51*, 6, 17–21.

Spiegel-McGill, P., Zippiroli, S. M., & Mistrett, S. G. (1989). Microcomputer as social facilitators in integrated preschools. *Journal of Early Intervention, 13*, 249–260.

Strain, P. S. (1981). Modifications of sociometric status and social interaction with mainstreamed developmentally disabled children. *Analysis and Intervention in Developmental Disabilities, 1*, 157–169.

Trefler, E. (1992). *Application and strategies for the education of children with severe disabilities, positioning, access, and mobility module.* Rockville, MD: American Speech-Language-Hearing Association.

Wilds, M. (1988, March). *The future role of technology/computer in the pre-school handicapped classroom.* Paper presented at the National Council for Exceptional Children Conference, Washington, DC.

Wolfberg, P. J. (1999). *Play and imagination in children with autism*. New York: Teachers College Press, Columbia University.

Wright, C., & Bigge, J. (1991). Avenues to physical participation. In J. Bigge (Ed.), *Teaching individuals with physical and multiple disabilities*. New York: Macmillan.

Cynthia Lau, *doctoral student, Department of Special Education, University of Nevada-Las Vegas.*

Address correspondence to the author at the Department of Special Education, University of Nevada-Las Vegas, 4505 Maryland Parkway, Las Vegas, NV 89154-3014 (e-mail: changlau@anv.net).

I would like to thank Kyle Higgins and Catherine Lyons of the University of Nevada-Las Vegas for their assistance with the preparation of this article.

Accommodations for Students with Disabilities: Removing Barriers to Learning

Secondary school principals frequently encounter questions about educating students with disabilities. Sometimes the questions revolve around seeking a deeper understanding of the disability and the best way to meet student needs. Other times, the questions focus on all the changes that must be made to ensure students receive an appropriate education. What questions do teachers ask about accommodations for students with a disability?

By MaryAnn Byrnes

Think about taking a driver's test without wearing glasses (if you do, that is). Not fair, you say; you need the glasses to see. You have just identified an accommodation that you need. Wearing glasses does not make a bad driver better or make driving easier; rather, wearing glasses makes driving possible. Glasses are so much a part of our lives that we do not even consider that they remove a barrier caused by a disability.

Secondary school teachers encounter students every day on an Individualized Education Plan (IEP) or 504 Plan, both of which address programs for students with disabilities. Most likely, the person charged with monitoring this plan has indicated that particular students need changes in teaching style, assignments, or testing strategies.

It is usually easy to understand the need for glasses or wheelchairs or hearing aids. These sound like changes the student must make. Other adjustments, modifications, or accommodations on these plans, such as extended time, may not be as clear.

What is an accommodation?

An accommodation is an adjustment, to an activity or setting, that removes a barrier presented by a disability so a person can have access equal to that of a person without a disability. An accommodation does not guarantee success or a specific level of performance. It should, however, provide the opportunity for a person with a disability to participate in a situation or activity.

Think of that pair of glasses, or the time you broke your leg and could not drive. Think of how your life was affected by these conditions. Your competence did not change. Your ability to think and work did not change. Your ability to interact with (have access to) the reading material may be very limited without your glasses. Your ability to get to (have access to) work or the grocery store may be very limited without someone to transport you. The support provided by the glasses—or the driver—made it possible for you to use your abilities without the barrier presented by less than perfect vision or limited mobility.

> An accomodation is an adjustment, to an activity or setting, that removes a barrier presented by a disability so a person can have access equal to that of a person without a disability.

The accommodations in IEPs or 504 Plans serve the same purpose. They identify ways to remove the barrier presented by a person's disability.

Why do we need to provide accommodations?

Accommodations are required under Section 504 of the Federal Rehabilitation Act of 1974 as well as the Americans with Disabilities Act. Both these federal laws prohibit discrimination against individuals who have a disability. Situations that limit access have been determined to be discriminatory.

Accommodations must be provided not just by teachers to students, but by employees for workers and governments for citizens. Curbs have been cut to provide access. Doors have been widened and door handles altered to provide access to people for whom the old designs posed a barrier. Employers provide computer adaptations or other adjustments in work schedules and circumstances.

For employers and schools, individuals with disabilities may have a document called a 504 Plan, which details the types of accommodations that are required. Students who have a 504 Plan will not require special education services, just changes to the environment or instructional situation.

Students who have a disability and require special education services in addition to accommodations will have this information contained in an IEP, which also details the types of direct services that need to be provided and the goals of these services. Accommodations will be listed within this IEP.

With the recent changes in IDEA '97, the federal law governing special education, you will be addressing accommodations that must be made so a student with a disability can participate in large-scale districtwide or statewide assessment systems as well as classwork and school life.

Who needs accommodations?

According to Section 504, an individual with a disability is any person who has "a physical or mental impairment that limits one or more major life activities." IDEA '97, the federal special education law, lists the following disabilities: autism, deaf-blindness, deafness, hearing impairment, mental retardation, multiple disabilities, orthopedic impairment, other health impairment, serious emotional disturbance, specific learning disability, speech or language impairment, traumatic brain injury, and visual impairment.

Students who have a 504 Plan will not require special education services, just changes to the environment or instructional situation.

Some conditions are covered by Section 504, but not special education. These can include attention deficit disorder—ADD, (also attention deficit hyperactivity disorder—ADHD); chronic medical conditions (such as cancer, Tourette Syndrome, asthma, or epilepsy); communicable diseases; some temporary medical conditions; physical impairments; and disorders of emotion or behavior. To qualify, there must be a demonstrated and substantial limitation of a major life activity.

Students (or adults) who have disabilities may require accommodations to have equal access to education. Not every student with a disability will require accommodations, and not every student with a disability requires the same accommodation all the time.

Think of Jim, a student who has limited mobility in his hands, affecting his ability to write. This disability will present a barrier in a class that requires the student to take notes quickly or write long essays in class. In a class that does not require either of these activities, no barrier may be present. Equal access is possible without accommodation. The student can learn and demonstrate what he knows and can do unaffected by his disability.

What kind of accommodations are there?

Just as there is no limit to the range of disabilities, there is no limit to the range of accommodations. The point is to understand disability and determine if it presents a barrier to equal access. If so, decide whether an accommodation can be identified to remove the barrier— and make sure the accommodation is implemented.

Not every student with a disability will require accomodations, and not every student with a disability requires the same accomodation all the time.

Think of the student described above. The limited mobility in Jim's hands presents a barrier in a class that requires rapid note taking or the writing of long essays in class. There are several accommodations that can result in equal access. Jim might tape the lesson and take notes later. These notes could be written or dictated into a computer. Essays could be composed verbally at a computer workstation or dictated into a tape recorder or to a scribe. A computer might be adapted so typing becomes an effective way to record information on paper. In yet another type of accommodation, essays could be replaced by oral reports.

Are there some accommodations that should not be used?

Like many difficult questions, the answer depends on the context. An accommodation should not alter the essential purpose of the assignment. If the skill you want to measure is the ability to make multiple rapid hand movements, then there is probably no accommodation that is appropriate. Jim will not do well because of his disability. Alternately, if the purpose of a task is to see if someone has perfect vision without glasses, using those glasses is not an appropriate accommodation. If the purpose is to see if you can read, the glasses become a reasonable accommodation.

Who decides about accommodations?

The team that writes IEPs and 504 Plans reviews the disability and determines what accommodations, if any, are necessary. These are then written into the EIP or 504 Plan.

Once more, return to Jim. As you consider the requirements of your class, think of the most appropriate way to remove the barrier that is presented by the limited mobility Jim has in his hands.

If we use accommodations, how will the student ever be prepared for independent life in college or the world of work?

Some people are concerned that the supports provided in school will result in the student being unable to work productively when he or she leaves school. As a matter of fact, Section 504 applies to colleges and employers as well. Colleges offer support centers and provide accommodations upon documentation that a disability exists. Employers are required to provide reasonable accommodations to any person who is otherwise qualified to fulfill the elements of the job.

If companies remove barriers at the workplace, educators should be willing and able to take barriers out of the school activities that prepare a student for the workplace. Teachers can help a student identify the type of accommodation that will be the least cumbersome for everyone, and those that will permit the student to be most independent.

Don't accommodations just make school easier?

That depends on how you view the world. Does wearing glasses make driving easier? Not really—for a person with limited vision, wearing glasses makes driving *possible*. With or without glasses, you need to be able to drive to pass the test. The same is true of an academic accommodation; whether or not the accommodation is provided, the students still must demonstrate that they know required material.

An accomodation should not alter the essential purpose of the assignment.

Think about the important elements of your class: Is it more important that Jim take notes in class or understand the material? Is it more important that Jim demonstrate good handwriting or the ability to communicate thoughts in print? Often, when you identify the main purpose of your assignments and consider the skills and abilities of a student, you will see that an accommodation lets you determine more clearly what a student knows, understands, and can do.

Does a student need to follow the IEP accommodations in all classes?

The IEP or 504 Plan needs to address any area in which the student's disability affects life in school. Sometimes this means in all classes, but not always. For example, a student who was blind would need to use Braille in all classes dealing with written material. Jim, our student with limited mobility in his hands, might not require accommodations in world languages or physical education.

Can we make accommodations without having students on an IEP?

Many accommodations are just different ways of teaching or testing. You should be able to have this freedom in your classes. In some cases, the way in which a class is taught makes accommodations unnecessary. Accommodations change the situation, not the content of the instruction. However, accommodations on standardized tests must be connected to IEP's or 504 Plans.

May teachers give different assignments on the same content as a way to meet the needs of different learning styles without lowering standards?

Absolutely. The point is to remove the barrier of the disability; this is one way to accomplish that. Some teachers find they tap student knowledge best in active projects; others find that written work is best. Many secondary schools are using portfolios or performance activities to document student learning.

These assessment activities can be very compelling and they do tap different methods of expression. A student like Jim, for example, might communicate depth of understanding and analysis to a social studies debate with a disability in the area of speech or language might find barriers in the performance activities that do not exist on a paper-and-pencil task.

... educators should be willing and able to take barriers out of the school activities that prepare a student for the workplace.

What if accommodations are not implemented?

Since accommodations allow equal access, refusing to provide them can be viewed as discrimination. Individuals who knowingly refuse to implement accommodations make themselves personally liable for legal suit.

This sounds serious, and it is serious. Once the accommodations are found to be necessary, everyone must implement them in situations where the student's disability poses a barrier that prevents equal access.

If no barrier exists in your class, the accommodation is not necessary. No one has the option, however, of deciding not to implement a necessary accommodation. Telling students they could not wear glasses or use a hearing aid is unthinkable. Just as inappropriate is a decision not to allow Jim to use accommodations to remove the barrier posed by his disability, even though it means making some changes to your own work.

Questions About Specific Accommodations

Now that the issues underlying accommodations have been addressed, it is time to talk about frequently-encountered accommodations that raise questions and concern. All these questions have come from secondary school faculty members in a variety of school systems.

Why is it fair to read material aloud to some students?

Some students have a learning disability that makes it difficult for them to decode print. They can understand the concepts; they can comprehend the material when they hear it; they can reason through the material. They just can't turn print into meaning. If the task is to determine if the student can read, you already know they will have difficulty. If the task is to determine if the student has content knowledge, reading material aloud removes the barrier of the learning disability. Reading material aloud to a student who does not understand the material will not result in a higher grade.

Why is it fair to give some students extra time on tests?

Some students have motor difficulties that make writing an enormous challenge. They may not be able to form the letters correctly. They may not be able to monitor their thoughts while they work on the physical act of writing. They understand the material, and they know what they want to respond; it just takes longer to write the answer. If the task is to determine how quickly the student can respond, you already know they will have difficulty. If the task is to determine if the student has the knowledge, providing extra time removes the

barrier of the motor disability. Providing extra time to a student who does not understand the material will not result in a higher grade.

Why is it fair to permit some students to respond orally to tests?

Think about the example above. For some students, responding orally would be a comparable accommodation. In this case, allowing an oral response will not result in a higher grade if the student does not know the material.

A student with a disability in the area of speech or language might find barriers in the performance activities that do not exist on a paper-and-pencil task.

The Bottom Line

It all comes down to deciding what is important. Think about your assignment and expectations. Think about the disability. If the disability provides a barrier, the accommodation removes it. The accommodation does not release a student from participating or demonstrating knowledge—it allows the student to be able to participate and demonstrate knowledge. And isn't that what school is all about?

References

Americans with Disabilities Act of 1990, P.L. 101–336, 2, 104 Stat. 328.1991.

Individuals with Disabilities Education Act Amendments of 1997, P.L. 105–17, 20 U.S. Code Sections 1401–1486.

Livovich, Michael P. *Section 504 of the Rehabilitation Act of 1973 and the Americans with Disabilities Act. Providing access to a free appropriate public education: a public school manual.* Indianapolis, Ind.: 1996.

Vocational Rehabilitation Act of 1973, 29 U.S.C. 794.

MaryAnn Byrnes (byrnes@mediaone.net) is assistant professor at the Graduate College of Education, University of Massachusetts-Boston.

From *NASSP Bulletin,* February 2000, pp. 21-27. © 2000 by NASSP Bulletin. Reprinted by permission. For more information concerning NASSP services and/or programs, please call (703) 860-0200.

Accessible Web Site Design

Stacy Peters-Walters

The World Wide Web (WWW) is a wonderful tool for classroom use. Students can explore many virtual libraries and museums and conduct research. The WWW has the ability to bring information to everyone who has access to a computer. The Web and other telecommunications applications like e-mail can help students with disabilities in many ways. When a Web site is designed correctly, there is very little discrepancy between users with disabilities and those people temporarily without disabilities. Computers and the WWW can be a great equalizer in the classroom and in the world. Figure 1 provides information about users with disabilities who have used telecommunications applications to overcome barriers (U.S. Department of Commerce, 1994).

The Importance of Web Site Design

Many people with disabilities have difficulties accessing information over the Internet because of poor Web site designs. Many of the site designs actually create barriers for information access (Paciello, 1996). Students with visual and cognitive disabilities have the greatest barriers to overcome to gain access to information (Paciello). There is very little that users can do to change site design to accommodate their own needs. Site designers must accommodate the user. Educators who wish to create Web sites that are accessible need to follow a few simple site design rules so that all students can access information.

- Educators can run "Bobby" (http://www.cast.org/bobby) to find out whether their site designs are accessible. "Bobby" is a Web site validator (Center for Applied Special Technology, 1997).

- Users who wish to validate their Web site with accessibility requirements type the specific URL they want validated into the form provided.

- "Bobby" goes to that URL and validates whether it meets the accessibility requirements. Images of a blue hat with the "handicapped" sign on them appear next to areas that are not accessible.

- "Bobby" also provides written reports as to what is wrong and how to fix the problem.

- "Bobby" also contains an advanced validator that validates the code for specific browser types.

Figure 1

Technology Can Break Down Barriers

Reduced Barriers to Full Participation in Society
I am a C7 quadriplegic who has completed a course in desktop publishing. I have been disabled for 2 years and am very eager to get back into the work force. I have learned I'm still employable regardless of my disability. I recently learned about telecommunications and the different networks for communicating. With electronic mail, I communicate with various people from all around the world. My life has really opened up with my career change and the electronic information systems.

Reduced Barriers to Business and Employment
I am a C5 quadriplegic living in the Silicon Valley and a current intern with the Networking and Communication Department. I have been disabled for 10 years from a motor vehicle accident in 1983. I use computer telecommunications daily in numerous functions. Telecommunications has opened up a new world, allowing me to communicate via e-mail with colleges, government agencies, and organizations. The future success of telecommunications is phenomenal, especially for the disabled community. It not only allows a person unable to go out into the community to access endless amounts of information, but also permits persons with disabilities, such as myself, to eventually return to the work force (via telecommuting) and become productive citizens again.

Reduced Communication Barriers
I am 17 years old. I am an oral, profoundly hearing impaired student who is fully mainstreamed in the 12th grade. I did not really have access to e-mail until early October, when a friend of mine proposed we e-mail each other. . . . E-mail turned out to be easier than I thought, and it has been wonderful because it has enabled me to communicate with my friends from around the Atlantic Seaboard region.
The "electronic super highway" is a boon for deaf/hearing impaired people because it enables them to communicate via the written word, which is a very effective alternate means of obtaining vital information in a relatively short period of time. It is my hope that the White House will make access to the information highway universal.

Reduced Barriers to the "Basics" in an Information Society
Rodney, a senior, has no use of his arms or legs and uses a mouth wand to operate a computer. He began using a computer at age 6, and learned to read and write in this manner.
When asked a question, Rodney balances his wand on a box strategically placed near his terminal. "A computer," he says, "is sort of like running water. You don't know what you'd do without it."

If a site meets with "Bobby" specifications, the site designers are invited to use the "Bobby Approved" logo on the site (Center for Applied Special Technology, 1997).

Second, educators can help students indirectly by educating site designers about information-access barriers on the WWW and how to overcome those barriers. A barrier that people with visual disabilities face is not being able to access the information because of its graphical format. People with auditory problems cannot access the information in sound files. People with attention-deficit disorder can become easily distracted from the information by the use of continual animations. Users with cognitive disabilities may become lost due to poor navigation controls.

People with physical disabilities face the barrier of not being able to run the browser that would give them access to the information.

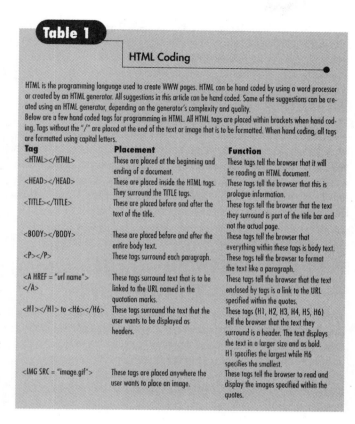

Table 1

HTML Coding

HTML is the programming language used to create WWW pages. HTML can be hand coded by using a word processor or created by an HTML generator. All suggestions in this article can be hand coded. Some of the suggestions can be created using an HTML generator, depending on the generator's complexity and quality.

Below are a few hand coded tags for programming in HTML. All HTML tags are placed within brackets when hand coding. Tags without the "/" are placed at the end of the text or image that is to be formatted. When hand coding, all tags are formatted using capital letters.

Tag	Placement	Function
<HTML></HTML>	These are placed at the beginning and ending of a document.	These tags tell the browser that it will be reading an HTML document.
<HEAD></HEAD>	These are placed inside the HTML tags. They surround the TITLE tags.	These tags tell the browser that this is prologue information.
<TITLE></TITLE>	These are placed before and after the text of the title.	These tags tell the browser that the text they surround is part of the title bar and not the actual page.
<BODY></BODY>	These are placed before and after the entire body text.	These tags tell the browser that everything within these tags is body text.
<P></P>	These tags surround each paragraph.	These tags tell the browser to format the text like a paragraph.
<A HREF = "url name"> </A>	These tags surround text that is to be linked to the URL named in the quotation marks.	These tags tell the browser that the text enclosed by tags is a link to the URL specified within the quotes.
<H1></H1> to <H6></H6>	These tags surround the text that the user wants to be displayed as headers.	These tags (H1, H2, H3, H4, H5, H6) tell the browser that the text they surround is a header. The text displays the text in a larger size and as bold. H1 specifies the largest while H6 specifies the smallest.
<IMG SRC = "image.gif">	These tags are placed anywhere the user wants to place an image.	These tags tell the browser to read and display the images specified within the quotes.

Visual Disabilities

People with visual disabilities have difficulties accessing information published on the WWW because the Web is a highly visual medium. Web pages are designed to be visually stimulating, which can make them difficult to read. Many people with visual disabilities access information from the WWW by using screen readers or refreshable Braille displays. These machines can only access and read text. When the machine arrives at a graphic, the machine either ignores the graphic or informs the user that it is reading a graphic and has no description to read. This cuts down on the usability of the WWW because graphics are used to convey much information.

Many people with disabilities have difficulties accessing information over the Internet because of poor Web site designs.

Graphics. Web site designers can alleviate the problem of interpreting graphics for people with visual disabilities by using the IMG ALT tag when creating WWW pages (see Table 1 for an illustration of this tag). This tag allows the designer to embed a text description of the image into the image source code so that a screen reader will be able to describe the picture. Example code for the IMG ALT tag is The IMG SRC = "*cat.gif*" is telling the browser that it will be viewing the picture cat.gif. The ALT tag tells the browser that if a user is browsing the Web in text mode or through a screen reader, instead of viewing the graphic, the text should read: "Graphic: A big black cat is perched on the windowsill looking outside at the trees blowing in the wind. It is a sunny day outside."

Web Barriers to Overcome

- Some barriers that people with *visual disabilities* face is not being able to access information because of its graphical format.
- People with *auditory problems* cannot access the information in sound files.
- People with *attention deficit disorder* can become easily distracted from the information by the use of continual animations.
- Users with *cognitive disabilities* may become lost due to poor navigation controls
- People with *physical disabilities* face the barrier of not being able to run the browser that would give them access to the information.

Graphic Links. Graphics that link one page to another page can be troublesome for people with visual disabilities. Because the screen reader cannot orally "read" the graphical link, people with visual disabilities do not have a description of the link that they will be visiting. The user will have to click the link and scan the page to decide whether the information on the page is what the user was looking for. This can amount to wasted time for the user when he or she is trying to access information. To help users with visual disabilities, all graphical links should have an alternate text link beside or beneath the graphical link.

Text links should be short yet descriptive. An example of a short descriptive link is "WWW and Visual Disabilities." Text links should not be placed in horizontal lines like Home Education Sites Student Work. While the screen reader can read the links, it can make comprehension difficult. The screen reader will not pause between the links, but read the links like a sentence (Paciello, 1996). It is difficult for the person listening to decide whether the link is the home page, which contains the educational sites and student work, or three separate links.

Video Files. More and more WWW pages are embedding video files that users can access. While a user with visual disabilities can hear the audio in the movie, the user will not be able to view the video. Because much of the information in video files is accessible only by viewing the video, without adaptations the user will be unable to use much of the informational content of the video. WWW designers can add a text file that gives the full transcription of the audio and a description of all visual elements in the video. Site designers can create a text file and then provide a link to it beside the link to the video.

Web Tutorials

There are many products on the market to help people build Web pages. When deciding what to purchase, educators must look at how much time and money they would like to invest in Web page development.

For those educators serious about Web page development and willing to learn how to hand code, Laura Lemay has published several informative tutorials on the different aspects of Web page design. Lemay speaks in layman's terms so that the user is not fumbling through computer jargon. Each book contains lessons for the user to try and examples for the user to view. Lemay's book *Learn HTML in 14 Days* covers the wide range of HTML programming that most beginners are willing to use.

While learning to hand code is beneficial for any HTML programmer, learning to hand code can be time-consuming. For those educators who do not have the time to learn hand coding, there are HTML generators. There are several types of HTML generators, most of which can be found in any software store. These programs range in price from thirty dollars to several hundred dollars. For the most part, the more a person pays for these programs, the more features the programs have.

HTML generators usually come with some type of documentation to explain how they work. There are also multitudes of books about each generator. Many of these books follow a lesson format like Lemay's books.

Imagemaps. Another problem for screen readers and other adaptive devices is reading imagemaps. An imagemap is a large picture that has hot spots, or links, embedded into the image. When a user runs a cursor over the imagemap, there are certain areas, the hot spots or links, where the cursor turns into a hand and can access another page of the site. Because screen readers and other adaptive devices cannot access pictures, the person with a visual disability will not be able to access the links. The user will not be able to follow the informational links if he or she cannot access the links within imagemaps. If WWW designers want to use imagemaps for their visual appeal, designers need to make text links that correspond

with the links in the imagemap and place those links beneath the imagemap.

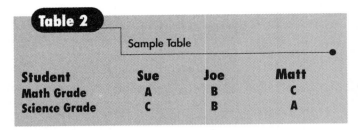

Student	Sue	Joe	Matt
Math Grade	A	B	C
Science Grade	C	B	A

Tables. Tables are another difficulty for screen readers and other adaptive devices to interpret. A screen reader will not read the information in each separate cell as one entity. The screen reader will read across the table from left to right. For example, a simple table like Table 2 will be difficult for the screen reader to interpret.

Other Devices to Enable People with Disabilities to Access Computers

- Dragon Dictate
- Dragon Naturally Speaking
- Microsoft "Access Pack"
- Mouth stick
- Switches (hand, head, mouth)
- Eyegaze
- Screen readers
- Stickybear ABC and Talking Stickybear
- Muppet Learning Keys
- IntelliKeys
- Touch Windows

Rather than reading that Sue received an A in math and a C in science, the user will read: "Student Sue Joe Matt Math Grade A B C Science Grade C B A." If possible, tables should be avoided. A designer who wants to use a table should also provide an alternate, text-only page that provides the same information but not in a table format. Some designers prefer to build their entire sites using tables. Users should be notified of the table format and a text-based site needs to be provided.

Use "Bobby" (http://www.cast.org/bobby) to find out whether their site designs are accessible.

Forms. Screen readers also have difficulty reading online forms. Online forms allow the user to enter information online in a guest book, request information through a form, use search engines, and register for shareware computer application. Forms should be available as a text file to download to the user's hard drive and then to be mailed either through e-mail or postal mail. All forms should list the e-mail address that the form is being sent to. Users who cannot download forms will then be able to write directly to the address.

Table 3		
Keyboard Commands for Tool Bar Functions in the Microsoft Internet Explorer		
Function	**Keyboard Commands**	**Description**
Access Menu Bar	F10	Open and view menus
Reload Page	F5	Reload current page
View Previous URLs	F4	View list of URLs previously visited
Help	F1	Access help menu
Stop	Esc	Stop page download
Open New Window	Ctrl + N	Open new window
Open URL	Ctrl + O	Type URL to visit
Print	Ctrl + P	Print current page
Save	Ctrl + S	Save current page
Find	Ctrl + F	Find keyword on current page
Go Back	Alt + Left Arrow	Move back a page
Go Forward	Alt + Right Arrow	Move forward a page
Next Anchor (Link)	Tab	Move to next anchor (link) and stop at end of document
Previous Anchor (Link)	Shift + Tab	Move to previous anchor and stop at beginning of document
Scroll Line Up	Up arrow key	Change view of document by one line up
Scroll Line Down	Down arrow key	Change view of document by one line down
Scroll Page Up	PageUp key	Change view of document by one height up
Scroll Page Down	PageDown key	Change view of document by one height down
Top of Page	Home key	Change view to beginning of document
Bottom of Page	End key	Change view to end of document

Colors and Backgrounds. Color and background patterns are another difficulty for people with visual disabilities. Pages with too many color combinations can be difficult to read for anyone, especially people with low vision and other visual disabilities. To decide whether the color combinations are difficult to read, designers need to view their pages in 256 shades of gray. Designers can adjust their monitors in the Control Panel to read only 256 shades of gray. While viewing the pages in gray, designers need to ask themselves whether they can read and distinguish the differences between colors on the basis of only lightness and darkness. Designers should also ask a person who has not helped to design the site to read the information on the site and to distinguish between the different shades of gray.

Sites that are meant to be wonders of design should have an alternate site built specifically for accessibility.

Another problem is the use of the color combinations of blue/yellow and red/green for text and backgrounds. People who are colorblind cannot see what is on these pages. Designers must never use these color combinations, unless they are providing an alternate site. The link to this alternate site should never be in blue, yellow, red, or green.

Background patterns can also create difficulty for people with low vision or other visual disabilities. A background that has many images on it or a pronounced texture is too decorative for the text to show well. Long pages of unbroken text are also a disadvantage for people with visual disabilities.

Unbroken Text. Long pages of unbroken text are difficult to skim for content for anybody, but especially for people with visual disabilities because it takes longer to read a passage. Long pages of text can be broken up by the use of headers (tags H1 to H6), which will help with the skimming process (see Table 1 for examples of tags used in HTML coding).

Frames. A major problem for people with visual disabilities is the use of frames. Although frames that are well designed can be visually stimulating, frames make an already small computer screen smaller. Also, frames act like tables for a screen reader, which causes confusion. Designers should avoid the use of frames. If frames must be used, designers need to provide an alternate site without frames.

Auditory Disabilities

Currently, people with auditory disabilities have few problems accessing information on the WWW. This is because Web design is primarily visual. More and more, however, Web designers are incorporating audio and video files into their pages. These formats pose problems for people with auditory disabilities.

Audio and video files should have full-text transcriptions of the audio. If possible, movies should be created that have a person signing the audio. The video of the person signing can either be added to the video file by using video editing software or as a separate file from the original video file. This will help the user—more than just reading the transcription—because the user can watch the movie and the signing at the same. Designers can also add closed captioning to the video.

Cognitive Disabilities

Navigating the WWW is currently very difficult; it is not an intuitive process. Not only are browsers difficult to use, but most Web page navigation is poorly designed. Site designers can make navigating a WWW page or site more intuitive by creating small menus at the top of the page for users to follow. Graphical "You Are Here" site maps can also be created using a graphics/drawing package and placed in each page.

Students who have difficulty reading will not receive much benefit from the WWW since the majority of the information is in a text format. Although it is extra work for Web designers, creating an audio file of the information on the page will alleviate the problem of long reading time or a lack of comprehension due to poor reading skills. The audio file can be designed as a downloadable option so that users who like to read text will not have to listen to the audio. Designers can add audio files by using sound recording and editing software and a computer microphone to create the files and then use an HTML generator to link the files into the site.

Table 4

Keyboard Commands for Tool Bar Functions in the Netscape Navigator

Function	Keyboard Commands	Description
Access Menu Bar	F10	Open and view menus
Reload Page	Ctrl + R	Reload current page
View Previous URLs	F4	View list of URLs previously visited
Help	F1	Access help menu
Stop	Esc	Stop page download
Open New Window	Ctrl + N	Open new window
Open URL	Ctrl + O	Type URL to visit
Print	Ctrl + P	Print current page
Save	Ctrl + S	Save current page
Find	Ctrl + F	Find keyword on current page
Increase Font	Ctrl +]	Increase font size
Decrease Font	Ctrl + [	Decrease font size
Page Source	Ctrl + U	View page source code
Page Info	Ctrl + I	View information about page
Next Anchor (Link)	Tab	Move to next anchor (link) and stop at end of document
Previous Anchor (Link)	Shift + Tab	Move to previous anchor and stop at beginning of document
Scroll Line Up	Up arrow key	Change view of document by one line up
Scroll Line Down	Down arrow key	Change view of document by one line down
Scroll Page Up	PageUp key	Change view of document by one height up
Scroll Page Down	PageDown key	Change view of document by one height down
Top of Page	Home key	Change view to beginning of document
Bottom of Page	End key	Change view of end of document

Long Web pages filled with unbroken text are difficult for users with cognitive disabilities to skim for information. Long pages of text can be broken up by the use of Headers (tags H1 to H6) and by graphics. Headers allow users to skim for the important parts of the document so that they will not have to read the entire document. Graphics break up the monotony of the pages and add another dimension to the user's understanding of the text.

Attention Deficit Disorder

The WWW has the ability to focus the attention of people with attention deficit disorder (ADD) by using graphics to lead the user through the information. But some Web designers create difficulties for people with ADD.

Multiple or long pages of unbroken text cannot keep people focused on the task of reading. Web designers can alleviate this problem by using descriptive headers (tags H1 to H6) to differentiate between important pieces in the document. Descriptive graphics can also be used to break up the monotony of long pages of text.

Many WWW pages are designed so that it is difficult to remain focused on an informational piece of text or graphic due to blinking text, scrolling marquees, or con-

tinual animation. This is a simple problem for Web designers to control. The designer can either not use the continual movements or can design an alternate page that does not contain the continual movements. Designers who wish to use continual movements for focusing the user's attention on one section can program the continual animations to stop after a few seconds. This will focus the user's attention to what the designer wants the user to view first, but will not become a distraction.

Physical Disabilities

Browsers make it difficult for people with limited mobility to access Web pages. Most browsers are designed for mainly mouse input. For people with limited mobility, mouses are difficult to use because they require fine motor skills of the fingers, hand, and arm.

For ease of navigation, many browsers are incorporating keyboard commands that function like mouse commands. Tables 3 and 4 list some of the keyboard commands for navigating the WWW with the Microsoft Internet Explorer and the Netscape Navigator.

Design and Accessibility

Because the WWW is a visual place where design is highly respected, many designers may want to focus more on design rather than accessibility. Sites that are meant to be wonders of design should have an alternate site built specifically for accessibility. These sites should allow users to access the alternate site or alternate pages on the first page of the site and then on every page throughout the site. For example, Page 1 of a site would contain a link to Page 1 of the alternate site. Page 2 of the graphical site would contain links to Pages 1 and 2 of the alternate site. Page 3 of the graphical site would contain links to Pages 2 and 3 of the alternate site, and so on. This enables users to move through sites at their ease, rather than at the designer's ease.

To many WWW designers, it may seem easier to create alternate text-only pages for users with disabilities. Though many users with disabilities (and users with slow modem connections) may use only the alternate pages, it is best to provide both alternate pages and the accessibility tips listed here. In this way, there will not be two standards and levels of quality for WWW design. All Web designs should be accessible to all people.

References

Center for Applied Special Technology. (1997, December 6). *Bobby* [Web site]. URL = http://www.cast.org/bobby/

Lemay, L. (1996). *Teach Yourself Web Publishing with HTML 3.2 in 14 Days* (Professional Reference Edition). [Web site]. URL = http://www.mcp.com/sansnet/

Paciello, Mike (1996; 1997, August 20). *Making the Web accessible for the blind and visually impaired* [Web site]. URL = http://www.yuri.org/webable/mp-blnax.html

Paciello, Mike (1996; 1997, August 20). *People with disabilities can't access the Web* [Web site]. URL = http://www.yuri.org/webable/mp-pwdca.html

Trace Research and Design Center. (1997, December 6). *Trace research and design* [Web site]. URL = http://www.trace.wisc.edu/

U.S. Department of Commerce, Technology Administration, National Institute of Standards and Technology. (1994; 1997, August 18). *People with disabilities and NII: Breaking down barriers, building choice* [Web site]. URL = http://www.itpolicy.gsa.gov/coca/SB_paper.htm

Stacy Peters-Walters, *Instructional Assistant, Governor's Technology for Teaching and Learning Academy, College of Education, Dakota State University, Madison, South Dakota.*

Address correspondence to the author at RR3, Box 28, Madison, SD 57042 (e-mail: peterss@triton.dsu.edu).

From *Teaching Exceptional Children*, May/June 1998, pp. 42-47. © 1998 by The Council for Exceptional Children. Reprinted by permission.

UNIT 10
Giftedness

Unit Selections

Key Points to Consider

- How can preschool teachers meet the needs of all students, including those with special gifts and talents?

- Is the Internet a useful tool for students with special gifts to communicate, collaborate, and develop higher-level thinking skills?

- How should gifted programs be assessed and how should schools change to meet the needs of high-ability students?

 **Links: www.dushkin.com/online/**
These sites are annotated in the World Wide Web pages.

Kenny Anthony's Gifted and Talented and General Educational Resources
http://www2.tsixroads.com/˜kva/

National Association for Gifted Children (NAGC)
http://www.nagc.org/home00.htm

The Individuals with Disabilities Education Act (IDEA) mandates special services for children with disabilities, but not for children with exceptional gifts or talents. The monies spent to provide special services for three children with high-cost disabilities could pay for accelerated lessons for a classroom full of college-bound students with intellectual giftedness. Should schools in the twenty-first century be more egalitarian? IDEA mandates appropriate education, but not sameness of quantity or degree of knowledge to be imported to every child. Are we inclined to push compensatory education of students with shortcomings in learning, while leaving students with a gift for learning to cope for themselves to counterbalance the equation? Do we want educational parity?

Since many textbooks on exceptional children include children with special gifts and talents, and since these children are exceptional, they will be included in this volume. Instructors who deal only with the categories of disabilities covered by IDEA may simply omit coverage of this unit.

The Omnibus Education Bill of 1987 provided modest support for gifted and talented identification and education of students with giftedness in the United States. It required, however, that each state foot the bill for the development of special programs for children with exceptional gifts and talents. Some states have implemented accelerated or supplemental education for the gifted. Most states have not.

Giftedness can be viewed as both a blessing and a curse. Problems of jealousy, misunderstanding, indignation, exasperation, and even fear are often engendered in people who live with, work with, or get close to a child with superior intelligence. Are children with giftedness at a disadvantage in our society? Children with special gifts and talents are deprived of some of the opportunities with which less exceptional children are routinely provided.

Students who are gifted tend to ask a lot of questions and pursue answers with still more questions. They can be incredibly persistent about gathering information about topics that interest them. They may, however, show no interest at all in learning about topics that do not. They may be very competitive in areas where they are especially skilled, competing even with teachers and other adults. They may seem arrogant about their skills, when, in their minds, they are only being honest.

Many children and youth with special gifts and talents have extraordinary sensitivity to how other people are reacting to them. As they are promoted through elementary school into middle school and high school, many such children learn to hide their accomplishments for the secondary gain of being more socially acceptable or more popular. Because they have been underchallenged and/or discouraged from achieving at their highest potentialities, underachievement becomes a problem. They have poor study habits as a result of not needing to study. They are unmotivated, intensely bored, and discouraged by the educational programs available to them.

Researchers who have studied creative genius have found that most accomplished high achievers share one childhood similarity. Their parents recognized their special abilities early and found tutors or mentors who would help them develop their skills. This is true not only of mathematicians and scientists but also of world-class sports players, musicians, artists, performers, writers, and other producers of note.

Educational programs that refuse to find tutors or mentors, or to encourage original work, or to provide special education in the skill areas of students with gifts are depriving the future of potential producers.

The earlier that children with special gifts and talents are recognized, the better. The sooner they are provided with enriched education, the more valuable their future contributions will become. Children from all ethnic backgrounds, from all socioeconomic levels, and from both sexes, can have exceptional gifts and talents. Researchers have reported that parents of gifted children seldom have any special creative skills or talents of their own.

The assessment of children with special gifts and talents, especially in the early childhood years, is fraught with difficulties. Should parents nominate their own children when they see extraordinary skills developing? How objective can parents be about their child's ability as it compares to the abilities of other same-aged children? Should measures of achievement be used (recitals, performances, art, reading levels, writings)? Many parents are embarrassed by their child's extraordinary aptitudes. They would rather have a popular child, or a child more like his or her peers.

The first article in this unit describes the uncommon talents of children who have been productive in exceptional ways; e.g., Mozart, Edison, Wang Yani, and some individuals with autistic savant syndrome. Ellen Winner reviews studies of giftedness such as Terman's famous study at Stanford University earlier in the twentieth century, and more contemporary research such as that by Csikszentmihalyi of the University of Chicago and Geschwind and Galaburda at Harvard University. The author points out the uneven development of many exceptionally gifted students. They may, for example, excel in spatial skills but have verbal deficits, or be high achievers in one area and unremarkable in others. In addition, many uncommonly talented youngsters suffer social problems. They may be misunderstood, neglected, or ridiculed as oddballs or nerds.

Angela Guptill, in the second article, describes how the Internet can be used to challenge and improve the performance of students with intellectual giftedness. Computer-based lessons allow students to pursue more work, find answers to questions, and spend evenings and weekends on learning adventures when and if they choose.

In the last article in this unit, Susan Winebrenner gives strong arguments for spending the time, effort, and money to ensure that our children with gifts and talents get all the education they need. Many students with special gifts and talents become underachievers. They rarely are challenged to learn above their current abilities. Because they score high on achievement tests it is assumed that they must be learning. An alternate explanation is that they already possessed these abilities. When they are not given a chance to pursue their special interests, and/or not requested to demonstrate increased excellence in an area, they lose confidence in their abilities to perform. This article urges that they be given a stimulating learning environment too.

Uncommon Talents:
Gifted Children, Prodigies and Savants

Possessing abilities well beyond their years, gifted children inspire admiration,
but they also suffer ridicule, neglect and misunderstanding

by Ellen Winner

One evening a few years ago, while I was attending a concert, a young boy in the audience caught my attention. As the orchestra played a Mozart concerto, this nine-year-old child sat with a thick, well-thumbed orchestral score opened on his lap. As he read, he hummed the music out loud, in perfect tune. During intermission, I cornered the boy's father. Yes, he told me, Stephen was really reading music, not just looking at it. And reading musical scores was one of his preferred activities, vying only with college-level computer programming manuals. At an age when most children concentrate on fourth-grade arithmetic and the nuances of playground etiquette, Stephen had already earned a prize in music theory that is coveted by adults.

Gifted children like Stephen are fascinating but also intimidating. They have been feared as "possessed," they have been derided as oddballs, they have been ridiculed as nerds. The parents of such young people are often criticized for pushing their children rather than allowing them a normal, well-balanced childhood. These children are so different from others that schools usually do not know how to educate them. Meanwhile society expects gifted children to become creative intellectuals and artists as adults and views them as failures if they do not.

Psychologists have always been interested in those who deviate from the norm, but just as they know more about psychopathology than about leadership and courage, researchers also know far more about retardation than about giftedness. Yet an understanding of the most talented minds will provide both the key to educating children and a precious glimpse of how the human brain works.

The Nature of Giftedness

Everyone knows children who are smart, hard-working achievers—youngsters in the top 10 to 15 percent of all students. But only the top 2 to 5 percent of children are gifted. Gifted children (or child prodigies, who are just extreme versions of gifted children) differ from bright children in at least three ways:

- *Gifted children are precocious.* They master subjects earlier and learn more quickly than average children do.
- *Gifted children march to their own drummer.* They make discoveries on their own and can often intuit the solution to a problem without going through a series of logical, linear steps.
- *Gifted children are driven by a "rage to master."* They have a powerful interest in the area, or domain, in which they can readily focus so intently on work in this domain that they lose sense of the outside world.

These are children who teach themselves how to read as toddlers, who breeze through college mathematics in middle school or draw more skillfully as second-graders than most adults do. Their fortunate combination of obsessive interest and an ability to learn easily can lead to high achievement in their chosen domain. But gifted children are more susceptible to interfering social and emotional factors than once was thought.

The first comprehensive study of the gifted, carried out over a period of more than 70 years, was initiated at Stanford University in the early part of this century by Lewis M. Terman, a psychologist with a rather rosy opinion of gifted children. His study tracked more than 1,500 high-IQ children over the course of their lives. To qualify for this study, the "Termites" were first nominated by their teachers and then had to score 135 or higher on the Stanford-Binet IQ test (the average score is 100). These children were precocious: they typically spoke early, walked early and read before they went to school. Their parents described them as being insatiably curious and as having superb memories.

Terman described his subjects glowingly, not only as superior in intelligence to other children but also as superior in health, social adjustment and moral attitude. This conclusion easily gave rise to the myth that gifted children are happy and well adjusted by nature, requiring little in the way of special attention—a myth that still guides the way these children are educated today.

In retrospect, Terman's study was probably flawed. No child entered the study unless nominated by a teacher as one of the best and the brightest; teachers probably overlooked those gifted children who were misfits, loners or problematic to teach. And the shining evaluations of social adjustment and personality in the gifted were performed by the same admiring teachers who had singled out the study subjects. Finally, almost a third of the sample came from professional, middle-class families. Thus, Terman confounded IQ with social class.

The myth of the well-adjusted, easy-to-teach gifted child persists despite more recent evidence to the contrary. Mihaly Csikszentmihalyi of the University of Chicago has shown that children with exceptionally high abilities in any area—not just in academics but in visual arts, music, even athletics—are out of step with their peers socially. These children tend to be highly driven, independent in their thinking and introverted. They spend more than the usual amount of time alone, and although they derive energy and pleasure from their solitary mental lives, they also report feeling lonely. The more extreme the level of gift, the more isolated these children feel.

Contemporary researchers have estimated that about 20 to 25 percent of profoundly gifted children have social and emotional problems, which is twice the normal rate; in contrast, moderately gifted children do not exhibit a higher than average rate. By middle childhood, gifted children often try to hide their abilities in the hopes of becoming more popular. One group particularly at risk for such underachievement is academically gifted girls, who report more depression, lower self-esteem and more psychosomatic symptoms than academically gifted boys do.

The combination of precocious knowledge, social isolation and sheer boredom in many gifted children is a tough challenge for teachers who must educate them alongside their peers. Worse, certain gifted children can leap years ahead of their peers in one area and yet fall behind in another. These children, the unevenly gifted, sometimes fall hopelessly out of sync.

The Unevenly Gifted

Terman was a proponent of the view that gifted children are globally gifted—evenly talented in all academic areas. Indeed, some special children have exceptional verbal skills as well as strong spatial, numerical and logical skills that enable them to excel in mathematics. The occasional child who completes college as an early teen—or even as a preteen—is likely to be globally gifted. Such children are easy to spot: they are all-around high achievers. But many children exhibit gifts in one area of study and are unremarkable or even learning disabled in others. These may be creative children who are difficult in school and who are not immediately recognized as gifted.

Unevenness in gifted children is quite common. A recent survey of more than 1,000 highly academically gifted adolescents revealed that more than 95 percent show a strong disparity between mathematical and verbal interests. Extraordinarily strong mathematical and spatial abilities often accompany average or even deficient verbal abilities. Julian Stanley of Johns Hopkins University has found that many gifted children selected for special summer programs in advanced math have enormous discrepancies between their math and verbal skills. One such eight-year-old scored 760 out of a perfect score of 800 on the math part of the Scholastic Aptitude Test (SAT) but only 290 out of 800 on the verbal part.

In a retrospective analysis of 20 world-class mathematicians, psychologist Benjamin S. Bloom, then at the University of Chicago, reported than none of his subjects had learned to read before attending school (yet most academically gifted children do read before attending school) and that six had had trouble learning to read. And a retrospective study of inventors (who presumably exhibit high mechanical and spatial aptitude) showed that as children these individuals struggled with reading and writing.

Indeed, may children who struggle with language may have strong spatial skills. Thomas Sowell of Stanford University, an economist by training, conducted a study of late-talking children after he raised a son who did not begin to speak until almost age four. These children tended to have high spatial abilities—they excelled at puzzles, for instance—and most had relatives working in professions that require strong spatial skills. Perhaps the most striking finding was that 60 percent of these children had engineers as first- or second-degree relatives.

The association between verbal deficits and spatial gifts seems particularly strong among visual artists. Beth Casey of Boston College and I have found that college art students make significantly more spelling errors than college students majoring in either math or in verbal areas such as English or history. On average, the art students not only misspelled more than half of a 20-word list but also made the kind of errors associated with poor reading skills—nonphonetic spelling such as "physicain" for "physician" (instead of the phonetic "fiscian").

The many children who posses a gift in one area and are weak or learning disabled in others presents a conundrum. If schools educate them as globally gifted, these students will continually encounter frustration in their weak areas; if they are held back because of their deficiencies, they will be bored and unhappy in their strong fields. Worst, the gifts that these children do possess may go unnoticed entirely when frustrated, unevenly gifted children wind up as misfits or troublemakers.

Savants: Uneven in the Extreme

The most extreme cases of spatial or mathematical gifts coexisting with verbal deficits are found in savants. Savants are retarded (with IQs between 40 and 70) and are either autistic or show autistic symptoms. "Ordinary" savants usually possess one skill at a normal level, in contrast to their otherwise severely limited abilities. But the rarer savants—fewer than 100 are known—display one or more skills equal to the prodigy level.

Savants typically excel in visual art, music or lightning-fast calculation. In their domain of expertise, they resemble child prodigies, exhibiting precocious skills, independent learning and a rage to master. For instance, the drawing savant named Nadia sketched more realistically at ages three and four than any known prodigy of the same age. In addition, savants will also surpass gifted children in the accuracy of their memories.

Savants are just like extreme versions of unevenly gifted children. Just as gifted children often have mathematical or artistic genius and language-based learning disabilities, savants tend to exhibit a highly developed visual-spatial ability alongside severe deficits in language. One of the most promising explanations for this syndrome posits atypical brain organization, with deficits in the left hemisphere of the brain (which usually controls language) offset by strengths in the right hemisphere (which controls spatial and visual skills).

According to Darold A. Treffert, a psychiatrist now in private practice in Fond du Lac, Wis., the fact that many savants were premature babies fits well with this notion of left-side brain damage and resultant right-side compensation. Late in pregnancy, the fetal brain undergoes a process called pruning, in which a large number of excess neurons die off [see "The Developing Brain," by Carla J. Shatz; SCIENTIFIC AMERICAN, September 1992]. But brain of babies born prematurely may not have been pruned yet; if such brains experience trauma to the left hemisphere near the time of birth, numerous uncommitted neurons elsewhere in the brain might remain to compensate for the loss, perhaps leading to a strong right-hemisphere ability.

Such trauma to a premature infant's brain could arise many ways—from conditions during pregnancy, from lack of oxygen during birth, from the administration of too much oxygen afterward. An excess of oxygen given to premature babies can cause blindness in addition to brain damage; many musical savants exhibit the triad premature birth, blindness and strong right-hemisphere skill.

Gifted children most likely possess atypical brain organization to some extent as well. When average students are tested to see which part of their brain controls their verbal skills, the answer in generally the left hemisphere only. But when mathematically talented children are tested the same way, both the left and right hemispheres are implicated in controlling language—the right side of their brains participates in tasks ordinarily reserved for the left. These children also tend not to be strongly right-handed, and indication that their left hemisphere is not clearly dominant.

The late neurologist Norman Geschwind of Harvard Medical School was intrigued by the fact that individuals with pronounced right-hemisphere gifts (that is, in math, music, art) are disproportionately nonright-handed (left-handed or ambidextrous) and have higher than average rates of left-hemisphere deficits such as delayed onset of speech, stuttering or dyslexia. Geschwind and his colleague Albert Galaburda theorized that this association of gift with disorder, which they called the "pathology of superiority," results from the effect of the hormone testosterone on the developing fetal brain.

Geschwind and Galaburda noted that the elevated testosterone can delay development of the left hemisphere of the fetal brain; this in turn might result in compensatory right hemisphere growth. Such "testosterone poisoning" might account for the larger number of males than females who exhibit mathematical and spatial gifts, nonright-handedness and pathologies of language. The researchers also noted that gifted children tend to suffer more than the usual frequency of immune disorders such as allergies and asthma; excess testosterone can interfere with the development of the thymus glad, which plays a role in the development of the immune system.

Testosterone exposure remains a controversial explanation for uneven gifts, and to date only scant evidence from the study of brain tissue exists to support the theory of damage and compensation in savants. Nevertheless, it seems certain that gifts are hardwired in the infant brain, as savants and gifted children exhibit extremely high abilities from a very young age—before they have spent much time working at their gift.

Emphasizing Gifts

Given that many profoundly gifted children are unevenly talented, socially isolated and bored with school, what is the best way to educate them? Most gifted programs today tend to target children who have tested above 130 or so on standard IQ tests, pulling them out of their regular classes for a few hours each week of general instruction or interaction. Unfortunately, these programs fail the most talented students.

Generally, schools are focusing what few resources they have for gifted education on the moderately gifted. These children make up the bulk of current "pull-out" programs: bright students with strong but not extraordinary abilities, who do not face the same challenges of precocity and isolation to the same degree as the profoundly gifted. These children—and indeed most children—would be better served if schools instead raised their standards across the board.

Other nations, including Japan and Hungary, set much higher academic expectations for their children than the U.S. does; their children, gifted or not, rise to the challenge by succeeding at higher levels. The needs of moderately gifted children could be met by simply teaching them a more demanding standard curriculum.

The use of IQ as a filter for gifted programs also tends to tip the programs toward the relatively abundant, moderately academically gifted while sometimes overlooking profoundly but unevenly gifted children. Many of these children do poorly on IQ tests because their talent lies either in math or language, but not both. Students whose talent is musical, artistic or athletic are regularly left out as well. It makes more sense to identify the gifted by examining past achievement in specific areas rather than on plain-vanilla IQ tests.

Schools should then place profoundly gifted children in advanced courses in their strong areas only. Subjects in which a student is not exceptional can be taught to the student in the regular classroom. Options for advanced classes include arranging courses especially for the gifted, placing gifted students alongside older students within their schools, registering them in college courses or enrolling them in accelerated summer programs that teach a year's worth of material in a few weeks.

Profoundly gifted children crave challenging work in their domain of expertise and the companionship of individuals with similar skills. Given the proper stimulation and opportunity, the extraordinary minds of these children will flourish.

ELLEN WINNER was a student of literature and painting before she decided to explore developmental psychology. Her inspiration was Harvard University's Project Zero, which researched the psychological aspects of the arts. Her graduate studies allowed her to combine her interests in art and writing with an exploration of the mind. She received her Ph.D. in psychology from Harvard in 1978 and is currently professor of psychology at Boston College as well as a senior research associate with Project Zero.

One of Winner's greatest pleasures is writing books; she has authored three, one on the psychology of the arts, another on children's use of metaphor and irony and, most recently, *Gifted Children, Myths and Realities*. "I usually have several quite different projects going on at once, so I am always juggling," she remarks. She is especially intrigued by unusual children—children who are gifted, learning disabled, gifted and learning disabled, nonright-handed or particularly creative. "The goal is to understand cognitive development in its typical and atypical forms."

When she has time to play, Winner devours novels and movies and chauffeurs her 13-year-old son on snowboarding dates. She is married to the psychologist Howard Gardner and has three grown stepchildren.

USING THE INTERNET
to Improve Student Performance

Angela M. Guptill

Use a search of the Web to draw associations between prior knowledge and new information

Individual or team collection of information

Classify information

Predict outcomes based on Web site search

Refine online search, as needed

Activities like these are essential parts of Internet-based lessons, and the activities are related to a well-known standard that teachers have relied on for years: *Bloom's Taxonomy*. These particular activities can be categorized as "application of knowledge," and teachers can assess the breadth and depth of their own lessons—and the performance of their students—by using a checklist like this one. This article shows how.

Challenges of New Technologies

Technology in the classroom creates new opportunities and challenges for educators. Skill-and-drill computer programs are being replaced by access to sites on the World Wide Web that allow students to use collaboration and multi-media to gather and demon-

strate knowledge. Technological resources have made it possible to develop lessons that promote critical, analytic, higher-order thinking skills and real-world problem-solving that are frequently found on assessments today (Blasi, Heinecke, Milman, & Washington, 1999). With the proper tools to monitor student performance, special educators have the opportunity to target individual needs and monitor progress as students progress through the curriculum using the Internet as a resource.

Challenges of the Standards Movement

As the focus on learning standards and outcomes prevails, educator concern has shifted from the multiple-choice standardized test to performance-based assessments. The possibilities for developing and strengthening higher-order thinking skills using the Internet has increased with the availability of interactive sites and classroom collaboration found on the Internet. Although research is inconclusive about the effect of technology on student performance, studies suggest that several outcome areas may be enhanced. According to Blasi et al. (1999), "These areas include higher order thinking skills, more sophisticated communication skills, research skills, and social skills" (p. 5).

This focus has challenged educators to develop lesson plans using the Internet that target the development of higher-order thinking skills required on many state assessments. For instance, the

Figure 1 Sample Internet Lesson Plan

The Structure of Matter   **Grade 8**

Unit Goals:
- Students will analyze the structures of matter by accessing their Hyperstudio stack titled "The Structure of Matter" and finding 3 Web sites that provide supporting information.
- Utilize Language Arts Skills—Complete Web site evaluation forms for 3 Web sites. Use information to prepare a newspaper article on the structure of matter. Send a copy to the assigned collaborative classroom. Respond to feedback and provide feedback to your collaborative partner.
- Prepare a multimedia presentation using your findings and the findings of your collaborative partner.
- Students will utilize technology skills—accessing programs, evaluating Web sites, toggle between programs, collaborate with other classrooms, prepare multimedia presentation.

Length of Unit: 8-12 days
Students should be able to:
- Classify objects by their properties
- Understand that matter exists in 3 states: solids, liquids, gases
- Understand the difference between chemical change and physical change (demonstrated through the newspaper article and presentation)
- Successfully collaborate with partner and provide feedback
- Prepare and present multimedia presentation
- Respond to questions from classmates and collaborative partner

Materials:
- Classroom computer lab with Internet access
- Software: Hyperstudio
- Web site evaluation form
- Technology taxonomy for assessment
- Web addresses for collaboration with other classrooms

Figure 2 Lesson Development and Assesment

1. For a lesson plan such as that in Figure 1, locate a collaborative classroom with a site on the Internet. This is a classroom working on the same topic in the same grade. Students can send and receive information (see http://www.epals.com/index.html).
2. Use a Web site evaluation form. Such a form gives the student the opportunity to critically analyze the information present on each Web site for timeliness and accuracy. These skills are addressed in the evaluation section of the technology taxonomy in Figure 3. See Web Site Evaluation form (Figure 2a).
3. Before presenting the lesson, assess whether it will provide students with the opportunity to progress up the technology taxonomy (Figure 3). Each lesson should facilitate demonstration of higher-level thinking skills.
4. Conduct performance measurement. At least quarterly, monitor the progress each student has made. This includes an assessment of progress using technology to develop critical-thinking and higher-order thinking skills. Careful documentation and charting of performance and progress is helpful for the student, parent, and the teacher. Use the technology taxonomy in Figure 3 to measure individual growth and performance.

ity of interactive sites and collaboration with other teachers and classrooms across all subjects and grades has made lesson planning easier (see Figures 1 and 2). More difficult has been the assessment of student performance using critical, higher-order, and problem-based inquiry skills. "It is clear that teaching and learning processes are embedded within complex systems. The challenge is to develop evaluation models that reflect this complexity" (Blasi et al., p. 4).

Figure 2a Web Site Evaluation: Junior High School

Student Information

Name: _____ Today's Date: _____

Topic: _____

Presentation of Information

URL of Web Page: _____
Name of Web Page: _____
Date the Web Page Was Made: _____
E-Mail Address of Author: _____
Was it easy to locate the Web Page ? __ Yes __ No
Did the Web Page give you a list of other good sites?
    __ Yes __ No
Did the pictures and sound help you to understand the information?
    __ Yes __ No
Did you find any spelling errors? __ Yes __ No
If yes, explain what errors you found:

Did you think that the information that you found was accurate?
Explain why or why not.

Notes

Notes:

Would you recommend this site to a classmate? __Yes __ No

World Wide Web can be used as a source of information for teachers and students to enhance classroom instruction and present knowledge using multimedia. Educators can evaluate these outcomes, but it is more complicated than the standardized testing route. According to Blasi et al. (1999), "Standardized tests are an efficient means for measuring certain types of learning outcomes but educators must ask if these are the outcomes valuable for the new millennium" (p. 3).

Classroom Collaboration

To share classroom ideas, projects, and communicate with teachers and students from around the world try... http://www.epals.com/index.html.

This Web site allows educators to locate classrooms to collaborate with by grade, location, and subject area.

Access to sites on the World Wide Web allows students to use collaboration and multimedia to gather and demonstrate knowledge.

Honey, McMillan, and Spielvogel (1995) have emphasized the real-world applications of modern technology: "Evidence indicates that when used effectively, technology applications can support higher-order thinking by engaging students in authentic, complex tasks within collaborative learning contexts" (p. 3). The availabil-

Benefits and Outcomes of Internet-Based Instruction

What are the benefits of Internet-based instruction, and what type of outcomes can be realized over traditional instruction? Accord-

Figure 3 Technology Taxonomy

Measuring Student Performance

Competence	Learning Hierarchy/Computer Application
Knowledge	• Search and reinforce . . . • Knowledge of major ideas • Knowledge of dates, events, places • Technological and academic concepts
Comprehension	• Surf (and sift) through information on the Web, and read for understanding • Identify valuable Web sites, record sites • Group Web sites into categories • Interpret, compare, and contrast facts • Predict consequences—use interactive Web sites to develop understanding of concepts • Contact experts to clarify understanding • Interpret information, provide perspectives
Application	• Draw together associations between prior knowledge and a search of the Web • Individual or team collection of information • Classify information • Predict outcomes based on Web site search • Refine online search, as needed • Select photographs, quotations, sound clips, virtual reality tours for use in presentation • Select format of presentation: newspaper, collage, Web page
Analysis	• Organization of information . . . (text, graphics, sound clips) • Sort and discern quality information from outdated or biased information • Find solutions to questions using collaboration and investigations with peers and experts
Synthesis	• Combine information from different Web sites • Modify information to meet assignment guidelines • Create and design Web sites, interactive projects, visual displays, and written text • Prepare essays, projects, visual displays, interactive presentations • Compose meaningful text from information gathered • Explain findings/synthesize findings
Evaluation	• Assess value and quality of presentation • Compare and discriminate between information from different sites • Verify value of information from various sources • Recognize the difference between subjective vs. objective information • Support information with prior knowledge • Summarize findings

Measuring individual growth and performance of students is a necessity when working with students with disabilities. To measure these elements when incorporating the use of technology into lessons, a taxonomy checklist is useful. This makes it possible to visualize student progress and provides excellent documentation.

Note: Adapted from *Bloom's Taxonomy* (adapted from Learning Skills Program, 1999. Available: http://www.coun.uvic.ca/learn/program/hndouts/ bloom.html).

Teachers and students can use the Internet to obtain feedback from other students—worldwide as well as to provide feedback to others.

Developing Internet-Based Lessons and Assessments

Access to the Internet provides educators with the opportunity to develop and implement lessons similar to the one that appears in Figure 1—a technology/science/language arts lesson selected from the Internet (http://www.d261.k12.id.us/tip/index.htm). The lesson was adapted to cover all levels on the "technology taxonomy" (adapted from *Bloom's Taxonomy*) in Figure 3. The lesson challenges students to use higher-level thinking skills as they use the World Wide Web to perform assignments and participate in activities.

Internet Resources for Educators

Awesome Library for Teachers, Students, and Parents
   http://www.neat-schoolhouse.org/awesome.html
Yahooligans!
   http://www.yahooligans.com/
The Global Classroom
   http://www/globalclassroom.org/projects.html
Index to Internet Lesson Plan Sites for K–12 Educators
   http://falcon.jmu.edu/~ramseyil/lesson.htm
Links to Educational Web Sites
   http://windsor.k12.co.us/links.htm
Internet Resources: Education Resources
   http://www.mcneese.edu/depts/library/int/educ.htm

The internet can help learners explore the world... by providing access to vast resources and information.

Educators can select similar lessons and adapt them for their own use (see Figure 2). Teachers can measure students' progress on the lesson by completing the "technology taxonomy" (Figure 3). This assessment model can be used to chart progress as students perform activities incorporated in the lesson using the Internet to access the World Wide Web.

Another boon to evaluation is the use of the Internet to obtain feedback from other students—worldwide—through collaboration, as well as to provide feedback to others. Teachers can access Web sites that provide instructional guidelines and can visit chat rooms that address Internet use in the classroom (see box, "Internet Resources"). Teachers can use the technology taxonomy in Figure 3 to check their lessons before class to ensure that learners gain exposure to each level of the taxonomy.

ing to Owston (cited in Pea & Roschelle, 1999), the Web can improve learning in three ways: "(a) by appealing to the learning styles of students, presumably increasing their motivation to learn; (b) by offering greater convenience through asynchronous communication; and (c) by providing a fertile ground for developing higher order thinking skills which are required to overcome the general lack of organization of knowledge in the Web" (p. 23). And don't forget the real-world applications: "The Internet can help learners explore the world beyond the classroom by providing access to vast resources and information, promoting scientific inquiry and discovery, and allowing students to communicate with experts" (Honey et al., 1995, p. 5).

Internet for Success

The Internet is an educational tool that can be used to expand learning opportunities and develop higher-order thinking skills. By adapting lessons found on the Web, collaborating with other classrooms, and obtaining feedback from other teachers and students, teachers can greatly expand their instructional strategies. Using a visual checklist such as the technology taxonomy (Figure 3) makes it possible to bring a level of classroom accountability to the application of advanced technology. It also serves as an instrument to measure individualized progress that may be incorporated in quarterly student progress reports to parents. Using the supports available on the Internet (see boxes), teachers have opportunities to develop lessons that provide students with effective instruction and enriched experiences.

"When used effectively, technology applications can support higher order thinking by engaging students in authentic, complex tasks within collaborative learning contexts."

References

Blasi, L., Heinecke, W., Milman, N., & Washington, L. (1999). New directions in the evaluation of the effectiveness of educational technology. The Secretary's Conference on Educational Technology 1999 [online]. Available: http://www.ed.gov/Technology/ Techconf/1999/whitepapers/ paper8.html.

Honey, M., McMillan, K., & Spielvogel, R. (1995). Critical issue: Using technology to improve student achievement. The Center for Children and Technology [online]. Available:http://www/ ncrel.org/sdrs/areas/issues/methods/technlgy/te800.htm.

Joint Jerome School District #261. (1999). Technology Integration Project: The structure of matter. Available: http://www/d261.id.us/ tip/index.htm.

Learning Skills Program, Bloom's Taxonomy [online]. Available: http://www.coun.uvic.ca/learn/program/hndouts/bloom.html.

Pea, R., & Roschelle, J. (1999). Trajectories from today's WWW to a powerful educational infrastructure. Educational Researcher, 26, 22–26.

Angela M. Guptill *(CEC Chapter #402), special education teacher, Shaker Junior High School, North Colonie Central School District, Latham, New York, and candidate, Certificate of Advanced Study in Educational Administration, State University of New York at Albany.*

Address correspondence to the author at 1260 Loudon Road, Apt. #C3, Cohoes, NY 12047 (e-mail: ANG111@aol.com).

This article was made possible in part by a grant from the AAUW Educational Foundation.

Gifted Students Need an Education, Too

Gifted children have the right to an education that takes into account their special needs. Here are suggestions for how to provide it.

Susan Winebrenner

Math time is beginning in Kate Ahlgren's primary grade classroom. Her objective is to teach several concepts relating to the base 10 method of counting and computing. Her first task is to assess her students' previous mastery of these concepts. She plans to allow those students who already have a clear understanding of this week's work to spend their math time applying what they have mastered about base 10 to learning about base 5.

Kate conducts a hands-on assessment by giving all students several tasks to complete with Cuisenaire rods. As she directs students to demonstrate what happens when they count past 10, she watches specifically for students who complete each directed task quickly and correctly. Fifteen minutes later, she has identified four children who clearly need more challenging content for the rest of this week's math work. She assigns a base 10 application task for most of the students to complete with partners and takes those four youngsters aside to briefly teach them the essential elements of base 5.

The four students practice excitedly for a few minutes under Kate's supervision. She explains that they will be working together for the rest of this week on learning about base 5 because that will challenge them. She assures them that all students should be working on challenging learning tasks.

Kate gives the four advanced students several tasks similar to those she has demonstrated. They practice together while she works with the rest of the students for the duration of the math period. Just before her instruction ends, she explains to the whole class that they will notice that not all students are working on the same tasks in math. She reassures them that this is perfectly all right and that her job is to make sure that all students are working on tasks that will help them move forward in their own learning. In this way, Kate makes differentiation the normal and acceptable condition of her classroom. She knows that when her students know something is all right with her, it will generally be all right with them, too.

Differentiated learning for high-ability students in heterogeneous classrooms is as important as it is for other children, yet the needs of the gifted are often misunderstood. Here are reasons why and suggestions for how teachers and administrators can differentiate the prescribed grade-level curriculum to meet the needs of high-ability students.

Why Provide Differentiated Learning for Gifted Students?

For the past 10 years, students who were not learning successfully were targeted for special attention. Sadly, during that same time, the needs of our most capable students have been overlooked. One reason for this neglect is the ability of gifted students to score high on assessments, which has led to the erroneous assumption that they must be learning. Another reason for ignoring their needs is that many educational leaders have misunderstood research on role modeling to mean that some gifted students should be present in all classrooms to facilitate forward progress for other students. Although students who struggle to learn can benefit from mixed-ability classes, they have plenty of positive role models in students who function well at the appropriate grade level, who are capable but not gifted learners. The discrepancy in learning ability between students who struggle to learn and gifted students is simply too wide to facilitate positive role modeling (Schunk, 1987).

Consider the range of abilities present in most classrooms. Visualize that both extremes of a learning curve are equally far removed from the norm. Students who fail to achieve the designated standards have received unprecedented attention during the past several years.

They are identified for special services before they start kindergarten, experience lower student-teacher ratios, and may even have a full-time aide assigned to them for the entire school day. School districts spend much more money educating this population than they designate for the usual per-pupil expenditure.

© Susie Fitzhugh

Teachers are expected to create numerous differentiation adjustments for low-achieving students by modifying the amount of work, depth, complexity, and content of the curriculum and by linking students' learning styles and interests to the prescribed learning tasks. Politicians, community members, and teachers avidly follow the progress of these students' learning for evidence that these students are indeed moving forward.

Contrast this with the situation for gifted students, whose natural learning abilities place them as far from average as their classmates who struggle to learn. In September, many of these youngsters could take the assessments that all students in their grade will take at the end of the year and still score at or above the 95th percentile. Simply in the interests of equity, these students are as entitled to receive the same types of differentiation so readily provided to the students who struggle to learn.

To assume that gifted students are learning because they achieve acceptable standards on state assessments is unrealistic. In Colorado, Oregon, and several other states, educators have realized that the learning progress of

gifted students cannot be adequately measured simply because the students meet or exceed minimum standards, so these states have specified learning expectations at exemplary levels. By setting exemplary standards, they can document the learning progress of gifted students.

Does the Promise of Education for All Apply to Gifted Students?

Every school district's mission statement promises its parents that "[a]ll students, including those who are exceptional, are entitled to a public-supported education in which instruction is geared to their needs, interests, and developmental levels" (Reis, Burns, & Renzulli, 1992, p. 3). Unfortunately, those at greatest risk of learning the least in classrooms are those at the top range of ability. Because a sense of confidence comes primarily from being successful at something perceived to be difficult (Rimm, 1990), gifted students who rarely undergo demanding learning experiences may lose confidence in their ability to perform well on challenging learning tasks. Many of these students learn to find the easiest way out, postponing their exposure to challenge in many patterns of underachievement (Rimm, 1990; Schmitz & Galbraith, 1985).

Either we must explain to parents that the promise of the school's mission statement does not apply to high-ability students, or we must commit ourselves to providing these students with appropriate and differentiated learning experiences. Whatever has been designated as suitable for students who are learning at a level commensurate with their age is not equally appropriate for students who learn at levels more typical of students several years older.

What Are the Characteristics and Needs of Gifted Students?

Gifted students learn differently from their classmates in at least five important ways. They learn new material in much less time. They tend to remember what they have learned, making spiral curriculums and reviewing previously mastered concepts a painful experience. They perceive ideas and concepts at more abstract and complex levels than do their peers. They become passionately interested in specific topics and have difficulty moving on to other learning tasks until they feel satisfied that they have learned as much as they possibly can about their passionate interest. Finally, gifted students are able to operate on many levels of concentration simultaneously, so they can monitor classroom activities without paying direct or visual attention to them.

Gifted students have already mastered much of the grade-level work, so they should have opportunities to function at more advanced levels of complexity and depth and to tie their own passionate interests into their schoolwork.

Why Are Many Educators Reluctant to Help Gifted Students?

Many teachers are reluctant to facilitate the needs of gifted students because of the lack of teacher training in this type of differentiation, a concern that other students or parents will accuse them of unfairness, or their belief that providing differentiation for this population is elitist.

Most preservice teachers take at least one course about meeting the needs of special–education students, but few states require teachers to take any courses in how to recognize and teach gifted students. Many teachers assume that gifted kids are highly productive, always complete their work on time, get consistently high grades, and will make it on their own without much assistance. Many educators believe that a student who is unproductive in school could not possibly be gifted.

Such misconceptions about how gifted students do their work are sources of great frustration for the students, their parents, and their teachers. Most teachers in my workshops are surprised when I tell them that gifted students often resist doing their assigned work because it is designed for age-appropriate learners and usually cannot provide the challenge and sense of accomplishment that would keep gifted learners motivated to work.

Another part of the problem is confusion about whether the mandated goals must actually be *taught* to students. Realistically, teachers are only required to demonstrate that all their students have *learned* the designated standards. Students who have already mastered the required content should be allowed to demonstrate their mastery before test-preparation sessions begin and to work on alternative activities because they already know the required content. When teachers learn how to plan and provide these alternative activities routinely to students who demonstrate prior mastery, these students can make progress in their own learning during more of their time in school.

How Can Teachers Provide Differentiation for Gifted Students?

The typical approach to differentiation for gifted students in heterogeneous classes has been to offer extra credit, an expectation that doesn't work because the only students eligible for extra credit are those who often have more than enough earned credit. The practice of offering extra credit should be replaced with approaches that can motivate gifted students to become enthusiastic learners.

Compact the curriculum. The most important needs of gifted students are to have regular opportunities to demonstrate what they already know, to receive full credit for content they have already mastered, and to spend their own learning time on challenging activities that accelerate and enrich the regular curriculum (Reis, Burns, & Renzulli, 1992). Compacting the curriculum can answer these needs.

To ascertain who would benefit from a compacted curriculum for a specific topic, teachers will want to provide interested students with pre-assessment opportunities for all learning activities. Teachers should use the same methods of assessment that they plan to use at the end of a learning unit, including written tests or observed performance on designated tasks. Because the preassessment is open to all students, the learning task itself can identify those who could benefit from the specific differentiated tasks regardless of whether particular students have been designated as gifted.

Students who can demonstrate previous mastery of upcoming content are expected to pay attention to direct instruction only when instruction includes concepts they have not yet mastered. On days when the lesson content is based on what these students have already mastered, they work instead on extension activities provided by the teacher or suggested by the students themselves. They receive full credit for what they have already mastered and earn daily credit for following the teacher's expectations about on-task behavior and productivity and by developing alternative projects and activities.

Design alternative learning experiences. As part of their regular lesson planning, teachers design alternative learning experiences. These provide differentiation opportunities in terms of *content, learning processes, products, learning environment*, and *assessment*.

The *content* is different because it moves students beyond grade-level standards or is connected to students' passionate interests. The *learning processes* called upon are different because they provide depth and complexity appropriate to these students' learning abilities. *Products* differ in that they demonstrate the students' learning at advanced levels, moving beyond typical research activities to the development of individual students' talents and curiosities and the presentation of their findings to appropriate audiences. Sometimes the *learning environment* is also different; students may pursue interests outside the regular classroom, work more independently on self-directed projects, or collaborate with other students. Even the *assessment process* is different because students receive full credit for what they have already mastered and do not have to complete all the work assigned to the rest of the class.

One particularly striking opportunity to provide alternative learning experiences presented itself when I discovered that James, one of my exceptionally gifted 6th graders, was writing a book at home on the anatomy and physiology of the human body. I pretested him and other interested students at the beginning of all language arts, reading, and writing units. James experienced differentiation in *content* because he wrote his book in class, in *learning processes* because he used sophisticated writing techniques, and in *assessment* because his grades for each unit were earned at the time of the pretest rather than at the end of the unit, with an overall grade that included an evaluation of his on-task behavior and project.

Allow differentiated pacing. For a curriculum that cannot be assessed beforehand because it is unfamiliar to all, gifted students work at their own pace to learn the required concepts and spend more time developing an expertise on a related topic of their choice.

Agree on expectations. Teachers and students work together to set up standards for evaluating productivity, behavior, and differentiated products and then agree to these standards in writing. Teachers should arrange to spend time with these students. It is important that gifted students not feel abandoned by the teacher and that they learn that everyone needs help on challenging tasks.

What Can Administrators Do To Facilitate Differentiation for Gifted Students?

Acknowledge the needs of gifted students. Acknowledge that the precedent for differentiation has been firmly set by the differentiation opportunities always available for students who struggle to learn. Because gifted learners are just as far removed from average as are children with learning problems, the differentiation that gifted students need is highly defensible and equitable.

Facilitate gifted education training for staff. Any strategies teachers learn for the benefit of their gifted students are applicable to many other students and tend to raise the learning bar for all students. One strategy, for example, is to allow students to get credit for an entire assignment by answering correctly at least four of the five most difficult problems first. This challenge motivates many students to listen more carefully to instructions so they can also qualify.

Investigate cluster grouping. Look into the practice of cluster grouping for gifted students. Cluster grouping is the practice of purposefully placing four to six gifted students together in an otherwise heterogeneous class. Their teacher must have some training in how to differentiate the curriculum for students who demonstrate previous mastery or who can learn new content faster than their classmates. Studies have demonstrated that

cluster grouping can lead to improved achievement for many students at all levels of learning ability (Gentry, 1999; Winebrenner & Devlin, 1996).

Communicate your expectations. Make clear your pledge that all students, including the most capable, will be able to learn something new and challenging every day. Clarify your commitment to the goal that all students will be expected to make continuous progress in their own learning. To that end, expect gifted students to demonstrate competencies that exceed those designated as basic.

Keep the Promise

Parents of gifted learners have a right to expect that schools will fulfill the promise made to all students that children will have consistent and daily opportunities for challenging learning experiences and will demonstrate continuous forward progress in their learning. This expectation requires providing gifted students with differentiation of the regular curriculum. To complacently accept their performance at regular competency levels is to deny their equal right to an appropriate education.

References

Gentry, M. L. (1999). *Promoting student achievement and exemplary classroom practices through cluster grouping: A research-based alternative to heterogeneous elementary classrooms.* Storrs, CT: National Research Center on the Gifted and Talented.

Reis, S. M., Burns, D. E., & Renzulli, J. S. (1992). *Curriculum compacting: The complete guide to modifying the regular curriculum for high ability students.* Mansfield Center, CT: Creative Learning Press.

Rimm, S. (1990). *How to parent so children will learn.* Watertown, WI: Apple Publishing.

Schunk, D. H. (1987). Peer models and children's behavioral change. *Review of Educational Research, 57,* 149–174.

Schmitz, C., & Galbraith, J. (1985). *Managing the social and emotional needs of the gifted.* Minneapolis, MN: Free Spirit Publishing.

Winebrenner, S., & Devlin, B. (1996). *Cluster grouping of gifted students: How to provide full-time services on a part-time budget.* Reston, VA: ERIC Clearinghouse on Disabilities and Gifted Education (ERIC Digest Document Reproduction Service No. 397618).

Susan Winebrenner is an educational consultant and author of *Teaching Gifted Kids in the Regular Classroom* (Free Spirit Publishing, 2000). She may be reached at P.O. Box 398, Brooklyn, MI 49230–0398 (e-mail: ecsfirst@aol.com)

Educational Leadership, September 2000, pp. 52-56. © 2000 by the Association for Supervision and Curriculum Development. All rights reserved. Reprinted by permission.

UNIT 11
Transition

Unit Selections

Key Points to Consider

- What services are needed to make the transition smoother from primary to middle school work for students with disabilities?
- What services are needed to make the transition smoother from high school to postsecondary programs for students with disabilities?
- What are the eight curricular components of a self-determination curriculum?

 **Links: www.dushkin.com/online/**
These sites are annotated in the World Wide Web pages.

National Transition Alliance (NTA) Home Page
http://www.dssc.org/nta/index.html

Special educational services are now mandated for students from the completion of their public school education through age 21 if they have a diagnosed condition of disability entitling them to assistance by the Individuals with Disabilities Education Act (IDEA). The extension of services to age 21 is to prepare students with disabilities to make a successful transition from the dependent status of student to a more independent status as community member and participant in the world of work.

The implementation of transitional services has been slow. The U.S. government defined transitional services as outcome-oriented, coordinated activities designed to move students with disabilities from school to activities such as college, vocational training, integrated employment, supported employment, adult education, adult services, independent living, and community participation. Choices are not either/or, but rather multiple: to help students with disabilities move from school to successful adulthood. While some students may only be able to achieve partial independence and supported employment, others may achieve professional degrees and complete self-sufficiency.

Every student with a disability should have an individualized transition plan (ITP) added to his or her individualized education plan (IEP) by age 16. This is the upper limit for beginning transition planning. It may begin in elementary school. Transitional services are more difficult to design than educational plans because of the nearly unlimited possibilities for the rest of one's life compared to the defined academic subjects possible to learn while in school.

The first step is to plan for an appropriate individualized transition plan for each unique student. Many teachers, special educators, vocational counselors, and employment mentors (job coaches) are not sure what kind of vocational preparation should be given in the public schools, or when. Should children with disabilities start planning for their futures in elementary school, in middle school, in high school, throughout their education, or just before they finish school? Should there be a trade-off between academic education and vocational education for these students? Should each student's vocational preparation be planned to meet the kind of needs and abilities of the individual, with no general rules about the wheres and whens of transitional services? Should students with disabilities be encouraged to seek out postsecondary education? The choices are legion. The necessity to rule out some possibilities and select others is daunting. Nobody on a team wants to make a mistake. Often the goals of the student are quite different from the goals of parents, teachers, counselors, and/or significant others. Compromises are necessary but may not please everyone, or anyone.

The transition from student to employee in the work world usually receives a great deal of attention. The transitions from child living at home to adult living away from parents, and from noncommunity participant to full participant in community activities, should get more attention in an ITP.

The transition to the world of work may take the form of supported employment (mobile work crew, clustered or enclave placement, on-site training and supervision by a job coach, group providing a specific service product) or sheltered employment (in a workshop). Many students with disabilities can make a transition from school to competitive employment. If they will

eventually work side by side with nondisabled coworkers, they may need transitional services such as assertiveness training, conflict resolution, negotiating skills, and personal empowerment counseling.

Just a few years ago, adults with disabilities were expected to live in institutions or with parents, siblings, or extended family members. This is no longer considered appropriate. Each individual with a disability should be encouraged to be as autonomous as possible in adulthood. Self-sufficiency is enhanced by providing education in life skills such as meal preparation and cleanup, home deliveries (for example, mail) and delivery pickups (for example, trash), using money and paying bills, making household repairs, and following home safety precautions.

The transition from noncommunity participant to fully participating member of society requires ITP modifications quite different from IEP academic goals. Students with exceptional conditions may need more than the usual amount of assistance in learning to drive a car or to use public transportation. They need to know how to read maps and schedules. They need to be able to assert their right to vote in secret (for instance, ballot in braille or computerized for their software), and to marry, divorce, reproduce, sue, defend themselves, or even run for public office. They should know social conventions (greetings, conversation skills, manners), grooming fashions, and clothing styles. They deserve to have the same access to health settings, religious locales, social activities, and information services (telephone, television, computer networks) as do persons without disabilities. Much is still left to be done to ensure a better life for adults with disabilities.

In the first article, Jean Lehmann, Timothy Davies, and Kathleen Laurin report on the transition needs of students with disabilities who go on to postsecondary institutions. Thirty-five such students attended a summit to discuss what would best meet their requirements in higher education. The ideas expressed most frequently were for more understanding of their disabilities, more services, more financial resources, and more self-advocacy training.

The second article in this unit deals with self-determination. This is one of the most important considerations for any ITP, yet one that is often forgotten as experts (parents, teachers, counselors, etc.) debate what would be most appropriate for a student with a disability. This selection describes a project whose goal was to promote each student's self-determination. It describes assessment and curriculum materials and strategies for implementing them. Eight self-determination components that should be in the curriculum were identified. Over 60 curricula that contain these components were found. The authors give Web sites, cost information, publishers, addresses, and phone numbers for obtaining these materials.

Listening to Student Voices About Postsecondary Education

Jean P. Lehmann • Timothy Gray Davies • Kathleen M. Laurin

Every year an increasing number of students with disabilities enter postsecondary education. Many of these students fail to successfully compete academically or simply leave before they complete their planned programs of study (Fairweather & Shaver, 1991; Wagner, 1989). In an effort to change the status quo, one community college and a university school of education program formed a collaborative support team to:

- Identify and systematically eliminate barriers to postsecondary education.
- Improve students' potential for having successful postsecondary experiences.

"Aiming for the Future," the project described here, is housed in a Midwestern community college in a rural area.

Using a systems-change model borrowed from Fullan (1993) that emphasizes the importance of listening to and acting on the ideas expressed by those most likely to be affected by change efforts, the collaborative support team sought information from the students' perspective. We asked students with disabilities currently attending postsecondary programs at the community college and university what they felt they needed to succeed. The process used to elicit these students' perceptions and ideas, which resulted in plans developed by the support team, is the focus of this article.

A Summit on "Aiming for the Future"

We invited 35 college students with a variety of disabilities—including hearing impairment, deafness, low vision, blindness, learning disabilities, traumatic brain injury, cerebral palsy, and paraplegia and quadriplegia—to attend a half-day focus group, which we called a *summit*. We asked the students to give us their perspectives on their personal and academic needs, barriers to their success, their support needs, and their visions for their future.

Using a nonthreatening group process designed to elicit a wealth of information in a short time, we ran-

domly placed the students in seven groups of five people each. We then asked each group to discuss questions aimed at helping students identify the barriers they have experienced as they attempt to successfully complete their educational and career goals. Students considered barriers encountered with admissions, financial assistance, and classes. They were asked to answer the following three questions:

- What are the most substantial barriers to your college experience?
- Are there special problems for students whose disability is not identified until posthigh school?
- What problems are encountered when making the transition from one college/university setting to another or into a job?

As students discussed their experiences, it became evident that the first question was central to understanding the realities and hopes of students receiving postsecondary training. Students perceived similar problems regardless of when their disability was identified, their year in college, or if they had entered the job market.

Next, we asked students to browse through magazines we placed on their table and select pictures representing barriers to their success in their current postsecondary institutions. We also asked them to select a second group of pictures representing strategies to support them in reaching their academic and career goals. Finally, we asked them to arrange these pictures to form a collage communicating their thoughts and ideas. Each group chose a spokesperson who interpreted the collage to the entire summit audience.

Student Barriers

As the students explained the experiences represented in their collages, four dominant themes emerged (see "Theme" boxes).

1. The lack of understanding and acceptance concerning disabilities in general, and their disabilities in

particular, on the part of people in general, fellow students, staff, and even faculty.

2. The lack of adequate services to assist in tackling academic and nonacademic responsibilities.
3. The lack of sufficient financial resources and the knowledge of how to acquire them, to live a more self-sufficient life.
4. The lack of self-advocacy skills and training needed to live independently.

Lack of Understanding and Acceptance

All the student groups emphasized two elements: the lack of acceptance and the lack of understanding of those with disabilities. One group's members strikingly portrayed how they felt about this lack of acceptance by placing a large picture of Tom Hanks in a trendy two-piece dress suit in its collage. Rather than leave the familiar face in place, however, they replaced it with a head disproportionately smaller. According to students, this picture "represents for us the small-minded people, small-minded students on campus; and every once in a while you run into a professor like that, too."

One member of the "summit" looks through magazines and selects pictures representing barriers to her success in her current postsecondary institution.

As groups shared their collages with other summit participants, they elaborated on their frustrations. For ex-

ample, another group shared that this lack of understanding and acceptance often resulted in a "crash and burn effect with the teachers; they don't understand you, and it gives you a sense of being out of order." Particularly troubling to students was the perception they had that society generally viewed disability to be associated with incompetence. Typifying this perception is the remark of one student, who stated: "Because of the problems we have, a lot of times people get mad that we are not doing things the way they do it and you always want to say, 'Yes, I will do it!'"

> **Theme 1. The lack of understanding and acceptance concerning disabilities by fellow students, staff, and faculty**
>
> - Small-mindedness.
> - Disability viewed as incompetence.
> - Instructor frustration.
> - Instructors can damage students.

Several groups of students expressed the difficulties they experience when instructors are not knowledgeable or experienced in modifying classroom environments, instructional strategies, or grading methods, For example, one group noted:

> We have to deal with professors, but they don't deal with us. They deal with the norm, and some are frustrated with us.

Another student expanded on this remark by saying: "Not only do we have a problem, we then have to alleviate accommodation anxiety [of instructors]." Perhaps the most poignant remark relative to this first barrier was from a student who stated:

> Some teachers and TA's [teaching assistants] don't have an understanding of students' needs. They cause damage to students with disabilities through their lack of understanding. It makes me think sometimes, so who has the real problem? Me or them?

Lack of Adequate Services

The second barrier identified by the students was the lack of adequate services available to assist them in tackling both academic and nonacademic challenges. These summit students realized that they were not alone in needing academic support outside the postsecondary classroom. Many of these students perceived that college educators and college-services staffs needed information, training, and ongoing support themselves to effectively teach students with disabilities. Perhaps that is why students expressed such disappointment in their traditional academic support laboratories, where tutoring in math, reading, writing, and computer literacy skills are available to all students. Their disappointments stem from the examples mentioned previously—that the staff and tutors knew little about these students' disabilities and thus could not communicate with them effectively.

Theme 2. The lack of adequate services to assist in tackling academic and non-academic responsibilities

- Teachers and support staff need information, training, and ongoing support themselves to effectively teach students with disabilities.
- Documentation of disability is not forwarded to postsecondary institutions.
- Students are unable to acquire medical and dental services because communication was difficult.
- Students felt need for increased access to transportation, buildings, and adaptive computers.

Further, students indicated that they literally were "searching for services" that were more appropriate to their needs but were beyond the scope of the support traditionally provided on campus. Examples of these needs included having adequate, reliable transportation to campuses, as well as on campus, and the need for networking and mentoring so that students could "learn from each other and reach their potential."

Theme 3: Lack of sufficient financial resources and the knowledge of how to acquire them to be self-sufficient

- Need reliable income to move out on their own and become more self-sufficient.
- Less on-campus opportunity to work compared to other students.
- Feeling insecure in their knowledge of time and money management.

Disabilities documentation was a major issue for many students. High school records of special education services received were not routinely given to students or passed along to the postsecondary institutions. Without this documentation, students were faced with several dilemmas, including having to prove their eligibility for postsecondary services. Often, students felt themselves to be unable to explain fully or even identify strategies previous educators had found to be helpful for enhancing their learning processes. Thus, students in several groups pointed out the need for more assessment opportunities at the postsecondary level so that incoming students could learn more about the extent of their disability and what assistance the support laboratories can provide on

an individual and group basis. Students reported that "disability changes the way you see life," but they needed to learn the accommodations and compensatory skills that might enhance their success.

It was not only the lack of academic support services and inadequate knowledge of their individual files that these students decried. For example, some students were upset at being unable to obtain service at local medical centers where neither doctors nor their staff could understand even basic signing, thus causing frustration and anxiety during examinations. Students said that there was no systematic career-services network to assist them in obtaining full-time employment. One student shared his appreciation for a counselor who was well connected with community employers; but when the counselor left, the contacts seemed to disappear.

Finally, students discussed the need for environmental support on campus and in the community so that they could more easily manage access to dependable transportation, buildings, restrooms, and adaptive computer technology on their campuses and at their banks.

Need for Financial Resources

The third barrier, insufficient financial resources, was a universal concern among students at the summit. They knew they needed a steady, reliable income for food, clothing, housing, transportation, and medical insurance so they could "move out on our own and be self-sufficient." Yet they were not sure they had the knowledge base to independently manage their time and budget their money effectively.

In addition, students' postsecondary experiences had taught them that, as students with disabilities, their opportunities for employment to work-study positions or student assistantships were limited and not on a par with their peers without disabilities. Further, the consequences of their disability often precluded the possibility of employment due to complicating factors of Social Security Disability Income (SSDI), Medicaid, or Vocational Rehabilitation Services. Often students' time was limited by constraints related to their disability, such as time scheduled for tutoring sessions and the need to reserve as much time as possible to studying.

Need for Self-advocacy Skills

The fourth barrier is a theme unto itself, yet is also a thread connecting the first three barriers. The students feel they lack self-advocacy skills. A constant cry from each of the groups at the summit was the need for respect: from their peers, their community, their professors, and from themselves. Students, however, also indicated that they had no training or experience in describing their disability to others. They wanted to learn how to advocate for themselves; to help educate their college community;

to be more assertive in gaining knowledge of their disability; to be forceful in communicating their strengths and weaknesses, abilities and inabilities; and to gain the necessary strength and courage to ask for what they needed to be able to succeed. In learning to advocate for themselves, they would continue to deepen their own self-understanding, increase their self-esteem and self-worth, and begin to develop "a positive attitude to live life to its potential!"

Theme 4. The lack of self-advocacy skills and training to live independently

- Need to gain respect from the college community.
- Need to learn to advocate for themselves.
- Need to be more assertive in gaining knowledge of their disability.
- Need to deepen their own self-understanding, self-esteem, and self-worth.

Visions for the Future

Although students expressed enormous frustration with the multiple barriers they encounter, they were positive in their outlook as they begin the "journey" to their futures. One student expressed this optimism by telling the group, "The dream begins as soon as you open the door." In describing their visions for the future, the students' statements signified the importance of self-advocacy skills. One group related that the key to breaking free of barriers was having "confidence, family, self-esteem, strength, and support." Another student stated that each day, "you get up in the morning, and you have to encourage yourself somehow." Other students discussed the importance of surrounding themselves with a supportive network of people. One student stated, "I didn't want to go to school, but I found out [that] more learning and knowledge make life easier."

Self-responsibility, interdependence, realistic goals, self-acceptance, positive self-esteem, knowledge of disability, communication skills, the ability to self-advocate, a supportive network of people, and a positive attitude—these were the elements that defined the students' perspective on self-determination.

Recommendations for Eliminating Barriers

In response to students' statements, the postsecondary education support team has planned a three-pronged approach that supports students, secondary teachers, and postsecondary faculty. The plan also addresses larger institutional issues regarding receptivity to recruiting and

serving students with disabilities (see box, "Tips for Eliminating Barriers").

The support team provides tuition waivers (using federally granted funds) for students who need financial assistance. The team also provides students with more intensive academic and nonacademic support. Specifically, the support team holds workshops throughout the state to recruit students with disabilities and inform them about higher education requirements. These workshops, for students, secondary teachers, and parents, are held on college and community college campuses. The workshops also help students gain insight into their responsibilities as college students, help them explore their learning styles, and provide students with self-determination training.

Tips for Eliminating Barriers

- Ask students to conduct workshops that describe the nature of various disabilities to faculty and staff.
- Provide staff development to postsecondary faculty regarding adaptations and accommodations they can implement.
- Reward faculty who are willing to adapt instruction to address the learning needs of students.
- Evaluate transportation availability to campus and on campus.
- Inform students about the documentation requirements of local postsecondary institutions before their senior year at high school.
- Identify potential financial resources for students entering into postsecondary settings.
- Teach high school students time and money management skills.
- Tour the college campus with interested students during transition planning.
- Provide summer classes addressing compensatory strategies on college campuses for high school students interested in obtaining a postsecondary education.
- Role-play with students ways of communicating to college faculty about students' disability and learning needs.
- Encourage networking between college students via focus groups, student meetings, and information workshops.

The support team also invites high school and college faculty members to training sessions regarding laws and accommodations for students with disabilities. To remind and assist institutions of higher education about the level of their commitment to teaching students with disabilities, the team is developing an evaluation instrument for postsecondary faculty members to use. The instrument addresses accessibility in terms of attitudes and architecture of many aspects of higher education: the college admissions office, career center, housing office, library, financial aid office, and student centers.

To gather more information, the team holds focus groups with community members, secondary teachers, and families. We hope to learn more about the specific types of support that these stakeholders perceive they need.

Final Thoughts

Students' perceptions solicited in the summit are consistent with research reported in recent years. Students in studies by Finn (1998) reported that receiving accommodations in courses and during testing were most beneficial to their success in postsecondary education. Finn (1998) concluded, as a result of these findings, that both staff development and student training in self-advocacy were therefore necessary (see box, "Why Involve Students?"). Research regarding faculty attitudes confirms that there is, in fact, a lack of understanding on the part of instructors relative to issues of disabilities (Hill, 1996; West et al., 1993).

One member from each group presented a collage communicating his or her thoughts and ideas to the entire "summit" audience.

What is unusual about the "Aiming for the Future" project? From the beginning, the support team solicited students' concerns and then designed the project's interventions in accordance with project goals *and* student responses generated during the focus group activities. This approach to changing systems is consistent with national

efforts to increase self-determination of students with disabilities.

Clearly, it is futile to create new student support services—or even enhance existing services—without gathering the opinions of all stakeholders, particularly students' opinions (Fullan, 1993). Excluding students from opportunities to articulate their needs is a recipe for failure. Not only do students lose a sense of ownership of the services (Smith, et al., 1995), but they also miss opportunities to practice self-determining skills, such a problem-solving and advocating for themselves (see box, "Why Involve Students?"). As noted by the students participating in the "Aiming for the Future" project, having a disability should not prevent you from having dreams and "going the distance."

Why Involve Students?

- *Increases knowledge of and ownership of the services offered.* According to Smith, Edelen-Smith, & Stodden (1995), excluding key participants in planning processes may increase resistance to ideas and decrease cooperation.
- *Enhances students' future success.* Reiff, Gerber, and Ginsberg (1997) found that successful adults with learning disabilities sought to and exerted control over their lives by making decisions about events in their lives. Further, Ward (1988) suggested that people who take control of their lives and can identify future goals will have greater future success.
- *Fosters high self-esteem.* Students whose opinions are valued, listened to, and acted upon become equal partners in the service delivery, thus increasing their sense of accomplishment and dignity (Lovett, 1996).
- *Provides students with opportunities to practice self-determination skills.* In a study by Lehmann, Bassett, and Sands (1999), students lack opportunities to engage in activities that facilitate the development of self-determination skills, such as articulating ideas, expressing needs, and acquiring leadership skills. Powers and her colleagues (1996) concluded that self-determination skills are learned and must be bolstered through application.
- *Encourages responsibility and decision-making skills.* Wehmeyer (1993) found that students who did not have opportunities to practice making choices tended to avoid making decisions and accepting responsibility.

References

Fairweather, J. S., & Shaver, D. M. (1991). Making the transition to postsecondary education and training. *Exceptional Children, 57*, 264–267.

Finn, L. (1998). Student's perceptions of beneficial LD accommodations and services at the postsecondary level. *Journal of
Postsecondary Education and Disability, 13,* 46–67.

Fullan, M. (1993). *Change forces: Probing the depths of educational
reform.* London: The Falmer Press.

Hill, J. L. (1996). Speaking out: Perceptions of students with disabilities regarding adequacy of services and willingness of
faculty to make accommodations. *Journal of Postsecondary
Education and Disability, 12,* 22–43.

Lehmann, J. P., Bassett, D. S., & Sands, D. J. (1999). Students' participation in transition-related actions: A qualitative study.
Remedial and Special Education, 20, 160–169.

Lovett, H. (1996). *Learning to listen: Positive approaches and people
with difficult behavior.* Baltimore: Paul H. Brookes.

Powers, L. E., Wilson, R., Matuszewski, J., Phillips, A., Rein, C.,
Schumacher, D., & Gensert, J. (1996). Facilitating adolescent
self-determination: What does it take? In D. J. Sands, & M.
L. Wehmeyer (Eds.), *Self-determination across the life span: In-
dependence and choice for people with disabilities* (pp. 257–284).
Baltimore: Paul H. Brookes.

Reiff, H. B., Gerber, P. J., & Ginsberg, R. (1997). *Exceeding expectations: Successful adults with learning disabilities.* Austin, TX:
PRO-ED.

Smith, G. J., Edelen-Smith, P. J., & Stodden, R. A. (1995). How to
avoid the seven pitfalls of systematic planning. A school
and community plan for transition. *Teaching Exceptional
Children, 27*(4), 42–47.

Wagner, M. (1989). *Youth with disabilities during transition: An
overview of descriptive findings from the National Longitudinal
Transition Study.* Menlo Park, CA: The National Longitudinal Study of Special Education Students.

Ward, M. J. (1998). *The many facets of self-determination: Transition
summary.* Washington, DC: National Information Center
for Children and Youth with Handicaps.

Wehmeyer, M. (1993). Perceptual and psychological factors in
career decision-making of adolescents with and without
cognitive disabilities. *Career Development for Exceptional Individuals, 16,* 135–146.

West, M., Kregel, J., Getzel, E. E., Zhu, M., Ipsen, S. M., & Martin,
E. D. (1993). Beyond Section 504: Satisfaction and empowerment of students with disabilities in higher education. *Exceptional Children, 59,* 456–467.

Jean P. Lehmann, *Associate Professor,* **Timothy Gray** Davies, *Associate
Professor, School of Education, Colorado State University, Fort Collins, Colo-
rado;* **Kathleen M.** Laurin, *Project Coordinator, Department of Health and
Human Services, The University of Northern Colorado, Greeley, Colorado.*

*Address correspondence to Jean P. Lehmann, School of Education, Colorado
State University, Fort Collins, CO 80523-1588 (e-mail: lehmann@CAHS.
colostate.edu).*

*Preparation of this article was funded in part through the support of Grant
HO78C60015 from the U.S. Department of Education, Office of Special Education and Rehabilitation Services. The contents of this article do not necessarily reflect the policies of the funding agency.*

Choosing a Self-Determination Curriculum

PLAN *for the Future*

David W. Test • Meagan Karvonen • Wendy M. Wood • Diane Browder • Bob Algozzine

Self-determination. In almost every special education publication, conference, or inservice workshop, someone mentions "self-determination." The popularity of this term is not surprising, considering the urgent need to improve postsecondary outcomes for students with disabilities (see box, "What Does the Literature Say About Self-Determination?"). Self-determination is certainly a factor in the success of all students.

This article describes a project to help educators improve the self-determination of students with disabilities. We conducted this project with support from the U.S. Department of Education, Office of Special Education Programs, to gather, evaluate, and disseminate information about curriculum/ assessment materials and strategies on promoting self-determination. In addition, we suggest a process other educators can use to select materials and curricula.

The Self-Determination Synthesis Project

The Self-Determination Synthesis Project (SDSP) has the objective of synthesizing and disseminating the knowledge base and best practices related to self-determination for students with disabilities. To this end, the purpose of the project was to improve, expand, and accelerate the use of this knowledge by the professionals who serve children and youth with disabilities; parents who rear, educate, and support their children with disabilities; and the students themselves.

We found 60 curricula designed to promote self-determination skills.

As part of the SDSP effort, we have conducted a comprehensive literature review of self-determination interventions research, visited school systems that exhibited exemplary self-determination outcomes, and gathered and catalogued published self-determination curricula. For more information on our exemplary sites and literature review visit our Web site at http://www.uncc.edu/sdsp.

Existing Self-Determination Curricula

To identify existing self-determination curricula, we reviewed the literature, conducted Web searches, asked experts in the area, and advertised in newsletters and at conferences. As a result, we found 60 curricula designed to promote self-determination skills. Table 1 shows a sampling of these curricula; other reviews are available from the authors (see Table 1). We compiled the name of each curriculum, the publisher, telephone number, and cost information for each curriculum. Further, we identified, for each curriculum, which of the eight self-determination components the curriculum included, based on the most commonly identified components of self-determination found in the literature (e.g., Field & Hoffman 1994; Mithaug, Campeau, & Wolman, 1992; Ward, 1988; Wehmeyer, 1996). The eight curricular components are as follows:
- Choice/decision-making.
- Goal setting/attainment.
- Problem-solving.
- Self-evaluation, observation, and reinforcement.
- Self-advocacy.
- Inclusion of student-directed individualized education programs (IEP).
- Relationships with others.
- Self-awareness.

Finally, we listed the materials included in each curriculum and the appropriate student audience identified by the author, and noted whether the curriculum had been field-tested.

Table 1. A Sample of Self-Determination Curricula and Components
(For a complete listing, see http://www.uncc.edu/sdsp)

TITLE	Choice/ Decision Making	Goal Setting/ Attainment	Problem Solving	Self Eval	Self Advocacy	IEP Plan	Relationships w/Others	Self Awareness
Next S.T.E.P.: Student transition and educational planning **Product Info:** Pro-Ed (800) 897-3202 Price: $144	X X	X		X		X		X
Contents: Video, Teacher manual, Student workbook **Audience:** Transition aged students with and without disabilities, and students at-risk **Other:** Adjustment, Employment, Education, Housing, Daily living, Community							*Field Test*	X
Self-advocacy strategy for education and transition planning **Product Info:** Edge Enterprises (785) 749-1473 Price: $15	X X				X	X		X
Contents: Instructor's manual **Audience:** Audience: Primary and secondary students with mild disabilities, and high risk students **Other:** Employment, Education, Housing, Daily living, Personal, Community							*Field Test*	X
Take action: Making goals happen [Choice-maker] **Product Info:** Sopris West Inc. (800) 547-6747 Price: $95	X X	X		X				
Contents: Teacher's manual, Reproducible lesson masters, Video **Audience:** Not specified **Other:** Adjustment, Employment, Education, Housing, Daily living, Personal, Community							*Field Test*	X
TAKE CHARGE for the future **Product Info:** OHSU Center on Self-Determination (503) 232-9154 Price: $45	X X	X		X	X	X		X
Contents: Student guide, Companion guide, Parent guide, Class guide **Audience:** Sophomores and juniors with disabilities **Other:** Adjustment, Employment, Education, Housing, Daily living, Personal, Community							*FieldTest*	X
Whose future is it anyway? A student-directed transition process **Product Info:** The Arc National Headquarters (888) 368-8009 Price $20	X X	X		X	X	X		X
Contents: Student manual with coach's guide **Audience:** Middle school and transition aged students with mild to moderate cognitive, developmental, or learning disabilities **Other:** Employment, Education, Housing, Daily living, Personal, Recreation, Community							*Field Test*	X

Choosing the Right Curriculum

We found many curricula that address the different components of self-determination. Some curricula teach specific skills, such as decision making or goal setting. Others include content intended to increase students' knowledge about their disabilities or about disability rights. Still others include learning approaches or processes by which students take greater ownership of their IEP planning process. With the variety of materials available, how do teachers know what will be most effective for use with their students? We suggest that the process begin with a careful review of the sampling in Table 1 to become familiar with the variety of resources that are available. In addition, you might want to gather other published descriptions/reviews of self-determination curriculum (see Field, 1996; Field et al., 1998).

What Does the Literature Say About Self-Determination?

Here are the current trends in self-determination research:

- Current research has referred to self-determination as the ultimate goal of education (Halloran, 1993).
- Research has demonstrated a positive relationship between self-determination and improved postsecondary outcomes. These outcomes include a higher rate of employment and higher wages 1 year after graduation for students with mild mental retardation and learning disabilities (Wehmeyer & Schwartz, 1997).
- Classroom teachers are recognizing that self-determination is an important skill to teach students (Agran, Snow, & Swaner, 1999; Wehmeyer, Agran, & Hughes, 2000).

Definition of Self-Determination. Beginning with the "normalization" movement in the early 1970s, many researchers, educators, and self-advocates have developed definitions of self-determination. According to a consensus definition by Field, Martin, Miller, Ward, and Wehmeyer, 1998, self-determination is

a combination of skills, knowledge, and beliefs that enable a person to engage in goal-directed, self-regulated, autonomous behavior. An understanding of one's strengths and limitations together with a belief in oneself as capable and effective are essential to self-determination. When acting on the basis of these skills and attitudes, individuals have greater ability to take control of their lives and assume the role of successful adults. (p. 2)

Conceptual models of self-determination have included knowing and valuing oneself (Field & Hoffman, 1994); skills and knowledge on topics such as choice and decision making, goal setting and attainment, problem-solving, and self-advocacy (Martin & Marshall, 1995; Wehmeyer, 1999); and recognition of the environment's role in supporting self-determination for people with disabilities (Abery & Stancliffe, 1996).

Need for Instruction in Self-Determination. Unfortunately, so far all the rhetoric, research, and recognition is not being translated into classroom instruction. For example, Agran et al. (1999) found that whereas over 75% of middle and secondary teachers rated self-determination skills as a high priority, 55% indicated that self-determination goals were either not included in their students' IEPs or only in some students' IEPs. This finding is supported by: (a) Wehmeyer and Schwartz (1998) who found no self-determination skills in 895 IEP transition goals; and (b) Wehmeyer et al. (2000) who found 31% of secondary-level teachers reported writing no self-determination goals in student IEPs, 47% reported writing self-determination IEP goals for some students, and only 22% reported writing self-determination IEP goals for all students.

Although many explanations may exist for why self-determination skills are not included in student IEPs, we believe a major reason is that teachers are unaware of what resources exist to help with the task. This is supported by Wehmeyer et al. (2000), who reported that 41% of teachers with secondary-aged students indicated that they did not have sufficient training or information on teaching self-determination, and 17% were unaware of curriculum/assessment materials/strategies.

Promoting self-determination also requires training those without disabilities to encourage and respect the decisions made by self-determining individuals with disabilities.

Figure 1 shows a curriculum materials review checklist that we have found useful when deciding what curriculum might be most appropriate. The information included in Figure 1 is summarized in the following set of questions:

Does the intended audience match my students?

Are the materials age-appropriate? Are they designed for use with students who have mild, moderate, or severe disabilities? Some materials that may have been originally designed for use with a specific group of students may have to be modified for use with other groups (including students without disabilities). Check the introductory section of the teacher's manual to see what the authors say.

Do the skills covered in this curriculum meet my students' needs?

You may find that your students are perfectly capable of setting goals, but they do not know enough about their rights under current legislation such as the Individuals with Disabilities Education Act or the Americans with Disabilities Act to be able to ask for reasonable accommodations in their postsecondary setting, or maybe they need a better understanding of how to run their IEP meeting. In some cases, the introduction or overview section of the teacher's manual will state the goals of the curriculum. For example, the Take Action curriculum states: "Students learn to act on their plans, evaluate their plan and results, and make any necessary adjustments" (Marshall, et al., 1999, p. 9). Do the goals of the curriculum match your instructional objectives?

Does the curriculum require prerequisite skills?

Some curricula may require relatively sophisticated reading levels, or assume that the students will already understand how to make choices for themselves. Both the teacher's manual and the student activities will give you a sense of what skill level is required for students to begin using the curriculum.

Figure 1. Curriculum Materials Review Checklist

CURRICULUM MATERIALS REVIEW CHECKLIST

Title:_____

Author:_____

Publisher's name contact/information:_____

Date of publication:_____ Cost of materials:_____

For what type of student is the curriculum designed (e.g., age, disability)?

_____

What types of materials are included (e.g., instructor manual, student workbook, video, alternate formats)

_____

Do the components of self-determination match my students' needs

Students' Needs	Included in Curriculum		Comments
Choice-making	YES	NO	
Decision-making	YES	NO	
Goal setting/attainment	YES	NO	
Problem solving	YES	NO	
Self-evaluation	YES	NO	
Self-advocacy	YES	NO	
Self-awareness	YES	NO	
Person-centered IEP Planning	YES	NO	
Relationship with Others	YES	NO	
Other:_____			

Rate each of the following on a scale from 1 (Excellent) to 4 (Poor) based on your students and yourself as a teacher.

	1 Excellent	2 Good	3 Fair	4 Poor	5 Can't tell
How easy is it to get materials?					
How well do the cost of materials fit my budget?					
Are the materials available in alternative formats?					
Are support materials provided?					
Are the instructions "teacher friendly"?					
Are the prerequisite skills delineated?					
Are there sufficient opportunities for practice?					
How relevant/motivating is the content for my students?					
How age-appropriate is the content for my students?					
How well do the materials match the academic level of my students?					
Is a system for assessing student progress included?					
Is the content based on research/field testing?					
How appealing are the videos and other materials?					
How well does the instructional time (number and length of sessions) fit with my schedule?					
Additional Comments:					

What types of materials are provided?

If you work with students who are visually or hearing impaired, does the curriculum have audiotape, closed-captioned, or Braille formats? Are the materials durable and easy to use? Do they provide enough variety or hold the interest of students? Is an assessment tool included?

How easy is it to follow the lesson plans?

Are the objectives for each lesson clearly stated? Is it easy to tell what materials you will need and how much time each lesson will require? Is the text formatted so you can easily find prompts? Is there flexibility in the order of the lesson plans?

Were the materials field-tested?

Has anyone collected information about whether students who used this curriculum improved their self-determination knowledge, skills, or behaviors? Just because someone is selling a product doesn't mean that it works. Many of the curricula we listed have been field-tested, but not all of them report the results of those tests. Sometimes authors report field-test results in a journal article or book chapter instead of the manual.

What are the time and financial obligations associated with this curriculum?

The costs of materials sampled in Table 1 range from nothing to more than $1,000. The time commitments also vary extensively. Is the financial cost of the curriculum appropriate to the length of instructional time you have available to teach the skills?

Important questions include: Are the materials age-appropriate? Are they designed for use with students who have mild, moderate, or severe disabilities? Do they provide enough variety or hold the interest of students? Is an assessment tool included?

Sample Curricula

We have selected five curricula which have published research documenting their effectiveness to describe in more detail here.

The Self-Advocacy Strategy for Education and Transition Planning

This curriculum was developed using a modified version of the Strategies Intervention Model (Ellis, Deshler, Lenz, Schumaker, & Clark, 1991) at the University of Kansas. The Self-Advocacy Strategy is a motivation strategy that teachers can use to help students prepare for any type of educational or transition planning meeting. The strategy, called I-PLAN, consists of five steps:

- *I*nventory your strengths, areas to improve, goals, needed accommodations, and choices for learning.
- *P*rovide your inventory information.
- *L*isten and respond.
- *A*sk questions.
- *N*ame your goals.

The instructor's manual contains step-by-step lesson plans and cue cards that you can use as transparencies, handouts, or worksheets. Finally, the Self-Advocacy Strategy has been field-tested with students with learning disabilities ages 14–21 (Van Reusen & Bos, 1994; Van Reusen, Deshler, & Schumaker, 1989).

Next S.T.E.P. (Student Transition and Education Planning)

Developed by Andrew Halpern and his colleagues at the University of Oregon, the purpose of the Next S.T.E.P. curriculum is to teach high school students how to begin planning for their lives after they leave school. Materials include a teacher's manual with lesson plans and necessary forms, a student workbook, and a videotape that contains an overview of the curriculum, as well as vignettes that address important issues from specific lessons. The Next S.T.E.P. curriculum has been field-tested with students with mild mental retardation ages 14–19 (Zhang, 2000).

Take Action: Making Goals Happen

Take Action is the last of the three strands of the Choice-Maker Self-Determination Curriculum designed by Laura Huber Marshall and Jim Martin and their colleagues at the University of Colorado at Colorado Springs. The first two strands are Choosing Goals and Expressing Goals (or Self-Directed IEP). Take Action is designed to provide teachers with a set of lessons to teach students a generalizable process for attaining their goals. Materials include a teacher's manual with reproducible lesson masters and a student instructional video. Take Action was field-tested with six students with mild or moderate mental retardation ages 16 to 18 (Jerman, Martin, Marshall, & Sale, 2000). Results indicated that all six students accomplished all goals set during maintenance.

TAKE CHARGE for the Future

This multicomponent curriculum was designed by Laurie Powers and her colleagues at Oregon Health Sciences University to assist students to become more involved in their transition planning process. The four components are coaching, mentorship, parent support, and staff training. Materials include a student guide, companion guide, parent guide, and class guide. TAKE CHARGE for the Future was field-tested with 43 students with specific learning disabilities, emotional disabilities, other health impairments, or orthopedic impairments ages 14–17 years (Powers, Turner, Matuszewski, Wilson, & Phillips, in press). Results indicated significant differences in education planning, transition awareness, family empowerment, and student participation in transition planning.

41% of teachers with secondary-aged students indicated that they did not have sufficient training or information on teaching self-determination.

Whose Future Is It Anyway? A Student-Directed Transition Planning Process

Developed by Michael Wehmeyer and his colleagues at the Arc National Headquarters, this curriculum is designed for middle school and transition-aged students with mild or moderate disabilities. The curriculum consists of a student manual, which includes a cut-out Coach's Guide. While the manual is written for students to read and work through at their own pace, the teacher's role is three part:

- To facilitate student success.
- To teach information requested by students.
- To advocate for a successful transition for students.

This curriculum was field-tested with 53 students with mild or moderate mental retardation ages 15–21 (Wehmeyer & Lawrence, 1995). Results indicate significant increases in self-efficacy and outcome expectancy measures.

For more information on our exemplary sites and literature review visit our World Wide Web site at http://www.uncc.edu/sdsp.

Final Thoughts

Self-determination develops over the life span as students gain self-awareness and learn to make increasingly important decisions about their lives with the guidance of their parents, teachers, and other adult mentors. Because traditionally other people (professionals) have made most major life decisions for them, students with disabilities often require instruction on the skills needed to be self-determining citizens. Promoting self-determination also requires training those without disabilities to encourage and respect the decisions made by self-determining individuals with disabilities.

Fortunately, many self-determination curricula are available from which to choose. We hope that the suggestions provided in this article will help you decide which curriculum will best promote self-determination for your students.

References

Abery, B., & Stancliffe, R. (1996). The ecology of self-determination. In D. J. Sands & M. Wehmeyer (Eds.), *Self-determination across the lifespan: Independence and choice for people with disabilities* (pp. 111–145). Baltimore: Paul H. Brookes.

Agran, M., Snow, K., & Swaner, J. (1999). Teacher perceptions of self-determination: Benefits, characteristics, strategies. *Education and Training in Mental Retardation and Developmental Disabilities, 34*, 293–301.

Ellis, E. S., Deshler, D. D., Lenz, B. K., Schumaker, J. B., & Clark, F. L. (1991). An instructional model for teaching learning strategies. *Focus on Exceptional Children, 23*(4), 1–24.

Field, S. (1996). Self-determination instructional strategies for youth with learning disabilities. *Journal of Learning Disabilities, 29*, 40–52.

Field, S., & Hoffman, A. (1994). Development of a model for self-determination. *Career Development for Exceptional Individuals, 17*, 159–169.

Field, S., Martin, J., Miller, R., Ward, M., & Wehmeyer, M. (1998). *A practical guide for teaching self-determination.* Reston, VA: Council for Exceptional Children.

Halloran, W. D. (1993). Transition service requirements: Issues, implications, challenge. In R. C. Eaves & P. J. McLaughlin (Eds.), *Recent advances in special education and rehabilitation* (pp. 210–224). Boston: Andover.

Jerman, S. L., Martin, J. E., Marshall, L. H., & Sale, P. R. (2000). Promoting self-determination: Using *Take Action* to teach goal attainment. *Career Development for Exceptional Individuals, 23*, 27–38.

Marshall, L. H., Martin, J. E., Maxson, L., Hughes, W., Miller, T., McGill, T., & Jerman, P. (1999). *Take action: Making goals happen.* Longmont, CO: Sopris West.

Martin, J. E., & Marshall L. H. (1995) Choicemaker: A comprehensive self-determination transition program. *Intervention in School and Clinic, 30*, 147–156.

Mithaug, D., Campeau, P., & Wolman, J. (1992). *Research on self-determination in individuals with disabilities.* Unpublished Manuscript.

Powers, L. E., Turner, A., Matuszewski, J., Wilson, R., & Phillips, A. (in press). TAKE CHARGE for the future: A controlled field-test of a model to promote student involvement in transition planning. *Career Development for Exceptional Individuals.*

Van Reusen, A. K., & Bos, C. S. (1994). Facilitating student participation in individualized education programs through motivation strategy instruction. *Exceptional Children, 60*, 466–475.

Van Reusen, A. K., Deshler, D. D., & Schumaker, J. B. (1989). Effects of a student participation strategy in facilitating the involvement of adolescents with learning disabilities in Individualized Education Program planning process. *Learning Disabilities, 1*, 23–34.

Ward, M. J. (1988). The many facts of self-determination. *NICHCY Transition Summary: National Information Center for Children and Youth with Disabilities, 5*, 2–3.

Wehmeyer, M. L. (1996). Self-determination in youth with severe cognitive disabilities: From theory to practice. In L. E. Powers, G. H. S. Singer, & J. Sowers (Eds.), *On the road to autonomy: Promoting self-competence for children and youth with disabilities* (pp. 17–36). Baltimore: Paul H. Brookes.

Wehmeyer, M. L. (1999). A functional model of self-determination: Describing development and implementing instruction. *Focus on Autism and Other Developmental Disabilities, 14,* 53–61.

Wehmeyer, M. L., Agran, M., & Hughes, C. A. (2000). A national survey of teachers' promotion of self-determination and student directed learning. *The Journal of Special Education, 34,* 58–68.

Wehmeyer, M., & Lawrence, M. (1995). Whose future is it anyway? Promoting student involvement in transition planning. *Career Development for Exceptional Individuals, 18,* 69–83.

Wehmeyer, M. L., & Schwartz, M. (1997). Self-determination and positive adult outcomes: A follow up study of youth with mental retardation or learning disabilities. *Exceptional Children, 63,* 245–255.

Wehmeyer, M. L., & Schwartz, M. (1998). The self-determination focus of transition goals for students with mental retardation. *Career Development for Exceptional Individuals, 21,* 75–86.

Zhang, D. (2000). The effects of self-determination instruction on high school students with mild disabilities. *Louisiana Education Research Journal, 25*(1), 29–54.

David W. Test *(CEC Chapter #147), Professor, Special Education Program;* **Meagan Karvonen**, *Project Coordinator, Special Education Program;* **Wendy M. Wood**, *Associate Professor, Special Education Program;* **Diane Browder**, *Snyder Distinguished Professor, Special Education Program; and* **Bob Algozzine**, *Professor, Department of Educational Administration, Research, and Technology, College of Education, University of North Carolina at Charlotte.*

Address correspondence to David Test, Special Education Program, University of North Carolina at Charlotte, 9201 University City Blvd., Charlotte, NC 28223 (e-mail: dwtest@email.uncc.edu; URL: http://www.uncc.edu/sdsp).

Index

Index

Test Your Knowledge Form

We encourage you to photocopy and use this page as a tool to assess how the articles in *Annual Editions* expand on the information in your textbook. By reflecting on the articles you will gain enhanced text information. You can also access this useful form on a product's book support Web site at *http://www.dushkin.com/online/*.

NAME:

DATE:

TITLE AND NUMBER OF ARTICLE:

BRIEFLY STATE THE MAIN IDEA OF THIS ARTICLE:

LIST THREE IMPORTANT FACTS THAT THE AUTHOR USES TO SUPPORT THE MAIN IDEA:

WHAT INFORMATION OR IDEAS DISCUSSED IN THIS ARTICLE ARE ALSO DISCUSSED IN YOUR TEXTBOOK OR OTHER READINGS THAT YOU HAVE DONE? LIST THE TEXTBOOK CHAPTERS AND PAGE NUMBERS:

LIST ANY EXAMPLES OF BIAS OR FAULTY REASONING THAT YOU FOUND IN THE ARTICLE:

LIST ANY NEW TERMS/CONCEPTS THAT WERE DISCUSSED IN THE ARTICLE, AND WRITE A SHORT DEFINITION:

We Want Your Advice

ANNUAL EDITIONS revisions depend on two major opinion sources: one is our Advisory Board, listed in the front of this volume, which works with us in scanning the thousands of articles published in the public press each year; the other is you—the person actually using the book. Please help us and the users of the next edition by completing the prepaid article rating form on this page and returning it to us. Thank you for your help!

ANNUAL EDITIONS: Educating Exceptional Children 02/03

ARTICLE RATING FORM

Here is an opportunity for you to have direct input into the next revision of this volume.
We would like you to rate each of the articles listed below, using the following scale:

1. **Excellent: should definitely be retained**
2. **Above average: should probably be retained**
3. **Below average: should probably be deleted**
4. **Poor: should definitely be deleted**

Your ratings will play a vital part in the next revision.
Please mail this prepaid form to us as soon as possible.
Thanks for your help!

RATING	ARTICLE
	1. What's Good? Suggested Resources for Beginning Special Education Teachers
	2. Here Comes the SUN Team! Collaborative Inclusion at Work
	3. Four Inclusion Models That Work
	4. Creating Culturally Responsive, Inclusive Classrooms
	5. From Philosophy to Practice in Inclusive Early Childhood Programs
	6. Together Is Better: Specific Tips on How to Include Children With Various Types of Disabilities
	7. Emergent Literacy in an Early Childhood Classroom: Center Learning to Support the Child With Special Needs
	8. Learning Disabilities
	9. Graphic Organizers to the Rescue! Helping Students Link—and Remember—Information
	10. Chaos in the Classroom: Looking at ADHD
	11. For the Love of Language
	12. Approaching Families: Facilitating Culturally/Linguistically Diverse Family Involvement
	13. Family and Cultural Alert! Considerations in Assistive Technology Assessment
	14. Collaborative Planning for Inclusion of a Student With Developmental Disabilities
	15. Don't Water Down! Enhance: Content Learning Through the Unit Organizer Routine
	16. Identifying Depression in Students With Mental Retardation
	17. Anger, Dismay, Guilt, Anxiety—The Realities and Roles in Reporting Child Abuse
	18. Wraparound Services for Young Schoolchildren With Emotional and Behavioral Disorders
	19. Student Mentors and Proteges Learning Together
	20. Schools for the Visually Disabled: Dinosaurs or Mainstays?
	21. Seeking the Light: Welcoming a Visually Impaired Student

RATING	ARTICLE
	22. Visual Teaching Strategies for Students Who Are Deaf or Hard of Hearing
	23. Training Basic Teaching Skills to Paraeducators of Students With Severe Disabilities
	24. The Unexpected Benefits of High School Peer Tutoring
	25. Using Technology to Construct Alternate Portfolios of Students With Moderate and Severe Disabilities
	26. I Learned How to Take Turns and Other Important Early Childhood Lessons Helped Along by Computers
	27. Accommodations for Students With Disabilities: Removing Barriers to Learning
	28. Accessible Web Site Design
	29. Uncommon Talents: Gifted Children, Prodigies and Savants
	30. Using the Internet to Improve Student Performance
	31. Gifted Students Need an Education, Too
	32. Listening to Student Voices About Postsecondary Education
	33. Choosing a Self-Determination Curriculum

(Continued on next page)

BUSINESS REPLY MAIL
FIRST-CLASS MAIL PERMIT NO. 84 GUILFORD CT

POSTAGE WILL BE PAID BY ADDRESSEE

McGraw-Hill/Dushkin
530 Old Whitfield Street
Guilford, Ct 06437-9989

ABOUT YOU

Name

Date

_____

Are you a teacher? ☐   A student? ☐
Your school's name

_____

Department

_____

Address   City   State   Zip

_____

School telephone #

_____

YOUR COMMENTS ARE IMPORTANT TO US!

Please fill in the following information:
For which course did you use this book?

_____

Did you use a text with this ANNUAL EDITION?   ☐ yes ☐ no
What was the title of the text?

_____

What are your general reactions to the *Annual Editions* concept?

_____

Have you read any pertinent articles recently that you think should be included in the next edition? Explain.

_____

Are there any articles that you feel should be replaced in the next edition? Why?

_____

Are there any World Wide Web sites that you feel should be included in the next edition? Please annotate.

_____

May we contact you for editorial input?   ☐ yes ☐ no
May we quote your comments? ☐ yes ☐ no